The Ultimate Scene Study Series
Volume III

103 Scenes for Three Actors

PN
2080
.U49
2001
V.3

Published by Smith and Kraus, Inc.
177 Lyme Road, Hanover, NH 03755
www.SmithandKraus.com

Copyright © 2001 by Smith and Kraus, Inc.
All rights reserved
Manufactured in the United States of America

First Edition: May 2001
9 8 7 6 5 4 3 2 1

Library of Congress cataloguing in publication data
The ultimate scene study series / edited by Wilma Marcus Chandler
p. cm. — (Scene study series)
Includes bibliographical references.
Contents: v.1. 101 scenes for groups — v.2. 102 short scenes for two actors —
v.3. 103 scenes for three actors — v.4. 104 scenes for four actors.
ISBN 1-57525-153-1 (v.2)
1. Acting. 2. English drama. 3. American drama. 4. Drama—Translations into English.
I. Chandler, Wilma Marcus II. Series.

PN2080.U49 1999
808.82—dc21 99-089197
ISBN-10: 1-57525-220-1
ISBN-13: 978-1-57525-220-9

NOTE: These scenes are intended to be used for audition and class study; permission is not required to use the material for those purposes. However, if there is a paid performance of any of the scenes included in this book, please refer to the permission acknowledgment pages 514-523 to locate the source who can grant permission for public performance.

The Ultimate
Scene Study Series
Volume III

103 Scenes
for Three Actors

edited by Wilma Marcus Chandler

SCENE STUDY SERIES

A SMITH AND KRAUS BOOK

To all my theater students over the years.
Over and over again—such bravery and such willingness
to receive the experiences that are brought forth
in the classroom and the rehearsal hall.

Contents

PART THREE: SCENES FOR TWO MEN/ONE WOMAN

PART FOUR: SCENES FOR TWO WOMEN/ONE MAN

Because we live on a level drastically reduced from what we can imagine, acting promises to represent a dynamic expression of the intense life. It is a way of making testimony to what we have witnessed—a declaration of what we know and what we can imagine.

Joseph Chaikin
The Presence of the Actor

Foreword

Most often in acting classes, students work in pairs on scenes from great plays and film scripts.

Two-person scenes provide a solid structure for exploring relationships and presence. They also provide a beginning director with intricacies of basic blocking and movement.

Three-person scenes are quite different. They provide unique problems of three-way focus, triangular blocking, and subtle interconnections among the characters. They also provide material for the classic situation in which one actor has lost a partner or there is an odd number of students working in class.

Three-person scenes have intrinsic movement. They are asymmetrical with conflict and focus bouncing among the players: as different as a 2/4 beat in music is from a 3/4 waltz. Many times there will be a "tearing" in a three-person scene; one character "torn" between the other two, either emotionally, physically, ethically, or economically.

The scenes presented here are diverse in style and content. Sometimes all three characters will take the stage simultaneously; other times sequentially. Not all three actors will have equal numbers of lines. This can provide opportunity for non-verbal acting, movement, stage business and exits and entrances worthy of the character.

All scenes are from the original plays, unedited. It is my hope that you will be inspired to seek out the entire play and read it thoroughly as you work. All scene study should include a solid beginning, a strong center, a climactic moment, and a substantial denouement. These can be built into each scene.

Create characters who speak and act truthfully.

And most of all, enjoy the process.

PART ONE:

SCENES FOR THREE MEN

Antigone

Sophocles
441 B.C.

Scene: In front of the Palace. Dawn, after the archive army has been repulsed. Kreon addresses the Citizenry. He has decreed that Polyneikês may not have an honorable burial.

Kreon, King of Thebes
A Sentry
Leader

> *(Kreon enters through the double door of the palace, surrounded by a full contingent of Guards.)*

LEADER: But here comes Kreon, son of Menoikeus,
New-crowned king of Thebes, our ruler.
What new fortunes have the gods in store?
What has he in mind to call this assembly of elders?
(The music fades out.)

KREON: Men of Thebes!
Our ship of state, so tossed on turbulent seas
In recent days by the gods, has once again
Found safe harbor by the same gods' help.
I have called you here, of all the men of Thebes,
Because I know the loyalty you proved
To old King Laïos; and later to his son
King Oedipus who also steered our land;
And when he fell, you loyally upheld his sons,
The princes Polyneikês and Eteoklês.

But now, as you have heard, those two sons
Have, in one day, in a double stroke of fate,
Slain each other, each his brother's murderer,
Each polluted with his brother's blood,
On the field of battle.

I, now, as next in blood,
Have taken to myself both throne and power
In Thebes. I know too well no man is tested
Except in action, for there is no other way
To divine the soul and mind and spirit of any—
And so of me.
But I say this:
No ruler who presumes to steer the state
And fails to heed the best counsel; who fears
And fails to speak; that man, I say, that man,
That man of all men, is the most base.
This I have always believed, and believe it now.
That man who places the good of a friend
Above the good of the state is beneath contempt.

I call on Zeus, all-seeing, to witness for me:
If ever I see my country headed for destruction,
And fail to speak, I would damn myself as well.
Nor would I make a friend of a state's enemy.
The state is our ship; and when that ship sails straight
And bears us safely, and prospers, then, only then,
Can we make true friends.

These are the laws by which I govern this state;
And these are the laws that led me to issue the edict
Relating to these two brothers, the sons of Oedipus.
Eteoklês, who died as a man should die,
In defense of his land, will be buried with full honors
And every rite that follows the noblest dead.
But Polyneikês, his brother, who returned
From exile in a rage of insane desire
To waste his father's land with fire and sword,
Upturn the shrines of his gods, batten on the blood
Of his people, and lead the remnant into slavery:
To that man I say: I deny burial
And every sign of ritual lamentation.

Let him lie on the open, barren field,
A naked corpse for birds and dogs to tear at:
A sight of unspeakable shame!
These are my orders:
While I am king, the patriot will always be honored
Above the traitor; and he who is loyal to the state
Will have my praise in life as well as death.

LEADER: If this is your will, Kreon son of Menoikeus,
Touching the city's enemies and friends,
So be it. As king, the power of law is yours
To enforce upon the dead as well as the living.

KREON: See to it, then, that my will is obeyed.

LEADER: We are old, Kreon; let younger men see to it.

KREON: No, not the body; I've posted guards.

LEADER: What would you have us do?

KREON: To side with no one who breaks this law.

LEADER: Only a fool is in love with death!

KREON: And death is the answer.
Yet many a man has been ruined by hope of gain.
(A Sentry has entered, left, during the above. When he reaches Kreon he salutes. He is a rough-hewn type, somewhat comic, and naturally direct in expressing himself.)

SENTRY: King, I won't say I'm breathless from running.
I haven't kicked up my heels, so to speak,
To get here faster. Fact is, I didn't want to come.
I stopped on the road time and again, thinking.
Doubled back and back more than once.
"Fool!" I said to myself, "where's the fire?"
And then: "Why rush smack into the lion's den?"
And: "Who needs the trouble?"

But then I thought: "What if there's someone else?"
What if someone else brings the news to Kreon?
Your neck's had it soldier!"

Well, my head whirls that around a while.

And my pace gets slower.
A mile becomes a league. But here I am,
Like it or not. Not that there's much to tell.
But I'll tell it anyway, whatever it costs me.
I mean, well, what happens, happens. You know?
(Kreon is at first amused by the Sentry's rough manner.)
KREON: What is all this? What's the problem?
SENTRY: First let me get myself off the hook, king.
I didn't do it and swear I don't know who did,
So please, sir, don't take it out on me!
KREON: You set up your defenses well, soldier.
It's clear that you have something important to say.
SENTRY: Serious matters can rattle a man's brain.
KREON: Come to the point, soldier, and get out!
SENTRY: Yes, sir! Right, sir! I sure will!
Well, here goes!
Just now—someone—out there—
The dead man?—Polyneikês?—Well, I mean—
Someone—someone buried the body—dust on it—
Scattered—and the rites—and then was gone—
KREON: What man would dare!
SENTRY: I don't know sir—no sign of digging—
No shovel, no pick, the earth hard and dry,
No cart tracks—nothing to tell who did it.
But then at sun-up the first watch came on,
And—well, the corporal points it out—
We're amazed, struck with wonder! There's the body,
You could still see it there, not buried yet,
Not all the way, covered with dust, just enough—
Like someone meant to lift the curse from a corpse
Left lying unburied in the field to escape pollution.
No tracks either, no dogs, wild animals,
No sign the body'd been torn—the skin—

And then it started. Words flew like stones.
"That one did it!" "No, him!" Each of us knew

It was the other, and it might have come to a fight,
Nothing to stop it, any of us could have done it,
No way to prove it! We'd each of us have picked up
Red-hot iron, walked through fire, sworn
We hadn't done it, or knew anyone who'd planned
Or done it, but there was no way out—

Then one of us said something—something—well, that—
That made us all shut up and stare in terror
At the ground. He was right, no argument there,
Not and come through it all in one piece.
Someone had to tell you, he said, report it.
So we threw the dice, and the lot fell to unlucky me,
And here I am, unwelcome as unwilling.
Bringers of bad news can't be choosy.
LEADER: It is possible my lord,
    The gods are involved in this?
KREON: Stop! I refuse to hear this senile drivel!
    Have you all gone mad in addition to your age!
    What can the gods care for a naked corpse?
    Would they bury him to honor his loyalty,
    His good deeds, the traitor who invaded their city,
    Who burned their pillared temples and sacred treasures,
    Savaged the land and cast its laws to the winds?
    When have you seen the gods honor traitors?
    No! Never!

    But I am aware that there are those here in Thebes
    Who have always opposed me, always opposed my authority.
    Heads together, murmuring against me,
    Refusing to keep their necks to the yoke,
    And submitting to *me*, their *king!* They're the ones
    Who have bribed my own sentries to bury that body!
    Money! What will men not do for money!
    What power corrupts men more! Cities fall,
    Men driven out, great houses collapse,

Honest minds depraved and led into villainy!
But every man bribed to this crime may be certain
That he will pay the full price for his treachery!
(Turning on the Sentry.)
You there! Listen carefully! I swear by Zeus,
Either you bring me the man guilty of this crime,
Or I will hang you alive till you beg for death!
I think then you'll find it easier to confess
Who bribed you to this act. And in the process
You may also learn that it isn't wise
To seek profit wherever you might fancy.
The price may be too great

SENTRY: Sir, have I leave to speak?

KREON: Every word you say grates me!

SENTRY: Grates your ears or tears your heart?

KREON: By god, he's going to analyze me!

SENTRY: Words don't hurt; what's done hurts.

KREON: Doesn't anything shut you up!

SENTRY: Yes; but I did nothing wrong!

KREON: Nothing but sold your soul for silver!

SENTRY: You think you know the truth, sir,
    But you're wide of the mark.

KREON: Play all you want with words! But play with this now!
    Either you catch the criminals and bring them to me,
    Or the bribes that bought you will bring more pain than pleasure.
    *(Kreon turns and enters the palace followed by his contingent of
    Guards. The Sentry speaks when Kreon is barely out of hearing.)*

SENTRY: "Find the criminals," he says! Oh, sure!
    What else! But found or not, I'm out of here!
    Luck or no luck, you'll never catch *me* here again!
    At least *my* neck's saved! Thank god!
    *(As the Sentry begins his hurried exit, left, in the direction of the
    plain, music begins, and at once the Chorus takes up a new posi-
    tion.)*

Oedipus Rex

Sophocles
430 B.C.

Scene: Tiresias, the blind prophet has said that Oedipus, himself, is the cause of the great plague that is devastating Thebes. Oedipus has sworn to uncover the causes but unjustly accuses Kreon for corrupting the prophet. All will not be well until the murderer of the old king, Laïos, is found. He had been slain while traveling on the roads by an unknown assailant.

Kreon, brother to Jocasta, brother-in-law to Oedipus the King.
Oedipus, King of Thebes—married to Jocasta for many years— proud, wise, and just, but filled with pride.
Choragos, leader of the chorus of Theban citizens.

KREON: Men of Thebes—I have heard the accusation
    King Oedipus makes against me, and I have come
    In haste, because I'm not a man to endure
    Such indignity!

    If, in the present crisis,
    He believes that I in any way
    Intended harm to him in word or deed,
    Then I would never choose a long life,
    For a life without honor is no life.
    This outrage to my name is no small matter.
    There is no more grievous charge, none
    More heinous than this: to be damned by my own city,
    By you, and those closest to me, as a traitor.
LEADER: He spoke in anger, not from careful thought.
KREON: And said that I persuaded the prophet to lie?
LEADER: Yes, but why, I don't know.
KREON: Did he look you straight in the eye?
    Was his mind steady?
LEADER: I can't say.

I don't judge the deeds of great men.
(Oedipus *enters from the palace.*)
But here he is now.
OEDIPUS: You, Kreon! You! Your have the gall
To come here! You! You have the audacity
To approach this house! You who openly plotted
Its master's murder! You who sought to steal
My throne, steal my power, like a bandit!
O by the gods, Kreon, were you so stupid
To think me a coward, a fool, blind to your plot
Against me? Did you think I had no eyes
To see your stealthy moves; that I would not
Without one moment's pause take arms against them
In my own defense? What a fool you are, Kreon!
What a fool! To set out hunting for throne
And power when throne and power need friends and funds;
When power and throne are caught with wealth and armies!
KREON: Finished? Then listen to me, I have listened to you,
And judge on the facts!
OEDIPUS: Ah, Kreon, you have a way with words,
But how do I listen to a known enemy?
KREON: First things first: listen for a change!
OEDIPUS: First things first, deny that you are a traitor!
KREON: If you think stubborn unreason a virtue,
Then you are a man who has lost his balance!
OEDIPUS: If you think you can wrong a kinsman
And escape the penalty, then I tell you
That *you* are a man who has lost his balance!
KREON: All right! There I agree: Only tell me
What this wrong is you say that I have done you?
OEDIPUS: Did you or did you not convince me to send
For that pious fraud of a prophet?
KREON: I did, yes, and I would do it again.
OEDIPUS: How long ago was it that Laïos—
KREON: That Laïos what? I don't understand.
OEDIPUS: Vanished, struck down in his tracks, murdered!

KREON: Years—many long years ago—
OEDIPUS: This prophet—was he practicing then?
KREON: Yes, with the same skill and honor.
OEDIPUS: And what did he say about me at the time?
KREON: Nothing—not while I was about.
OEDIPUS: And you never hunted the king's killer?
KREON: We did, but came away with nothing.
OEDIPUS: Why didn't your prophet accuse me then?
KREON: When I don't know, I prefer to keep silent.
OEDIPUS: But *this* you'd tell, if you were honest.
KREON: What would that be? If I know, I'll tell.
OEDIPUS: If you and he hadn't schemed together,
    He would never have said I murdered Laïos.
KREON: If this is what he said, well then—
    who would know better than you?
    But now it is my turn to question.
OEDIPUS: Ask away. But I'm not a murderer.
KREON: Very well.—Is my sister your wife?
OEDIPUS: Now there's a fact I can't deny.
KREON: And you rule together, equal in power?
OEDIPUS: Everything she wants, she has.
KREON: And I'm the third? We're all of us equal?
OEDIPUS: And that is where you are proven a traitorous friend!
KREON: Not if you see it as I do, rationally.
    Why would a man in his right mind ever choose
    The distressing cares of kingship over untroubled sleep,
    Especially if he has equal power and rank?
    Certainly not I. I have never longed to wield
    Royal power. Why should I? I live like a king.
    Any man with reason would choose as I have.
    As it is, I have everything from you.
    My life is free. I live unburdened by the demands
    Put upon kingship.
    But if I were king,
    I should be bound to act as a king must act:
    Against his will and pleasure. So what could kingship

Give me that I don't have: unruffled power
And influence, without the care, without
The pain, without the threat.
I'm not so insane
Yet to seek out other honors than those
That bring advantage. I'm welcome everywhere.
And those who court your favor, curry mine:
Their success depends on me.
Why give up comfort for worry?
No sane mind is treasonous.
No. I have no leanings in that direction,
And I would never deal with a man who did.
Test me, why don't you? Go to the Pythia at Delphi.
Ask the goddess if I reported correctly.
And if I didn't, if I'm found to be in league
With the prophet, plotting treason, then have me executed!
But not on your vote only; on mine as well:
A double charge. Just don't convict without proof,
on a mere guess.

It is just as wrong to think a bad man good,
As it is a good man bad.
To reject a loyal friend is to tear life
Out of your own breast: there is nothing more precious!
Only time will tell, and time will tell
For certain who is just and who is not;
The traitor is easily spotted.
LEADER: Good advice for a careful man.
Hasty judgment is often dangerous.
OEDIPUS: Hasty conspiracy is hastily met.
If I delay, he wins, I lose.
KREON: What do you want? Say it! Banishment?
OEDIPUS: Banishment? No! It is your head I want!
KREON: You refuse to believe! You refuse to yield!
(Iokastê enters from the palace with a women Attendant and
approaches them.)

OEDIPUS: You don't persuade me you're worthy of belief!
KREON: Quite frankly, I think you've lost your wits!
OEDIPUS: In *my* interest, yes!
KREON: And what about mine?
OEDIPUS: But you're a traitor!
KREON: What if you're wrong?
OEDIPUS: But I *must* rule!
KREON: When your rule is evil?
OEDIPUS: Think of the city!
KREON: It is *my* city, too!
LEADER: Please, my lords, no more!
    Look, Iokastê, just in time!
    Let her end this. ·

Phormio

Terence
161 B.C

Scene: Antipho, son of Demipho, marries a poor but respectable young woman, Phanium, while his father is away. Phaedria supports the marriage for his own interests, for his is in love with a young lady who is also poor and is less than appropriate. Geta always serves his own best interests. Now Demipho has returned and is very upset. He walks down the street.

Demipho, respected man—gone to Egypt for three years.
Phaedria, Demipho's nephew.
Geta, Demipho's servant.

DEMIPHO: Is it so, is Antipho marry'd without my consent? Shou'd not my authority—but I wave authority—shou'd not he have feared my displeasure at least? Is he not asham'd? Audacious act! O! Geta, thou tutor! *(To himself, not seeing them.)*
GETA: He's out at last. *(Aside to Phaedria.)*
DEMIPHO: I wonder what they'll say to me, or what excuse they'll find. *(To himself, not seeing them.)*
GETA: I've found one already: look you for another. *(Aside to Phaedria.)*
DEMIPHO: Will he excuse himself by saying, "I did it against my will, the law compell'd me?" I hear him, and allow it to be so. *(To himself, not seeing them.)*
GETA: Well say'd. *(Aside.)*
DEMIPHO: But knowingly, without speaking a word, to give up his cause to his adversaries! Did the law compel him to that too? *(To himself, not seeing them.)*
PHAEDRIA: That strikes home. *(Aside to Geta.)*
GETA: I'll find an excuse for that: leave it to me: *(Aside to Phaedria.)*
DEMIPHO: I know not what to do, because this has happen'd beyond my expectation or belief: I'm so provok'd, that I am scarcely capable of thinking: ev'ry one therefore, in the heighth of his prosperity, should then think within himself how he cou'd bear

adversity; let him always, as he returns home, consider thus, I may meet with dangers, losses, a disobedient son, a dead wife, or a sick daughter, and these are misfortunes common to all men, there's nothing new or strange in either of them, therefore whatever happens beyond his expectation he should account as gain. *(To himself, not seeing them.)*

GETA: O! Phaedria, 'tis scarcely to be believ'd how much wiser I am than my master: I have consider'd of all the inconveniences which can happen to me, if my master shou'd return, I concluded that I should be condemn'd to perpetual imprisonment to grind there, to be well drubbed, to be fettered, or sentenced to work in the fields; neither of which wou'd be new or strange to me; therefore whatever happens beyond my expectation I shall account as gain: but why don't you go up to the old gentlemen, and speak him fair? *(Aside to Phaedria.)*

DEMIPHO: There's Phaedria my brother's son, I see, coming this way. *(To himself.)*

PHAEDRIA: Uncle, your servant.

DEMIPHO: Your servant: but where's Antipho?

PHAEDRIA: I'm glad to see you safe return'd.

DEMIPHO: I believe you: but give me an answer to what I ask.

PHAEDRIA: He's very well; and he's not far off; but are all things as you'd have 'em?

DEMIPHO: I wish they were.

PHAEDRIA: What's the matter?

DEMIPHO: Do you ask, Phaedria: Ye've patch'd up a fine marriage here in my absence.

PHAEDRIA: O, what, are you angry with him for that?

GETA: He manages him dextrously! *(To himself.)*

DEMIPHO: Ought I not to be angry with him? I wish he'd come into my presence, that he may see now how he has provok'd a good-natured father by his offence.

PHAEDRIA: But he has done nothing, uncle, to merit your displeasure.

DEMIPHO: See how they hang together; they're all alike; know one, you know all.

PHAEDRIA: Indeed you mistake us.

DEMIPHO: Let one commit a fault, and the other's ready to defend him; if one's here, the other's not far off; so they help one another.

GETA: The old man has spoke the truth of them without knowing it. *(To himself.)*

DEMIPHO: For if it was not so, you wou'd not stand up for him, Phaedria.

PHAEDRIA: Uncle, if Antipho had been so much his own enemy as to have been guilty of any fault, contrary to his interest or honour, I would not open my lips in his behalf, but give him over to what he might deserve; but supposing any one, by his malicious strategems, has lay'd a snare for us youth, and has caught us in it, are we to be blam'd or the judges, who often thro envy take from the rich, and as often thro pity add to the poor?

GETA: If I did not know the affair, I shou'd believe what he's saying to be true. *(Aside.)*

DEMIPHO: How should any judge know your right, when you don't speak a word for yourself, as he did not?

PHAEDRIA: He behav'd like a gentleman; when he came before the judges, he was unable to utter what he had premeditated, his modesty and fear so confounded him.

GETA: Well defended: but why don't I go directly up to the old man? *(To himself.)* Your servant, Sir: I'm glad to see you safe return'd.

DEMIPHO: Oh! thou excellent guardian your servant, thou prop of our family, to whose care I committed my son when I went from hence.

GETA: I hear you have been accusing us all undeservedly, and me most undeservedly of all; for what wou'd you have me do for you in this affair? The laws don't allow a servant to plead, nor is his evidence taken.

DEMIPHO: Well, be it so: grant besides that the young man was foolishly fearful, I allow it, you're but a servant; however, if she was ever so near related, there was no occasion for him to marry her; but, as the law requires, you shou'd have giv'n her a portion; and she might look out for another husband: what reason had he to take a beggar home?

GETA: We did not want reason, but money.

DEMIPHO: He shou'd have borrow'd it anywhere.

GETA: Anywhere? Nothing more easily said.

DEMIPHO: If he cou'd not borrow it on other terms, he shou'd have took it up on interest.

GETA: Huy! that's well said: as if any one would lend him money, while you are alive.

DEMIPHO: No, no, it must not be so, it never can: shall I suffer her to live with him one day? There's no temptation for it. I wish that fellow was brought before me, or that I knew where he lives.

GETA: You mean Phormio.

DEMIPHO: The woman's friend.

GETA: I'll bring him here presently.

DEMIPHO: Where's Antipho now?

GETA: Within.

DEMIPHO: Go, Phaedria, look for him, and bring him hither.

PHAEDRIA: I'll go directly.

GETA: Yes to Pamphila. *(Aside.)*

(Phaedria and Geta go.)

The Little Clay Cart

Anonymous
800 A.D.

Scene: By the river.

Of Note: A scene which emphasizes the concept of status.

Monk
Sansthanaka, King Palaka's brother-in-law.
Courtier

MONK: Ye ignorant, lay by a store of virtue!
    Restrain the belly; watch eternally,
    Heeding the beat of contemplation's drum.
    For else the senses—fearful thieves they be—
    Will steal away all virtue's hoarded sum.
    And further: I have seen that all things are transitory, so
    that now I am become the abode of virtues alone.
    Who slays the Five Men, and the Female Bane,
    By whom protection to the Town is given,
    By whom the Outcaste impotent is slain,
    He cannot fail to enter into heaven.
    Though head be shorn and face be shorn,
    The heart unshorn, why should man shave him?
    But he whose inmost heart is shorn
    Needs not the shaven head to save him.
    I have dyed this robe of mine yellow. And now I will go
    into the garden of the king's brother-in-law, wash it in the
    pond, and go away as soon as I can.
    (He walks about and washes the robe.)
    (A voice behind the scenes.) Shtop, you confounded monk, shtop!
MONK: *(Discovers the speaker. Fearfully.)* Heaven help me!
    Here is the king's brother-in-law, Sansthanaka. Just be-
    cause one monk committed an offense, now, wherever he
    sees a monk, whether it is the same one or not, he bores

a hole in his nose and drives him around like a bullock.
Where shall a defenseless man find a defender? But after
all, the blessèd Lord Buddha is my defender.
(Enter the courtier, carrying a sword, and Sansthânaka.)
SANSTHANAKA: Shtop, you confounded monk, shtop! I'll
pound your head like a red radish at a drinking party.
(He strikes him.)
COURTIER: You jackass, you should not strike a monk who wears the
yellow robes of renunciation. Why heed him? Look rather upon
this garden, which offers itself to pleasure.

To creatures else forlorn, the forest trees
Do works of mercy, granting joy and ease;
Like a sinner's heart, the park unguarded lies,
Like some new-founded realm, an easy prize.

MONK: Heaven bless you! Be merciful, servant of the Blessèd One!
SANSTHANAKA: Did you hear that, shir? He's inshulting me.
COURTIER: What does he say?
SANSTHANAKA: Shays I'm a shervant. What do you take me for? a
barber?
COURTIER: A servant of the Blessèd One he calls you, and this is
praise.
SANSTHANAKA: Praise me shome more, monk!
MONK: You are virtuous! You are a brick!
SANSTHANAKA: Shee? He shays I'm virtuous. He shays I'm a brick.
What do you think I am? a materialistic philosopher? or a water-
ing-trough? or a pot-maker?
COURTIER: You jackass, he praises you when he says that you are vir-
tuous, that you are a brick.
SANSTHANAKA: Well, shir, what did he come here for?
MONK: To wash this robe.
SANSTHANAKA: Confound the monk! My shishter's husband gave
me the finesht garden there is, the garden Push-pakaranda. Dogs
and jackals drink the water in thish pond. Now I'm an arishtocrat,
I'm a man, and I don't even take a bath. And here you bring your
shtinking clothes, all shtained with shtale bean-porridge, and
wash 'em! I think one good shtroke will finish you.

COURTIER: You jackass, I am sure he has not long been a monk.

SANSTHANAKA: How can you tell, shir?

COURTIER: It doesn't take much to tell that. See!

His hair is newly shorn; the brow still white;
The rough cloak has not yet the shoulder scarred;
He wears it awkwardly; it clings not tight;
And here above, the fit is sadly marred.

MONK: True, servant of the Blessèd One. I have been a monk but a short time.

SANSTHANAKA: Then why haven't you been one all your life?
(He beats him.)

MONK: Buddha be praised!

COURTIER: Stop beating the poor fellow. Leave him alone. Let him go.

SANSTHANAKA: Jusht wait a minute, while I take counshel.

COURTIER: With whom?

SANSTHANAKA: With my own heart.

COURTIER: Poor fellow! Why didn't he escape?

SANSTHANAKA: Blesshèd little heart, my little shon and mashter, shall the monk go, or shall the monk shtay? *(To himself.)* Neither go, nor shtay. *(Aloud.)* Well, shir, I took counshel with my heart, and my heart shays—

COURTIER: Says what?

SANSTHANAKA: He shall neither go, nor shtay. He shall neither breathe up, nor breathe down. He shall fall down right here and die, before you can shay "boo."

MONK: Buddha be praised! I throw myself upon your protection.

COURTIER: Let him go.

SANSTHANAKA: Well, on one condition.

COURTIER: And what is that?

SANSTHANAKA: He musht shling mud in, without making the water dirty. Or better yet, he musht make the water into a ball, and shling it into the mud.

COURTIER: What incredible folly!

The patient earth is burdened by
So many a fool, so many a drone,
Whose thoughts and deeds are all awry—

These trees of flesh, these forms of stone.
(The monk makes faces at Sansthanaka.)
SANSTHANAKA: What does he mean?
COURTIER: He praises you.
SANSTHANAKA: Praise me shome more! Praise me again!
(The monk does so, then exits.)
COURTIER: See how beautiful the garden is, you jackass.
See yonder trees, adorned with fruit and flowers,
O'er which the clinging creepers interlace;
The watchmen guard them with the royal powers;
They seem like men whom living wives embrace.
SANSTHANAKA: A good deshcription, shir.
The ground is mottled with a lot of flowers;
The blosshom freight bends down the lofty trees;
And, hanging from the leafy tree-top bowers,
The monkeys bob, like breadfruit in the breeze.
COURTIER: Will you be seated on this stone bench, you jackass?
SANSTHANAKA: I am sheated. *(They seat themselves.)* Do you know,
shir, I remember that Vasantasena even yet. She is like an inshult.
I can't get her out of my mind.
COURTIER: *(Aside).* He remembers her even after such a repulse. For
indeed,
The mean man, whom a woman spurns,
But loves the more:
The wise man's passion gentler burns,
Or passes o'er.
SANSTHANAKA: Shome time has passhed, shir, shince I told my sher-
vant Sthavaraka to take the bullock-cart and come as quick as he
could. And even yet he is not here. I've been hungry a long time,
and at noon a man can't go a-foot. For shee!
The shun is in the middle of the shky,
And hard to look at as an angry ape;
Like Gandhari, whose hundred shons died die,
The earth is hard dishtresshed and can't eshcape.
COURTIER: True.
The cattle all—their cuds let fall—

Lie drowsing in the shade;
In heated pool their lips to cool,
Deer throng the woodland glade;
A prey to heat, the city street
Makes wanderers afraid.

The Second Shepherd's Play

Anonymous
15th Century

Scene: In the fields. The story of the Nativity from the Gospel of Luke.

Three Shepherds

FIRST SHEPHERD
Lord, but these weathers are cold! And I am ill wrapped.
I am near-hand dold, so long have I napped;
My legs they fold, my fingers are chapped.
It is not as I would, for I am all lapped
In sorrow.
In storms and tempest,
Now in the east, now in the west,
Woe is him has never rest
Midday nor morrow!

But we simple husbands that walk on the moor,
In faith we are near-hands out of the door.
No wonder, as it stands, if we be poor,
For the tilth of our lands lies fallow as the floor,
As ye ken.
We are so lamed,
O'ertaxed and maimed,
We are made hand-tamed
By these gentlery men.

Thus they rob us our rest, our Lady them harry!
These men that are lord-fast, they make the plough tarry.
What men say is for the best, we find it contrary.
Thus are husbands oppressed, about to miscarry
In life.
Thus hold they us under,
Thus they bring us in blunder;

It were great wonder
If ever should we thrive.

There shall come a swain as proud as a po;
He must borrow my wain, my plough also;
Then I am full fain to grant ere he go.
Thus live we in pain, anger, and woe,
By night, and day.
He must have it for sure,
Though I remain poor;
I'll be pushed out of door
If I once say nay.

If he has braid on his sleeve or a badge nowadays,
Woe to him that him grieve or ever gainsays!
No complaint he'll receive, whatever his ways.
And yet may none believe one word that he says,
No letter.
He can make his demands
With boats and commands,
And all because he stands
For men who are greater.

It does me good, as I walk thus by mine own,
Of this world for to talk in manner of moan.
To my sheep will I stalk, and hearken anon,
And there will I halt and sit on a stone
Full soon.
For I trust, pardie,
True men if there be,
We get more company
Ere it be noon.
(Enter the Second Shepherd, who does not see the First Shepherd.)

SECOND SHEPHERD
Blessings upon us, what may this be-mean?

Why fares this world thus? Such we seldom have seen.
Lord, these weathers are spiteous, and the winds full keen,
And the frosts so hideous they water mine eyne,
No lie!
Now in dry, now in wet,
Now in snow, now in sleet,
When my shoes freeze to my feet
It is not all easy.

But as far as I've been, or yet as I know,
We poor wedded-men suffer great woe;
We sorrow now and again; it falls oft so.
Silly Caple, our hen, both to and fro
She cackles;
But begins she to croak,
To groan or to cluck,
Woe is him, our cock,
For he is in her shackles.

These men that are wed have not all their will;
When they're full hard bestead, they sign full still.
God knows they are led full hard and full ill;
In bower nor in bed they say nought theretil.
This tide
My part have I found,
I know my ground!
Woe is him that is bound,
For he must abide.

But now late in our lives—a marvel to me,
That I think my heart rives such wonders to see;
Whate'er destiny drives, it must so be—
Some men will have two wives, and some men three
In store;
Some are grieved that have any.
But so far ken I—

Woe is him that has many,
For he feels sore.

(Addresses the audience.)

But, your men, of wooing, for God who you bought,
Be well ware of wedding, and think in your thought,
"Had I known" is a thing that serves us of nought.
Much constant mourning has wedding home brought,
And griefs,
With many a sharp shower;
For thou may catch in an hour
What shall savor full sour
As long as thou lives.

For, as e'er read I epistle, I have one for my dear
As sharp as thistle, as rough as a brier;
She is browed like a bristle, with a sour-looking cheer;
Had she once wet her whistle, she could sing full clear
Her Paternoster.
She is as great as a whale,
She has a gallon of gall;
By Him that died for us all,
I would I had run till I had lost her!
(The First Shepherd interrupts him.)
FIRST SHEPHERD: The like I never saw! Full dearly ye stand.
SECOND SHEPHERD: Be the devil in thy maw, so tariand!
Saw thou ought of Daw?
FIRST SHEPHERD: Yea, on pasture-land
Heard I him blaw. He comes here at hand,
Not far.
Stand still.
SECOND SHEPHERD: Why?
FIRST SHEPHERD: For he comes here, think I.
SECOND SHEPHERD: He will tell us both a lie
Unless we beware.

(Enter the Third Shepherd, a boy, who does not see the others.)

THIRD SHEPHERD
    Christ's cross, my creed, and Saint Nicholas!
    Thereof had I need; it is worse than it was.
    Whoso could take heed and let the world pass,
    It is ever in dread and brittle as glass
    And slides.
    This world fared never sure,
    With marvels more and more—
    Now with rich, now with poor,
    Nothing abides.

    Never since Noah's flood were such floods seen,
    Winds and rains so rude, and storms so keen—
    Some stammered, some stood in fear, as I ween,
    Now God turn all to good! I say as I mean,
    For, ponder:
    These floods so they drown,
    Both in fields and in town,
    And bear all down;
    And that is a wonder.
    (He sees the others.)
    We that walk in the nights, our cattle to keep,
    We see sudden sights when other men sleep.
    Yet methinks my heart lights; I see rogues peep.
    Ye are two tall wights —I will give my sheep
    A turn.
    But much ill have I meant;
    As I walk on this bent,
    I may lightly repent,
    My toes if I spurn.
    (The other two advance.)
    Ah, sir, God you save, and master mine!
    A drink fain would I have, and somewhat to dine.
FIRST SHEPHERD: Christ's curse, my knave, thou art lazy, I find!

SECOND SHEPHERD: How the boy will rave! Wait for a time;
    You have fed.
    Bad luck on your brow;
    The rogue came just now,
    Yet would he, I vow.
    Sit down to his bread.
THIRD SHEPHERD: Such servants as I, that sweats and swinks,
    Eats our bread full dry, a sorrow methinks.
    We are oft wet and weary when master-men winks;
    Yet comes full tardy both dinners and drinks.
    But truly.
    Both our dame and our sire,
    When we have run in the mire,
    They can nip at our hire,
    And pay us full slowly.

    But hear my mind, master: for the bread that I break,
    I shall toil thereafter—work as I take.
    I shall do but little, sir, and always hold back,
    For yet lay my supper never on my stomach
    In fields.
    Why should I complain?
    With my staff I can run;
    And men say, "A bargain
    Little profit yields."
FIRST SHEPHERD: You'd be a poor lad to go a-walking
    With a man that had but little for spending.
SECOND SHEPHERD: Peace, boy, I said. No more jangling,
    Or I shall make thee afraid, by the heaven's king!
    Thy joke—
    Where are our sheep boy?—we scorn.
THIRD SHEPHERD: Sir, this same day at morn
    I them left in the corn,
    When the dawn broke.
    They have pasture good, they can not go wrong.
FIRST SHEPHERD: That is right. By the rood, these nights are long!

Ere we went, how I would, that one gave us a song.

SECOND SHEPHERD: So I thought as I stood, to mirth us among.

THIRD SHEPHERD: I grant.

FIRST SHEPHERD: Let me sing the tenory.

SECOND SHEPHERD: And I the treble so high.

THIRD SHEPHERD: Then the mean falls to me.

Let see how ye chant.

(They sing.)

The Killing of Abel

Anonymous
15th Century

Scene: A field. Abel warns Cain to live a righteous life.

Cain
Abel, Cain's brother.
God

ABEL: Cain, I warn thee, tithe aright,
    For dread of his so powerful might.
CAIN: The way I tithe tax not your head,
    But tend they scabby sheep instead;
    If my tithes you think not true,
    It will be the worse for you.
    Would thou I gave him this sheaf or this sheaf?
    But neither of these two will I leave:
    But take this; now has he two,
    By my soul, that's more than due,
    But it goes sore against my will,
    And he shall like this tithe but ill.
ABEL: Cain, better tithe thou, to the end
    That God of heaven rest your friend.
CAIN: My friend? Nay not unless he will!
    Reason only rules me still.
    If I need not dread him sore,
    I were a fool to give him more.
ABEL: If right thou tithed, such must thou find.
CAIN: Yea, kiss the devil's arse behind!
    The devil hang thee by the neck!
    How I may tithe never thou reck;
    Wilt thou not yet hold thy peace?
    Of this jangling I bid thee cease.
    And tithed I well or tithed I ill,
    To thee it's one; keep thy tongue still.

But now since thou hast offered thine,
Now will I set fire to mine.
(Choking smoke comes from the offering.)
Alas! Harrow! Help to blow!
For me it burns no more than snow;
Puff! This smoke does me much shame—
Burn now in the devil's name!
Ah, what devil of hell is it!
Almost had my lungs been split.
Had I blown then one blast more
I had been choked to death full sore.
It stank like the devil in hell,
That longer there I might not dwell.
ABEL: Cain, this is not worth one leek;
Such smoky offering who should seek?
CAIN: Come kiss the devil right in the arse,
For this smoke is slow to pass;
I would that it were in thy throat,
Fire and sheaf, and wheat and oat.
(God appears above.)
GOD: Cain, why art thou such a rebel
Against they brother, Abel?
To jeer and gibe there is no need,
If thou tithe right thou getst they meed;
But be thou sure if thou tithe ill,
Repaid thou shalt be thy evil
(God withdraws.)
CAIN: *(Sarcastic.)*
Why, who is the hob-over-the-wall?
Alas, who was that that piped so small?
Come go we hence from perils all;
God is out of his wit.
Come forth, Abel, and let us go;
I find that God will be my foe,
From here then must I flit.
(They leave the hill.)

ABEL: Oh, Cain, brother, that is ill done.
CAIN: No, but fast hence let us run;
    And if I may, there shall I be
    Where God's eye shall not see me.
ABEL: Dear brother, I will be at hand
    In the field where our beasts stand,
    To see if they be well or sick.
CAIN: Nay, nay, abide, we have a bone to pick.
    Hark, speak with me ere thou go;
    What, thinkst thou thus to escape so?
    Nay a deep debt owe I thee by right,
    And now is time I thee requite.
ABEL: Brother, to me why show you so much spleen?
CAIN: Out, thief, why burnt thy tithe so clean,
    When mine but foully smoked
    As if it would us both have choked?
ABEL: God's will, I trust was here
    That made mine burn so clear.
    If thine smoked, am I to blame?
CAIN: Why, yea, and thou shalt smart with shame;
    With cheek-bone ere my hand I slay
    I shall have torn thy life away.
    (Cain strikes Abel with a cheek-bone.)
    So lie down there and take they rest,
    Thus braying curs are chastised best.
ABEL: Vengeance, vengeance, Lord, I cry!
    For I am slain and not guilty.
    (Abel dies.)
CAIN: Yea, lie thou there, wretch, lie there, lie;
    (To the spectators.)
    And if any of you think I did amiss,
    I shall amend it, worse than it is,
    That all men may it see:
    (Menacingly.)
    Much worse than it is
    Right so shall it be.

But now since he is brought to sleep
Into some hole I fain would creep;
For I fear I quake in so sore dread,
For be I taken I be but dead;
Here will I lie these forty days,
And curse him who may first me raise.
(God appears above.)

GOD: Cain, Cain!

CAIN: Who is that that calls me?
Look, I am here, may thou not see?

GOD: Where is thy brother, Abel?

CAIN: Why ask of me? I think in hell,
I trust in hell he be—
As any there might see—
Or somewhere fallen a-sleeping;
When was he in my keeping?

GOD: Cain, Cain, thou art caught in a fierce flood;
The voice of they brother's blood
That thou hast slain in such false wise,
From earth to heaven vengeance cries.
And for thou hast brought they brother down,
Under the flood of my fury drown.

CAIN: Yea, deal out curses, I will none,
Or give them back when thou hast done.
Since I have done so great a sin,
That I may not thy mercy win,
And thus thou thrust me from thy grace,
I shall hide me from thy face;
And if any man may me find,
Let him slay me and not mind;
Wheresoever he may me meet,
Either by sty or in the street;
And harshly, when that I am dead,
Bury me in Goodybower at the Quarry Head;
If safe I can this place depart,
By all men set I not a fart.

GOD: It is not so, Cain, nay.
   No man may another slay,
   For he that slays thee, young or old,
   He shall be punished sevenfold.
   (God withdraws.)
CAIN: No matter, I know where I shall go;
   In hell for me the fire will glow;
   For mercy now to wail is vain,

   For that would but increase my pain;
   But this corpse I would were hid,
   For suddenly might come a swain
   And cry "False wretch, now God forbid,
   Thou hast thy very brother slain."
   If only Pickbrain, my boy, were here,
   We both should bury him without a tear.
   How, Pickbrain, scape-grace, Pickbrain, how!

Gorbuduc

Thomas Norton and Thomas Sackville
1561

Scene: The Court of Ferrex. The King has decided to divide his lands between his two sons, Ferrex and Porrex, while he is still alive. Great dissention has occurred because of this.

Ferrex, elder son of King Gorbuduc.
Hermon, a parasite.
Dordan, a wise counsellor assigned by the king to his son.

> *(The Court of Ferrex. Enter Ferrex attended by Hermon the parasite and Dordan the wise counsellor.)*

FERREX: I marvel much what reason led the king,
    My father, thus without all my desert,
    To reave me half the kingdom, which by course
    Of law and nature should remain to me.
HERMON: If you with stubborn and untamed pride
    Had stood against him in rebelling wise;
    Or if, with grudging mind, you had envied
    So slow a sliding of his aged years;
    Or sought before your time to haste the course
    Of fatal death upon his loyal head;
    Or strain'd your stock with murder of your kin;
    Some face of reason might perhaps have seem'd
    To yield some likely cause to spoil ye thus.
FERREX: The wreakful gods pour on my cursed head
    Eternal plagues and never-dying woes,
    The hellish prince adjudge my damned ghost
    To Tantale's thirst, or proud Ixion's wheel,
    Or cruel Gripe to gnaw my growing heart,
    To during torments and unquenched flames,
    If ever I conceiv'd so foul a thought,
    To wish his end of life, or yet of reign.
DORDAN: Ne yet your father, O most noble prince,

Did ever think so foul a thing of you;
For he, with more than father's tender love,
While yet the fates do lend him life to rule.
(Who long might live to see your ruling well)
To you, my lord, and to his other son,
Lo, he resigns his realm and royalty;
Which never would so wise a prince have done,
If he had once misdeem'd that in your heart
There ever lodged so unkind a thought.
But tender love, my lord, and settled trust
Of your good nature, and your noble mind,
Made him to place you thus in royal throne,
And now to give you half this realm to guide;
Yea, and that half which, in abounding store
Of things that serve to make a wealthy realm,
In stately cities, and in fruitful soil,
In temperate breathing of the milder heaven,
In things of needful use, which friendly sea
Transports by traffic from the foreign parts,
In flowing wealth, in honour, and in force,
Doth pass the double value of the part
That Porrex hath allotted to his reign.
Such is your case, such is your father's love.
FERREX: Oh love, my friends! Love wrongs not whom he love.
DORDAN: Ne yet he wrongeth you, that giveth you
    So large a reign ere that the course of time
    Bring you to kingdom by descended right,
    Which time perhaps might end your time before.
FERREX: Is this no wrong, say you, to reave from me
    My native right of half so great a realm,
    And thus to match his younger son with me
    In equal pow'r, and in as great degree?
    Yea, and what son? The son whose swelling pride
    Would never yield one point of reverence,
    When I the elder and apparent heir
    Stood in the likelihood to possess the whole;

Yea, and that son which from his childish age
Envieth mine honour and doth hate my life.
What will he now do, when his pride, his rage,
The mindful malice of his grudging heart
Is arm'd with force, with wealth, and kingly state?
HERMON: Was this not wrong? yea, ill advised wrong,
To give so mad a man so sharp a sword,
To so great peril of so great mishap,
Wide open thus to set so large a way?
DORDAN: Alas, my lord, what griefful thing is this,
That of your brother you can think so ill?
I never saw him utter likely sign,
Whereby a man might see or once misdeem
Such hate of you, ne such unyielding pride.
Ill is their counsel, shameful be their end,
That raising such mistrustful fear in you,
Sowing the seed of such unkindly hate,
Travail by treason to destroy you both.
Wise is your brother, and of noble hope,
Worthy to wield a large and mighty realm.
So much a stronger friend have you thereby,
Whose strength is your strength if you 'gree in one.
HERMON: If Nature and the Gods had pinched so
Their flowing bounty, and their noble gifts
Of princely qualities, from you, my lord,
And pour'd them all at once in wasteful wise
Upon your father's younger son alone;
Perhaps there be, that in your prejudice
Would say that birth should yield to worthiness.
Bit sith in each good gift and princely art
Ye are his match, and in the chief of all
In mildness and in sober governance
Ye far surmount; and sith there is in you
Sufficing skill and hopeful towardness
Io wield the whole, and match your elder's praise;
I see no cause why ye should lose the half,

Ne would I wish you yield to such a loss:
Lest your mild sufferance of so great a wrong,
Be deemed cowardice and simple dread,
Which shall give courage to the fiery head
Of your young brother to invade the whole.
While yet therefore sticks in the people's mind
The loathed wrong of your disheritance;
And ere your brother have, by settled power,
By guileful cloak of an alluring show,
Got him some force and favour in the realm;
And while the noble queen, your mother, lives,
To work and practise all for your avail;
Attempt redress by arms, and wreak yourself
Upon his life that gaineth by your loss,
Who now to shame of you, and grief of us,
In your own kingdom triumphs over you.
Show now your courage meet for kingly state,
That they which have avow'd to spend their goods,
Their lands, their lives and honours in your cause,
May be the bolder to maintain your part,
When they do see that coward fear in you
Shall not betray, ne fail their faithful hearts.
If once the death of Porrex end the strife,
And pay the price of his usurped reign,
Your mother shall persuade the angry king,
The lords, your friends, eke shall appease his rage.
For they be wise, and well they can foresee,
That ere long time your aged father's death
Will bring a time when you shall well requite
Their friendly favour, or their hateful spite,
Yea or their slackness to advance your cause.
"Wise men do not so hang on passing state
Of present princes, chiefly in their age,
But they will further cast their reaching eye,
To view and weigh the times and reigns to come."
Ne is it likely, though the king be wroth,

That he yet will, or that the realm will bear,
Extreme revenge upon his only son:
Or, if he would, what one is he that dare
Be minister to such an enterprise?
And here you be now placed in your own,
Amid your friends, your vassals, and your strength:
We shall defend and keep your person safe,
Till either counsel turn his tender mind,
Or age or sorrow end his weary days.
But if the fear of gods, and secret grudge
Of nature's law, repining at the fact,
Withhold your courage from so great attempt,
Know ye, that lust of kingdoms hath no law.
The gods do bear, and well allow in kings,
The things that they abhor in rascal routs.
"When kings on slender quarrels run to wars,
And then in cruel and unkindly wise,
Command thefts, rapes, murders of innocents,
The spoil of towns, ruins of mighty realm;
Think you such princes do suppose themselves
Subject to laws of kind, and fear of gods?"
Murders and violent thefts in private men
Are heinous crimes, and full of foul reproach;
Yet none offence, but decked with glorious name
Of noble conquests in the hands of kings.
But if you like not yet so hot devise,
Ne list to take such vantage of the time,
But, though with peril of your own estate,
You will not be the first that shall invade;
Assemble yet your force for your defence,
And for your safety stand upon your guard.
DORDAN: O heaven! was there ever heard or known,
So wicked counsel to a noble prince?
Let me, my lord, disclose unto your grace
This heinous tale, what mischief it contains;
Your father's death, your brother's, and your own,

Your present murder, and eternal shame.
Hear me, O king, and suffer not to sink
So high a treason in your princely breast.
FERREX: The mighty gods forbid that ever I
Should once conceive such mischief in my heart.
Although my brother hath bereft my realm,
And bear, perhaps, to me an hateful mind,
Shall I revenge it with his death therefore?
Or shall I so destroy my father's life
That gave me life? The gods forbid, I say:
Cease you to speak so any more to me;
Ne you, my friend, with answer once repeat
So foul a tale. In silence let it die.
What lord or subject shall have hope at all,
That under me they safely shall enjoy
Their goods, their honours, lands, and liberties,
With whom, neither one only brother dear,
Ne father dearer, could enjoy their lives?
But, sith I fear my younger brother's rage,
And sith, perhaps, some other man may give
Some like advice, to move his grudging head
At mine estate; which counsel may perchance
Take greater force with him, than this with me;
I will in secret so prepare myself,
As, if his malice or his lust to reign
Break forth in arms or sudden violence,
I may withstand his rage and keep mine own.
(Exeunt Ferrex and Hermon.)
DORDAN: I fear the fatal time now draweth on
When civil hate shall end the noble line
Of famous Brute, and of his royal seed.
Great Jove, defend the mischiefs now at hand!
O that the secretary's wise advice
Had erst been heard when he besought the king
Not to divide his land, nor send his sons
To further parts, from presence of his court,

Ne yet to yield to them his governance.
Lo, such are they now in the royal throne
As was rash Phaeton in Phoebus' car;
Ne then the fiery steeds did draw the flame
With wilder random through the kindled skies,
Than traitorous counsel now will whirl about
The youthful heads of these unskilful kings.
But I hereof their father will inform;
The reverence of him perhaps shall stay
The growing mischiefs, while they yet are green.
If this help not, then woe unto themselves,
The prince, the people, the divided land!
(Exit.)

The Interlude of the Four PP

John Heywood
1544

Scene: An "interlude" can be performed anywhere: in a home, out-doors, on a platform or a stage. There is a minimum of action and the characters represent their vocations.

Of Note: This is considered a "merry interlude" and it provides opportunity for monologue-length speeches.

A Palmer
A Pardoner
A Pothecary

PALM.: Now God be here! Who keepeth this place?
    Now, by my faith, I cry you mercy!
    Of reason I must sue for grace,
    My rudeness showeth me now so homely.
    Whereof your pardon axed and won,
    I sue you, as courtesy doth me bind,
    To tell this which shall be begun
    In order as may come best in mind.
    I am a palmer, as ye see,
    Which of my life much part hath spent
    In many a fair and far country,
    As pilgrims do of good intent.
    At Jerusalem have I been
    Before Christ's blessèd sepulture;
    The Mount of Calvary have I seen,
    A holy place, ye may be sure;
    To Josophat and Olivet
    On foot, God wot, I went right bare,
    Many a salt tear did I sweat
    Before this carcase could come there.
    Yet have I been at Rome also,

And gone the stations all arow,
Saint Peter's shrine, and many mo
Than, if I told, all ye do know,
Except that there be any such
That hath been there and diligently
Hath taken heed and markèd much,
Then can they speak as much as I.
Then at the Rhodes also I was,
And round about Amias;
At Saint Toncomber; and Saint Trunnion;
At Saint Botolph, and Saint Anne of Buxton;
On the hills of Armony, where I see Noe's ark;
With holy Job; and Saint George in Southwark;
At Waltham; and at Walsingham;
And at the good Rood of Dagenham;
At Saint Cornelius; at Saint James in Gales;
And at Saint Winifred's Well in Wales;
At Our Lady of Boston; at Saint Edmundsbury;
And straight to Saint Patrick's Purgatory;
At Redburne; and at the Blood of Hales,
Where pilgrims' pains right much avails;
At Saint Davy's; and at Saint Denis;
At Saint Matthew; and Saint Mark in Venice;
At Master John Shorn; at Canterbury;
The great God of Catwade; at King Henry;
At Saint Saviour's; at Our Lady of Southwell;
At Crome; at Willesden; and at Muswell;
At Saint Richard; and at Saint Roke;
And at Our Lady that standeth in the oak.
To these, with other many one,
Devoutly have I prayed and gone,
Praying to them to pray for me
Unto the Blessed Trinity;
By whose prayers and my daily pain
I trust the sooner to obtain
For my salvation grace and mercy.

For, be ye sure, I think surely
Who seeketh saints for Christ's sake
And namely such as pain do take
On foot to punish their frail body
Shall thereby merit more highly
Than by anything done by man.

PARD.: And when ye have gone as far as ye can,
For all your labour and ghostly intent
Yet welcome home as wise as ye went!

PALM.: Why, sir, despise ye pilgrimage?

PARD.: Nay, 'fore God, sir! Then did I rage!
I think ye right well occupied
To seek these saints on every side.
Also your pain I not dispraise it;
But yet I discommend your wit;
And, ere we go, even so shall ye,
If ye in this will answer me:
I pray you, show what the cause is
Ye went all these pilgrimages.

PALM.: Forsooth, this life I did begin
To rid the bondage of my sin;
For which these saints, rehearsed ere this,
I have both sought and seen, iwis,
Beseeching them to be record
Of all my pain unto the Lord
That giveth all remission
Upon each man's contrition.
And by their good mediation,
Upon mine humble submission,
I trust to have in very deed
For my soul's health the better speed.

PARD.: Now is your own confession likely
To make yourself a fool quickly!
For I perceive ye would obtain
None other thing for all your pain
But only grace your soul to save.

Now, mark in this what wit ye have
To seek so far, and help so nigh!
Even here at home is remedy,
For at your door myself doth dwell,
Who could have saved your soul as well
As all your wide wandering shall do,
Though ye went thrice to Jericho.
Now, since ye might have sped at home,
What have ye won by running at Rome?
PALM.: If this be true that ye have moved,
Then is my wit indeed reproved!
But let us hear first what ye are.
PARD.: Truly, I am a pardoner.
PALM.: Truly a pardoner, that may be true,
But a true pardoner doth not ensue!
Right seldom is it seen, or never,
That truth and pardoners dwell together;
For, be your pardons never so great,
Yet them to enlarge ye will not let
With such lies that oft-times, Christ wot,
Ye seem to have that ye have not.
Wherefore I went myself to the self thing
In every place, and, without faining,
Had as much pardon there assuredly
As ye can promise me here doubtfully.
Howbeit, I think ye do but scoff.
But if ye had all the pardon ye speak of,
And no whit of pardon graunted
In any place where I have haunted,
Yet of my labour I nothing repent.
God hath respect how each time is spent;
And, as in his knowledge all is regarded,
So by his goodness all is rewarded.
PARD.: By the first part of this last tale
It seemeth you come late from the ale!
For reason on your side so far doth fail

That ye leave reasoning and begin to rail;
Wherein ye forget your own part clearly,
For ye be as untrue as I;
And in one point ye are beyond me,
For ye may lie by authority,
And all that hath wandered so far
That no man can be their controller.
And, where ye esteem your labour so much,
I say yet again my pardons be such
That, if there were a thousand souls on a heap,
I would bring them all to heaven as good cheap
As ye have brought yourself on pilgrimage
In the last quarter of your voyage,
Which is far a this side heaven, by God!
There your labour and pardon is odd,
With small cost and without any pain,
These pardons bringeth them to heaven plain.
Give me but a penny or two pence,
And as soon as the soul departeth hence,
In half an hour—or three quarters at most—
The soul is in heaven with the Holy Ghost!
(While he is speaking, enter the Pothecary.)
POT.: Send ye any souls to heaven by water?
PARD.: If we did, sir, what is the matter?
POT.: By God, I have a dry soul should thither!
 I pray you let our souls go to heaven togither.
 So busy you twain be in souls' health,
 May not a pothecary come in by stealth?
 Yes, that I will, by Saint Anthony!
 And, by the leave of this company,
 Prove ye false knaves both, ere we go,
 In part of your sayings, as this, lo:
 (To the Palmer.)
 Thou by they travel thinkest heaven to get;
 (To the Pardoner.)
 And thou by pardons and relics countest no let

To send thine own soul to heaven sure,
And all other whom thou list to procure.
If I took an action, then were they blank;
For, like thieves, the knaves rob away my thank.
All souls in heaven having relief,
Shall they thank your crafts? Nay, thank mine, chief!
No soul, ye know, entereth heaven-gate
Till from the body he be separate;
And whom have ye known die honestly
Without help of the pothecary?
Nay, all that cometh to our handling,
Except ye hap to come to hanging—
That way, perchance, ye shall not mister
To go to heaven without a glister!
But, be ye sure, I would be woe
If ye should chance to beguile me so.
As good to lie with me a-night
As hang abroad in the moonlight!
There is no choice to flee my hand
But, as I said, into the band.
Since of our souls the multitude
I send to heaven, when all is viewed,
Who should but I, then, altogither
Have thank of all their coming thither?

PARD.: If ye killed a thousand in an hour's space,
    When come they to heaven, dying from state of grace?

POT.: If a thousand pardons about your necks were tied,
    When come they to heaven if they never died?

PALM.: Long life after good works, indeed,
    Doth hinder man's receipt of meed,
    And death before one duty done
    May make us think we die too soon.
    Yet better tarry a thing, then have it,
    Than go too soon and vainly crave it.

PARD.: The longer ye dwell in communication,
    The less shall you like this imagination;

For ye may perceive, even at the first chip,
Your tale is trapped in such a stop
That, at the least, ye seem worse than we.
POT.: By the Mass, I hold us naught, all three!

Hamlet

William Shakespeare
1604

Scene: In the Palace. Rosenkranz and Guildenstern have been sent by King Claudius to try to discover the cause of Hamlet's unusual behavior.

Hamlet, Prince of Denmark.
Rosenkranz, Courtier and previously friend of Hamlet.
Guildenstern, Courtier and previously friend of Hamlet.

GUILDENSTERN: My honored lord!

ROSENKRANZ: My most dear lord!

HAMLET: My excellent good friends! How dost thou, Guilderstern?
   O, Rosenkranz! Good lads, how do you both?

ROSENKRANZ: As the indifferent children of the earth.

GUILDENSTERN: Happy in that we are not overhappy,
   On Fortune's cap we are not the very button.

HAMLET: Nor the soles of her shoe?

ROSENKRANZ: Neither, my lord.

HAMLET: Then you live about her waist, or in the middle of her favors?

GUILDENSTREN: Faith, her privates we.

HAMLET: In the secret parts of Fortune? O, most true, she is a strumpet. What's the news?

ROSENKRANZ: None, my lord, but that the world's grown honest.

HAMLET: Then is doomsday near. But your news is not true. Let me question more in particular. What have you, my good friends, deserved at the hands of Fortune, that she sends you to prison hither?

GUIDENSTERN: Prison, my lord?

HAMLET: Denmark's a prison.

ROSENKRANZ: Then is the world one.

HAMLET: A goodly one, in which there are many confines, wards, and dungeons, Denmark being one o'th' worst.

ROSENKRANZ: We think not so, my lord.

HAMLET: Why, then 'tis none to you; for there is nothing either good or bad, but thinking makes it so. To me it is a prison.

ROSENKRANZ: Why, then, your ambition makes it one; 'tis too narrow for your mind. O God I could be bounded in a nutshell and count myself a king of infinite space, were it not that I have bad dreams.

GUILDENSTERN: Which dreams, indeed, are ambition; for the very substance of the ambitious is merely the shadow of a dream.

HAMLET: A dream itself is but a shadow.

ROSENKRANZ: Truly, and I hold ambition of so airy and light a quality, that it is but a shadow's shadow.

HAMLET: Then are our beggars bodies, and our monarchs and outstretched heroes the beggars' shadows. Shall we to th'court? For, by my fay, I cannot reason.

ROSENKRANZ AND GUILDENSTERN: We'll wait upon you.

HAMLET: No such matter. I will not sort you with the rest of my servants, for, to speak to you like an honest man, I am most dreadfully attended. But, in the beaten way of friendship, what make you at Elsinore?

ROSENKRANZ: To visit you, my lord, no other occasion.

HAMLET: Beggar that I am, I am even poor in thanks, but I thank you. And sure, dear friends, my thanks are too dear a halfpenny. Were you not sent for? Is it your own inclining? Is it a free visitation? Come, deal justly with me. Come, come. Nay, speak.

GUILDENSTERN: What should we say, my lord?

HAMLET: Why, anything but to the purpose. You were sent for, and there is a kind of confession in your looks, which your modesties have not craft enough to color. I know the good King and Queen have sent for you.

ROSENKRANZ: To what end, my lord?

HAMLET: That you must teach me. But let me conjure you, by the rights of our fellowship, by the consonancy of our youth, by the obligation of our ever-preserved love, and by what more dear a better proposer could charge you withal, be even and direct with me whether you were sent for or no.

ROSENKRANZ: *(Aside to Guildenstern.)* What say you?

HAMLET: *(Aside.)* Nay, then, I have an eye of you. If you love me, hold not off.

GUILDENSTERN: My lord, we were sent for.

HAMLET: I will tell you why. So shall my anticipation prevent your discovery and your secrecy to the King and Queen moult no feather. I have of late—but wherefore I know not—lost all my mirth, forgone all custom of exercises; and, indeed, it goes so heavily with my disposition that this goodly frame, the earth, seems to me a sterile promontory. This most excellent canopy, the air, look you, this brave o'erhanging firmament, this majestical roof fretted with golden fire—why, it appears no other thing to me than a foul and pestilent congregation of vapors. What a piece of work is man, how noble in reason, how infinite in faculty, in form and moving how express and admirable, in action how like an angel, in apprehension how like a god—the beauty of the world, the paragon of animals! And yet, to me, what is this quintessence of dust? Man delights not me—no, nor woman neither, though by your smiling you seem to say so.

ROSENKRANZ: My lord, there was no such stuff in my thoughts.

HAMLET: Why did you laugh, then, when I said "Man delights not me"?

ROSENKRANZ: To think, my lord, if you delight not in man, what lenten entertainment the players shall receive from you. We coted them on the way, and higher are they coming, to offer you service.

HAMLET: He that plays the King shall be welcome—his majesty shall have tribute of me; the Adventurous Knight shall use his foil and target, the Lover shall not sigh gratis; the Humorous Man shall end his part in peace; the Clown shall make those laugh whose lungs are tickle o'th'sere; and the Lady shall say her mind freely, or the blank verse shall halt for't. What players are they?

ROSENKRANZ: Even those you were wont to take such delight in, the tragedians of the city.

HAMLET: How chances it they travel? Their residence, both in reputation and profit, was better both ways.

ROSENKRANZ: I think their inhibition comes by the means of the late innovation.

HAMLET: Do they hold the same estimation they did when I was in the city? Are they so followed?

ROSENKRANZ: No, indeed, they are not.

HAMLET: How comes it? Do they grow rusty?

ROSENKRANZ: Nay, their endeavour keeps in the wonted pace. But there is, sir, an aerie of children, little eyases, that cry out on the top of question, and are most tyrannically clapped for't. These are now the fashion, and so berattle the common stages—so they call them—that many wearing rapiers are afraid of goose-quills, and dare scarce come thither.

HAMLET: What, are they children? Who maintains 'em? How are they escoted? Will they pursue the quality no longer than they can sing? Will they not say afterwards, if they should grow themselves to common players—as it is most like, if their means are no better—their writers do them wrong to make them exclaim against their own succession?

ROSENKRANZ: Faith, there has been much to do on both sides; and the nation holds it no sin to tar them to controversy. There was, for a while, no money bid for argument, unless the poet and the player went to cuffs in the question.

HAMLET: Is't possible?

GUILDENSTERN: O, there has been much throwing about of brains.

HAMLET: Do the boys carry it away?

ROSENKRANZ: Ay, that they do, my lord—Hercules and his load too.

HAMLET: It is not very strange; for my uncle is King of Denmark, and those that would make mouths at him while my father lived, give twenty, forty, fifty, a hundred ducats a piece for his picture in little. 'Sblood, there is something in this more than natural, if philosophy could find it out.

(Flourish of trumpets.)

The Spanish Wives

Mary Griffith Pix
1696

Scene: A Hall in the Governor's Palace—Barcelona.

Governor of Barcelona, a merry old Lord who gives his wife much
  liberty.
Marquess of Moncada, a jealous Lord, guest of the Governor.
Hidewell, retained by the Count Camillus, who is in love with the
  Marquess's wife (disguised as a Country Fellow).

(Enter the Governor of Barcelona and the Marquess of Moncada.)
GOVERN: Prithee, my Lord Marquess, don't trouble me with they jealous whims: You say, there was masqueraders last night under the
  windows,—why there let 'em be a God's name! I am sorry 'twas
  such a cold raw night for the honest lads. By the honor of Spain,
  if I had heard 'em, I would ha' sent the rogues a glass of malaga
  to warm 'em.
MARQUESS: O Lard! O Lard! I shall run mad! Sure, my Lord Governor,
  your horns will exceed the largest in the Palace Hall.—Oh! that
  my wife were out of your house, and Barcelona! Methinks I am
  not secure, though she's under eleven locks.
GOV: By my Holy Dame, I am of your mind: I don't think you are
  secure.
MARQ: How! Do you know anything to the contrary?
GOV: Why, by th' mass, this I believe: her head's at work; And, I dare
  say, she has made ye a cuckold, in imagination, with every Don
  she has through any peep-hole seen, since your first marriage.
MARQ: Oh! damn her! damn her!
GOV: You'll never take my advice. *(Sings.)*
  —Give but a woman her freedom still,
  Then she'll never act what's ill:
  'Tis crossing her, makes her have the will.
  —Phough! I have been in England—There they are the happiest
  husbands—If a man does happen to be a cuckold, which, by the

way, is almost as rare as in Spain: But, I say, if it does fall out, all his wife's friends are his; and he's caressed,—nay, Gadzooks, many times rises to his preferment by it.

MARQ: Oh, insufferable! I am not able to bear your discourse.

(Enter a Country Fellow.)

—A man coming from my wife's apartments!—Oh, the Devil! the Devil!

GOV: I see no cloven foot he has.

MARQ: No; but he is one of his imps; a letter-carrier. I read it in his face.

GOV: Oh! I begin to perceive it now,—here's the superscription writ in his forehead:—*To the beauteous Donna Elenora, Marchioness of, & C,* Ay, 'tis very plain.

MARQ: Well, Governor, these jeers won't' be put up so.

COUNTRY FELLOW: What a wanion ails ye, trow? What do ye mean by letters: Ich am no schollard; my calling is to zell fruit; and sum o' the meads o' this hause (meads Ich think 'em) beckoned me in;—I zould 'em zum; and that's all I knaw.

GOV: Ay, honest fellow, I dare swear 'tis: —why, if thou wert a monkey, he'd be jealous on thee.

MARQ: You may think what you please, but I fear other things. Therefore, if, as a guest, you will let me have the freedom of your house, I'll take this fellow in, and search him.

GOV: Ay, with all my heart.—Oh these jealous fools! *(Aside.)*

MARQ: Come along, sirrah; I'll look as much in thy mouth.

GOV: Ay, for fear there should be a note in a hollow tooth.

COUNT. FELLOW: Why,—de ye zee, as for matter o' that,—ye ma' look in my a—

GOV: Hold, Beast, 'tis a man of quality you speak to.

COUNT. FELLOW: Zooks, I think 'tis a madman.

MARQ: Come your ways, Impudence!

COUNT. FELLOW: But, Sir, Sir,—must the meads zerch me, or the men?

MARQ: I'll tell you presently, ye wanton rogue.

(Exit. Driving him before him.)

The Spanish Wives

Mary Griffith Pix
1696

Scene: A palace in Barcelona—Camillus's lodgings.

Count Camillus, a Roman Count following the Marquess' wife.
Friar Andrew, one who attends the Count.
Hidewell, retained by the Count.

FRIAR: Well, my Lord! now we are come to Barcelona, I fear this devil of a Marquess will be too hard for us.

CAM: How, Father Andrew, desponding!—'Twas but this morning, over your Malaga, you swore by the Eleven Thousand Virgins, and all your catalogue of saints, you'd bring my Elenora to my arms.

FRIAR: And by fifty thousand more, so I will, if it be possible: If not, my oath is void: You know the Marquess hates me heartily, as I do him, because once he caught me carrying your letter to his wife.

CAM: For the good office, I think, used ye most scurvily.

FRIAR: Scurvily! basely, barbarously; without respect to these sacred robes; tossed me in a blanket; covered me with filth and dust; and so sent me by force to our convent. For which, and my natural inclination to cuckoldom, I have joined in your attempts, and waited on you to Barcelona, to be revenged.

CAM: You know there's justice in my cause.—Elenora was, by contract, mine, at Rome, before this old Marquess had her. And could I again recover her, I don't question but to get leave of his Holiness for a divorce, and marry her myself.

FRIAR: Nay, that's as you please; when she's in your possession, marry or not, 'tis all one to Father Andrew; it never shall trouble my conscience. I must own, were I in your condition, I should not marry; because daily experience shows, a wife's a cloy, and a mistress a pleasure.

CAM: Well, we'll discourse that when we have the lady; and in the mean time, good Father, be diligent.

FRIAR: I think I am diligent; I am sure, I am worn to mere skin and bone in your service. This morning I found for ye a Mercury, a letter-carrier, that can slip through a key-hole to deliver a billet-doux to a fair lady.

CAM: I wish he were returned; I fear some misfortune has befallen him.

FRIAR: O! here he comes, sound wind and limb!
(Enter Hidewell [the Country Fellow before].)
—So, my dear tool of gallantry! how hast thou sped?

HIDEWELL: Gad, the hardest task I ever undertook.—Sir, you gave me five ducats,—as I hope for preferment, and to be made pimp-master general, it deserves double the sum.

CAM: Nor shalt thou fail of it, Boy, if thou hast succeeded.

HIDEW: First then, the damned old jealous Marquess caught me, and notwithstanding my counterfeit speech and simplicity, had me amongst his varlets, to be searched. They knew his custom, and no sooner, but they flew upon me like so many furies: I feared it had been to tear me limb from limb; but it proved only to tear my clothes off; which was done in a twinkling, and I left as naked as my mother bore me; whilst the old Marquess groveled all over my habiliments, and run pins in 'em, so thick that a poor louse would not have 'scaped spitting. The only thing which pleased me, was to observe a peep-hole the maids (knowing this to be their master's searching-room) had made; and sometimes one eye, sometimes another, viewing my proportions.

CAM: But had you any letter? was that safe? Satisfy me there.

HIDEW: Pray let me take my own method.—Nothing being found, they gave me again my clothes, and the Marquess a ducat for my trouble: Yet I had a letter—

CAM: Which thou ingeniously swallowedst.

HIDEW: No; which I more ingeniously brought.

CAM: What, in thy hat?

HIDEW: My hat had the same severe trial.

CAM: Thy shoes—

HIDEW: They passed the same scrutiny,—impossible in any of them to hide a scrip, the least shred of paper.

CAM: How then?

HIDEW: My Lord, do ye observe this stick?

CAM: *(Viewing it.)* Yes; 'tis an honest crabtree-stick—I see no more in it.

FRIAR: *(Taking the stick and putting on his spectacles to view it.)* Come, come, let me see it; I can smell out a note that comes from a fair hand;—By St. Dominic, here's neither paper not writing upon it.

HIDEW: Give it me. *(He unscrews the ferrule at the bottom, takes out the letter, and gives it to Camillus.)*

FRIAR: Thou dear abstract of invention, let me kiss thee.

CAM: Excellent Hidewell! if thou wilt stay with me, whilst I am in Barcelona, I'll satisfy thy utmost wishes.

HIDEW: Most willingly.

CAM: Here Father, here dear confidant! Orada writes that the tormented Marquess has removed her from those apartments that were next the streets to some that overlook the gardens,—thither, she says, my Elenora would have me come this night; And if they can find a place to 'scape at, before the lodgings are better secured, they will: If not, we shall hear of them,—a gentle whistle is the sign.—Hidewell, you shan't appear in this, because if seen, you'd be known again.

FRIAR: Pray let me go: Gad, if the business should be done without my help, I should take it very ill.

CAM: Well, well, we'll in, and consider on't. *(Exeunt.)*

A Bold Stroke for a Wife

Susanna Centlivre
1718

Scene: A tavern

Colonel Fainwell
Freeman, his friend.
Mr. Sackbut, a tavern keeper.
Brief entrance of Drawer, a servant.

FREEMAN: Come, Colonel, his Majesty's health! You are as melancholy as if you were in love; I wish some of the beauties at Bath ha'n't snapped your heart.

COLONEL: Why faith, Freeman, there is something in't; I have seen a lady at Bath who has kindled such a flame in me that all the waters there can't quench.

FREEMAN: Women, like some poisonous animals, carry their antidote about 'em. Is she not to be had, Colonel?

COLONEL: That's a difficult question to answer; however, I resolve to try. Perhaps you may be able to serve me; you merchants know one another.—The lady told me herself she was under the charge of four persons.

FREEMAN: Odso! 'Tis Mrs. Ann Lovely.

COLONEL: The same; do you know her?

FREEMAN: Know her! Ay—faith, Colonel, your condition is more desperate than you imagine; why she is the talk and pity of the whole town; and it is the opinion of the learned that she must die a maid.

COLONEL: Say you so? That's somewhat odd in this charitable city. She's a woman, I hope.

FREEMAN: For aught I know; but it had been as well for her had nature made her any other part of the creation. The man which keeps this house served her father; he is a very honest fellow and may be of use to you; we'll send for him to take a glass with us. He'll give you the whole history, and 'tis worth your hearing.

COLONEL: But may one trust him?

FREEMAN: With your life; I have obligations enough upon him to make him do anything; I serve him with wine. *(Knocks.)*

COLONEL: Nay, I know him pretty well myself; I once used to frequent a club that was kept here.

(Enter Drawer.)

DRAWER: Gentlemen, d'you call?

FREEMAN: Ay, send up your master.

DRAWER: Yes, sir *(Exit.)*

COLONEL: Do you know any of this lady's guardians, Freeman?

FREEMAN: Yes, I know two of them very well.

COLONEL: What are they?

(Enter Sackbut.)

FREEMAN: Here comes one will give you an account of them all—Mr. Sackbut, we sent for you to take a glass with us. 'Tis a maxim among the friends of the bottle that as long as the master is in company one may be sure of good wine.

SACKBUT: Sir, you shall be sure to have as good wine as you send in.—Colonel, your most humble servant; you are welcome to town.

COLONEL: I thank you, Mr. Sackbut.

SACKBUT: I am as glad to see you as I should a hundred ton of French claret custom free. My service to you, sir *(Drinks.)* You don't look so merry as you used to do; are you not well, Colonel?

FREEMAN: He has got a woman in his head, landlord; can you help him?

SACKBUT: If 'tis in my power, I shan't scruple to serve my friend.

COLONEL: 'Tis one perquisite of your calling.

SACKBUT: Ay, at t'other end of the town, where you officers use, women are good forcers of trade; a well-customed house, a handsome barkeeper, with clean, obliging drawers, soon get the master an estate; but our citizens seldom do anything but cheat within the walls.—But as to the lady, Colonel, point you at particulars, or have you a good champagne stomach? Are you in full pay, or reduced, Colonel?

COLONEL: Reduced, reduced, landlord.

FREEMAN: To the miserable condition of a lover!

SACKBUT: Pish! That's preferable to half pay; a woman's resolution may break before the peace; push her home, Colonel; there's no parleying with that sex.

COLONEL: Were the lady her own mistress I have some reasons to believe I should soon command in chief.

FREEMAN: You know Mrs. Lovely, Mr. Sackbut?

SACKBUT: Know her! Ay, poor Nancy; I have carried her to school many a frosty morning. Alas, if she's the woman, I pity you, Colonel. Her father, my old master, was the most whimsical, out-of-the-way tempered man I ever heard of, as you will guess by his last will and testament. This was his only child. I have heard him wish her dead a thousand times.

COLONEL: Why so?

SACKBUT: He hated posterity, you must know, and wished the world were to expire with himself. He used to swear if she had been a boy, he would have qualified him for the opera.

FREEMAN: 'Tis a very unnatural resolution in a father.

SACKBUT: He died worth thirty thousand pounds, which he left to this daughter provided she married with the consent of her guardians. But that she might be sure never to do so, he left her in the care of four men, as opposite to each other as light and darkness. Each has his quarterly rule, and three months in a year she is obliged to be subject to each of their humors, and they are pretty different, I assure your. She is just come from Bath.

COLONEL: 'Twas there I saw her.

SACKBUT: Ay, sir the last quarter was her beau guardian's. She appears in all public places during his reign.

COLONEL: She visited a lady who boarded in the same house with me. I liked her person and found an opportunity to tell her so. She replied she had no objection to mine, but if I could not reconcile contradictions, I must not think of her, for that she was condemned to the caprice of four persons who never yet agreed in any one thing, and she was obliged to please them all.

SACKBUT: 'Tis most true, sir; I'll give you a short description of the men and leave you to judge of the poor lady's condition. One is a kind of a virtuoso, a silly, half-witted fellow but positive and surly; fond of nothing but what is antique and foreign, and wears his clothes of the fashion of the last century; dotes upon travelers and believes Sir John Mandeville more than the Bible.

COLONEL: That must be a rare old fellow!

SACKBUT: Another is a changebroker, a fellow that will outlie the devil for the advantage of stock and cheat his father that got him in a bargain. He is a great stickler for trade and hates everything that wears a sword.

FREEMAN: He is a great admirer of the Dutch management and swears they understand trade better than any nation under the sun.

SACKBUT: The third is an old beau that has May in his fancy and dress but December in his face and his heels; he admires nothing but new fashions, and those must be French; loves operas, balls, masquerades, and is always the most tawdry of the whole company on a birthday.

COLONEL: These are pretty opposite to one another, truly. And the fourth, what is he, landlord?

SACKBUT: A very rigid Quaker, whose quarter begun this day. I saw Mrs. Lovely go in not above two hours ago. Sir Philip set her down. What think you now, Colonel; is not the poor lady to be pitied?

COLONEL: Ay, and rescued too, landlord.

FREEMAN: In my opinion, that's impossible.

COLONEL: There is nothing impossible to a lover. What would not a man attempt for a fine woman and thirty thousand pounds? Besides, my honor is at stake; I promised to deliver her, and she bade me win her and take her.

SACKBUT: That's fair, faith.

FREEMAN: If it depended upon knight-errantry, I should not doubt your setting free the damsel; but to have avarice, impertinence, hypocrisy, and pride at once to deal with requires more cunning than generally attends a man of honor.

COLONEL: My fancy tells me I shall come off with glory; I resolve to try, however.—Do you know all the guardians, Mr. Sackbut?

SACKBUT: Very well, sir; they all use my house.

COLONEL: And will you assist me, if occasion be?

SACKBUT: In everything I can, Colonel.

FREEMAN: I'll answer for him; and whatever I can serve you in, you may depend on. I know Mr. Periwinkle and Mr. Tradelove; the latter has a very great opinion of my interest abroad. I happened to have a letter from a correspondent two hours before the news arrived of the French king's death; I communicated it to him; upon which he bought up all the stock he could, and what with that and some wagers he laid he told me he had got to the tune of five thousand pounds; so that I am much in his good graces.

COLONEL: I don't know but you may be to service of me, Freeman.

FREEMAN: If I can, command me, Colonel.

COLONEL: Is it not possible to find a suit of clothes ready-made at some of these sale shops, fit to rig out a beau, think you, Mr. Sackbut?

SACKBUT: O hang 'em, no, Colonel; they keep nothing ready-made that a gentleman would be seen in. But I can fit you with a suit of clothes, if you'd make a figure—velvet and gold brocade— they were pawned to me by a French count who had been stripped at play and wanted money to carry him home; he promised to send for them, but I have heard nothing from him.

FREEMAN: He has not fed upon frogs long enough yet to recover his loss, ha, ha.

COLONEL: Ha, ha; well, those clothes will do, Mr. Sackbut, though we must have three or four fellows in tawdry liveries. Those can be procured, I hope.

FREEMAN: Egad, I have a brother come from the West Indies that can match you and, for expedition sake, you shall have his servants. There's a black, a tawny-moor, and a Frenchman. They don't speak one word of English, so can make no mistake.

COLONEL: Excellent. Egad, I shall look like an Indian prince. First I'll attach my beau guardian. Where lives he?

SACKBUT: Faith, somewhere about St. James's; though to say in what street, I cannot. But any chairman will tell you where Sir Philip Modelove lives.

FREEMAN: O, you'll find him in the Park at eleven every day; at least I never passed through at that hour without seeing him there. But what do you intend?

COLONEL: To address him in his own way and find what he designs to do with the lady.

FREEMAN: And what then?

COLONEL: Nay, that I can't tell, but I shall take my measures accordingly.

SACKBUT: Well, 'tis a mad undertaking, in my mind; but here's to your success, Colonel. *(Drinks.)*

COLONEL: 'Tis something out of the way, I confess; but fortune may chance to smile, and I succeed. Come, landlord, let me see those clothes—Freeman, I shall expect you'll leave word with Mr. Sackbut where one may find you upon occasion; and send my equipage of India immediately, do you hear?

FREEMAN: Immediately. *(Exit.)*

COLONEL: Bold was the man who ventured first to sea,
But the first vent'ring lovers bolder were.
The path of love's a dark dangerous way,
Without a landmark, or one friendly star,
And he that runs the risk, deserves the fair. *(Exit with Sackbut.)*

Woyzeck

Georg Buchner
1836

Scene: Three short scenes from the fragmented and unfinished play by Buchner. Woyzeck has volunteered his body for scientific experimentation and has been on a diet of green peas for several weeks. He is increasingly hallucinatory and paranoid. He is supporting a common-law wife and new baby but suspects her of infidelities.

Of Note: These scenes may be performed in any order. Each is complete within itself.

Woyzeck, early 30s, a barber in the army.
The Captain
The Doctor

(The Captain in a chair, Woyzeck shaves him.)
CAPTAIN: Take it easy, Woyzeck, take it easy. One thing at a time. You're making me dizzy. You're going to finish early today—what am I supposed to do with the extra ten minutes? Woyzeck, just think, you've still got a good thirty years to live, thirty years! That's 360 months, and days, hours, minutes! What are you going to do with that ungodly amount of time? Get organized, Woyzeck.
WOYZECK: Yes, Cap'n.
CAPTAIN: I fear for the world when I think about eternity. Activity, Woyzeck, activity! Eternal—that's eternal—that is—eternal—you realize that, of course. But then again it's not eternal, it's only a moment, yes, a moment. Woyzeck, it frightens me to think that the earth rotates in one day. What a waste of time! What will come of that? Woyzeck, I can't look at a mill wheel anymore or I get melancholy.
WOYZECK: Yes, Cap'n.
CAPTAIN: Woyzeck, you always look so upset. A good man doesn't

act like that, a good man with a good conscience. Say something, Woyzeck. What's the weather like?

WOYZECK: It's bad, Cap'n, bad—wind.

CAPTAIN: I can feel it, there's something rapid out there. A wind like that reminds me of a mouse. *(Cunningly.)* I believe it's coming from the south-north.

WOYZECK: Yes, Cap'n.

CAPTAIN: Ha-ha-ha! South-north! Ha-ha-ha! Oh, are you stupid, terribly stupid! *(Sentimentally.)* Woyzeck, you're a good man, a good man—*(With dignity.)* but Woyzeck, you've got no morality. Morality—that's when you are moral, you understand. It's a good word. You have a child without the blessing of the church, as our Reverend Chaplain says, without the blessing of the church. *I* didn't make that up.

WOYZECK: Cap'n, the good Lord isn't going to look at a poor worm only because amen was said over it before it was created. The Lord said: "Suffer little children to come unto me."

CAPTAIN: What's that you're saying? What kind of a crazy answer is that? You're getting me all confused. When I say you, I mean you—you!

WOYZECK: Us poor people. You see, Cap'n—money, money. If you don't have money . . . Just try to raise your own kind on morality in this world. After all, we're flesh and blood. The likes of us are unhappy in this world and in the next. I guess if we ever got to Heaven, we'd have to help with the thunder.

CAPTAIN: Woyzeck, you have no virtue. You're not a virtuous person. Flesh and blood? When I'm lying at the window after it has rained, and I watch the white stockings as they go tripping down the street—damn it, Woyzeck, then love comes all over me. I've got flesh and blood, too. But Woyzeck, virtue, virtue! How else could I make time go by? I always say to myself: you're a virtuous man, *(Sentimentally.)* a good man, a good man.

WOYZECK: Yes, Cap'n, virtue! I haven't figured it out yet. You see, us common people, we don't have virtue. We act like nature tells us. But if I was a gentleman, and had a hat and a watch and a topcoat and could talk refined, then I'd be virtuous, too. Virtue must be nice, Cap'n. But I'm just a poor guy.

CAPTAIN: That's fine, Woyzeck. You're a good man, a good man. But you think too much, that's unhealthy. You always look so upset. This discussion has really worn me out. You can go now—and don't run like that! Slowly, nice and slow down the street.

(At the Doctor's.)

DOCTOR: What is this I hear. Woyzeck? A man of honor!

WOYZECK: What is it, Doctor?

DOCTOR: I saw it, Woyzeck. You pissed on the street, you pissed on the wall like a dog. And you get two cents a day. Woyzeck, that's bad. The world's getting bad, very bad.

WOYZECK: But Doctor, the call of nature . . .

DOCTOR: The call of nature, the call of nature! Nature! Haven't I proved that the *musculus constrictor vesicae* is subject to the will? Nature! Woyzeck, man is free. In man alone is individuality exalted to freedom. Couldn't hold it in! *(Shakes his head, puts his hands behind his back, and paces back and forth.)* Did you eat your peas already, Woyzeck? I'm revolutionizing science, I'll blow it sky-high. Urea ten per cent, ammonium chloride, hyperoxide. Woyzeck try pissing again. Go in there and try.

WOYZECK: I can't, Doctor.

DOCTOR: *(With emotion.)* But pissing on the wall! I have it in writing. Here's the contract. I saw it all—saw it with my own eyes. I was just holding my nose out the window, letting the sun's rays hit it, so as to examine the process of sneezing. *(Goes up to him.)* No, Woyzeck, I'm not getting angry. Anger is unhealthy, unscientific. I am calm, perfectly calm. My pulse is beating at its usual sixty, and I tell you this in all cold-bloodedness. Now, who would get excited about a human being, a human being? If it were a Proteus that were dying—! But you shouldn't have pissed on the wall . . .

WOYZECK: You see, Doctor, sometimes you've got a certain character, a certain structure. But with nature, that's something else, you see, with nature. *(He cracks his knuckles.)* That's like—how should I put it—for example. . .

DOCTOR: Woyzeck, you're philosophizing again.

WOYZECK: *(Confidingly.)* Doctor, have you ever seen anything of double nature? When the sun's standing high at noon and the world seems to be going up in flames, I've heard a terrible voice talking to me!

DOCTOR: Woyzeck, you've got an *aberratio!*

WOYZECK: *(Puts his finger to his nose.)* The toadstools, Doctor. There—that's where it is. Have you seen how they grow in patterns? If only someone could read that.

DOCTOR: Woyzeck, you've got a marvelous *aberratio mentalis partialis,* second species, beautifully developed. Woyzeck, you're getting a raise. Second species: fixed idea with a generally rational condition. You're doing everything as usual? Shaving your captain?

WOYZECK: Yes, sir.

DOCTOR: Eating your peas?

WOYZECK: Same as ever, Doctor. My wife gets the money for the household.

DOCTOR: Going on duty.

WOYZECK: Yes, sir.

DOCTOR: You're an interesting case. Subject Woyzeck, you're getting a raise. Now behave. Show me your pulse! Yes.

(Street.)

(The Captain comes panting down the street, stops, pants, looks around.)

CAPTAIN: Doctor, I feel sorry for horses when I think that the poor beasts have to go everywhere on foot. Don't run like that! Don't wave your cane around in the air like that! You'll run yourself to death that way. A good man with a good conscience doesn't go so fast. A good man . . . *(He catches the Doctor by the coat.)* Doctor, allow me to save a human life. You're racing . . . Doctor, I'm so melancholy. I get so emotional. I always start crying when I see my coat hanging on the wall—there it is.

DOCTOR: Hm! Bloated, fat, thick neck, apoplectic constitution. Yes, Captain, you might be stricken by an *apoplexia cerebralis.* But you might get it just on one side and be half paralyzed, or—best of all—you might become mentally affected and just vegetate from then on. Those are approximately your prospects for the next four weeks. Moreover, I can assure you that you will be a most interesting case, and if, God willing, your tongue is partialy paralyzed, we'll make immortal experiments.

CAPTAIN: Doctor, don't frighten me! People have been known to die of fright, of pure, sheer fright. I can see them now, with flowers in their hands—but they'll say, he was a good man, a good man. You damn coffin nail!

DOCTOR: *(Holds out his hat.)* What's this, Captain? That's brain-less!

CAPTAIN: *(Makes a crease.)* What's this, Doctor? That's increase!

DOCTOR: I take my leave, most honorable Mr. Drillprick.

CAPTAIN: Likewise, dearest Mr. Coffin Nail.

(Woyzeck comes running down the street.)

CAPTAIN: Hey, Woyzeck, why are you running past us like that? Stay here, Woyzeck. You're running around like an open razor blade. You might cut someone! You're running like you had to shave a regiment of castrates and would be hanged while the last hair was disappearing. But about those long beards—what was I going to say? Woyzeck—those long beards . . .

DOCTOR: A long beard on the chin. Pliny speaks of it. Soldiers should be made to give them up.

CAPTAIN: *(Continues.)* Hey? What about those long beards? Say, Woyzeck, haven't you found a hair from a beard in your soup bowl yet? Hey! You understand, of course, a human hair, from the beard of an engineer, a sergeant, a—drum major? Hey, Woyzeck? But you've got a decent wife. Not like others.

WOYZECK: Yes, sir! What are you trying to say, Cap'n?

CAPTAIN: Look at the face he's making! Now, it doesn't necessarily have to be in the soup, but if you hurry around the corner, you might find one on a pair of lips—a pair of lips, Woyzeck. I know what love is, too, Woyzeck. Say! You're as white as chalk!

WOYZECK: Cap'n, I'm just a poor devil—and that's all I have in the world. Cap'n, if you're joking . . .

CAPTAIN: Joking? Me? Who do you think you are?

DOCTOR: Your pulse, Woyzeck, your pulse—short, hard, skipping, irregular.

WOYZECK: Cap'n, the earth is hot as hell—for me it's ice cold! Ice cold—hell is cold. I'll bet. It can't be! God! God! It can't be!

CAPTAIN: Listen, fellow, how'd you like to be shot, how'd you like to have a couple of bullets in your head? You're looking daggers at me; but I only mean well, because you're a good man, Woyzeck, a good man.

DOCTOR: Facial muscles rigid, tense, occasionally twitching. Posture erect, tense.

WOYZECK: I'm going. A lot is possible. A man! A lot is possible. The weather's nice, Cap'n. Look: such a beautiful, hard, rough sky—you'd almost feel like pounding a block of wood into it and hanging yourself on it, only because of the hyphen between yes, and yes again—and no. Cap'n, yes and no? Is no to blame for yes, or yes for no? I'll have to think about that. *(Goes off with long strides, first slowly, then ever faster.)*

DOCTOR: *(Races after him.)* A phenomenon! Woyzeck! Another raise!

CAPTAIN: These people make me dizzy. Look at them go—that tall rascal takes off like the shadows before a spider, and the short one—he's trotting along. The tall one is lightning and the short one is thunder. Ha-ha! After them.

The Father

August Strindberg
1887

Scene: The Captain's home in a remote district of Sweden. The Captain, Adolph, has asked that his brother-in-law, the Pastor of the village, speak to Nojd about a personal matter.

The Captain, a cavalry officer.
The Pastor, his brother-in-law.
Nöjd, a younger cavalry soldier.

PASTOR: *Now* what's the trouble?

CAPTAIN: Been at it with the serving girl again! Got her pregnant! Damn him!

PASTOR: Nöjd? Same as last year?

CAPTAIN: What else! Have a word with him, won't you? Something friendly. Maybe it'll take this time. I've about run the gamut. Sworn at him, thrashed him—he couldn't care less.

PASTOR: I see. Read him a sermon. Hm. May I ask what effect the word of God will have on a cavalryman?

CAPTAIN: Yes, well, as my brother-in-law you know the effect it's had on me

PASTOR: Only too well.

CAPTAIN: Well, it might on him. At least give it a try. *(Nöjd enters.)* So, what have you been up to now, Nöjd, my man?

NÖJD: Excuse me, Captain, sir, I really shouldn't say, what with the Pastor here.

PASTOR: No need to be embarrassed, my boy.

CAPTAIN: All right, let's have it, the whole story—or you know what to expect.

NÖJD: Well, sir, you see, well—I mean, we were dancing up at Gabriel's—and the, well, Ludwig said—

CAPTAIN: Ah! Ludwig! The facts, man, the facts!

NÖJD: Well sir—I mean, well, then Emma got it in her head to—to go down to the barn and—

CAPTAIN: Aha! So then it was Emma who seduced you!

NÖJD: Well, you're not too far off the mark there, sir, if you know what I mean. If a girl doesn't want to, you can just kiss the whole thing off—if you know what I—

CAPTAIN: I know exactly what your mean! Are you the child's father or aren't you?

NÖJD: Well, sir, how do you know a thing like that, sir?

CAPTAIN: How do you—? What do you mean, how do you know a thing like that!

NÖJD: Well, I mean, that's something you can never be sure of, sir.

CAPTAIN: You weren't the only one, then?

NÖJD: Well, that time, sure, sir, but that's no proof that other times—

CAPTAIN: Ah, so you're blaming Ludwig now, is that it?

NÖJD: It's hard to know exactly who to blame, sir.

CAPTAIN: Then why did you tell Emma you wanted to marry her?

NÖJD: Well, sir, I mean—I mean, it's just—what you say—

CAPTAIN: *(To the Pastor.)* I can't believe this!

PASTOR: The same old story! But, Nöjd, listen to me—you have to be man enough to know if you're the father.

NÖJD: Well, I mean—well, we did it—sure—you know—but that doesn't mean anything has to come of it.

PASTOR: Listen to me now, young man, this is you we're talking about here! Surely you're not going to abandon that girl with a child to take care of! I dare say we can't force you to marry her, but I assure you, you *will* pay for the child's upkeep! That I promise you!

NÖJD: Maybe so, but Ludwig pays his share, too.

CAPTAIN: Well, then, it goes to court! Let them settle it! This has nothing to do with me, and I couldn't care less! Now get out of here!

PASTOR: Nöjd! One more thing! Hm! Doesn't it disturb you leaving the girl in the lurch like that with a child to take care of? Doesn't it? Have you no sense of honor? Doesn't such behavior strike you as—as—well—?

NÖJD: If I really knew I was the father, then, sure, but I don't know that, no one can. I mean, slaving away for somebody else's kid.

I'm not made for that—not me, no, sir! I mean, you and the Captain, sir, can understand that, I know.

CAPTAIN: Get out!

NÖJD: Sir! *(Goes out.)*

CAPTAIN: And stay out of the kitchen, you hear?—*(To the Pastor.)* Fine scourge of God, you are!

PASTOR: What? I thought I laid into him with real gusto.

CAPTAIN: Laid into him! You sat there muttering to yourself!

PASTOR: To be honest about it, I really don't know what to say. There's no question I pity the girl, but I pity the boy, too. And what if he isn't the father? The girl can nurse the child for four months at the orphanage, and then the child is permanently taken care of. Can the boy do as much? Is he a wet nurse? Afterwards she'll find a good position with a respectable family, but the boy's future is as good as washed up if he's discharged from the regiment.

CAPTAIN: One thing's for certain, I wouldn't want to judge the case. The boy isn't exactly innocent, I suppose; it's not something we can prove. But the girl's guilt can't be doubted—if in fact it's guilt we're looking for.

PASTOR: Yes, well, I don't presume to judge anyone. But what were we talking about when this messy little story interrupted us? Ah! Bertha and her confirmation! That was it!

CAPTAIN: Actually it was less about her confirmation than about her whole upbringing. This house is filled with women, everyone of whom wants to bring up my little girl. My mother-in-law wants to turn her into a spiritualist; Laura insists she become an artist; the governess is determined to make a Methodist of her; old Margret, a Baptist; and the kitchen help already have her marching to the Salvation Army drum. Who ever patched a soul together like that! The trouble is that I, who am solely responsible for her education, am thwarted no matter what I do. I have to get her out of this house.

PASTOR: The trouble is you have too many women running this house.

CAPTAIN: You can say that again! It's a cage of tigers! If I don't hold red-hot irons under their noses, they tear me to bits on the spot! Sure, go on, laugh, you bastard! It wasn't enough I married your sister, you had to foist your old stepmother off on me, too!

A Cry in the Streets

Rolf Lauckner
1922

Scene: Fenced-off corner of a courtyard to a Home for the Blind, leading on to a passageway into the street. Buildings, chimneys, and so on, all around. New Year's Eve. Moonlight. The bells ring out the hour of twelve. Various New Year's greetings are heard from the buildings. Three blind men have sneaked out of the Home and, overjoyed at their escape into the fenced-off courtyard, join in the New Year's greetings, mumbling first, then calling out loud: "Happy New Year!"

Three blind men:
    Sasha
    Konzel
    Wolf

SASHA: And the moon! And the moon! The walls swept away. And every crack resounding with the jingle of full glasses.

KONZEL: Do you see?. . .

SASHA: I hear it—feel it, wrap it around my fingers like a leaf, taste it with my tongue, swallow it. . .

KONZEL: The nerves take the toll!

WOLF: That's what I mean! With you it's the nerves, and with Sasha it's the memory that blinds! . . .So which is the healthy one?. . .

SASHA: Oh, Wolf, let's live tonight! I never felt better! Without walls! And all around—life— brimming over!. . .

KONZEL: The city celebrates—you feel it. . . .A cloud of lust hovers over the beds of stone!. . .

WOLF: Lust five flights high breaks loose on all the streets, until the New Year is sweated out! The muscles are taut with life. . .

SASHA: The whole world swells up . . . at the bountiful tables of the night. . .

KONZEL: Secret guests—the three of us. . .

SASHA: Out of a sleepy shaft, moon-crazy, and free as a bird, strangely awakened, suddenly plopped into light! Thousandfold life foaming up! . . .The year staggers by bawling at the night. . . We break the fence and swirl after it! . . .Space is lust! . . .Out into space.

WOLF: Are you being carried away again? . . .Just don't forget, Shorty, you walk with a cane! We blind ones. . .

SASHA: We blind ones. . .

KONZEL: We blind have it all over the others in the dark! They see only the small halos around the lamps out there! But we shovel out long stretches with our ears and find things where no beam of light ever falls!. . .

WOLF: But they find their way about town!. . .

KONZEL: And us they hide in cramped holes! . . .We should sleep during the day, and at night, light out—*our* realm. Before long, we'd serve as guides to the seeing!. . .

SASHA: The town will never be ours. Town is light. . .Town is like water gurgling over an abyss constantly threatening us without eyes. Town is glass-thin over blood-filled veins that cracks under crutches, that needs dancers!

WOLF: Well, let it crack! . . .Blood is warm! Blood shouldn't scare us—worms housed in the world's intestines!

KONZEL: Shorty is scared. . .

WOLF: And therefore he brags. Liberty makes him anxious.

SASHA: It's just that I have better ears for the night. And every breeze brings me images. . .

KONZEL: Not us?. . .

SASHA: Then they don't grow so big in your brain. . .

WOLF: As if our ears weren't good enough!

SASHA: Psst! . . .Well, what do you hear?. . .

KONZEL: Now? . . .Nothing!

SASHA: I hear footsteps!

WOLF: Sure! He's right!

(A "loaded gentleman" comes through the passageway. The Blind Men listen.)

KONZEL: Well who's that? . . .

SASHA: He's looking in every corner.

WOLF: Too much celebrating. . . *He* doesn't see us. Let's just stand silent here!. . .

KONZEL: Let's scare him! And line up quietly along the fence. . .

SASHA: He'll think it's a spook. . .

KONZEL: Maybe this will sober him up. . .

WOLF: How tepid the night is, as if it were already spring. . .People strolling. . .

SASHA: *(Jubilant and loud.)* Happy New Year!

KONZEL: Are you mad?. . .Do you want to wake up the old man?

WOLF: Oh, he'll make sure not to come home before sunrise. . .He's taken the Matron along!. . .It's seething out there tonight!. . .

KONZEL: The Matron? Where?

WOLF: To bed! Into the hotbed of passion! Onto the mattress of lust!

KONZEL: The old lady?. . .

WOLF: As if *he* were a young man. . .They sing into each other's ears in the dark until youth stirs between the sheets. . .And besides. . .

SASHA: The whole city burns in beds of sin tonight!. . .

WOLF: Old?. . .Her hair is still long and beautiful, let me tell you. . .

KONZEL: Who told you that?

WOLF: Nobody. I felt it with my hands. . .After all, if she didn't sleep upstairs. . .

SASHA: You've touched her hair?. . .Tell us, Wolf. . .

WOLF: I wouldn't think of it. . .So that next time you'll—

KNOZEL: Tell us! Tell us!

WOLF: Well, here goes! Because it's New Year's Eve. . .Though really I should keep it to myself. Still, maybe all three of us. . .Well, anyway, two weeks ago, on Saturday, she's taking a bath—I hear this very distinctly under her room. . .Two weeks ago, the old man was out—that I knew. Why shouldn't I go up and ask her something?. . .So I dress, and, softly, up I go. The door wasn't bolted yet. I grope my way through the rooms until I feel her sitting there. All the doors open. I see her clearly, and simply knock at the last door. . .She's terrified! Quickly, I tell her something I made up about the laundry, and hold a book out toward her. Now she doesn't know whether to stay or to . . . Her hair is undone, I feel that quite distinctly! And nothing on! Only a towel! You see, she had just taken a bath!. . .And upset!. . .Should she put something on?. . .The head moves back and forth. At last she can't help laughing at herself: The blind man! she thinks! Stays seated as she is, in the nude, and bends over the extended book! I'm standing behind her and see everything. She still smells fresh from the warm water. . .Now cautiously I stretch out my arms and—finger her long, beautiful hair!. . .She cries out, just to pretend. . .Every woman cries out a little!. . .But just then somebody's on the stairs. . .Excuse me, I say simply, playing dumb; she returned the book to me, I think. . .Otherwise, fellows, I'd be having my love here in the Home!. . .

KONZEL: Some guy, this Wolf! Some guy. . .And did she say anything afterwards?

WOLF: Now a word to me. . .But Monday morning she did dish out something on temptation from the Bible to all of us!. . .Of course, she continues to live her "sin"!. . .She's aroused, that I feel. And that makes sense. Sensual, like any woman her age. . .Once kindled—it burns!. . .Now she's at loose ends and fights her flesh. She's lost her poise and avoids meeting me. . .She's completely thrown by the kiss. . .

SASHA: You kissed her?. . .

WOLF: Kissed her?. . .I held her head in my arm—like this—almost on my chest. . .And am about to feel my way further down when someone disturbs us. . .She hardly resisted any more!. . .

KONZEL: Some guy! Simply goes up there, picks up love in the room, and doesn't even let us in on it. . .

WOLF: She squawked like a loon. . .When a woman's ripe for love and utters a sound, half frightened and irritated, half craving, that tickles you right down to the ass, I'm telling you!. . .And here I wait. . .And if you care to, we can join forces!. . .Then each one can still have something!. . .

SASHA: Up to now, I've always heard her only from a distance. . .One of these days I'll approach her. But first I must sniff her!. . .

WOLF: No one's begging you to come along—just keep your mouth shut, Shorty! The two of us will win her over all right, won't we, Konzel?. . .

KONZEL: Sasha wouldn't stay away!

SASHA: Just watch out I don't outsmart you! I'm the youngest; I'll say no more. . .

WOLF: Shares will be determined right from the start. And whoever cheats and gets too passionate will be cooled off by the other two. . .

SASHA: Barely in the saddle, he's worried already whether his love will be true to him!

WOLF: Shorty: I can still ride home without a saddle!

SASHA: So much success with women and he still can't take any ribbing!

WOLF: Why should I?. . .As if mature women would laugh! That only cuts wrinkles in the face. . .You joke with kids. But purpose guides women! They want money or they want men.

SASHA: Then you've got money?. . .

(Laughter)

WOLF: I'll show you, buddy, what I've got. . .

(They scuffle.)

SASHA: Let go!

KONZEL: Quiet now! Somebody's coming!. . .

(Listening. . .footsteps.)

KONZEL: The police?

(Listening.)

SASHA: The police!

WOLF: Get behind the walls!

(An officer in uniform slowly passes by. Then the blind men reappear.)

KONZEL: That one makes an extra round on holidays. Ordinarily he'd've been sitting for some time now down in the cellar over there!. . .

SASHA: We're free!. . .Just think, we're free! Then why do we stay here? Let's clear out! Dance over the fence and celebrate New Year's on the town. . .

WOLF: But where?. . .They know us here in the neighborhood. And further down?. . .

KONZEL: Between the houses?. . .Us?. . .

SASHA: Then let's look for someone to guide us. . .

WOLF: And rob us snugly around the next corner!. . .You can't even yell for help!. . .Listen to me, Shorty, stay with us.

SASHA: But not alone!. . .Naturally, only together!

WOLF: You always get carried away! Fidgety and excited like someone out there on the street! As if you had eyes. . .

SASHA: Well, once I did see. . .

WOLF: What you saw in those few years couldn't amount to very much. . .The sluice with the little stretch of woods behind it, and the red fence around your yard, right?. . .

SASHA: And yet I won't ever explain to you these two—the only visual impressions that have remained with me! They certainly make me richer than either of you, and I'd rather give away anything but this bit of light behind the veils. . .

KONZEL: How long could you see?. . .

SASHA: Until I was four. . .

WOLF: And that keeps you hopped up all the rest of your life!. . .An old fence dangles in your mind, luring you beyond your limitations! Better to have been born blind like the two of us.

KONZEL: Well, properly speaking, I'm not. . .Now and then a tinge of light flashes through my brain. . .

WOLF: Then drives you completely out of your mind! On your "light days" you're not good for anything at all!

Blood Wedding

Federico Garcia Lorca
1933

Scene: Spain. A poetic scene in the forest. They are discussing the scandal of the Bride running away with a former suitor (Leonardo) on the day of her wedding.

Of Note: The Three Woodcutters are as a chorus and provide an interesting opportunity to develop characters where none is provided by the author.

Three Woodcutters

(A forest. Night. Large moist tree trunks. A gloomy atmosphere. Two violins are heard. Three Woodcutters enter.)

FIRST WOODCUTTER: And have they found them?

SECOND WOODCUTTER: No. But they look for them everywhere.

THIRD WOODCUTTER: They'll find them.

SECOND WOODCUTTER: Shh!

THIRD WOODCUTTER: It's as if they're getting closer and closer on all sides.

FIRST WOODCUTTER: When the moon comes out, they'll see them.

SECOND WOODCUTTER: They should leave them alone.

FIRST WOODCUTTER: It's a big world. Everyone can live in it.

THIRD WOODCUTTER: They'll kill them.

SECOND WOODCUTTER: You have to follow your desire: They've done well in running away.

FIRST WOODCUTTER: They were lying to each other, but in the end blood got the best of them.

THIRD WOODCUTTER: Blood!

FIRST WOODCUTTER: One must follow blood's path.

SECOND WOODCUTTER: Blood that sees light is swallowed by the earth.

FIRST WOODCUTTER: What of it? It's better to be dead drained of blood than alive with it rotting.

THIRD WOODCUTTER: Hush!

FIRST WOODCUTTER: What? You hear something?

THIRD WOODCUTTER: I hear the crickets, the toads, the ambush of the night.

FIRST WOODCUTTER: But you can't hear the horse.

THIRD WOODCUTTER: No.

FIRST WOODCUTTER: He must be making love to her now.

SECOND WOODCUTTER: Her body is his, and his body is hers.

THIRD WOODCUTTER: They'll find them and they will kill them.

FIRST WOODCUTTER: But their blood will be one and they'll be like two empty jars, two dry streams.

SECOND WOODCUTTER: There are many clouds. It would be easy for the moon not to come out.

THIRD WOODCUTTER: The bridegroom will find them with or without the moon. I saw him leave. Like a raging star. His face the color of ash. He wore on it the fate of his whole clan.

FIRST WOODCUTTER: The clan of the dead in the middle of the road.

SECOND WOODCUTTER: Just so!

THIRD WOODCUTTER: You think they will be able to break through?

SECOND WOODCUTTER: It's hard to say. There are knives and shotguns ten leagues around.

THIRD WOODCUTTER: He's riding a swift horse.

SECOND WOODCUTTER: But he has a woman with him.

FIRST WOODCUTTER: We're closer now.

SECOND WOODCUTTER: A tree with forty branches. We'll cut it down soon.

THIRD WOODCUTTER: The moon's coming out now. Let's hurry.

(A light shines from the left.)

FIRST WOODCUTTER:
Oh rising moon!
Moon among great leaves.

SECOND WOODCUTTER:
Cover their blood with jasmine!

FIRST WOODCUTTER:
Oh lonely moon!

Moon among green leaves!

SECOND WOODCUTTER:
Silver on the bride's face.
THIRD WOODCUTTER:
Oh cursed moon!

Leave for their love the shadowed branch.
FIRST WOODCUTTER:
Oh weeping moon!

Leave for their love a branch in shadow.
(They exit. From left, the Moon appears through the brilliant light.)

Death of a Salesman

Arthur Miller
1949

Scene: Charley's office. Willy asks Bernard what he remembers about
growing up with Willy's son Biff who somehow has never made
the grade in any sort of career.

Willy Loman, a salesman, 50s-60s, weary, filled with false dreams.
Charley, his neighbor and friend, 60s, has been lending Willy money
for a long time.
Bernard, Charlie's son, 30s, a lawyer home for a short visit.

BERNARD: You still with the old firm, Willy?
WILLY: *(After a pause.)* I'm—I'm overjoyed to see how you made the
grade, Bernard, overjoyed. It's an encouraging thing to see a
young man really—really— Looks very good for Bill—very—*(He
breaks off, then:)* Bernard— *(He is so full of emotion, he breaks
off again.)*
BERNARD: What is it, Willy?
WILLY: *(Small and alone.)* What—what's the secret?
BERNARD: What secret?
WILLY: How—how did you? Why didn't he ever catch on?
BERNARD: I wouldn't know that, Willy,
WILLY: *(Confidentially, desperately.)* You were his friend, his boyhood
friend. There's something I don't understand about it. His life
ended after that Ebbets Field game. From the age of seventeen
nothing good ever happened to him.
BERNARD: He never trained himself for anything.
WILLY: But he did, he did. After high school he took so many corre-
spondence courses. Radio mechanics; television; God knows
what, and never made the slightest mark.
BERNARD: *(Taking off his glasses.)* Willy, do you want to talk candidly?
WILLY: *(Rising, faces Bernard.)* I regard you as a very brilliant man,
Bernard. I value your advice.
BERNARD: Oh, the hell with the advice, Willy. I couldn't advise you.

There's just one thing I've always wanted to ask you. When he was supposed to graduate, and the math teacher flunked him—
WILLY: Oh, that son-of-a-bitch ruined his life.
BERNARD: Yeah, but, Willy, all he had to do was go to summer school and make up that subject.
WILLY: That's right, that's right.
BERNARD: Did you tell him not to go to summer school?
WILLY: Me? I begged him to go. I ordered him to go!
BERNARD: Then why wouldn't he go?
WILLY: Why? Why! Bernard, that question has been trailing me like a ghost for the last fifteen years. He flunked the subject, and laid down and died like a hammer hit him!
BERNARD: Take it easy, kid.
WILLY: Let me talk to you—I got nobody to talk to. Bernard, Bernard, was it my fault? Y'see? It keeps going around in my mind, maybe I did something to him. I got nothing to give him.
BERNARD: Don't take it so hard.
WILLY: Why did he lay down? What is the story there? You were his friend!
BERNARD: Willy, I remember, it was June, and our grades came out. And he'd flunked math.
WILLY: That son-of-a-bitch.
BERNARD: No, it wasn't right then. Biff just got very angry, I remember, and he was ready to enroll in summer school.
WILLY: (Surprised.) He was?
BERNARD: He wasn't beaten by it at all. But then, Willy, he disappeared from the block for almost a month. And I got the idea that he'd gone up to New England to see you. Did he have a talk with you then?
(Willy stares in silence.)
BERNARD: Willy?
WILLY: (With a strong edge of resentment in his voice.) Yeah, he came to Boston. What about it?
BERNARD: Well, just that when he came back—I'll never forget this, it always mystifies me. Because I'd thought so well of Biff, even though he'd always taken advantage of me. I loved him, Willy,

y'know? And he came back after that month and took his sneakers—remember those sneakers with "University of Virginia" printed on them? He was so proud of those, wore them every day. And he took them down in the cellar, and burned them up in the furnace. We had a fist fight. It lasted at least half an hour. Just the two of us, punching each other down the cellar, and crying right through it. I've often thought of how strange it was that I knew he'd given up his life. What happened in Boston, Willy? *(Willy looks at him as at an intruder.)*

BERNARD: I just bring it up because you asked me.

WILLY: *(Angrily.)* Nothing. What do you mean, "What happened?" What's that got to do with anything?

BERNARD: Well, don't get sore.

WILLY: What are you trying to do, blame it on me? If a boy lays down is that my fault?

BERNARD: Now, Willy, don't get—

WILLY: Well, don't—don't talk to me that way! What does that mean, "What happened?"

(Charley enters. He is in his vest, and he carries a bottle of bourbon.)

CHARLEY: Hey, you're going to miss that train. *(He waves the bottle.)*

BERNARD: Yeah, I'm going. *(He takes the bottle.)* Thanks, Pop. *(He picks up his rackets and bag.)* Good-bye, Willy, and don't worry about it. You know, "If at first you don't succeed . . . "

WILLY: Yes, I believe in that.

BERNARD: But sometimes, Willy, it's better for a man just to walk away.

WILLY: Walk away?

BERNARD: That's right.

WILLY: But it you can't walk away?

BERNARD: *(After a slight pause.)* I guess that's when it's tough. *(Extending his hand.)* Good-bye, Willy.

WILLY: *(Shaking Bernard's hand.)* Good-bye, boy.

CHARLEY: *(An arm on Bernard's shoulder.)* How do you like this kid? Gonna argue a case in front of the Supreme Court.

BERNARD: *(Protesting.)* Pop!

WILLY: *(Genuinely shocked, pained, and happy.)* No! The Supreme Court!

BERNARD: I gotta run. 'Bye, Dad!

CHARLEY: Knock 'em dead, Bernard!

(Bernard goes off.)

WILLY: *(As Charley takes out his wallet.)* The Supreme Court! And he didn't even mention it!

CHARLEY: *(Counting out money on the desk.)* He don't have to—he's gonna do it.

WILLY: And you never told him what to do, did you? You never took any interest in him.

CHARLEY: My salvation is that I never took any interest in anything. There's some money—fifty dollars. I got an accountant inside.

WILLEY: Charley, look . . . *(With difficulty.)* I got my insurance to pay. If you can manage it—I need a hundred and ten dollars.

(Charley doesn't reply for a moment; merely stops moving.)

WILLEY: I'd draw it from my bank but Linda would know, and I . . .

CHARLEY: Sit down, Willy.

WILLY: *(Moving toward the chair.)* I'm keeping an account of everything, remember. I'll pay every penny back. *(He sits.)*

CHARLEY: Now listen to me, Willy.

WILLY: I want you to know I appreciate . . .

CHARLEY: *(Sitting down on the table.)* Willy, what're you doin'? What the hell is goin' on in your head?

WILLY: Why? I'm simply . . .

CHARLEY: I offered you a job. You can make fifty dollars a week. And I won't send you on the road.

WILLY: I've got a job.

CHARLEY: Without pay? What kind of a job is a job without pay? *(He rises.)* Now, look, kid, enough is enough. I'm no genius but I know when I'm being insulted.

WILLY: Insulted!

CHARLEY: Why don't you want to work for me?

WILLY: What's the matter with you? I've got a job.

CHARLEY: Then what're you walkin' in here every week for?

WILLY: *(Getting up.)* Well, if you don't want me to walk in here—

CHARLEY: I am offering you a job.

WILLY: I don't want your goddam job!

CHARLEY: When the hell are you going to grow up?

WILLY: *(Furiously.)* You big ignoramus, if you say that to me again I'll rap you one! I don't care how big you are! *(He's ready to fight.)* *(Pause.)*

CHARLEY: *(Kindly, going to him.)* How much do you need, Willy?

WILLY: Charley, I'm strapped, I'm strapped. I don't know what to do. I was just fired.

Rashomon

Fay and Michael Kanin
1959

Scene: The Rashomon Gate on the outskirts of the city. It has been raining all night and the three men have been sharing their own versions of an incident of the murder of a Samurai and the rape of his bride that they all witnessed. Now it is dawn, and the rain is stopping. The woodcutter is describing his view of the bandit Tajomaru whom he believes did the murder.

Of Note: The Wigmaker may also be played by a woman. In the original stories she is a female character. In the Broadway play it is played as a male character.

The Woodcutter, a family man with several children, poor, kindly.
The Monk, disillusioned by humanity.
The Wigmaker, a scoundrel who earns money by cutting and selling the hair of corpses found in the Rashomon gate.

WOODCUTTER: passed by me so close I could have touched him. I didn't move a hair—not until the last echo of his footsteps died away. Then I jumped up and ran as fast as I could—out of the forest.

WIGMAKER: Straight to the Police.

WOODCUTTER: Yes.

WIGMAKER: Only on the way you happened to forget part of the story.

WOODCUTTER: No, I didn't forget. I— *(Rubbing his forehead.)* I don't know—maybe I should have spoken up at Court, but—all those different stories—I began to doubt my own senses. I couldn't understand—I still can't understand—why they all lied.

WIGMAKER: *(Teasingly.)* Did they? *(The sound of the Crows is heard again.)*

WOODCUTTER: They must have! I know what I saw with my own eyes.

WIGMAKER: Why should I trust *your* eyes any more than those of the other three? Like I told you—people see what they want to see and say what they want to hear. *(As the Woodcutter starts to protest, he holds up a hand, grinning.)* But don't worry—if I believed any story, it would be yours. Not because of you, but only because it has the smell of truth. It's disappointing, isn't it? You'd like to think people are big—big heroes, big villains, big anything. But no—this is the way they are—small, weak, selfish, cowardly—faithless— *(He looks at the* Priest's *back with a smile of triumph.)* There's your miracle, holy man.

(The Priest's face is bleak, empty. Picking up his staff and pack, he moves toward the rear of the Gate, stands looking off down the road leading away from the city. The Woodcutter turns on the Wigmaker angrily.)

WOODCUTTER: Why do you keep chopping to bits everything that's good?

WIGMAKER: *(Starting to douse the fire.)* It's all in the way you look at it. Some people think *trees* are good—yet you chop them down. Me—I have nothing, I am nothing—and I've long since given up deluding myself. To me, truth is a firefly—now you see it, now you don't. And lies—they're no more than the little bugs that go to bed with me. I swat them for amusement— *(With a shrug.)* It's the only form of cleanliness I can afford.

(There's a sound suddenly, from somewhere in the back —the odd, choked sound of a Baby's crying. The three men turn, looking around questioningly.)

WOODCUTTER: Listen?! That's not a crow! *(The Wigmaker runs off, disappearing behind some large beams.)* What is it?

(In a moment, the Wigmaker returns, carrying a blanket wrapped bundle.)

PRIEST: *(Dropping his pack and coming over.)* A baby!

WIGMAKER: They're always dumping them here. *(Examining the blanket.)* Look at this blanket. Wool—real wool. *(Quickly stripping the blanket off the Baby.)* It must be worth at least—

PRIEST: *(Outraged.)* What are you doing? Give me that child! *(He tears* the Baby away from the Wigmaker, who manages to hang on to the precious blanket.)

WOODCUTTER: What a vile thing—stripping an infant!

WIGMAKER: Someone's bound to do it. Why not me?

WOODCUTTER: I ought to break your bones.

WIGMAKER: (Moving away.) Oh, stop being such a hero.

WOODCUTTER: You're just a ghoul—a ghoul!

WIGMAKER: (Turning, stung.) Then what would you call its parents? They had themselves a little pleasure, then dumped the consequences—like some rubbish. If I'm a ghoul, what are they?

WOODCUTTER: What do *you* know of parents and children?

WIGMAKER: (With a shrug.) What's there to know? Sometimes they throw you away—sometimes you throw them away.

WOODCUTTER: Your mind is so twisted! (Crossing to look at the Baby in the Priest's arms.) Can't you see this isn't a newborn infant? It must be four or five months old. What agonies these people must have suffered—to abandon such a child!

WIGMAKER: (Pained.) Please—I've heard enough sad stories for one day.

(The Baby begins to whimper again.)

PRIEST: It's shivering—

WOODCUTTER: It'll die of cold. (Advancing on the Wigmaker.) Give me back that blanket! (As the Wigmaker ignores him, folding it deliberately.) Give it back, I tell you!

WIGMAKER: (Dismissingly.) Oh, go away—

(The Woodcutter tries to snatch the blanket away from him. They grapple for it—falling to the floor—struggling for its possession. The Priest takes a step toward them helplessly. With the child in his arms, there's nothing he can do.)

WOODCUTTER: (As they scuffle.) Let go of it!

WIGMAKER: Get away!

WOODCUTTER: Let go—or I'll—I'll call the Police!

WIGMAKER: Call them! Go ahead and call them! (Struggling to disengage himself.) There are—other things—they might like know. About—you. (The Woodcutter stops fighting—stares at him.) That's right—you! (Scrambling to his feet, still clutching the blan-

ket.) You'd *better* leave me alone. I've been very generous to you—so far.

WOODCUTTER: *(Uncertainly.)* Generous?

WIGMAKER: Very generous, my friend—my good, honest, self-right-eous friend—*(Comtemptuously.)*—considering that you're a lying hypocrite like all the rest of them! *(Backing off, as the Woodcutter springs to his feet.)* You may have fooled the Magistrate—but not me.

(The Woodcutter stops in his tracks, his face going pale. The Priest looks from one to the other in bewilderment.)

PRIEST: What are you talking about?

WIGMAKER: He knows well enough. Ask him—just ask him! *(The Priest looks at the Woodcutter, who doesn't meet his eyes. Pointedly, to the Woodcutter.)* Where is the husband's sword, that fancy sword with the silver handle? Tell me that. No one took it from the scene of the murder—yet the Police couldn't find it. What happened? Did it melt away? Was it swallowed up into the earth?

WOODCUTTER: I—don't know.

WIGMAKER: You don't know! *(To the Priest.)* Just look at his face. *(To the Woodcutter, relentlessly.)* What was it the Medium said?— "Someone approached softly—drew the sword out of the dead man's breast—even before he was cold—"

WOODCUTTER: *(Desperately, shaking his head.)* No—!

WIGMAKER: *(Cocky now, he pokes him in the chest with a bony finger.)* How much did you get for it? Plenty, I'll bet. And you call *me* a ghoul! *(The Woodcutter turns to meet the anguished, questioning eyes of the Priest. Suddenly, he wilts, his head dropping down against his chest. To the Woodcutter.)* You were so eager to spare his feelings, I thought I'd help you cover up. You know, as one thief to another. But that's what you get when you try to do someone a good turn. *(The Priest has turned away, brokenly. The Wigmaker moves to the rear of the Gate, looks off.)* Looks like a break in the storm. *(He turns back. The Woodcutter is slump against the pillar.)* Oh, don't take it so hard. *(Friendlier now.)* I once saw a painting—a man hanging by a rope over a precipice. On top were wild beasts ready to devour him if he went up. Down below lay a dragon waiting to catch him if he fell. And all the time a white rat, representing day, and a black rat, representing night, were gnawing away at the rope. *(Patting him on the shoulder, encouragingly.)* That's the way it is, my friend. So let's not argue about right and wrong, the few minutes we're dangling here. Anyway, my thanks to you—both—for such an entertaining afternoon. *(Holding up the blanket.)* And profitable, too. *(He laughs, tucking the folded blanket into his shirt as he hurries away through the rear of the Gate and out of sight.)*

(For a long while, the Two Men stand silently, not looking at each other. Then the Priest crosses to get his pack. As he bends to pick it up, the Baby begins to cry again. He straightens quickly, shifting the Baby in his arms. The Woodcutter has raised his head and it watching as the Priest tries inexpertly to comfort the infant with awkward pats.)

WOODCUTTER: *(Draws back, his lips trembling.)* I know. And I don't blame you. Why should you trust me? But—*(As always, the words come hard.)* I have six of my own at home. Hungry, sometimes—cold, frightened. They cry, too. *(The Priest turns back slowly, beginning to take in the meaning behind the words. Under his gaze, the Woodcutter lowers his eyes apologetically.)* What can I say? *(A helpless gesture.)* A silver-handled sword can dry a lot of tears. *(The Baby's crying becomes more violent, choked.*

The Woodcutter *finds it impossible to do nothing. Tentatively, he reaches out his arms toward the child again.)* Please— *(This time the Priest makes no move to stop him as he takes the Baby. Expertly, yet tenderly, he puts it over his shoulder, patting and rubbing its back as he makes comforting little sounds. The Baby's crying trickles off and stops. The Woodcutter looks over at the Priest reassuringly.)* Gas. *(He removes the Baby from his shoulder and cradles it in his arms.)* It will be hard for you to travel—with an infant. The road is often steep—lonely— *(Hesitantly.)* Maybe— I could take it home with me. There's little enough, but— *(Looking down at the Baby, he smiles.)* How much can such a small mouth eat? *(The Priest stands looking at him, wordless suddenly in the midst of an immense, dawning comprehension. At his silence, the Woodcutter holds out the child.)* I'm sorry—I shouldn't have asked.

PRIEST: No—keep it. *(As the Woodcutter stares at him.)* Take it with you.

WOODCUTTER: But—you heard it yourself—I'm a coward, a thief, a liar—

PRIEST: *(Nodding.)* You're many things. A man—like all men.

WOODCUTTER: *(His eyes slowly fill with tears.)* Then you—forgive me?

PRIEST: Forgive you? *(Looking off toward the city.)* I'm the one who must go back to be forgiven. I thought only of how much I could teach the people. *(He looks at the Woodcutter.)* But it is you who teach me.

WOODCUTTER: *(Shaking his head dumbly.)* I'm afraid I—I'm still too ignorant to understand.

PRIEST: *(With a half-smile.)* I thank Buddha for such ignorance. *He bows respectfully. Embarrassed, the Woodcutter bows back.)*

WOODCUTTER: *(Peering off.)* The rain has stopped. *(As the* Priest *goes to pick up his staff and pack.)* The sun will soon dry the ground, the trees—*(Looking around him.)*—the Gate.

PRIEST: *(Following the* Woodcutter's *eyes.)* The Rashomon. Somehow, it's no longer so fearsome—with all its crows and corpses and jackals. *(Looking down at the baby.)* Even out of its crumbling ruins can come—life.

(The Temple bells sound the hour. As the Woodcutter looks off, the Priest understands.) It's late. They'll be looking for you at home.

WOODCUTTER: I'd better go. *(The* Priest *smiles at him. The Woodcutter smiles back—then goes down the steps of the Gate. There he turns to look back at the Priest.)*

PRIEST: And thank you.

(At a loss for words, the Woodcutter bows. The Priest returns the bow even more deeply. Shifting the baby in his arms, the Woodcutter turns and hurries away, disappearing into the forest.

The Priest stands looking after the Woodcutter until he is out of sight. Then he turns, his face at peace for the first time since we've seen him. He glances off at the road he was heading for— turns forward and moves to the top of the steps. The air is clean and sweet after the rain. He takes a deep breath, hoists his pack over his shoulder—then starts back toward the Temple bells, toward the teeming city and his unfinished work.)

The Disposal

William Inge
1968

Scene: Death Row. A Midwestern penitentiary. Three Cells. Jess in the
center cell. Luke is just walking up. Jess has yelled for his breakfast. Archie has suggested lavish foods for Jess's last meal. Today
he is destined to go to the gas chamber.

Archie, 20s, effeminate.
Luke, middle-aged.
Jess, 30, acts like a boy despite his age.

ARCHIE: I head you ranting a while ago, praying for God or the governor to intervene and save you from frying tonight.
JESS: I suppose you're looking forward to when it happens to you?
ARCHIE: I'm really not very concerned.
JESS: That's because you're a goddamn psycho, on top of being a fag-
got, and you've got no human feelings about *any*thing.
ARCHIE: What you call "human feelings" are only the product of cen-
turies of conventional thinking that society has instilled in us in
order to divert us from discovering the real crimes that they per-
form in the name of *law*.
JESS: I don't know what you're talking about.
ARCHIE: The world itself is the great criminal.
JESS: Bullshit!
ARCHIE: And we are like insects that got caught in the world's web,
and had to commit some violent act to get out. I feel no guilt
whatever for my supposed *crimes*. And I regard my rapidly
approaching death philosophically.
JESS: You're a freak.
ARCHIE: Perhaps it takes a freak to face reality. For instance, just look
at the freakish irony of our situation. If we had the forethought
to *plan* our murders across the border in one of our neighboring
states, we would not now be on Death Row, but serving life sen-

tences, working contentedly at some usual craft or employment to keep our evil minds occupied.

JESS: A lotta good it does to think about that now.

ARCHIE: True. It's merely an idle thought that sheds some light upon the incongruities of human justice.

JESS: I wanna see my old man!

ARCHIE: Why can you not admit to yourself by this time that your old man is not going to show up, anymore than Christ is going to appear out of the clouds with a band of angels and carry us all up to heaven?

JESS: I hate talk like that.

ARCHIE: You hate it because it's true.

JESS: *You* say it's true. But you don't know *every*thing.

ARCHIE: Oh, I humbly admit that.

JESS: Then admit that you don't know whether my old man is coming or not.

ARCHIE: If he comes, I'll say a thousand *Hail, Mary's! (Pause) Princess Lukemia!* Do *you* want to place a bet with me.

LUKEL What on?

ARCHIE: That *Miss Jessica* doesn't crap her pants tonight when they take her off to fry!

(Luke is silent for several long moments.)

JESS: Take the sonuvabitch up on it. Luke, I'm not gonna. You can count on *that!*

LUKE: Sure. I'll take your bet . . . *Dragon Lady.* (Archie *laughs.*) How much do ya wanna bet?

ARCHIE: Anything you say, *Dearest.*

LUKE: I've got five bucks.

ARCHIE: It's a deal. I'll bet five bucks *she* does.

LUKE: Okay.

JESS: *(Under his breath.)* Dirty . . . !

ARCHIE: What's that, *Sweetie?*

JESS: *You* heard me.

ARCHIE: Mad?

JESS: I hate guys like you, think they know everything.

LUKE: *(Sitting on his cot, eating his breakfast with the calm of one who has accepted his fate.)* Pay no 'tention to him, Jess.

JESS: He riles me.

LUKE: That's all he wants to do. Don't give him the satisfaction of payin' any 'tention to him.

JESS: You're right, Luke.

ARCHIE: Holy Mother! All I'm trying to do is to drill an ounce or two of realism into your immature brain. It'll be so much easier tonight, when the guards come and lead you away. . .

JESS: Shut up, Goddamn you!

ARCHIE: It'll be so much easier if you just admit that that's what's gonna happen, and neither the governor, nor God, nor Jesus, nor the Holy Virgin is going to come down and stop it.

JESS: Shut up, Just shut up, will ya?

ARCHIE: Very well.

JESS: I'll face . . . whatever I've got to face . . . my own way.

ARCHIE: I never tried to kid myself. After I shot my old lady and Gran', I just sat down and said, "Well, I've done it. I had to do it some time. There's no point in running away because *Miss Lily Law* would catch up with me in time. So I'll call them and tell them." That's what I did. I picked up the telephone and called the sheriff's office and said: "Mary, I've done it. Come on out and get me. And bring a couple of stretchers to carry them away in." And then I sat down and waited. They could hardly believe I'd really done it, I'd always been known around home as such a goody-good. But I *had* done it. Finally, they came to their senses and realized I wasn't kidding. Jesus! When they got a look at those bloody corpses in the kitchen, there was no denying anything. *(He laughs.)* One of the cops was a young fellow, new on the force. He vomited when he saw them. Oh dear! I've never had much patience with squeamish people.

JESS: You wanna know something. I wanna vomit, just listening to you talk.

LUKE: Me, too.

Streamers

David Rabe
1976

Scene: The cadre room. Basic training. All these men are preparing to be shipped out to Vietnam. There is a feeling of fear everywhere, and a desperate wanting to know what is what and who is who.

Of Note: The reference to Martin, another character, refers to the opening scene of the play in which Martin had attempted to cut his wrists and Richie came to his aid.

Roger, black, very neat, plays by the rules.
Billy, white, concerned, apparently straightforward.
Richie, white, a tease, gay, honest, and friendly.

BILLY: Roger . . . you ever ask yourself if you'd rather fight in a war where it was freezin' cold or one where there was awful snakes? You ever ask that question?

ROGER: Can't say I ever did.

BILLY: We used to ask it all the time. All the time. I mean, us kids sittin' out on the back porch tellin' ghost stories at night. 'Cause it was Korea time and the newspapers were fulla pictures of soldiers in snow with white frozen beards; they got these rags tied around their feet. And snakes. We hated snakes. Hated 'em. I mean, it's bad enough to be in the jungle duckin' bullets, but then you crawl right into a goddamn snake. That's awful. That's awful.

ROGER: It don't sound none too good.

BILLY: I got my draft notice, goddamn Vietnam didn't even exist. I mean, it existed, but not as in a war we might be in. I started crawlin' around the floor at this house where I was stayin' 'cause I'd dropped outa school, and I was goin' "Bang, bang," pretendin'. Jesus.

ROGER: *(Continuing with his laundry, he tries to joke.)* My first goddamn formation in basic, Billy, this NCO's up there jammin' away about how some a us are goin' to be dyin' in the war. I'm sayin', "What war? What that crazy man talkin' about?"

BILLY: Us, too. I couldn't believe it. I couldn't believe it. And now we got three people goin' from here.

ROGER: Five.

(They look at each other, and then turn away, each returning to his task.)

BILLY: It don't seem possible. I mean, people shootin' at you. Shootin' at you to kill you. *(Slight pause.)* It's somethin'.

ROGER: What did you decide you preferred?

BILLY: Huh?

ROGER: Did you decide you would prefer the snakes or would you prefer the snow? 'Cause it look like it is going be the snakes.

BILLY: I think I had pretty much made my mind up on the snow.

ROGER: Well, you just let 'em know that, Billy. Maybe they get one goin' special just for you in Alaska. You can go to the Klondike. Fightin' some snowmen.

(Richie bounds into the room and shuts the door as if to keep out something dreadful. He looks at Roger and Billy and crosses to his wall locker, pulling off his tie as he moves. Tossing the tie into the locker, he begins unbuttoning the cuffs of his shirt.)

RICHIE: Hi, hi, hi, everybody. Billy, hello.

BILLY: Hey.

ROGER: What's happenin' Rich?

(Moving to the chair beside the door, Richie picks up the pie Billy left there. He will place the pie atop the locker, and then sitting, he will remove his shoes and socks.)

RICHIE: I simply did this rather wonderful thing for a friend of mine, helped him see himself in a clearer, more hopeful light—little room in his life for hope? And I feel very good. Didn't Billy tell you?

ROGER: About what?

RICHIE: About Martin.

ROGER: No.

BILLY: *(Looking up and speaking pointedly.)* No. *(Richie looks at Billy and then at Roger. Richie is truly confused.)*

RICHIE: No? No.?

BILLY: What do I wanna gossip about Martin for?

RICHIE: *(He really can't figure out what is going on with Billy. Shoes and socks in hand, he heads for his wall locker.)* Who was planning to gossip? I mean, it did happen. We could talk about it. I mean, I wasn't hearing his goddamn confession. Oh, my sister told me Catholics were boring.

BILLY: Good thing I ain't one anymore.

RICHIE: *(Taking off his shirt, he moves toward Roger.)* It really wasn't anything, Roger, except Martin made this rather desperate, pathetic gesture for attention that seems to have brought to the surface Billy's more humane and protective side.

(Reaching out, he tousles Billy's hair.)

BILLY: Man, I am gonna have to obliterate you.

RICHIE: *(Tossing his shirt into his locker.)* I don't know what you're so embarrassed about.

BILLY: I just think Martin's got enough trouble without me yappin' to everybody. *(Richie has moved nearer Billy, his manner playful and teasing.)*

RICHIE: "Obliterate"? "Obliterate," did you say? Oh, Billy, you better say "shit," "ain't" and "motherfucker" real quick now or we'll all know just how far beyond the fourth grade you went.

ROGER: *(Having moved to his locker, in which he is placing his folded clothes.)* You hear about the ole sarge, Richard?

BILLY: *(Grinning.)* You ain't . . . shit . . . motherfucker.

ROGER: *(Laughing.)* All right.

RICHIE: *(Moving center and beginning to remove his trousers.)* Billy, no, no. Wit is my domain. You're in charge of sweat and running around the block.

ROGER: You hear about the ole sarge?

RICHIE: What about the ole sarge? Oh, who cares? Let's go to a movie. Billy, wanna? Let's go. C'mon.

(Trousers off, he hurries to his locker.)

BILLY: Sure. What's playin'?

RICHIE: I don't know. Can't remember. Something good, though.

(With a Playboy *magazine he has taken from his locker, Roger is setting down on his bunk, his back toward both Billy and Richie.)*

BILLY: You wanna go, Rog?

RICHIE: *(In mock irritation.)* Don't ask Roger! How are we going to kiss and hug and stuff if he's there?

BILLY: That ain't funny, man.

(He is stretched out on his bunk, and Richie comes bounding over to flop down and lie beside him.)

RICHIE: And what time will you pick me up?

BILLY: *(He pushes at Richie, knocking him off the bed and onto the floor.)* Well, you just fall down and wait, all right?

RICHIE: Can I help it if I love you?

(Leaping to his feet, he will head to his locker, remove his shorts, put on a robe.)

ROGER: You gonna take a shower, Richard?

RICHIE: Cleanliness is nakedness, Roger.

ROGER: Is that right? I didn't know that. Not too many people know that. You may be the only person in the world who knows that.

RICHIE: And godliness is in there somewhere, of course.

(Putting a towel around his neck, he is gathering toiletries to carry to the shower.)

ROGER: You got your own way a lookin' at things, man. You cute.

RICHIE: That's right.

ROGER: You g'wan, have a good time in that shower.

RICHIE: Oh, I will.

BILLY: *(Without looking up from his feet, which he is powdering.)* And don't drop your soap.

RICHIE: I will if I want to.

(Already out the door, he slams it shut with a flourish.)

BILLY: Can you imagine bein' in combat with Richie—people blastin' away at you—he'd probably want to hold your hand.

ROGER: Ain't he somethin'?

BILLY: Who's zat?

ROGER: He's all right.

BILLY: *(Rising, he heads toward his wall locker, where he will put the powder and Dopp kit.)* Sure he is, except he's livin' under water.

(Looking at Billy, Roger senses something unnerving; it makes Roger rise, and return his magazine to his footlocker.)
ROGER: I think we oughta do this area, man. I think we oughta do our area. Mop and buff this floor.
BILLY: You really don't think he means that shit he talks, do you?
ROGER: Huh? Awwww, man . . . Billy, no.
BILLY: I'd put money on it, Roger, and I ain't got much money.
(Billy is trying to face Roger with this, but Roger, seated on his bed, has turned away. He is unbuttoning his shirt.)
ROGER: Man, no, no. I'm tellin' you, lad, you listen to the ole Rog. You seen that picture a that little dolly he's got in his locker? He aint' swish, man, believe me—he's cool.

Master Harold and the Boys

Athol Fugard
1982

Scene: The St. George's Park Tea Room on a wet and windy Port
Elizabeth afternoon. Tables and chairs have been cleared and are
stacked on one side except for one that stands apart with a single chair. On this table a knife, fork, spoon, and side plate in
anticipation of a simple meal, together with a pile of comic
books. Other elements: a serving counter with a few stale cakes
under glass and a not-very-impressive display of sweets, cigarettes, and cool drinks, etc.; a few cardboard advertising hand-
outs—Cadbury's Chocolate, Coca-Cola—and a blackboard on
which an untrained hand has chalked up the prices of Tea,
Coffee, Scones, Milkshakes—all flavors—and Cool Drinks; a few
sad ferns in pots; a telephone; an old-style jukebox. There is an
entrance on one side and an exit into a kitchen on the other.
Leaning on the solitary table, his head cupped in one hand as he
pages through one of the comic books, is Sam. A black man in
his mid-forties. He wears the white coat of a waiter. Behind him
on his knees, mopping down the floor with a bucket of water
and a rag, is Willie. Also black and about the same age as Sam.
He has his sleeves and trousers rolled up.

Willie, mid-forties, black.
Sam
Hally, 17, white.

WILLIE: *(Singing as he works)*
   "She was scandalizz in' my name,
   She took my money
   She called my honey
   But she was scandalizz in' my name.
   Called it love but was playin' a game . . .
   (He gets up and moves the bucket. Stands thinking for a
   moment, then, raising his arms to hold an imaginary partner, he

launches into a intricate ballroom dance step. Although a mildly comic figure, he reveals a reasonable degree of accomplishment.)
Hey, Sam.
(Sam, absorbed in the comic book, does not respond.)
(Sam looks up.)
I'm getting it. The quickstep. Look now and tell me. *(He repeats the step.)* Well?

SAM: *(Encouragingly.)* Show me again.

WILLIE: Okay, count for me.

SAM: Ready?

WILLIE: Ready.

SAM: Five, six, seven, eight . . . *(Willie starts to dance.)* A-n-d one two three four . . . and one two three four . . . *Ad-libbing as* Willie *dances.)* Your shoulders, Willie . . . your shoulders! Don't look down! Look happy, Willie! Relax, Willie!

WILLIE: *(Desperate but still dancing.)* I am relax.

SAM: No. you're not.

WILLIE: *(He falters.)* Ag no man, Sam! Mustn't talk. You make me make mistakes.

SAM: But you're stiff.

WILLIE: Yesterday I'm not straight . . . today I'm too stiff!

SAM: Well, you are. You asked me and I'm telling you.

WILLIE: Where?

SAM: Everywhere. Try to glide through it.

WILLIE: Glide?

SAM: Ja, make it smooth. And give it more style. It must look like you're enjoying yourself.

WILLIE: *(Emphatically.)* I wasn't.

SAM: Exactly.

WILLIE: How can I enjoy myself? Not straight, too still and now it's also glide, give it more style, make it smooth . . . Haai! Is hard to remember all those things, Boet Sam.

SAM: That's your trouble. You're trying too hard.

WILLIE: I try hard because it *is* hard.

SAM: But don't let me see it. The secret is to make it look easy.

Ballroom must look happy. Willie, not like hard work. It must . . . Ja! . . . it must look like romance.

WILLIE: Now another one! What's romance?

SAM: Love story with happy ending. A handsome man in tails, and in his arms, smiling at him, a beautiful lady in evening dress!

WILLIE: Fred Astaire, Ginger Rogers.

SAM: You got it. Tap dance or ballroom, it's the same. Romance. In two weeks' time when the judges look at you and Hilda, they must see a man and a woman who are dancing their way to a happy ending. What I saw was you holding her like you were frightened she was going to run away.

WILLIE: Ja! Because that is what she wants to do! I got no romance left for Hilda anymore, Boet Sam.

SAM: Then pretend. When you put your arms around Hilda, imagine she is Ginger Rogers.

WILLIE: With no teeth? You try.

SAM: Well, just remember, there's only two weeks left.

WILLIE: I know, I know! *(To the jukebox.)* I do it better with music. You got sixpence for Sarah Vaughan?

SAM: That's a slow foxtrot. You're practicing the quickstep.

WILLIE: I'll practice slow foxtrot.

SAM: *(Shaking his head.)* It's your turn to put money in the jukebox.

WILLIE: I only got bus fare to go home. *(He returns disconsolately to his work.)* Love story and happy ending! She's doing it all right, Boet Sam, but is not me she's giving happy endings. Fuckin' whore! Three nights now she doesn't come practice. I wind up gramophone, I get record ready and I sit and wait. What happens? Nothing. Ten o'clock I start dancing with my pillow. You try and practice romance by yourself, Boet Sam. Struesgod, she doesn't come tonight I take back my dress and ballroom shoes and I find me new partner. Size twenty-six. Shoes size seven. And now she's also making trouble for me with the baby again. Reports me to Child Wellfed, that I'm not giving her money. She lies! I am giving her money for milk. And how do I know it is my baby? Only his hair look like me. She's fucking around all the time I turn my back. Hilda Samuels is a bitch! *(Pause.)* Hey, Sam!

SAM: Ja.

WILLIE: You listening?

SAM: Ja.

WILLIE: So what you say?

SAM: About Hilda?

WILLIE: Ja.

SAM: When did you last give her a hiding?

WILLIE: *(Reluctantly.)* Sunday night.

SAM: And today is Thursday.

WILLIE: *(He knows what's coming.)* Okay.

SAM: Hiding on Sunday night, then Monday, Tuesday, and Wednesday she doesn't come to practice . . . and you are asking me why?

WILLIE: I said okay, Boet Sam!

SAM: You hit her too much. One day she's going to leave you for good.

WILLIE: So? She makes me the hell-in too much.

SAM: *(Emphasizing his point.)* *Too* much and *too* hard. You had the same trouble with Eunice.

WILLIE: Because she also make the hell-in, Boet Sam. She never got the steps right. Even the waltz.

SAM: Beating her up every time she makes a mistake in the waltz? *(Shaking his head.)* No Willie! That takes the pleasure out of ball-room dancing.

WILLIE: Hilda is not too bad with the waltz, Boet Sam. Is the quick-step where the trouble starts.

SAM: *(Teasing him gently.)* How's your pillow with the quickstep?

WILLIE: *(Ignoring the tease.)* Good! And why? Because it got no legs. That's her trouble. She can't move them quick enough, Boet Sam. I start the record and before halfway Count Basie is already win-ning. Only time we catch up with him is when gramophone runs down. *(Sam laughs.)* Haaikona, Boet Sam, is not funny.

SAM: *(Snapping his fingers.)* I got it! Giver her a handicap.

WILLIE: What's that?

SAM: Giver he a ten-second start and them let Count Basie go. Then

I put my money on her. Hot favorite in the Ballroom Stakes: Hilda Samuels ridden by Willie Malopo.

WILLIE: *(Turning away.)* I'm not talking to you no more.

SAM: *(Relating.)* Sorry, Willie . . .

WILLIE: It's finish between us.

SAM: Okay, okay . . . I'll stop.

WILLIE: You can also fuck off.

SAM: Willie, listen! I want to help you!

WILLIE: No more jokes?

SAM: I promise.

WILLIE: Okay. Help me.

SAM: *(His turn to hold an imaginary partner.)* Look and learn. Feet together. Back straight. Body relaxed. Right hand placed gently in the small of her back and wait for the music. Don't start worrying about making mistakes or the judges or the other competitors. It's just you, Hilda, and the music, and you're going to have a good time. What Count Basie do you play?

WILLIE: "You the cream in my coffee, you the salt in my stew."

SAM: Right. Give it to me in strict tempo.

WILLIE: Ready?

SAM: Ready.

WILLIE: A-n-d . . . *(Singing.)*

You the cream in my coffee.
You the salt in my stew.
You will always be my necessity.
I'd be lost without you . . . (etc.)

(Sam launches into the quickstep. He is obviously a much more accomplished dancer than Willie. Hally enters. A seventeen-year-old white boy. Wet raincoat and school case. He stops and watches Sam. The demonstration comes to an end with a flourish. Applause from Hally and Willie.)

HALLY: Bravo! No question about it. First place goes to Mr. Sam Semela.

WILLIE: *(In total agreement.)* You was gliding with style, Boet Sam.

HALLY: *(Cheerfully.)* How's it, chaps?

SAM: Okay, Hally.

WILLIE: (Springing to attention like a soldier and saluting.) At your service, Master Harold!

HALLY: Not long to the big event, hey!

SAM: Two weeks.

HALLY: You nervous?

SAM: No.

HALLY: Think you stand a chance?

SAM: Let's just say I'm ready to go out there and dance.

HALLY: It looked like it. What about you, Willie? (Willie groans.) What's the matter?

SAM: He's got leg trouble.

HALLY: (Innocently.) Oh, sorry to hear that, Willie.

WILLIE: Boet Sam! You promised. (Willie returns to his work.)
(Hally deposits his school case and takes off his raincoat. His clothes are a little neglected and untidy: black blazer with school badge, gray flannel trousers in need of an ironing, khaki shirt and tie, black shoes. Sam has fetched a towel for Hally to dry his hair.)

HALLY: God, what a lousy bloody day. It's coming down cats and dogs out there. Bad business, chaps. . . . (Conspiratorial whisper.) . . . but it also means we're in for a nice quiet afternoon.

SAM: You can speak loud. Your Mom's not here.

HALLY: Out shopping?

SAM: No. The hospital.

HALLY: But it's Thursday. There's no visiting on Thursday afternoons. Is my Dad okay?

SAM: Sounds like it. In fact, I think he's going home.

HALLY: (Stopped short by Sam's remark.) What do you mean?

SAM: The hospital phoned.

HALLY: To say what?

SAM: I don't know. I just heard your Mom talking.

HALLY: So what makes you say he's going home?

SAM: It sounded as if they were telling her to come and fetch him.
(Hally thinks about what Sam has said for a few seconds.)

HALLY: When did she leave?

SAM: About an hour ago. She said she would phone you. Want to eat? (Hally doesn't respond.) Hally, want your lunch?

HALLY: I suppose so. *(His mood has changed.)* What's on the menu? . . . as if I don't know.

SAM: Soup, followed by meat pie and gravy.

HALLY: Today's?

SAM: No.

HALLY: And the soup?

SAM: Nourishing pea soup.

HALLY: Just the soup. *(The pile of comic books on the table.)* And these?

SAM: For your Dad. Mr. Kempston brought them.

HALLY: You haven't been reading them, have you?

SAM: Just looking.

HALLY: *(Examing the comics.)* Jungle Jim . . . Batman and Robin . . . Tarzan . . . God, what rubbish! Mental pollution. Take them away. *(Sam exits waltzing into the kitchen. Hally turns to Willie.)*

HALLY: Did you hear my Mom talking on the telephone, Willie?

WILLIE: No, Master Hally. I was at the back.

HALLY: And she didn't say anything to you before she left?

WILLIE: She said I must clean the floors.

HALLY: I mean about my Dad.

WILLIE: She didn't say nothing to me about him, Master Hally.

HALLY: *(With conviction.)* No! It can't be. They said he needed at least another three weeks of treatment. Sam's definitely made a mistake. *(Rummages through his school case, finds a book and settles down at the table to read.)* So, Willie!

WILLIE: Yes, Master Hally! Schooling okay today?

HALLY: Yes, okay . . . *(He thinks about it.)* . . . No, not really. Ag, what's the difference? I don't care. And Sam says you've got problems.

WILLIE: Big problems.

HALLY: Which leg is sore? *(Willie groans.)* Both legs.

WILLIE: There is nothing wrong with my legs. Sam is just making jokes.

HALLY: So then you *will* be in the competition.

WILLIE: Only if I can find a partner.

HALLY: But what about Hilda?

SAM: *(Returning with a bowl of soup.)* She's the one who's got trouble with her legs.

HALLY: What sort of trouble, Willie?

SAM: From the way he describes it, I think the lady has gone a bit lame.

HALLY: Good God! Have you taken her to see a doctor?

SAM: I think a vet would be better.

HALLY: What do you mean?

SAM: What do you call it again when a racehorse goes very fast?

HALLY: Gallop?

SAM: That's it!

WILLIE: Boet Sam!

HALLY: "A gallop down the homestretch to the winning post." But what's that got to do with Hilda?

SAM: Count Basie always gets there first.

(Willie lets fly with his slop rag. It misses Sam and hits Hally.)

HALLY: *(Furious.)* For Christ's sake, Willie! What the hell do you think you're doing?

WILLIE: Sorry, Master Hally, but it's him . . .

HALLY: Act your bloody age! *(Hurls the rag back at Willie.)* Cut out the nonsense now and get on with your work. And you too, Sam. Stop fooling around. *(Sam moves away.)* No. Hang on. I haven't finished! Tell me exactly what my Mom said.

SAM: I have. "When Hally comes, tell him I've gone to the hospital and I'll phone him."

HALLY: She didn't say anything about taking my Dad home?

SAM: No. It's just that when she was talking on the phone . . .

HALLY: *(Interrupting him.)* No, Sam. They can't be discharging him. She would have said so if they were. In any case, we saw him last night and he wasn't in good shape at all. Staff nurse even said there was talk about taking more X rays. And now suddenly today he's better? If anything, it sounds more like a bad turn to me . . . which I sincerely hope it isn't. Hang on . . . how long ago did you say she left?

SAM: Just before two . . . *(His wristwatch.)* . . . hour and a half.

HALLY: I know how to settle it. *(Behind the counter to the telephone.*

Talking as he dials.) Let's give her ten minutes to get to the hospital, ten minutes to load him up, another ten, at the most, to get home, and another ten to get him inside. Forty minutes. They should have been home for at least half an hour already. *(Pause—he waits with the receiver to his ear.)* No reply, chaps. And you know why? Because she's at his bedside in hospital helping him pull through a bad turn. You definitely heard wrong.

SAM: Okay.

> *(As far as Hally is concerned, the matter is settled. He returns to his table, sits down, and divides his attention between the book and his soup. Sam is at his school case and picks up a textbook.)* Modern Graded Mathematics for Standards, Nine and Ten. *(Opens it at random and laughs at something he sees.)* Who is this supposed to be?

HALLY: Old fart-face Prentice.

SAM: Teacher?

HALLY: Thinks he is. And believe me, that is not a bad likeness.

SAM: Has he seen it?

HALLY: Yes.

SAM: What did he say?

HALLY: Tried to be clever, as usual. Said I was no Leonardo da Vinci and the bad art had to be punished. So, six of the best, and his are bloody good.

SAM: On your bum?

HALLY: Where else? The days when I got them on my hands are gone forever, Sam.

SAM: With your trousers down!

HALLY: No. He's not quite that barbaric.

SAM: That's the way they do it in jail.

HALLY: *(Flicker of morbid interest.)* Really?

SAM: Ja. When the magistrate sentences you to "strokes with a light cane."

HALLY: Go on.

SAM: They make you lie down on a bench. One policeman pulls down your trousers and holds your ankles, another one pulls your shirt over your head and holds your arms . . .

HALLY: Thank you! That's enough.

SAM: . . . and the one that gives you the strokes talks to you gently and for a long time between each one. *(He laughs.)*

HALLY: I've heard enough. Sam! Jesus! It's a bloody awful world when you come to think of it. People can be real bastards.

SAM: That's the way it is, Hally.

HALLY: It doesn't *have* to be that way. There is something called progress, you know. We don't exactly burn people at the stake anymore.

SAM: Like Joan of Arc.

HALLY: Correct. If she was captured today, she'd be given a fair trial.

SAM: And then the death sentence.

HALLY: *(A world-weary sigh.)* I know, I know! I oscillate between hope and despair for this world as well, Sam. But things will change, you wait and see. One day somebody is going to get up and give history a kick up the backside and get it going again.

SAM: Like who?

HALLY: *(After thought.)* They're called social reformers. Every age, Sam, has got its social reformer. My history book is full of them.

SAM: So where's ours?

HALLY: Good question. And I hate to say it, but the answer is: I don't know. Maybe he hasn't even been born yet. Or is still only a babe in arms at his mother's breast. God, what a thought.

SAM: So we just go on waiting.

HALLY: Ja, looks like it. *(Back to his soup and the book.)*

Finding the Sun

Edward Albee
1983

Scene: An episode at a beach. Summer.

Fergus, 20s–30s.
Benjamin, 20s–30s.
Daniel

FERGUS: Let's play catch.

DANIEL: I *beg* your pardon!

FERGUS: Let's play *catch*. Here; I have a ball. *(Throws and catches a beach ball.)*

BENJAMIN: Hey! Why not?

DANIEL: Why *not*? You? Catch something? Herpes is about the only thing you can catch.

FERGUS: Who's that?

BENJAMIN: *(To Daniel.)* As opposed to *you*—who comes down with *every*thing: herpes, hepatitis . . .

FERGUS: *(Helping.)* Harelip, halitosis. This is fun!

DANIEL: *(To Benjamin.)* Never mind now; not in front of a child.

BENJAMIN: *(Mocking imitation of Daniel.)* And all I did was go to confession: The wafer must have been contaminated.

DANIEL: I said: never mind!

FERGUS: May we play?

BENJAMIN: Okay! Okay!

DANIEL: *(To Benjamin.)* Be sure to put your glasses on: You *do* want to catch the ball.

FERGUS: *(To Daniel.)* I'll throw it to you and you throw it to him and he'll throw it to me.

DANIEL: *(Mildly sarcastic.)* Won't this be fun!

BENJAMIN: It *will* be!

FERGUS; Okay; here we go. *(Throws at Daniel.)* Catch!

DANIEL: *(Catching.)* Ow! Jesus!

BENJAMIN: *(Parody of baseball player.)* C'mon, guy; heave her over here!

DANIEL: *(Disbelief.)* *Heave* her over *here*?

BENJAMIN: Come on; have fun!

DANIEL: Who ever heard of anybody saying anything like that? *(Underhand toss.)* Here!

BENJAMIN: *(Sibilant comment.)* Ooooooh! My gracious! Such force!

FERGUS: You guys are *fun!* *(Catches Benjamin's fair throw.)* Hey! That's good!

DANIEL: *(Jock imitation.)* What's ya name, kid? *(Benjamin giggles; Fergus throws sort of hard to Daniel.)* Ow!

FERGUS: Fergus. Was that too hard?

BENJAMIN: *(Jock imitation.)* For a guy like him, kid? You kidding? *(Daniel throws very hard.)* Ow!

FERGUS: You guys *are* fun!

(Natural, casual throwing now; unobtrusive.)

DANIEL: What kind of name is Fergus?

FERGUS: Scots, I believe.

BENJAMIN: I'm Benjamin.

FERGUS: Hi!

DANIEL: And I'm Lucille.

FEGUS: *(No change in friendly tone.)* Hi!

DANIEL: *(Awe at Fergus's aplomb.)* Wow! No, actually I'm Daniel.

FERGUS: I know. You two are presently married to those ladies over there, although . . . since the two of *you* have been . . . uh . . . intimately involved? . . . there is a question floating around this particular area of the beach as to whether these marriages were made in heaven. I have no opinion on the matter.

BENJAMIN: *(To Daniel; false sotto voce.)* The "in-laws" have been talking again.

FERGUS: Are you all good friends, you four? You and your wives?

DANIEL: It varies; it varies.

FERGUS: I . . . wondered.

(Pause.)

BENJAMIN: Oh?

DANIEL: Oh?

FERGUS: I was having a little chat with . . . well, I guess *your* wife, Benjamin; uh . . . Abigail is *yours*?

DANIEL: Oh, yes; Abigail is his and he is Abigail's.

BENJAMIN: Enough!

DANIEL: Desist? Hold? *Basta?*

FERGUS: You guys are really *fun*?

BENJAMIN: What *about* Abigail?

FERGUS: She's . . . *(Tosses ball above his head; catches it.)* . . . well, she's . . . unhappy?

DANIEL: No kidding!

BENJAMIN: *(Gently.)* I *know.*

FERGUS: I'd take care if I were you.

DANIEL: *(To no one.)* What*ever* can he mean?

BENJAMIN: *(Ignoring Daniel's tone.)* Whatever *can* you mean?

FERGUS: I'd be careful of her; that's all. *(Quick subject switch.)* Which one of you guys married first?

BENJAMIN: *I* did.

FERGUS: *(Some surprise.)* Really?

DANIEL: I was planning to when this one decided to do something precipitous. "I'll show *you*!"—*that* sort of thing.

BENJAMIN: Untrue! Untrue!

DANIEL: . . . when he realized that I was serious—that Cordelia and I were going to be married. When *that* sank in, he sort of ran out in the street and hooked on to the first gullible girl he could find.

BENJAMIN: Unclean! Unclean!

DANIEL: *(Naggy tone.)* "I'll show you! I'll show you!"

FERGUS: *(To Benjamin.)* I'd worry about her a little if I were you.

DANIEL: With any luck she might just . . . walk out of our lives, you mean?

FERGUS: Something like that.

BENJAMIN: *(More or less to himself.)* That *is* something to think about.

FERGUS: *(Starting to leave, still tossing to himself; a kind of "Okay you guys" tone.)* Okay. Okay.

BENJAMIN: Where are you going?

DANIEL: Where are you taking the ball?

FERGUS: You guys don't need the ball; you've got your own game
   going.
   *(As Fergus leaves, a combination of regret and something private
   and not too nice.)*
BENJAMIN AND DANIEL: *Aaaaawwwwwwwwwwwwwwwwwwww!*

I Hate Hamlet
Paul Rudnick

Scene: Andrew's girlfirend, Dierdre, will not have a sexual relationship with him unless he plays Hamlet in New York. She feels it will reveal his true artistry as an actor. Andrew is terrified of the prospect, but has come to New York and even rented an apartment that is haunted by the ghost of John Barrymore. The ghost cannot rest until Barrymore passes the "mantle" of Hamlet to a new, younger actor. Gary has come to New York to tempt Andrew to return to L.A. to do a television sitcom and go for the sure money.

Andrew, a young actor 20s– 30s.
Gary, his agent, based in Hollywood, 20s – 30s.
John Barrymore, a ghost, the deceased actor, elegant, suave and brilliant.

GARY: Andy—are you in some sort of trouble?
ANDREW: Yes Gary, that's it, you finally hit it. Joe Papp has my parents.
GARY: Hamlet. Andy, I have to say this 'cause we're buds—and I cherish that budship—but think reputation. Word on the street. When folks—let's call 'em Hollywood—when they hear that you're doing the greatest play in the English-speaking world, they're gonna know you're washed up!
ANDREW: Gary . . .
GARY: I'm serious. You haven't had offers? Nothing? What about the commercials? That Trailburst crap?
ANDREW: Gary, have you ever seen those ads? Have you seen what I have to work with?
BARRYMORE: What?
GARY: A puppet. A furry little chipmunk. It's cute.
ANDREW: It's a *hand puppet. (To Barrymore.)* Have you ever worked with a puppet? There's some guy, kneeling down near your crotch, working the puppet. And he's doing a chipmunk voice

into a microphone. And the guy, the chipmunk operator, he says, *(In a high-pitched, cutesy chipmunk voice.)* "Oh Andy, can I have a Trailburst Nugget?" and I say. "No, they're for people, not chipmunks." And he starts . . . to cry. And I . . . *(Andrew can't quite continue.)*

BARRYMORE: You what?

ANDREW: *(Mortified.)* I . . . kiss him. On the top of his little chipmunk head.

GARY: It's great!

ANDREW: It's disgusting! It's humiliating! I didn't spend four years in college and two in drama school to end up comforting someone's fist! It's not even a decent product. Trailburst Nuggets are like sawdust dipped in chocolate and they have more calories than lard.

GARY: And that's why you're doing *Hamlet?*

ANDREW: Gary, you don't understand, about the theatre. And why people do Shakespeare.

BARRYMORE: They do it because . . . it's art.

GARY *(After a beat:)* Andy. Andy my honey, Andy my multitalented prime-time delight. You don't do art. You buy it. You do TV or a flick, you make a bundle and you nail a Monet. I was at this producer's place in Brentwood on the weekend. Incredible. Picassos. Van Gogh. A Rembrandt. And all from his TV shows.

ANDREW: But Gary, I don't want to just buy art. I mean, which would you rather do, paint a Picasso or own one?

GARY: Are you kidding? I'd like to sell one. At auction. Cash flow. See, that's what I like—balls in the air. Activity. You're my Rembrandt.

ANDREW: I am?

GARY: How much are you gonna clear from this Shakespeare deal? Zip, right? Actually, you're paying them because your time is valuable. A pilot and five episodes, high six figures. And if it hits, you get participation.

ANDREW *(Impressed:)* Participation? In syndication?

GARY: Yup. You'll get paid every time it airs, first run, rerun, four A.M. in Singapore in the year 3000. Basically, you'll be able to afford to buy England, dig up Shakespeare, and get him to write the Christmas show!

BARRYMORE: The television program you're promoting, the gold mine—what is it exactly?

GARY: Okay—the pitch. Gather ye round. It's not crops, it's not young doctors, none of that TV crap.

ANDREW: Great.

GARY: You're a teacher. Mike Sullivan. You're young idealistic, new to the system. Inner-city high school. Rough. Dope, M–1s. Teen sex.

ANDREW: Wow . . .

GARY: No one cares. All the other teachers are burnouts. Not you.

BARRYMORE: Why not?

GARY: Because . . . you care. You grew up in the neighborhood. You want to give something back.

ANDREW *(Sincerely:)* You know, that sounds sort of . . . okay. It's almost realistic. I mean, you could deal with real problems. I could be vulnerable. I could mess up sometimes.

GARY: And at night, after the sun goes down, you have superpowers.

BARRYMORE: Superpowers?

GARY: Sure. I mean, who wants to watch that caring–feeling–unwed mothers bullshit? It's over. But after sundown, you're invincible. Modified X ray vision. You can fly, but only about ten feet up. See, we're keeping it real. Gritty. And so after dark, you help the community, you help the kids, with your powers.

ANDREW: Do they know it's me? When I have superpowers?

GARY: No. You're in leather, denim, they just think it's some great dude. Great title, killer title—"Night School." Dolls. Posters. The clothes. You could get an album, easy.

ANDREW: But . . . I can't sing.

GARY: Someone can. You can keep the Trailburst gig, there's no conflict—they'll probably extend, 'cause now you're a teacher! So think about it. What's to think, you've got a network commitment. Just forget this Hamlet crap—I mean, who are you kidding?

ANDREW: What do you mean?

GARY: Andy, I know you. I gave you your break. You're no actor.

ANDREW: What?

GARY: You're better than that. An actor, what, that's just some English guy who can't get a series. Look, I'm in town, I'm at the Ritz. I'll talk to Lillian, get things rolling. *(Gary hugs Andrew. He shakes Barrymore's hand.)* Great to meet you. You act, right?

BARRYMORE: John Sidney Barrymore.

GARY: We'll keep you in mind. Barrymore—any relation to the dead guy?

BARRYMORE: Distant.

GARY *(At the door:)* Death. Man. Think about it—the third coast. *(Gary exits, out the front door.)*

ANDREW *(Defensively:)* Don't say it! He's right, he's totally right!

BARRYMORE: "Night School"?

ANDREW: I don't know what to do! Think about the money—you had that kind of money!

BARRYMORE: Yes, as I grew older. Wealth is obscene in the young, it stunts ambition.

ANDREW: But . . . but . . . what about security?

BARRYMORE: What is this mania for security? What's the worst that can happen?

ANDREW: That I play Hamlet and Gary's right. And no one will hire me and soon I'm face down in the gutter, wearing rags, without a job or anywhere to go.

BARRYMORE: Shouldn't every evening end like that?

William Tell

Johann Christoph and Fredrich Schiller
1804

Scene: The home of Walter Furst, in Uri, Switzerland. Melchthal has
escaped from the governor's men and hidden in the home of his
friend. He worries of the welfare of his father, whom the governor hates for his rebellious spirit. The country is torn apart by
Austrian invasion, and each of the Swiss cantons is attempting to
hold out against the interlopers.

Walter Furst, 40s.
Arnold of Melchthal, 20s–30s.
Werner Stauffacher, 40s, comrade to Furst.

*(Walter Furst and Arnold von Melchthal enter simultaneously at
different sides.)*
MELCHTHAL: Good Walter Furst.
FURST: If we should be surprised! Stay where you are. We are beset
    with spies.
MELCHTHAL: Have you no news for me from Unterwald?
    What of my father? 'Tis not to be borne,
    Thus to be pent up like a felon here!
    What have I done of such a heinous stamp,
    To skulk and hide me like a murderer?
    I only laid my staff across the fingers
    Of the pert varlet, when before my eyes,
    By order of the governor, he tried
    To drive away my handsome team of oxens.
FURST: You are too rash by far. He did no more.
    Than what the governor had ordered him.
    You had transgreass'd, and therefore should have paid
    The penalty, however hard, in silence.
MELCHTHAL: Was I to brook the fellow's saucy words?
    "That if the peasant must have bread to eat,
    Why, let him go and draw the plough himself!"

It cut me to the very soul to see
My oxen, noble creatures, when the knave
Unyoked them from the plough. As though they felt
The wrong, they lowed and butted with their horns.
On this I could contain myself no longer,
And, overcome by passion, struck him down.
FURST: O, we old men can scarce command ourselves!
And can we wonder youth should break its bounds?
MELCHTHAL: I'm only sorry for my father's sake!
To be away from him, that needs so much
My fostering care! The governor detests him,
Because he hath, whene'er occasion served,
Stood stoutly up for right and liberty.
Therefore they'll bear him hard—the poor old man!
And there is none to shield him from their gripe.
Come what come may, I must go home again.
FURST: Compose yourself, and wait in patience till
We get some tidings o'er from Unterwald.
Away! away! I hear a knock! Perhaps
A message from the Viceroy! Get thee in.
You are not safe from Landenberger's arm
In Uri, for these tyrants pull together.
MELCHTHAL: They teach us Switzers what *we* ought to do.
FURST: Away! I'll call you when the coast is clear. *(Melchthal retires.)*
Unhappy youth! I dare not tell him all
The evil that my boding heart predicts!
Who's there? The door ne'er opens, but I look
For tidings of mishap. Suspicion lurks
With darkling treachery in every nook.
Even to our inmost rooms they force their way,
These myrmidons of power; and soon we'll need
To fasten bolts and bars upon our doors.
(He opens the door, and steps back in surprise as Werner Stauffacher enters.)
What do I see? You, Werner? Now, by Heaven!
A valued guest, indeed. No man e'er set

His foot across this threshold, more esteem'd.
Welcome! thrice welcome, Werner, to my roof!
What brings you here? What see you here in Uri?
STAUFFACHER: *(Shakes Furst by the hand.)* The olden times and olden
    Switzerland.
FURST: You bring them with you. See how I'm rejoiced.
    My heart leaps at the very sight of you.
    Sit down—sit down, and tell me how you left
    Your charming wife, fair Gertrude Iberg's child?
    And clever as her father. Not a man
    That wends from Germany, by Meinrad's Cell,
    To Italy, but praises far and wide
    Your house's hospitality. Buy say,
    Have you come here direct from Flüelen,
    And have you noticed nothing on your way,
    Before you halted at my door?
STAUFFACHER: *(Sits down.)* I saw
    A work in progress, as I came along,
    I little thought to see—that likes me ill.
FURST: O friend! you've lighted on my thought at once.
STAUFFACHER: Such things in Uri ne'er were known before.
    Never was prison here in man's remembrance,
    Nor ever any stronghold but the grave.
FURST: You name it well. It is the grave of freedom.
STAUFFACHER: Friend, Walter Furst, I will be plain witn you.
    No idle curiosity it is
    That brings me here, but heavy cares. I left
    Thraldom at home, and thraldom meets me here.
    Our wrongs, e'en now, are more than we can bear,
    And who shall tell us where they are to end?
    From eldest time the Switzer has been free,
    Accustom'd only to the mildest rule.
    Such things as now we suffer ne'er were known
    Since herdsmen first drove cattle to the hills.
FURST: Yes, our oppressions are unparallel'd!
    Why even our own good lord of Attinghaus,

Who lived in olden times, himself declares
They are no longer to be tamely borne.
STAUFFACHER: In Unterwalden yonder, 'tis the same;
And bloody has the retribution been.
The imperial Seneschal, the Wolfshot, who
At Rossberg dwelt, long'd for forbidden fruit—
Baumgarten's wife, that lives at Alzellen,
He wished to overcome in shameful sort,
On which the husband slew him with his axe.
FURST: O, Heaven is just in all its judgments still!
Baumgarten, say you? A most worthy man.
Has he escaped, and is he safely hid?
STAUFFACHER: Your son-in-law conveyed him o'er the lake,
And he lies hidden in my house at Steinen.
He brought the tidings with him of a thing
That has been done at Sarnen, worse than all,
A thing to make the very heart run blood!
FURST: *(Attentively.)* Say on. What is it?
STAUFFACHER: There dwells in Melchthal, then,
Just as you enter by the road from Kerns,
An upright man, named Henry of the Halden,
A man of weight and influence in the Diet.
FURST: Who knows him not? But what of him? Proceed.
STAUFFACHER: The Landenberg, to punish some offence,
Committed by the old man's son, it seems,
Had given command to take the youth's best pair
Of oxen from his plough; on which the lad
Struck down the messenger and took to flight.
FURST: But the old father—tell me, what of him?
STAUFFACHER: The Landenberg sent for him, and required
He should produce his son upon the spot;
And when th' old man protested, and with truth,
That he knew nothing of the fugitive,
The tyrant call'd his torturers.
FURST: *(Springs up and tries to lead him to the other side.)* Hush, no
more!

STAUFFACHER: *(With increasing warmth.)* "And though thy son," he
cried, "has 'scaped me now,
I have thee fast, and thou shalt feel my vengeance."
With that they flung the old man to the earth,
And plunged the pointed steel into his eyes.
FURST: Merciful Heaven!
MELCHTHAL *(Rushing out.)* Into his eyes, his eyes?
STAUFFACHER: *(Addresses himself in astonishment to Walter Furst.)*
Who is this youth?
MELCHTHAL: *(Grasping him convulsively.)* Into his eyes? Speak! speak!
FURST: Oh, miserable hour!
STAUFFACHER: Who is it, tell me?
(Furst makes a sign to him.) It is his son! All righteous heaven!
MELCHTHAL: And I
Must be from thence! What! into both his eyes?
FURST: Be calm, be calm; and bear it like a man!
MELCHTHAL: And all for me—for my mad, wilful folly!
Blind, did you say? Quite blind—and both his eyes?
STAUFFACHER: Ev'n so. The fountain of his sight's dried up.
He ne'er will see the blessed sunshine more.
FURST: Oh, spare his anguish!
MELCHTHAL: Never, never more! *(Presses his hands upon his eyes and
is silent for some moments; then turning from one to the other,
speaks in a subdued tone, broken by sobs.)*
O the eye's light, of all the gifts of Heaven
The dearest, best! From light all beings live—
Each fair created thing—the very plants
Turn with a joyful transport to the light,
And he—he must drag on through all his days
In endless darkness! Never more for him
The sunny meads shall glow, the flow'rets bloom;
Nor shall he more behold the roseate tints
Of the ice mountain top! To die is nothing,
But to have life, and not have sight,—oh, that
Is misery indeed! Why do you look
So piteously at me? I have two eyes,

Yet to my poor blind father can give neither!
No, not one gleam of that great sea of light,
That with its dazzling splendor floods my gaze.
STAUFFACHER: Ah, I must swell the measure of your grief,
Instead of soothing it. The worst, alas!
Remains to tell. They've stripp'd him of his all;
Nought have they left him, save his staff, on which,
Blind, and in rags, he moves from door to door.
MELCHTHAL: Nought but his staff to the old eyeless man!
Stripp'd of his all—even of the light of day.
The common blessing of the meanest wretch.
Tell me no more of patience, of concealment!
Oh, what a base and coward thing am I,
That on mine own security I thought,
And took no care of thine! Thy precious head
Left as a pledge within the tyrant's grasp!
Hence, craven-hearted prudence, hence! And all
My thoughts be vengeance and the despot's blood!
I'll seek him straight—no power shall stay me now—
And at his hands demand my father's eyes.
I'll beard him 'mid a thousand myrmidons!
What's life to me, if in his heart's best blood
I cool the fever of this mighty anguish.
(He is going.)
FURST: Stay, this is madness, Melchthal! What avails
Your single arm against his power? He sits
At Sarnen high within his lordly keep,
And, safe within its battlemented walls,
May laugh to scorn your unavailing rage.
MELCHTHAL: And though he sat within the icy domes
Of yon far Schreckhorn—ay, or higher, where,
Veil'd since eternity, the Jungfrau soars,
Still to the tyrant would I make my way;
With twenty comrades minded like myself
I'd lay his fastness level with the earth!
And if none follow me, and if you all,

In terror for your homesteads and your herds,
Bow in submission to the tyrant's yoke,
I'll call the herdsmen on the hills around me,
And there beneath heaven's free and boundless roof,
Where men still feel as men, and hearts are true,
Proclaim aloud this foul enormity!

STAUFFACHER: *(To Furst.)* 'Tis at its height—and are we then to wait.
Till some extremity—

MELCHTHAL: What extremity remains for apprehension, when men's
eyes
Have ceased to be secure within their sockets?
Are we defenceless? Wherefore did we learn
To bend the cross-bow,—wield the battleaxe?
What living creature but, in its despair,
Finds for itself a weapon of defence?
The baited stag will turn, and with the show
Of his dread antlers hold the hounds at bay;
The chamois drags the huntsman down th' abyss
The very ox, the partner of man's toil,
The sharer of his roof, that meekly bends
The strength of his huge neck beneath the yoke,
Springs up, if he's provoked, whets his strong horn,
And tosses his tormentor to the clouds.

FURST: If the three Cantons thought as we three do,
Something might, then, be done, with good effect.

STAUFFACHER: When Uri calls, when Unterwald replies,
Schwyz will be mindful of her ancient league.

MELCHTHAL: I've many friends in Unterwald, and none
That would not gladly venture life and limb,
If fairly backed and aided by the rest.
Oh, sage and reverend fathers of this land,
Here do I stand before your riper years,
An unskill'd youth, whose voice must in the Diet
Still be subdued into respectful silence.
Do not, because that I am young, and want
Experience, slight my counsel and my words.

'Tis not the wantonness of youthful blood
That fires my spirit, but a pang so deep
That e'en the flinty rocks must pity me.
You, too, are fathers, heads of families,
And you must wish to have a virtuous son,
To reverence your grey hairs, and shield your eyes
With pious and affectionate regard.
Do not, I pray, because in limb and fortune
You still are unassail'd, and still your eyes
Revolve undimm'd and sparkling in their spheres,
Oh, do not, therefore, disregard our wrongs!
Above you, too, doth hang the tyrant's sword.
You, too, have striven to alienate the land
From Austria. This was all my father's crime:
You share his guilt, and may his punishment.
STAUFFACHER: *(To Furst.)* Do thou resolve! I am prepared to follow.
FURST: First let us learn what steps the noble lords
    Von Sillinen and Attinghaus propose.
    Their names would rally thousands in the cause.
MELCHTHAL: Is there a name within the Forest Mountains
    That carries more respect than thine—and thine?
    To names like these the people cling for help
    With confidence—such names are household words.
    Rich was your heritage of manly virtue,
    And richly have you added to its stores.
    What need of nobles? Let us do the work
    Ourselves. Although we stood alone, methinks,
    We should be able to maintain our rights.
STAUFFACHER: The nobles' wrongs are not so great as ours.
    The torrent, that lays waste the lower grounds,
    Hath not ascended to the uplands yet.
    But let them see the country once in arms,
    They'll not refuse to lend a helping hand.
FURST: Were there an umpire 'twixt ourselves and Austria,
    Justice and law might then decide our quarrel.
    But our oppressor is our emperor too,

And judge supreme. 'Tis God must help us, then.
And our own arm! Be yours the task to rouse
The men of Schwyz; I'll rally friends in Uri.
But whom are we to send to Unterwald?

MELCHTHAL: Thither send me. Whom should it more concern?

FURST: No, Melchthal, no; thou art my guest, and I
Must answer for thy safety.

MELCHTHAL: Let me go. I know each forest track and mountain pass;
Friends too I'll find, be sure, on every hand,
To give me willing shelter from the foe.

STAUFFACHER: Nay, let him go; no traitors harbor there:
For tyranny is so abhorred in Unterwald,
No minions can be bound to work her will.
In the low valleys, too, the Alzeller
Will gain confederates and rouse the country.

MELCHTHAL: But how shall we communicate, and not
Awaken the suspicion of the tyrants?

STAUFFACHER: Might we not meet at Brunnen or at Treib,
Hard by the spot where merchant vessels land?

FURST: We must not go so openly to work.
Hear my opinion. On the lake's left bank,
As we sail hence to Brunnen, right against
The Mytenstein, deep-hidden in the wood
A meadow lies, by shepherds called the Rootli,
Because the wood has been uprooted there.
'Tis where our Canton bound'ries verge on yours;—
(To Melchthal.) Your boat will carry you across from Schwyz.
(To Stauffacher.) Thither by lonely bypaths let us wend.
At midnight, and deliberate o'er our plans.
Let each bring with him there ten trusty men,
All one at heart with us; and then we may
Consult together for the general weal,
And, with God's guidance, fix our onward course.

STAUFFACHER: So let it be. And now your true right hand!
Yours, too, young man! and as we now three men
Among ourselves thus knit our hands together

In all sincerity and truth, e'en so
Shall we three Cantons, too, together stand
In victory and defeat, in life and death.
FURST and MELCHTHAL: In life and death.
(They hold their hands clasped together for some moments in silence.)
MELCHTHAL: Alas, my old blind father!
Thou canst no more behold the day of freedom;
But thou shalt hear it. When from Alp to Alp
The beacon fires throw up their flaming signs.
And the proud castles to the tyrants fall,
Into they cottage shall the Switzer burst,
Bear the glad tidings to thine ear, and o'er
Thy darken'd way shall Freedom's radiance pour.

PART TWO:

SCENES FOR
THREE WOMEN

The Libation Bearers

Aeschylus
458 B.C.

Scene: Electra is in mourning for her father who has been brutally murdered by her mother, Clytemnestra and her mother's lover Aegisthus. She waits the return of her brother Orestes to assist her in avenging the murder. The chorus has assembled and awaits Electra.

Electra, a young woman, daughter of the recently murdered King Agamemnon—grief-stricken.
Chorus, serving women attendant upon Electra. (Chorus should be divided between two speakers.)

STROPHE I: Missioned from these halls I come
  In the sable pomp of woe,
  Here to wail and pour libations,
  With the bosom-beating blow;
  And my cheeks, that herald sorrow,
  With the fresh-cut nail-ploughed furrow,
  Grief's vocation show.

  See! my rent and ragged stole
  Speaks the conflict of my soul;
  My vex'd heart on grief is feeding,
  Night and day withouten rest;
  Riven with the ruthless mourning,
  Hangs the linen vest, adorning
  Woefully my breast.

ANTISTROPHE I: Breathing wrath through nightly slumbers,
  By a dream-encompassed lair,
  Prophet of the house of Pelops,
  Terror stands with bristling hair.
  Through the dark night fitful yelling,

He within our inmost dwelling
Did the sleeper scare.
Heavily, heavily terror falls
On the women-governed halls!
And, instinct with high assurance,
Speak the wise diviners all;
"The dead, the earth-hid dead are fretful,
And for vengeance unforgetful,
From their graves they call."

STROPHE II: This graceless grace to do, to ward
What ills the dream portendeth
This pomp—O mother Earth!—and me
The godless woman sendeth.
Thankless office! Can I dare,
Naming thee, to mock the air?
Blood that stains with purple track
The ground, what price can purchase back?
O the hearth beset with mourning!
O the proud halls' overturning!
Darkness, blithe sight's detestation,
Sunless sorrow spread
Round the house of desolation,
Whence the lord is fled.

ANTISTROPHE II: The kingly majesty that was
The mighty, warlike-hearted,
That swayed the general ear and will,
The unconquered, hath departed.
And now fear rules, and we obey,
Unwilling, a loveless sway.
Who holds the key of plenty's portals
Is god, and more than god to mortals;
But justice from her watchful station,
With a sure-winged visitation
Swoops; and some in blazing noon

She for doom doth mark,
Some in lingering eve, and some
In the deedless dark.

EPODE: When mother Earth hath drunk black gore,
    Printed on the faithful floor,
    The staring blot remaineth;
    There the deep disease is lurking;
    There thrice double-guilt is working
    Woes that none restraineth.
    As virgin-chambers once polluted
    Never may be pure again,
    So filthy hands with blood bedabbled
    All the streams of all the rivers
    Flow to wash in vain.
    For me I suffer what I must;
    By ordinance divine,
    Since Troy was levelled with the dust
    The bondman's fate is mine.
    What the masters of my fate
    In their strength decree,
    Just or unjust, matters not,
    Is the law to me.
    I must look content; and chain
    Strongest hate with tightest rein;
    I for my mistress' woes must wail,
    And for my own, beneath the veil;
    I must sit apart,
    And thaw with tears my frozen heart,
    When no eye may see.
    (Enter Electra.)
ELECT: Ye ministering maids with dexterous heed
    That tend this household, as with me ye share
    This pomp of supplication, let me share
    In your good counsel. Speak, and tell me how,
    This flood funereal pouring on the tomb,

I shall find utterance in well-omened words?
Shall I declare me bearer of sweet gifts
From a dear wife to her dear lord? I fear
To mingle falsehood with libations pure,
Poured on my father's tomb. Or shall I pray,
As mortals wont to pray, that he may send
Just retribution, and a worthy gift
Of ill for ill to them that sent these garlands?
Or shall I silent stand, nor with my tongue
Give honour, as in dumb dishonoured death
My father died, and give the Earth to drink
A joyless stream, as who throws lustral ashes
With eyes averse, and flings the vase away?
Your counsel here I crave; ye are my friends,
And bear with me, within these fated halls
A common burden. Speak, and no craven fear
Lurk in your breasts! The man that lives most free,
And him to sternest masterdom enthrolled,
One fate abides. Lend me your wisdom, friends.
CHORUS: Thy father's tomb shall be to me an altar;
As before God I'll speak the truth to thee.
ELECT: Speak thus devoutly, and thou'lt answer well.
CHORUS: Give words of seemly honour, as thou pourest,
To all that love thy father.
ELECT: Who are they?
CHORUS: Thyself the first, and whoso hates Ægisthus.
ELECT: That is myself and thou.
CHORUS: Thyself may'st judge.
ELECT: Hast thou none else to swell the scanty roll?
CHORUS: One far away, thy brother, add—Orestes.
ELECT: 'Tis well remembered, very well remembered.
CHORUS: Nor them forget that worked the deed of guilt.
ELECT: Ha! what of them? I'd hear of this more nearly.
CHORUS: Pray that some god may come, or mortal man.
ELECT: Judge or avenger?
CHORUS: Roundly pray the prayer,

Some god or man may come to slay the slayer.

ELECT: And may I pray the gods such boon as this?

CHORUS: Why not? What other quittance to a foe
  Than hate repaid with hate, and blow with blow?

ELECT: *(Approaching to the tomb of Agamemnon.)* Hermes, that
  swayest underneath the ground.
  Of powers divine, Infernal and Supernal,
  Most weighty herald, herald me in this,
  That every subterranean god, and earth,
  Even mother earth, who gave all things their birth,
  And nurseth the reviving germs of all,
  May hear my prayer, and with their sleepless eyes
  Watch my parental halls. And while I dew
  Thy tomb with purifying stream, O father,
  Pity thou me, and on thy loved Orestes
  With pity look, and to our long lost home
  Restore us!—us, poor friendless outcasts both,
  Bartered by her who bore us, and exchanged
  Thy love for his who was thy murderer.
  Myself do menial service in this house;
  Orestes lives in exile; and they twain
  In riot waste the fruits of thy great toils.
  Hear thou my prayers, and quickly send Orestes
  With happy chance to claim his father's sceptre!
  And give thou me a wiser heart, and hand
  More holy-functioned than the mother's was
  That bore thy daughter. Thus such for myself,
  And for my friends. To those that hate my father,
  Rise thou with vengeance mantled-dark to smite
  Those justly that unjustly smote the just.
  These words of evil imprecation dire,
  Marring the pious tenor of my prayer,
  I speak constrained: but thou for me and mine
  Send good, and only good, to the upper air,
  The gods being with thee, mother Earth, and Justice
  With triumph in her train. This prayer receive

And these libations. Ye, my friends, the while
Let your grief blossom in luxuriant wail,
Lifting the solemn pæan of the dead.
CHORUS: Flow! in plashing torrents flow!
Wretched grief for wretched master!
O'er this heaped mound freely flow,
Refuge of my heart's disaster!
O thou dark majestic shade,
Hear, O hear me! While anear thee
Pours this sorrow-stricken maid
The pure libation,
May the solemn wail we lift
Atone the guilt that taints the gift
With desecration!
O that some god from Scythia far,
To my imploring,
Might send a spearman strong in war,
Our house restoring!
Come Mars, with back-bent bow, thy hail
Of arrows pouring,
Or with the hilted sword assail,
And in the grapple close prevail;
Of battle roaring!
ELECT: These mild libations, earth-imbibed, my father
Hath now received. Thy further counsel lend.
CHORUS: In what? Within me leaps my heart for fear.
ELECT: Seest thou this lock of hair upon the tomb?
CHORUS: A man's hair is it, or a low-zoned maid's?
ELECT: Few points there are to hit. 'Tis light divining.
CHORUS: I am thine elder; yet I fain would reap
Instruction from young lips.
ELECT: If it was clipt
From head in Argos, it should be my own.
CHORUS: For they that should have shorn the mourning lock
Are foes, not friends.
ELECT: 'Tis like, O strange! how like!

CHORUS: Like what? What strange conception stirs thy brain?
ELECT: 'Tis like—O strange!—to these same locks I wear.
    And yet—
CHORUS: Not being yours, there's none, I know,
    Can claim it but Orestes.
ELECT: In sooth, 'tis like.
    Trimmed with one plume Orestes was and I.
CHORUS: But how should he have dared to tread this ground?
ELECT: Belike, he sent it by another's hand,
    A votive lock to grace his father's tomb.
CHORUS: Small solace to my grief, if that he lives,
    Yet never more may touch his native soil.
ELECT: I, too, as with a bitter wave was lashed,
    And pierced, as with an arrow, at the sight
    Of this loved lock; and from my thirsty eyne
    With troubled overflowings unrestrained
    The full tide gushes: for none here would dare
    To gift a lock to Agamemnon's grave;
    No citizen, much less the wife that slew him.
    My mother most unmotherly, her own children
    With godless hate pursuing, evil-minded:
    And though to think this wandering lock have graced
    My brother's head—even his—my loved Orestes,
    Were bliss too great, yet will I hold the hope.

Dulcitius

Hrotsvitha
900 A.D.

Scene: In the apartment where the young women are being held. It is dark. The governor, Dulcitius has sneaked in and is acting demented, embracing and kissing the pots and pans, thinking they are the young virgins.

Of Note: A brief scene, in a brief "martyrdom" play. It is a comic moment in an otherwise serious play about the death of the young women as Christian martyrs.

Agape
Irena
Chionia

AGAPE: What is that clattering noise outside the door?

IRENA: That wretched Dulcitius has come it.

CHIONIA: May God protect us!

AGAPE: So be it.

CHIONIA: What is this clashing of pots and kettles and frying pans?

IRENA: I will look out.

IRENA: Come, I beg you and peek through this small crack.

AGAPE: What is it?

IRENA: Look, the foolish fellow must be out of his mind; he thinks he is embracing us.

AGAPE: What is he doing?

IRENA: Now he hugs the kettle, now the frying pays, and now he hugs the pots, caressing them with soft kisses.

CHIONA: How ridiculous!

IRENA: His face, his hands, his clothes! They are soiled and dirty. With the soot clinging to them he looks like an Ethiopian.

AGAPE: That's fine, his body should turn as black as his soul which is possessed by the devil.

IRENA: He seems to be going. Let us see what the soldiers who are waiting for him are going to do when he goes outside.

Ralph Roister Doister

Nicholas Udall
1400s

Scene: Ralph, madly in love with Christian Custance, spies on her serving women to gain information about her and her household. Even though he is a presence here, it is primarily a scene for the three servants as they spin, mend, and knit.

Margery Mumblecrust
Tibet Talkapace
Annot Alyface

(Roister Doister in the background. Enter Margery Mumblecrust, spinning on the distaff, and Tibet Talkapace, sewing.)

M. MUMBLECRUST: If this distaff were spun, Margery Mumblecrust—

TIB. TALKAPACE: Where good stale ale is, will drink no water, I trust.

M. MUMBLECRUST: Dame Custance hath promised us good ale and white bread—

TIB. TALKAPACE: If she keep not promise I will beshrew her head!
But it will be stark night before I shall have done.

ROISTER DOISTER: I will stand here awhile, and talk with them anon.
I hear them speak of Custance, which doth my heart good;
To hear her name spoken doth even comfort my blood.

M. MUMBLECRUST: Sit down to your work, Tibet, like a good girl.

TIB. TALKAPACE: Nurse, meddle you with your spindle and your whirl!
No haste but good, Madge Mumblecrust; for whip and whur,
The old proverb doth say, never made good fur.

M. MUMBLECRUST: Well, ye will sit down to your work anon, I trust.

TIB. TALKAPACE: Soft fire maketh sweet malt, good Madge Mumblecrust.

M. MUMBLECRUST: And sweet malt maketh jolly good ale for the nones.

TIB. TALKAPACE: Which will slide down the lane without any bones.
(Sings.)
Old brown bread-crusts must have much good mumbling.

But good ale down your throat hath good easy tumbling.

ROISTER DOISTER: The jolliest wench that ere I heard! little mouse!
May I not rejoice that she shall dwell in my house?

TIB. TALKAPACE: So, sirrah, now this gear beginneth for to frame.

M. MUBLECRUST: Thanks to God, though your work stand still, your
tongue is not lame!

TIB. TALKAPACE: And, though your teeth be gone, both so sharp and
so fine,
Yet your tongue can run on pattens as well as mine.

M. MUMBLECRUST: Ye were not for nought named Tib. Talkapace.

TIB. TALKAPACE: Doth my talk grieve you? Alack, God save your
grace!

M. MUMBLECRUST: I hold a groat ye will drink anon for this gear.

TIB. TALKAPACE: And I will pray you the stripes for me to bear.

M. MUMBLECRUST: I hold a penny, ye will drink without a cup.

TIB. TALKAPACE: Wherein so e'er ye drink, I wot ye drink all up.

(Enter Annot Alyface, knitting.)

ANN. ALYFACE: By Cock! and well sewed, my good Tibet Talkapace!

TIB. TALKAPACE: And e'en as well knit, my nown Annot Alyface!

ROISTER DOISTER: See what a sort she keepeth that must be my wife.
Shall not I, when I have her, lead a merry life?

TIB. TALKAPACE: Welcome, my good wench, and sit here by me just.

ANN. ALYFACE: And how doth our old beldame here, Madge
Mumblecrust?

TIB. TALKAPACE: Chide, and find faults, and threaten to complain.

ANN. ALYFACE: To make us poor girls shent, to her is small gain.

M. MUMBLECRUST: I did neither chide, nor complain, nor threaten.

ROISTER DOISTER: It would grieve my heart to see one of them
beaten.

M. MUMBLECRUST: I did nothing but bid her work and hold her
peace.

TIB. TALKAPACE: So would I, if you could your clattering cease;
But the devil cannot make old trot hold her tong.

ANN. ALYFACE: Let all these matters pass, and we three sing a song!
So shall we pleasantly both the time beguile now
And eke dispatch all our works ere we can tell how.

TIB. TALKAPACE: I shrew them that say nay, and that shall not be I.

M. MUMBLECRUST: And I am well content.

TIB. TALKAPACE: Sing on then, by-and-by.

ROISTER DOISTER: And I will not away, but listen to their song,

Yet Merrygreek and my folks tarry very long.

(Tib. Talkapace, Ann. Alyface, and Margery do sing here.)

Pipe, Merry Annot, & c.

Trilla, trilla, trillary.

Work, Tibet; work, Annot; work, Margery!

Sew, Tibet; knit, Annot; spin, Margery!

Let us see who shall win the victory.

TIB. TALKAPACE: This sleeve is not willing to be sewed, I trow.

A small thing might make me all in the ground to throw!

(Then they sing again.)

Pipe, merry Annot, & c.

Trilla, trilla, trillary.

What, Tibet? what, Annot? what, Margery?

Ye sleep, but we do not; that shall we try.

Your fingers be numbed, our work will not lie.

TIB. TALKAPACE: If ye do so again, well, I would advise you nay.

In good sooth, one stop more, and I make holiday.

(They sing the third time.)

Pipe, merry Annot, & c.

Trilla, trilla, trillary.

Now, Tibet; now, Annot; now, Margery;

Now whippet apace for the mastery,

But it will not be, our mouth is so dry.

TIB. TALKAPACE: Ah, each finger is a thumb to-day methink,

I care not to let all alone, choose it swim or sink.

(They sing the fourth time.)

Pipe, Merry Annot, & c.

Trilla, trilla, trillary.

When, Tibet? when, Annot? when, Margery?

I will not! I cannot, no more can I!

Then give we all over, and there let it lie.

(Let her cast down her work.)

TIB. TALKAPACE: There it lieth! The worst is but a curried coat.
Tut, I am used thereto; I care not a groat!
ANN. ALYFACE: Have we done singing since? Then will I in again.
Here I found you, and there I leave both twain. *(Exit.)*
M. MUMBLECRUST: And I will not be long after. Tib. Talkapace.
(Spying Roister Doister.)
TIB. TAKAPACE: What is the matter?
M. MUMBLECRUST: Yond stood a man all this space,
And hath heard all that ever we spake together.
TIB. TALKAPACE: Marry! the more lout he for his coming hither!
And the less good he can, to listen maidens' talk!
I care not an I go bid him hence for to walk.
It were well done to know that he maketh here away.

King Richard the Third

Shakespeare

Scene: Queen Margaret withdraws to eavesdrop on the conversation between Queen Elizabeth and the Duchess. Queen Elizabeth is worried about the future, for Edward is gravely ill and their young son is to be placed under the protection of the scheming Richard.

Queen Margaret, widow of King Henry VI.
Queen Elizabeth, queen to Edward IV.
The Duchess of York, mother to Edward IV, Clarence, and Gloster.

(Before the palace. Enter Queen Margaret.)
QUEEN MARGARET: So, now prosperity begins to mellow,
    And drop into the rotten mouth of death.
    Here is these confines slily have I lurkt,
    To watch the waning of mine enemies.
    A dire induction am I witness to,
    And will to France; hoping the consequence
    Will prove as bitter, black and tragical.—
    Withdraw thee, wretched Margaret: who comes here? *(Retires.)*
    (Enter Queen Elizabeth and the Duchess of York.)
QUEEN ELIZABETH: Ah, my poor princes! ah, my tender babes!
    My unblown flowers, new-appearing sweets!
    If yet your gentle souls fly in the air,
    And be not fixt in doom perpetual,
    Hover about me with your airy wings,
    And hear your mother's lamentation!
QUEEN MARGARET: *(Aside.)* Hover about her; say, that right for right
    Hath dimm'd your infant morn to aged night.
DUTCHESS OF YORK: So many miseries have crazed my voice,
    That my woe-wearied tongue is still and mute.—
    Edward Plantagenet, why art thou dead?
QUEEN MARGARET: *(Aside.)* Plantagenet doth quit Plantagenet,
    Edward for Edward pays a dying debt.
QUEEN ELIZABETH: Wilt Thou, O God, fly from such gentle lambs,

And throw them in the entrails of the wolf?
When didst Thou sleep, when such a deed was done?
QUEEN MARGARET: *(Aside.)* When holy Harry died, and my sweet
son.
DUTCHESS OF YORK: Dead life, blind sight, poor mortal living ghost,
Woe's scene, world's shame, grave's due by life usurpt,
Brief abstract and record of tedious days,
Rest thy unrest on England's lawful earth, *(Sitting down.)*
Unlawfully made drunk with innocents' blood!
QUEEN ELIZABETH: Ah, that thou wouldst as soon afford a grave
As thou canst yield a melancholy seat!
Then would I hide my bones, not rest them here.
Ah, who hath any cause to mourn but I? *(Sitting down by her.)*
QUEEN MARGARET: *(Coming forward.)* If ancient sorrow be most rev-
erend,
Give mine the benefit of seniory,
And let my griefs frown on the upper hand.
If sorrow can admit society, *(Sitting down with them.)*
Tell o'er your woes again by viewing mine:—
I had an Edward, till a Richard kill'd him;
I had a Harry, till a Richard kill'd him:
Thou hadst an Edward, till a Richard kill'd him;
Thou hadst a Richard, till a Richard kill'd him.
DUCHESS OF YORK: I had a Richard too, and thou didst kill him;
I had a Rutland too, thou holp'st to kill him.
QUEEN MARGARET: Thou hadst a Clarence too, and Richard kill'd him.
From forth the kennel of thy womb hath crept.
A hell-hound that doth hunt us all to death:
That dog, that had his teeth before his eyes,
To worry lambs, and lap their gentle blood;
That foul defacer of God's handiwork;
That excellent grand tyrant of the earth,
That reigns in galled eyes of weeping souls,—
Thy womb let loose, to chase us to our graves.—
O upright, just, and true-disposing God,
How do I thank thee, that this carnal cur

Preys on the issue of his mother's body,
And makes her pew-fellow with others' moan!
DUCHESS OF YORK: O Harry's wife, triumph not in my woes!
God witness with me, I have wept for thine.
QUEEN MARGARET: Bear with me; I am hungry for revenge,
And now I cloy me with beholding it.
Thy Edward he is dead, that kill'd my Edward;
Thy other Edward dead, to quit my Edward;
Young York he is but boot, because both they
Match not the high perfection of my loss:
Thy Clarence he is dead that stabb'd my Edward;
And the beholders of this tragic play,
Th' adulterate Hastings, Rivers, Vaughan, Grey,
Untimely smother'd in their dusky graves.
Richard yet lives, hell's black intelligencer;
Only reserved their factor, to buy souls,
And send them thither;—but at hand, at hand.
Ensues his piteous and unpitied end:
Earth gapes, hell burns, fiends roar, saints pray,
To have him suddenly convey'd from hence.—
Cancel his bond of life, dear God, I pray,
That I may live to say, "The dog is dead!"
QUEEN ELIZABETH: O, thou didst prophesy the time would come
That I should wish for thee to help me curse
That bottled spider, that foul bunch-backt toad!
QUEEN MARGARET: I call'd thee then vain flourish of my fortune;
I call'd thee then poor shadow, painted queen;
The presentation of but what I was;
The flattering index of a direful pageant;
One heaved a-high, to be hurl'd down below;
A mother only mockt with two sweet babes;
A dream of what thou wast; a breath, a bubble;
A sign of dignity, a garish flag
To be the aim of every dangerous shot;
A queen in jest, only to fill the scene.
Where is they husband now? where be thy brothers

Where be thy two sons? wherein dost thou joy?
Who sues to thee, and cries, "God save the queen"?
Where be the bending peers that flattered thee?
Where be the thronging troops that followed thee?
Decline all this, and see what now thou art:
For happy wife, a most distressed widow;
For joyful mother, one that wails the name;
For one being sued-to, one that humbly sues;
For queen, a very caitiff crown'd with care;
For one that scorn'd at me, now scorn'd of me:
For one of being fear'd of all, now fearing one;
For one commanding all, obey'd of none;
Thus hath the course of justice wheel'd about,
And left thee but a very prey to time;
Having no more but thought of what thou wast,
To torture thee the more, being what thou art.
Thou didst usurp my place, and dost thou not
Usurp the just proportion of my sorrow?
Now thy proud neck bears half my burden'd yoke;
From which even here I slip my wearied head,
And leave the burden of it all on thee.
Farewell, York's wife; and queen of sad mischance:
These English woes will make me smile in France.
QUEEN ELIZABETH: O thou well-skill'd in curses, stay awhile,
And teach me how to curse mine enemies!
QUEEN MARGARET: Forbear to sleep the night, and fast the day;
Compare dead happiness with living woe;
Think that thy babes were fairer than they were,
And he that slew them fouler than he is:
Bettering thy loss makes the bad causer worse:
Revolving this will teach thee how to curse.
QUEEN ELIZABETH: My words are dull; O, quicken them with thine!
QUEEN MARGARET: Thy woes will make them sharp, and pierce like mine.
(Exit.)
DUCHESS OF YORK: Why should calamity be full of words?

QUEEN ELIZABETH: Windy attorneys to their client woes,
    Airy succeeders of intestate joys,
    Poor breathing orators of miseries!
    Let them have scope: though what they do impart
    Help nothing else, yet do they ease the heart.
DUCHESS OF YORK: If so, then be not tongue-tied: go with me,
    And in the breath of bitter words let's smother
    My damned son, that thy two sweet sons smother'd. *(Drum within.)*
    I hear his drum:—be copious in exclaims.

Romeo and Juliet

Shakespeare

Scene: Act One, Scene Three, Verona, The Capulet's House. Lady
Capulet suggests that Juliet consider Paris for her future husband.

Juliet, age 14.
Lady Capulet, her mother.
Nurse

(Verona. Capulet's house. Enter Lady Capulet and Nurse.)
LADY CAPULET: Nurse, where is my daughter? Call her forth to me.
NURSE: Now by my maidenhead—at twelve year old—I bade
   her come. What lamb! What lady-bird! God forbid!
   Where's this girl? What, Juliet! *(Enter Juliet.)*
JULIET: How now? Who calls?
NURSE: Your mother.
JULIET: Madam, I am here, what is your will?
LADY CAPULET: This is the matter—nurse, give leave awhile,
   We must talk in secret. Nurse, come back again,
   I have remembered me. Thou's hear our counsel.
   Thou knowest my daughter's of a pretty age.
NURSE: Faith I can tell her age unto a hour.
LADY CAPULET: She's not fourteen.
NURSE: I'll lay fourteen of my teeth, and yet to my teen be
   it spoken, I have but four, she's not fourteen. How
   long is it now to Lammas-tide?
LADY CAPULET: A fortnight and odd days.
NURSE: Even or odd, of all days in the year,
   Come Lammas Eve at night shall she be fourteen.
   Susan and she—God rest all Christian souls—
   Were of an age. Well, Susan is with God,
   She was too good for me. But as I said,
   On Lammas Eve at night shall she be fourteen;
   That shall she marry, I remember it well.
   'Tis since the earthquake now eleven years,

And she was weaned—I never shall forget it—
Of all the days of the year, upon that day.
For I had then laid wormwood to my dug,
Sitting in the sun under the dove-house wall.
My lord and you were then at Mantua—
Nay I do bear a brain—but as I said
When it did taste the wormwood on the nipple
Of my dug, and felt it bitter, pretty fool,
To see it tetchy and fall out with the dug!
Shake, quoth the dove-house; 'twas no need I trow
To bid me trudge.
And since that time it is eleven years,
For then she could stand high-lone; nay by th' rood,
She could have run and waddled all about;
For even the day before, she broke her brow,
And then my husband—God be with his soul,
'A was a merry man—took up the child.
Yea, quoth he, dost thou fall upon thy face?
Thou wilt fall backward when thou has more wit,
Wilt thou not Jule? And by my holidame,
The pretty wretch left crying, and said ay.
To see now how a jest shall come about!
I warrant, an I should live a thousand years,
I never should forget it. Wilt thou not Jule, quoth he,
And pretty fool it stinted, and say ay.
LADY CAPULET: Enough of this, I pray thee hold thy peace.
NURSE: Yes madam, yet I cannot choose but laugh,
To think it should leave crying, and say ay.
And yet I warrant it had upon it brow
A bump as big as a young cockerel's stone.
A perilous knock, and it cried bitterly.
Yea, quoth my husband, fall'st upon thy face?
Thou wilt fall backward when thou comest to age;
Wilt thou not Jule? It stinted, and said ay.
JULIET: And stint thou too, I pray thee nurse, say I.
NURSE: Peace, I have done. God mark thee to his grace;

Thou wast the prettiest babe that e'er I nursed;
An I might live to see thee married once.
I have my wish.
LADY CAPULET: Marry, that marry is the very theme
I came to talk of. Tell me daughter Juliet,
How stands your dispositions to be married?
JULIET: It is an honour that I dream not of.
NURSE: An honour? Were not I thine only nurse,
I would say thou hadst sucked wisdom from thy teat.
LADY CAPULET: Well, think of marriage now. Younger than you,
Here in Verona, ladies of esteem,
Are made already mothers. By my count,
I was your mother much upon these years
That you are now a maid. Thus then in brief—
The valiant Paris seeks you for his love.
NURSE: A man, young lady; lay, such a man
As all the world—why he's a man of wax.
LADY CAPULET: Verona's summer hath not such a flower.
NURSE: Nay he's a flower, in faith a very flower.
LADY CAPULET: What say you, can you love the gentlemen?
This night you shall behold him at our feast,
Read o'er the volume of young Paris' face,
And find delight writ there with beauty's pen;
Examine every married lineament,
And see how one another lends content;
And what obscured in this fair volume lies
Find written in the margent of his eyes.

This precious book of love, this unbound lover,
To beautify him only lacks a cover.
The fish lives in the sea, and 'tis much pride
For fair without the fair within to hide.
That book in many's eyes doth share the glory,
That in gold clasps locks in the golden story;
So shall you share all that he doth possess,
By having him, making yourself no less.

NURSE: No less, nay bigger; women grow by men.
LADY CAPULET: Speak briefly, can you like of Paris' love?
JULIET: I'll look to like, if looking liking move.
     But no more deep will I endart mine eye
     Than your consent gives strength to make it fly.

Macbeth

Shakespeare

Scene: Scene One—the witches' first manifestation.
Scene Three—on the Heath.

Of Note: Two short scenes, yet vital to the play. The witches can be interpreted many ways but always portend the future and create a powerful supernatural force.

Three witches

SCENE I
(Thunder and lightning. Enter Three Witches.)
FIRST WITCH: Then shall we three meet again?
In thunder, lightning, or in rain?
SECOND WITCH: When the hurlyburly's done,
When the battle's lost and won.
THIRD WITCH: That will be ere the set of sun.
FIRST WITCH: Where the place?
SECOND WITCH: Upon the heath.
THIRD WITCH: There to meet with Macbeth.
FIRST WITCH: I come, Graymalkin.
SECOND WITCH: Paddock calls.
THIRD WITCH: Anon!
ALL: Fair is foul, and foul is fair.
Hover through the fog and filthy air. *(Exeunt.)*

SCENE III
(Thunder. Enter the Three Witches.)
FIRST WITCH: Where hast thou been, sister?
SECOND WITCH: Killing swine.
THIRD WITCH: Sister, where thou?
FIRST WITCH: A sailor's wife had chestnuts in her lap,
And mounched, and mounched, and mounched.
"Give me," quoth I.

"Aroint thee, witch!" the rump-fed ronyon cries.
Her husband's to Aleppo gone, master o' th' Tiger:
But in a sieve I'll thither sail,
And, like a rat without a tail,
I'll do, I'll do, and I'll do.
SECOND WITCH: I'll give thee a wind.
FIRST WITCH: Th'art kind.
THIRD WITCH: And I another.
FIRST WITCH: I myself have all the other;
And the very ports they blow
All the quarters that they know
I' th' shipman's card.
I'll drain him dry as hay:
Sleep shall neither night nor day
Hang upon his penthouse lid;
He shall live a man forbid:
Weary sev'nights nine times nine
Shall be dwindle, peak, and pine:

Though his bark cannot be lost,
Yet it shall be tempest-tossed.
Look what I have.
SECOND WITCH: Show me, show me.
FIRST WITCH: Here I have a pilot's thumb,
Wracked as homeward he did come.
(Drum within.)
THIRD WITCH: A drum, a drum!
Macbeth doth come.
ALL: The weird sisters, hand in hand,
Posters of the sea and land,
Thus do go about, about:
Thrice to thine, and thrice to mine,
And thrice again, to make up nine.
Peace! The charm's wound up.

Offering Flowers

Traditional Aztec
Jerome Rothenberg

Scene: In the ninth month of the year the Aztecs had a feast which they called The Flowers Are Offered.

Of Note: This is a ritual that I have included here because it lends itself to Readers' Theateror Movement work. It is appropriate for women's voices.

And two days before the feast, when flowers were sought, all scattered over the mountains, that every flower might be found.

And when these were gathered, when they had come to the flowers and arrived where they were, at dawn they strung them together; everyone strung them.

And when the flowers had been threaded, then these were twisted and wound in garlands—long ones, very long, & thick— very thick.

And when morning broke the temple guardians then ministered to Uitzilopochtli; they adorned him with garlands of flowers; and placed flowers upon his head.

And before him they spread, strewed, and hung rows of all the various flowers, the most beautiful flowers, the threaded flowers

then flowers were offered to all the rest of the gods

they were adorned with flowers; they were girt with garlands of flowers

flowers were placed upon their heads, there in the temples.

And when midday came, they all sang and danced
quietly, calmly, evenly they danced

they kept going as they danced.

I offer flowers. I sow flower seeds. I plant flowers. I assemble flowers. I pick flowers. I pick different flowers. I remove flowers. I seek flowers. I offer flowers. I arrange flowers. I thread a flower. I string flowers. I make flowers. I form them to be extending, uneven, rounded, round bouquets of flowers.

I make a flower necklace, a flower garland, a paper of flowers, a bouquet, a flower shield, hand flowers. I thread them. I string them. I provide them with grass. I provide them with leaves. I make a pendant of them. I smell something. I smell them. I cause one to smell something. I cause him to smell. I offer flowers to one. I offer him flowers. I provide him with flowers. I provide one with flowers. I provide one with a flower necklace. I provide him with a flower necklace. I place a garland on one. I provide him a garland. I clothe one in flowers. I clothe him in flowers. I cover one with flowers. I cover him with flowers. I destroy one with flowers. I destroy him with flowers. I injure one with flowers. I injure him with flowers.

I destroy one with flowers; I destroy him with flowers; I insure one with flowers: with drink, with food, with flowers, with tobacco, with capes, with gold. I beguile, I incite him with flowers, with words; I beguile him, I say, "I caress him with flowers. I seduce one. I extend one a lengthy discourse. I induce him with words."

I provide one with flowers. I make flowers, or I give them to one that someone will observe a feastday. Or I merely continue to give one flowers; I continue to place them in one's hand, I continue to offer them to one's hands. Or I provide one with a necklace, or I provide one with a garland of flowers.

The Rivals

Richard Brinsley Sheridan
1775

Scene: A dressing room in Mrs. Malaprop's Lodgings. Lucy has been
to the library for Lydia.

Lydia Languish, a wealthy young woman.
Lucy, her young maid.
Julia Melville, Lydia's cousin.

> *(A dressing room in Mrs. Malaprop's lodgings, second grooves;
> discovered, Lydia Languish sitting on a sofa, R. C. with a book in
> her hand; Lucy as if just returned from a message, on her R.)*

LUCY: Indeed, ma'am, I traversed half the town in search of it; I don't
believe there's a circulating library in Bath I ha'n't been at.

LYD: And could you not get *The Reward of Constancy?*

LUCY: No, indeed, ma'am.

LYD: Nor *The Fatal Connexion?*

LUCY: No, indeed, ma'am.

LYD: Nor *The Mistakes of the Heart? (Ready knock, L.)*

LUCY: Ma'am, as ill-luck would have it, Mr. Bull said, Miss Sukey
Saunter had just fetched it away.

LYD: Heigho! Did you inquire for *The Delicate Distress?*

LUCY: Or, *The Memoirs of Lady Woodford?* Yes, indeed, ma'am, I
asked everywhere for it; and I might have brought it from Mr.
Frederick's, but Lady Slattern Lounger, who had just sent it home,
had so soiled and dog's-eared it, it wa'n't fit for a Christian to
read.

LYD: Heigho! Yes, I always know when Lady Slattern has been before
me. She has a most observing thumb, and, I believe, cherishes her
nails for the convenience of making marginal notes. Well, child,
what have you brought me?

LUCY: Oh, here, ma'am! *(Takes books from under her cloak and from
her pockets.)* This is *The Man of Feeling.* and this, *Peregrine Pickle*

—here are *The Tears of Sensibility,* and *Humphrey Clinker. (Knock, L.)*

LYD: Hold! here's someone coming—quick, see who it is. *(Exit Lucy, L.I.E.)*

JUL: *(Heard outside.)* Very well, Lucy.

LYD: Surely I heard my cousin Julie's voice! *(Re-enter Lucy, L.I.E.)*

LUCY: Lud, ma'am, here is Miss Melville!

LYD: Is it possible! *(Enter Julia, L.I.E.)*

LYD: *(Rising.)* My dearest Julia, how delighted I am! *(They embrace.)* How unexpected was this happiness! *(Exit Lucy, L.I.E.)*

JUL: True, Lydia, and our pleasure is the greater. But what has been the matter? You were denied to me at first.

LYD: *(Reseating herself, and drawing Julia beside her on sofa; Lydia, R.; Julia, L.)* Ah, Julia, I have a thousand things to tell you! But first inform me what has conjured you to Bath? Is Sir Anthony here?

JUL: He is. We are arrived within this hour, and I suppose he will be here to wait on Mrs. Malaprop as soon as he is dressed.

LYD: Then before we are interrupted, let me impart to you some of my distress; I know your gentle nature will sympathize with me, though your prudence may condemn me. My letters have informed you of my whole connection with Beverley, but I have lost him, my Julia—my aunt has discovered our intercourse, by a note she intercepted, and has confined me ever since. Yet would you believe it? She has fallen absolutely in love with a tall Irish baronet she met one night since we have been here, at Lady MacShuffle's court.

JUL: You jest, Lydia.

LYD: No, upon my word. She really carries on a kind of correspondence with him, under a feigned name, though, till she chooses to be known to him; but it is a Delia, or a Celia, I assure you.

JUL: Then surely she is now more indulgent to her niece?

LYD: Quite the contrary; since she has discovered her own frailty, she has become ten times more suspicious of mine. Then I must inform you of another plague; that odious Acres is to be in Bath to-day, so that, I protest, I shall be teased out of all spirits.

JUL: Come, come, Lydia, hope for the best. Sir Anthony shall use his interest with Mrs. Malaprop.

LYD: But you have not heard the worst. Unfortunately I had quarrelled with my poor Beverley, just before my aunt made the discovery, and I have not seen him since to make up.

JUL: What was his offence?

LYD: Nothing at all; but I don't know how it was, as often as we had been together, we had never had a quarrel; and, somehow, I was afraid he would never give me an opportunity; so, last Thursday I wrote a letter to myself, to inform myself that Beverley was, at that time, paying his addresses to another woman. I signed it "Your unknown friend," showed it to Beverley, charged him with his falsehood, put myself in a violent passion, and vowed I'd never see him more.

JUL: And you let him depart so, and have not seen him since?

LYD: 'Twas the next day my aunt found the matter out; I intended only to have teazed him three days and a half, and now I have lost him forever.

JUL: If he is as deserving and sincere as you have represented him to me, he will never resign you so. Yet consider, Ldia, you tell me he is but an ensign—and you have thirty thousand pounds!

LYD: But, you know, I lose most of my fortune if I marry without my aunt's consent till of age; and that is what I have determined to do ever since I knew the penalty; nor could I love the man who would wish to wait a day for the alternative.

JUL: Nay, this is caprice!

LYD: What, does Julia tax me with caprice? I thought her lover Faulkland had inured her to it.

JUL: I do not love even his faults. They, I own, have cost me many unhappy hours; but I have learned to think myself his debtor for those imperfections which arise from the ardour of his attachment.

LYD: Well, I cannot blame you for defending him; but, tell me candidly, Julia—had he never saved your life, do you think you should have been attached to him as you are? Believe me, the rude blast that overset your boat was a prosperous gale of love to him.

JUL: Gratitude may have strengthened my attachment to Mr. Faulkland, but I loved him before he had preserved me; yet, surely, that alone were an obligation sufficient—

LYD: Obligation! Why, a water spaniel would have done as much! Well, I should never think of giving my heart to a man because he could swim! What's here? *(Enter* Lucy, *in a hurry, L.I.E.)*

LUCY: Oh, ma'am, here is Sir Anthony Absolute, just come home with your aunt.

LYD: They'll not come here; Lucy, do you watch. *(Exit Lucy, L.I.E.)*

JUL: Yet I must go; Sir Anthony does not know I am here, and if we meet, he'll detain me, to show me the town. *(Rising.)* I'll take another opportunity of paying my respects to Mrs. Malaprop, when she shall treat me, as long as she chooses, with her select words, so ingeniously misapplied, without being mispronounced. *(Crosses, R.) (Enter Lucy, L.I.E.)*

LUCY: Oh, lud, ma'am! They are both coming up stairs!

LYD: Well, I'll not detain you. *(Rising, and crossing to door at R.)* Adieu, my dear Julia. I'm sure you are in haste to send to Faulkland. There—*(Indicating door, R.)* through my room you'll find another staircase.

JUL: Adieu! *(Exit, R.I.E.)*

LYD: Here, my dear Lucy, hide these books. Quick—quick! Fling *Peregrine Pickle* under the toilet—throw *Roderick Randow* into the closet—put *The Innocent Adultery* into *The Whole Duty of Man*—thrust *Lord Aimworth* under the sofa—cram *Ovid* behind the bolster—there—put *The Man of Feeling* into your pocket. Now for them!

Riders to the Sea

John Millington Synge
1904

Scene: The cottage kitchen in the Aran Islands, off the West Coast of
Ireland. Nets, oilskins, and some new boards standing by the wall.
It is a fishing village and Mauyra has lost her husband and several
sons to the sea. Her son Michael is missing and the youngest son,
Bartley, has insisted on catching the last boat to the mainland to
sell a horse, despite his mother's protests. Mauyra is angry as
Bartley leaves for his trip. Earlier, Cathleen and Nora have hidden
a bundle of washed-up clothing that they fear belongs to
Michael. They do not want their Mother to know that he, too,
has surely drowned.

Mauyra, the matriarch of the family.
Cathleen, her daughter, 20s.
Nora, her younger daughter.

MAUYRA: *(Crying out as he is in the door.)* He's gone now, God spare
us, and we'll not see him again. He's gone now, and when the
black night is falling I'll have no son left me in the world.

CATHLEEN: Why wouldn't you give him your blessing and he looking
round in the door? Isn't it sorrow enough is on everyone in this
house without your sending him out with an unlucky word
behind him, and a hard word in his ear?
*(Mauyra takes up the tongs and begins raking the fire aimlessly
without looking round.)*

NORA: *(Turning towards her.)* You're taking away the turf from the
cake.

CATHLEEN: *(Crying out.)* The Son of God forgive us, Nora, we're after
forgetting his bit of bread. *(She comes over to the fire.)*

NORA: And it's destroyed he'll be going till dark night, and he after
eating nothing since the sun went up.

CATHLEEN: *(Turning the cake out of the oven.)* It's destroyed he'll be
surely. There's no sense left on any person in a house where an

old woman will be talking forever. *(Mauyra sways herself on her stool.)* *(Cutting off some of the bread and rolling it in a cloth; to Mauyra.)* Let you go down now to the spring well and give him this and he passing. You'll see him then and the dark word will be broken, and you can say "God speed you," the way he'll be easy in his mind.

MAUYRA: *(Taking the bread.)* Will I be in it as soon as himself?

CATHLEEN: If you go now quickly.

MAUYRA: *(Standing up unsteadily.)* It's hard set I am to walk.

CATHLEEN: *(Looking at her anxiously.)* Give her the stick, Nora, or maybe she'll slip on the big stones.

NORA: What stick?

CATHLEEN: The stick Michael brought from Connemara.

MAUYRA: *(Taking a stick Nora gives her.)* In the big world the old people do be leaving things after them for their sons and children, but in this place it is the young men do be leaving things behind for them that do be old. *(She goes out slowly. Nora goes over to the ladder.)*

CATHLEEN: Wait, Nora, maybe she'd turn back quickly. she's that sorry, God help her, you wouldn't know the thing she'd do.

NORA: Is she gone round by the bush?

CATHLEEN: *(Looking out.)* She's gone now. Throw it down quickly, for the Lord knows when she'll be out of it again.

NORA: *(Getting the bundle from the loft.)* The young priest said he'd be passing to-morrow, and we might go down and speak to him below if it's Michael's they are surely.

CATHLEEN: *(Taking the bundle.)* Did he say what way they were found?

NORA: *(Coming down.)* "There were two men," said he, "and they rowing round with poteen before the cocks crowed, and the oar of one of them caught the body, and they passing the black cliffs of the north."

CATHLEEN: *(Trying to open the bundle.)* Give me a knife, Nora; the string's perished with the salt water, and there's a black knot on it you wouldn't loosen in a week.

NORA: *(Giving her a knife.)* I've heard tell it was a long way to Donegal.

CATHLEEN: *(Cutting the string.)* It is surely. There was a man in here a while ago—the man sold us that knife—and he said if you set off walking from the rocks beyond, it would be in seven days you'd be in Donegal.

NORA: And what time would a man take, and he floating?
(Cathleen opens the bundle and takes out a bit of a shirt and a stocking. They look at them eagerly.

CATHLEEN: *(lin a low voice.)* The Lord spare us, Nora! isn't it a queer hard thing to say if it's his they are surely?

NORA: I'll get his shirt off the hook the way we can put the one flannel on the other. *(She look through some clothes hanging in the corner.)* It's not with them, Cathleen, and where will be it?

CATHLEEN: I'm thinking Bartley put it on him in the morning, for his own shirt was heavy with the salt in it. *(Pointing to the corner.)* There's a bit of a sleeve was of the same stuff. Give me that and it will do. *(Nora brings it to her and they compare the flannel.)* It's the same stuff, Nora; but if it is itself, aren't there great rolls of it in the shops of Galway, and isn't it many another man may have a shirt of it as well as Michael himself?

NORA: *(Who has taken up the stocking and counted the stitches, crying out.)* It's Michael, Cathleen, it's Michael; God spare his soul, and what will herself say when she hears this story, and Bartley on the sea?

CATHLEEN: *(Taking the stocking.)* It's a plain stocking.

NORA: It's the second one of the third pair I knitted, and I put up three-score stitches, and I dropped four of them.

CATHLEEN: *(Counts the stitches.)* It's that number is in it. *(Crying out.)* Oh Nora, isn't it a bitter thing to think of him floating that way to the far north, and not one to keen him but the black hags that do be flying on the sea?

NORA: *(Swinging herself half round, and throwing out her arms on the clothes.)* And isn't it a pitiful thing when there is nothing left of a man who was a great rower and fisher but a bit of an old shirt and a plain stocking?

CATHLEEN: *(After an instant.)* Tell me is herself coming, Nora? I hear a little sound on the path.

NORA: *(Looking out.)* She is, Cathleen. She's coming up to the door.

CATHLEEN: Put these things away before she'll come in. Maybe it's easier she'll be after giving her blessing to Bartley, and we won't let on we've heard anything the time he's on the sea.

NORA: *(Helping Cathleen to close the bundle.)* We'll put them here in the corner.

(They put them into a hole in the chimney corner. Cathleen goes back to the spinning wheel.) Will she see it was crying I was?

CATHLEEN: Keep your back to the door the way the light'll not be on you. *(Nora sits down at the chimney corner, with her back to the door. Mauyra comes in very slowly, without looking at the girls, and goes over to her stool at the other side of the fire. The cloth with the bread is still in her hand. The girls look at each other, and Nora points to the bundle of bread.)* *(After spinning for a moment.)* You didn't give him his bit of bread? *(Mauyra begins to keen softly, without turning round.)* Did you see him riding down? *(Mauyra goes on keening.)* *(A little impatiently.)* God forgive you; isn't it a better thing to raise your voice and tell what you seen, than to be making lamentation for a thing that's done? Did you see Bartley, I'm saying to you?

MAUYRA: *(With a weak voice.)* My heart's broken from this day.

CATHLEEN: *(As before.)* Did you see Bartley?

MAUYRA: I seen the fearfullest thing.

CATHLEEN: *(Leaves her wheel and looks out.)* God forgive you; he's riding the mare now over the green head, and the grey pony behind him.

MAUYRA: *(Starts so that her shawl falls back from her head and shows her white tossed hair. With a frightened voice.)* The grey pony behind him . . .

CATHELEEN: *(Coming to the fire.)* What is it ails you at all?

MAUYRA: *(Speaking very slowly.)* I've seen the fearfullest thing any person has seen since the day Bride Dara seen the dead man with the child in his arms.

CATHLEEN and NORA: Uah.

(They crouch down in front of the old woman at the fire.)

NORA: Tell us what it is you seen.

MAUYRA: I went down to the spring well, and I stood there saying a prayer to myself. Then Bartley came along, and he riding on the red mare with the grey pony behind him. *(She puts up her hands, as if to hide something from her eyes.)* The Son of God spare us, Nora!

CATHLEEN: What is it you seen?

MAUYRA: I seen Michael himself.

CATHLEEN: *(Speaking softly.)* You did not, mother. It wasn't Michael you seen, for his body is after being found in the far north, and he's got a clean burial, by the grace of God.

MAUYRA: *(A little defiantly.)* I'm after seeing him this day, and he riding and galloping. Bartley came first on the red mare, and I tried to say "God speed you," but something choked the words in my throat. He went by quickly; and "The blessing of God on you," says he, and I could say nothing. I looked up then, and I crying, at the grey pony, and there was Michael upon it—with fine clothes oh him, and new shoes on his feet.

CATHLEEN: *(Begins to keen.)* It's destroyed we are from this day. It's destroyed, surely.

NORA: Didn't the young priest say the Almighty God won't leave her destitute with no son living?

MAUYRA: *(In a low voice, but clearly.)* It's little the like of him knows of the sea . . . Bartley will be lost now, and let you call in Eamon and make me a good coffin out of the white boards, for I won't live after them. I've had a husband, and a husband's father, and six sons in this house—six fine men, though it was a hard birth I had with every one of them and they coming into the world—and some of them were found and some of them were not found, but they're gone now the lot of them . . . There were Stephen and Shawn were lost in the great wind, and found after in the Bay of Gregory of the Golden Mouth, and carried up the two of them on one plank, and in by that door. *(She pauses for a moment; the girls start as if they heard something through the door that is half open behind them.)*

NORA: *(In a whisper.)* Did you hear that, Cathleen? Did you hear a noise in the north-east?

CATHLEEN: *(In a whisper.)* There's someone after crying out by the seashore.

The Cherry Orchard

Anton Chekhov
1904

Scene: The action takes place on the estate of Mme. Ranevsky, owner of the cherry orchard. It is May. The cherry trees are in flower. Mme. Ranevsky and Anya have returned to the country after a five-year absence. Dunyasha and Varya have remained on the land. It is the first few moments that Anya is home. They are in her old nursery.

Of Note: Lopahin, a merchant who has come to greet them, makes a Baa-ing sound from offstage in this scene.

Dunyasha, a maid, dressed up, hair all fixed, nervous.
Anya, a young woman, age 17, daughter of Mme. Ranevsky.
Varya, an adopted daughter, age 24, of Mme. Ranevsky, serious and religious.

DUNYASHA: We've been waiting forever . . . *(Takes Anya's coat and hat.)*

ANYA: I didn't sleep one moment that whole journey long, four whole nights . . . and now I'm absolutely frozen!

DUNYASHA: You left during Lent, we had snow then, and frost, and now! My darling! *(Bursts out laughing, kisses her.)* I've waited forever for you, my precious, my joy . . . and I've got something to tell you, I can't wait one minute longer . . .

ANYA: *(Listlessly.)* Now what . . .

DUNYASHA: Yepikhodov, the clerk, proposed to me just after Easter.

ANYA: Not again . . . *(Adjusts her hair.)* I've lost all my hairpins . . . *(She is exhausted; she almost sways on her feet.)*

DUNYASHA: No, really, I don't know what to think any more. He adores me, God, how he adores me!

ANYA: *(Gazes at the door to her room, tenderly.)* My very own room, my windows, it's as if I never left. I'm home! And tomorrow I'll wake up, and I'll run out into the orchard . . . Oh, if only I could rest! I'm so exhausted—I didn't sleep one moment the whole way, I was so worried.

DUNYASHA: Pyott Sergeich arrived the day before yesterday.

ANYA: *(Overjoyed.)* Petya!

DUNYASHA: He's out in the bathhouse, asleep, that's where he's staying. "I'm afraid of being in the way," he said. *(Glances at her pocket watch.)* We ought to wake him up, but Varvara Mikhailovna gave us strict orders not to. "Don't you dare wake him up," he said.

(Enter Varya, a bunch of keys hanging from her belt.)

VARYA: Dunyasha, go, quickly, bring the coffee . . . Mamochka wants coffee.

DUNYASHA: Right away. *(Exits.)*

VARYA: So, thank God, you're here. You're home at last! *(Embracing her.)* My darling's home! My angel is home!

ANYA: I've been through so much.

VARYA: I can imagine.

ANYA: I left during Holy Week, it was so cold then, remember? And Charlotta Ivanovna talked the whole way, talked and played card tricks. How could you have stuck me with Charlotta! . . .

VARYA: You can't travel alone, darling, At seventeen!

ANYA: When we arrived in Paris, it was cold there, too, and snowing. My French is terrible. Mama lived on the fifth floor, and when I finally got there, the flat was filled with all sorts of French people, ladies, and an old Catholic priest with a little book, and, oh, it was so uncomfortable there, so stuffy, the room was filled with smoke. And suddenly I felt sorry for Mama, so very sorry, I threw my arms around her neck, I held her so tight, I couldn't let go. And Mama kept clinging to me, and weeping . . .

VARYA: *(In tears.)* Enough, enough . . .

ANYA: She had already sold the dacha near Menton, she had nothing left, nothing at all. And neither did I, not a single kopek, we hardly had enough money to get home. And Mama just doesn't understand it, still! There we are, sitting in the station restaurant, and she orders the most expensive thing on the menu, she gives the waiter a ruble tip for tea. Charlotta, too. And Yasha orders a complete dinner, it's simply terrible. Yasha is Mama's butler, you know. We brought him with us . . .

VARYA: I'm seen him, the devil . . .

ANYA: So, tell me! Have we paid the interest yet?

VARYA: With what?

ANYA: Dear God, dear God . . .

VARYA: And in August, the estate will be sold . . .

ANYA: Dear God . . .

LOPAKHIN: *(Peeks through the door and makes a "bleating" sound.)* Ba-a-a . . . *(Exits.)*

VARYA: *(In tears.)* I'd like to give him such a . . . *(Makes a threatening gesture with his fist.)*

ANYA: *(Embraces Varya, softly.)* Varya, has he proposed yet? *(Varya shakes her head "no.")* But he loves you, he does . . . Why don't you talk about it, what are you two waiting for?

VARYA: I know nothing will ever come of it, nothing. He's so busy, he has no time for me, really . . . he pays no attention to me at all. Well, God bless him, but it's too painful for me even to look at him . . . Everyone talks about our wedding, everyone congratulates us, but the fact is, there's absolutely nothing to it, it's all a dream . . . *(Changes tone.)* Your brooch looks just like a little bee.

ANYA: *(Sadly.)* Mama bought it. *(She goes to her room, speaking in a gay, childlike voice.)* And in Paris, I went up in a hot air balloon!

VARYA: My darling's home! My angel is home! *(Dunyasha has already returned with the coffeepot and prepares the coffee.)* *(Stands by the doorway.)* All day long, darling, I go about my business, I run the household, I do my chores, but all the time I'm thinking, dreaming. If only we could marry you off to a rich man, then I'd find peace, I'd go to a cloister, and then on a pilgrimage to Kiev, to Moscow, and on and on, from one holy place to the next . . . on and on. A blessing!

ANYA: The birds are singing in the orchard. What time is it?

VARYA: After two, it must be . . . Time for you to sleep, darling. *(Goes into* Anyas's *room.)* Yes, a blessing!

Yerma

Federico Garcia Lorca
1934

Scene: Yerma, married and childless, longs for a baby. Here, she meets two women on the road and is upset with the one for leaving her baby alone in the house. The other represents another perspective: that to be childless is to be free for fun and a life unburdened by responsibility.

Yerma
First Girl
Second Girl

FIRST GIRL: Everywhere we go we run into people.

YERMA: With all the work that needs to be done, the men have to be in the olive groves, and we must bring them food. The only people left in their homes are the old people.

SECOND GIRL: Are you on your way back to the village?

YERMA: That's where I'm headed.

FIRST GIRL: I'm in a great hurry. I've left my baby sleeping, and there's no one in the house.

YERMA: Then hurry up, woman. You can't leave children alone. Are there pigs at your place?

FIRST GIRL: No, but you're right. I should hurry.

YERMA: Go ahead. That's how things happen. Surely, you've locked the door, though.

FIRST GIRL: Naturally.

YERMA: Yes, but even so, we don't understand what a small child really is. Something that seems perfectly harmless to us can destroy him: a tiny needle, a sip of water.

FIRST GIRL: You're right. I'll run on. I don't think of these things.

YERMA: Go on.

SECOND GIRL: If you had four or five, you wouldn't talk like that.

YERMA: Why not? Even if I had forty.

SECOND GIRL: Anyway, you and I, by not having any, live a more peaceful life.

YERMA: Not I.

SECOND GIRL: Well, I do. What a fuss! My mother, on the other hand, does nothing but give me herbs so I will have children, and in October we'll go to a saint who they say gives to those who beg to him with fervor. My mother will ask him for me. Not I.

YERMA: Why did you get married?

SECOND GIRL: Because it was arranged. Everyone gets married. If we keep on like this, the only unmarried ones will be little girls. Well, and besides . . . in reality one gets married long before going to church. But the old women keep worrying about all these things. I'm nineteen years old and I don't like to cook or clean. Well, now I spend the entire day doing what I like the least. And what for? What need does my husband have to be my husband? We did the same thing as sweethearts as we do now. It's all just old folks' nonsense.

YERMA: Be quiet. Don't say such things.

SECOND GIRL: You'll be calling me crazy as well. That crazy girl, that crazy girl. *(She laughs.)* I can tell you the only thing I've learned in this life: Everyone is stuck inside their houses doing what they don't wish to do. How much better it is to be out in the street! I can go to the river, I can go up to the tower and ring the bells, or I can drink a glass of anisette.

YERMA: You're just a girl.

SECOND GIRL: Yes, but I'm not crazy. *(She laughs.)*

YERMA: Doesn't your mother live up on the highest point of the village?

SECOND GIRL: Yes.

YERMA: In the last house?

SECOND GIRL: Yes.

YERMA: What's her name?

SECOND GIRL: Dolores. Why do you ask?

YERMA: No reason.

SECOND GIRL: You ask for a reason!

YERMA: I don't know . . . I've heard say . . .

SECOND GIRL: Well, that's your concern . . . Look, I'm going to take my husband his food. *(She laughs.)* That's something to see. A pity I can't say he's my sweetheart, isn't it? *(She laughs.)* The crazy girl goes on! *(She leaves, laughing joyfully.)* Good-bye!

The House of Bernarda Alba

Federico Garcia Lorca
1936

Scene: The house of the matriarch Bernarda Alba whose husband has just died.

Maid
Poncia, a maid, 60s.
A beggar woman.

> *(A very white room in Bernarda Alba's house. Thick walls. Arched doorways with jute curtains tied back with tassles and ruffles. Wicker chairs. On the walls hang paintings of improbable landscapes of nymphs and kings of legend. It is summer. A great brooding silence fills the stage. As the curtain rises, the stage is empty. The tolling of bells can be heard. The maid enters.)*

MAID: I've the tolling of those bells inside my brain.

PONCIA: *(Appears eating sausage and bread.)* More than two hours of mocking funeral chants. Priests have come from all over. The church looks beautiful. At the first responsary Magdalena fainted.

MAID: She is the one who will be the most alone.

PONCIA: She was the only one who loved her father. Oh! Thank God we're alone for a bit! I've come to eat.

MAID: If Bernarda were to see you .. .!

PONCIA: Since she's not eating today, she'd have us all die of hunger! Domineering tyrant! Well, she'll have to put up with it! I've opened the sausage pot.

MAID: *(Sadly, anxiously.)* Why don't you give me some for my daughter, Poncia?

PONCIA: Go ahead and take a fistful of peas while you're at it. She won't know the difference today!

MAID: *(From inside.)* Bernarda!

PONCIA: The old woman. Is she locked up?

MAID: Two turns of the key.

PONCIA: You best put the cross-bar up as well. She has the fingers of a lock-picker.

VOICE: Bernarda!

PONCIA: *(Shouting.)* She's coming! *(To the Maid.)* Make sure everything's clean. If Bernarda doesn't see everything sparkling, she'll tear out what little hair I've got left.

MAID: What a woman!

PONCIA: Tyrant of all who surround her. She's capable of sitting on your heart and watching you die for a whole year without ever once erasing that cold smile she wears on her cursed face. Scrub, scrub the dishes!

MAID: I've blood on my hands from scouring everything.

PONCIA: She's the cleanest, the most decent, the most everything. Her husband earned his rest! *(The bells cease ringing.)*

MAID: Did all the relatives come?

PONCIA: Hers. His family hates her. They came to pay their respects and made the sign of the cross over him.

MAID: Are there enough chairs?

PONCIA: More than enough. Let them sit on the floor. Ever since Bernarda's father died no one has come into this house. She doesn't want people to see her in her realm. Curse her!

MAID: She's been good to you.

PONCIA: Thirty years washing her sheets; thirty years eating her leftovers; sleepless nights when she coughs; entire days spent looking through the crack in the shutters so I could spy on the neighbors and go to her with all the gossip; a life without secrets, and yet, curse her! May a piercing pain strike her eyes!

MAID: Woman!

PONCIA: But I'm a good dog; I bark when I'm told and I bite the heels of the beggars when she sets me on them; my sons work her lands and they're both married already, but one day I'll have enough.

MAID: And on that day . . .

PONCIA: On that day I will lock myself up in a room with her and I will spit on her for a whole year. "Bernarda, this is for this, and for that, and for everything," until she's like a lizard the children squash under their feet, because that's what she is, Bernarda and her whole family. Not that I envy her life. She's left with five daughters, five ugly daughters, who, except for Angustias, the eldest, who is the daughter of her first husband and the one who had the money, may do a lot of embroidery, and wear fine linen clothes, but when it comes to an inheritance, they've nothing but grapes and bread.

MAID: Well, I'd like to have what they have!

PONCIA: We have our hands and a hole in God's earth.

MAID: It's the only earth those who have nothing can have.

PONCIA: *(At the cupboard.)* This glass has some specks.

MAID: Neither soap nor a good rag will get rid of them. *(The bells ring.)*

PONICA: The last prayer! I'm going over to hear it. I like how our priest sings. In the Pater Noster, his voice went higher, and higher until he seemed like a water jar filling itself up slowly; of course in the end his voice cracked, but it was still glorious to listen to it. Of course, there was nobody like the old sexton Tronchapinos. At my mother's Mass, may she rest in peace, he sang . . . the walls shook, and when he said "Amen" it was as if a wolf had come into the church. *(Imitating him.)* A-a-a-a-amen! *(She begins to cough.)*

MAID: You're going to strain your windpipe.

PONCIA: I used to strain something else! *(She exits, laughing.)*
(The Maid cleans. The bells ring.)

MAID: *(Accompanying the bells.)* Ding, ding, dong. Ding, ding, dong. May God forgive him!

BEGGAR WOMAN: *(With a child.)* Blessed be God!

MAID: Ding, ding, dong. I hope he waits for us for many years! Ding, ding, dong.

BEGGAR WOMAN: *(Loudly and a little annoyed.)* Blessed by God!

MAID: *(Annoyed.)* Forever and ever!

BEGGAR WOMAN: I came for the scraps.
(The bells cease ringing.)

MAID: Go out the same way you came in. Today's scraps are for me.

BEGGAR WOMAN: But, woman, you have someone to take care of you. My little girl and I are alone!

MAID: So are dogs and they live.

BEGGAR WOMAN: They always give them to me.

MAID: Get out of here. Who told you could come in here? You've already left tracks on the floor. (*They exit. The Maid cleans.*) Floors finished with oil, cupboards, pedestals, iron beds—so that those of us who live in mud huts can swallow our hunger with a plate and a spoon. I hope one day no one will be left to tell the tale. (*The bells ring.*) Yes yes, let the bells ring! Let the gold-inlaid coffin pass! You're no less dead than I will be! Take what's coming to you, Antonio Maria Benavides—you're nothing but a stiff now in your broadcloth suit and high boots! Take what's coming to you! You'll never be able to lift my skirts behind the corral door!

The Madwoman of Chaillot

Jean Giraudoux
1945

Scene: The ladies have come for tea. Constance is dressed all in white and has brought along her imaginary dog, Dickie. Gabrielle is dressed with the affected simplicity of the 1880s: with toque, muff, and garish makeup. Aurelia has uncovered a terrible conspiracy that she means to reveal to her friends at tea today.

Of Note: Irma, the maid, has a brief moment on stage.

Countess Aurelia, the Madwoman of Chaillot.
Mme. Constance, the Madwoman of Passy.
Mme. Gabrielle, the Madwoman of St. Suplice.

CONSTANCE: Aurelia! Here we are! Don't tell us they've found your boa?

GABRIELLE: You don't mean Adolphe Bertaut has proposed at last! I knew he would.

COUNTESS: How are you, Constance? *(She shouts.)* How are you, Gabrielle? Thank you both so much for coming.

GABRIELLE: You needn't shout today, my dear. It's Wednesday. Wednesdays, I hear perfectly.

CONSTANCE: It's Thursday. *(To an imaginary dog who has stopped on landing L.)* Come along, Dickie. Come along. And stop barking. What a racket you're making! Come on, darling—we've come to see the longest boa and the handsomest man in Paris. Come on. *(Crossing to R. chair.)*

COUNTESS: Constance, it's not a question of my boa today. Nor of Adolphe. It's a question of the future of the human race.

CONSTANCE: You think it has a future?

COUNTESS: Don't make silly jokes. Sit down and listen to me. *(Constance and Gabrielle sit.)* We have got to make a decision today, which may alter the fate of the world.

CONSTANCE: Couldn't we do it tomorrow? I want to wash my slippers. Now, Dickie, please!

COUNTESS: We haven't a moment to waste. Where is Josephine? Well, we'd better have our tea, and as soon as Josephine comes—

GABRIELLE: Josephine is sitting on her bench by the palace waiting for President Wilson to come out. She says she's sorry, but she must see him today.

CONSTANCE: Dickie!

COUNTESS: What a pity she had to see him today! She has a first-class brain *(She gets tea things from a side table, pours tea, and serves cake and honey.)*

CONSTANCE: Well, go ahead, dear. We're listening. *(To Dickie.)* What is it, Dickie? You want to sit in Aunt Aurelia's lap? All right, darling. Go on. Jump, Dickie.

COUNTESS: Constance, we love you dearly, as you know. And we love Dickie, too. But this is too serious a matter. So let's stop being childish for once.

CONSTANCE: And what does that mean, if you please?

COUNTESS: It means Dickie. You know perfectly well that we love him and fuss over him just as if he were still alive. He's a sacred memory and we wouldn't hurt his feelings for the world. But please don't plump him in my lap when I'm settling the future of mankind. His basket is in the corner—he knows where it is, and he can just go and sit in it. *(Tea to Constance.)*

CONSTANCE: So you're against Dickie, too!

COUNTESS: I'm not in the least bit against Dickie. I adore Dickie. But you know as well as I that Dickie is only a convention with us. It's a beautiful convention. But that doesn't mean it has to bark all the time. Besides, it's you that spoil him. The time you went to visit your niece and left him with me, we got along marvellously together. When you're not there, he's a model dog—he doesn't bark, he doesn't tear things, he doesn't even eat. But with you around him, one really can't pay attention to anything else. I'm not going to take Dickie in my lap at a solemn moment like this— no, not for anything in the world—and that's that!

GABRIELLE: *(Very sweetly.)* Constance, dear, I don't mind taking him in my lap. He loves to sit in my lap, don't you, darling?

CONSTANCE: Kindly stop putting on angelic airs, Gabrielle. I know you very well. You're much too sweet to be sincere. There's plenty of times that I make believe that Dickie is here, when really I've left him home, and you cuddle and pet him just the same.

GABRIELLE: I adore animals.

CONSTANCE: If you adore animals, you shouldn't pet them when they're not there. It's a form of hypocrisy.

COUNTESS: Now, Constance, Gabrielle has as much right as you—

CONSTANCE: Gabrielle has no right to do what she does. Do you know what she does? She invites people to come to tea with us. People whom we know nothing about, people—who exist only in her imagination.

COUNTESS: You think that's not an existence?

GABRIELLE: I don't invite them at all. They come by themselves. What can I do?

CONSTANCE: You might introduce us.

COUNTESS: If you think they're imaginary, what do you want to meet them for?

CONSTANCE: Of course they're imaginary. But who likes to have imaginary people staring at one? Especially strangers.

GABRIELLE: Oh, they're really very nice—

CONSTANCE: Tell me one thing, Gabrielle.—Are they here now?

COUNTESS: Am I to be allowed to speak? Or is this going to be the same as the argument about inoculating Josephine's cat, when we didn't get to the subject at all?

CONSTANCE: Never! Never! I'll never give my consent to that. *(To Dickie.)* I'd never do a thing like that to you, Dickie sweet—*(She begins to weep softly.)*

COUNTESS: Good Heavens! Now she's in tears. What an impossible creature! Everything will be spoiled because of her. All right, all right, Constance, stop crying. I'll take him in my lap.

CONSTANCE: *(Rises.)* No. He won't go now.—Oh, how can you be so cruel? Don't you suppose I know about Dickie? Don't you think I'd rather have him here alive and woolly and frisking around the way he used to? You have your Adolphe. Gabrielle has her birds. But I have only Dickie. Do you think I'd be so silly about him if it wasn't that it's only by pretending that he's here all the time that I get him to come sometimes, really? Next time I won't bring him! *(Sits.)*

COUNTESS: *(Rises, crossing L.)* Now let's not get excited over nothing at all! Come here, Dickie. Irma is going to take you for a walk. Irma! *(Rings bell. Irma appears.)*

CONSTANCE: *(Crossing L. to below Countess.)* No. He doesn't want to go. Besides, I didn't bring him today. So there! *(Back to her chair R.)*

COUNTESS: Irma, make sure the door is locked. *(Irma nods and exits.)*

CONSTANCE: What do you mean? Why locked? Who's coming?

COUNTESS: *(Crosses to iron chair c.)* You'd know by now, if you'd let me get a word in. A horrible thing has happened.—This very morning, exactly at noon—

CONSTANCE: Oh, how exciting!

COUNTESS: Be quiet!—this morning, exactly at noon, thanks to a young man, who drowned himself in the Seine.—Oh yes, while I think of it—do you know a mazurka called "La Belle Polonaise"?

CONSTANCE: Yes, Aurelia.

COUNTESS: Could you sing it now, this very minute?

CONSTANCE: Yes, Aurelia.

COUNTESS: All of it?

CONSTANCE: Yes, Aurelia. But who's interrupting now, Aurelia?

COUNTESS: You're right. Well, this morning exactly at noon, I discovered a terrible plot. There is a group of men who want to destroy the whole city.

CONSTANCE: Is that all?

GABRIELLE: But I don't understand, Aurelia. Why should men want to destroy the city? It was they themselves who put it up.

COUNTESS: There are people in the world who want to destroy everything. They have the fever of destruction. Even when they pretend that they're building, it's only in order to destroy. When they put up a new building, they quietly knock down two old ones. They build cities in order to destroy the countryside.—They destroy space with telephones, and time with airplanes. Humanity is now dedicated to a task of universal demolition! I speak, of course, primarily of the male sex—

GABRIELLE: *(Shocked.)* Oh—!

CONSTANCE: Aurelia! Must you talk sex in front of Gabrielle?

COUNTESS: After all, there are two sexes.

CONSTANCE: Gabrielle is a virgin!

COUNTESS: Oh, she can't be that innocent. She keeps canaries.

GABRIELLE: I think you're being very cruel about men, Aurelia. Men are big and beautiful, and as loyal as dogs. I preferred not to marry, it's true. But I hear excellent reports of them from friends who have had an opportunity to observe them closely.

COUNTESS: My poor darling! You are still living in a dream. But one day, you will wake up, as I have, and then you will see what is happening in the world. The tide has turned. Men are changing back into beasts. I remember a time when the hungriest man was the one who took the longest to pick up his fork. The one who put on the broadest grin was the one who needed most to go to the bathroom. I remember, it was such fun to keep them grinning like that for hours. But now they no longer pretend. Just look at them—snuffling their soup like pigs, tearing their meat like tigers, crunching their lettuce like crocodiles!—A man doesn't take your hand nowadays—he gives you his paw.

CONSTANCE: Would that bother you so much if they changed into animals? Personally, I think it's a good idea.

GABRIELLE: Oh, I'd love to see them like that. They'd be sweet.

CONSTANCE: It might be the salvation of the human race.

COUNTESS: *(Rises, crosses down R. to Constance.)* You'd make a fine rabbit, wouldn't you?

CONSTANCE: I?

COUNTESS: Naturally, You don't think it's only the men who are changing? You'd change along with them. Husbands and wives together. We're all one race, you know.

CONSTANCE: You think so. And why would my husband have to be a rabbit if he were alive?

COUNTESS: Remember his front teeth? When he nibbled his celery?

CONSTANCE: I remember, I'm happy to say, absolutely nothing about him. All I remember is the time that Father Lacordaire tried to kiss me in the park.

COUNTESS: Yes, yes, of course.

CONSTANCE: And what does that mean, if you please? "Yes, yes, of course"?

COUNTESS: *(By her.)* Constance, just this once, look us in the eye and tell us truly—did that really happen or did you read about it in a book?

CONSTANCE: Now I'm being insulted!

COUNTESS: We promise faithfully that we'll believe it all over again after, won't we, Gabrielle? But just tell us the truth this once.

CONSTANCE: How dare you question my memories? Suppose I said your pearls were false!

COUNTESS: *(Moves above iron chair.)* They were.

CONSTANCE: I'm not asking what they were. I'm asking what they are. Are they false, or are they real?

The Killing of Sister George

Frank Marcus
1965

Scene: The apartment of June and Alice. June is afraid she is being "killed off" the show and is beside herself with rage and fear. Mrs. Croft has just phoned to say she would like to come over for "a chat" with Sister George about a serious matter and Alice has prepared a tea. The doorbell rings.

June, a radio soap star known as Sister George, a British Nursing Sister.
Alice, her lover and housemate.
Mrs. Mercy Croft, the assistant head of the station who has her own radio show, "Woman's Hour."

(The doorbell rings.)
ALICE: *(Suddenly scared.)* Let's not open the door!
(June throws Alice a glance expressing contempt, and strides out to open the door.)
JUNE: *(Offstage.)* Oh, hello, Mrs. Croft! I'm so sorry—I'd only just remembered that the lift was out of order . . .
MRS. CROFT: *(Entering, cheerfully.)* Not at all—I never use the lift. *(Seeing Alice.)* Oh?
(Mrs. Croft is a well-groomed lady of indeterminate age, gracious of manner, and freezingly polite. She is wearing a gray two-piece suit, matching hat and accessories, and a discreet double string of pearls around her neck. She carries a briefcase.)
JUNE: May I introduce—Miss Alice McNaught, Mrs. Croft.
MRS. CROFT: *(Extending her hand.)* How do you do? *(Turning to June)* Yes, I always say: We get far too little exercise these days. If we walked the stairs, instead of using lifts, those extra inches would disappear.
ALICE: *(Trying to be helpful.)* I sometimes walk—
MRS. CROFT: You don't need to lose any weight, my dear—
JUNE: Alice is just preparing the tea—

MRS MERCY: Oh, that is nice. I do hope I haven't put you to any trouble—inviting myself out of the blue.

JUNE: Rubbish.

ALICE: Not at all. *(Goes to the kitchen.)*

MRS. CROFT: May I look around? I *adore* looking at other people's flats—they do reflect their occupier's personalities in an uncannily accurate way. *(Looking around.)* To be perfectly honest, I imagined your home to be . . . different.

JUNE: Really?

MRS. CROFT: This charming Victoriana . . . the dolls . . . Somehow—

JUNE: *(Slightly embarrassed.)* They're Miss McNaught's.

MRS. CROFT: Oh, of course, that would explain it. They just weren't *you*. I don't know—

JUNE: *(Rather sheepishly.)* Yes, I have a flatmate . . .

MRS. CROFT: *(Sympathetically.)* How nice. It's so important to have . . . companionship—especially when one's an artist . . .

JUNE: These are mine—I collect brasses.

MRS. CROFT: How useful . . . May I look out from your window? I love overlooking things. I've always adored heights; in my young days, my husband and I often used to go mountaineering—in the Austrian Alps for preference. *(She has gone to the window.)* Oh! *(A sudden yell of delight.)* There's BH! You can see Broadcasting House from the window—isn't that . . . *super!* To have that reassuring presence brooding over you, seeing that you don't get into mischief!

ALICE: *(Lifting the hatch and looking into the room.)* Ready in a minute.

MRS. CROFT: Oh—good!

JUNE: Would you kindly close the hatch. *(Alice shuts the hatch.)* There are times when I have an almost irresistible urge to decapitate her.

MRS MERCY: Oh, poor Miss McNaught. I do like your settee cover—a homely pattern. I love floral design—I know it's old-fashioned, but . . .

JUNE: Childie—Miss McNaught—made them.

MRS. CROFT: Really. How clever of her—they're beautifully fitted. You're fortunate to have such a handy companion.

JUNE: *(With a bitter look at the trophies.)* Yes, she's good with the needle, I'll say that for her.

MRS. CROFT: *(Lightly.)* That was Sister George speaking.

JUNE: *(Self-consciously.)* One can't helping slipping—

MRS. CROFT: But you are Sister George far more than Miss June Buckridge to all of us at BH.

JUNE: Jolly nice of you to say so. *(Motions her to sit.)*

MRS. CROFT: Thank you. You have made the part completely your own—it was obvious—even at the first auditions. I remember it quite clearly, although it must be, oh—

JUNE: Almost six years ago. I was scared stiff, too.

MRS MERCY: How charming! One can't imagine you scared stiff!

JUNE: I don't mind physical danger, I even like it. I manned an anti-aircraft during the war.

MRS. CROFT: Lovely!

JUNE: None of that sissy troop entertainment for yours truly!

MRS. CROFT: It wasn't that bad. As a matter of fact, I did a bit of organizing of ENSA myself . . .

JUNE: I'm sorry. No offense meant.

MRS MERCY: None taken. Now, Miss Buckridge—or may I call you Sister George, like everybody else

JUNE: Certainly.

MRS. CROFT: As you know, I hold a monthly surgery in my office, when I welcome people to come to me with their problems. I've always made it a rule to be approachable. In some cases, involving matters of special importance, I prefer to visit the subjects in their own homes, so that we can talk more easily without any duress. That's why I'm here today.

JUNE: *(In her country accent.)* Ah well, farmer's footsteps are the best manure!

MRS MERCY: Quite. There's rather a serious matter I wish to discuss with you.

ALICE: *(Entering with tea.)* Sorry I took so long.

MRS. CROFT: Ah, *lovely!* *(To June.)* We'll continue our little chat after tea.

ALICE: If you'd rather—

JUNE: You can speak quite freely, Mrs. Mercy. Miss McNaught and I have no secrets from each other.

MRS. CROFT: Well, let's all have tea first . . . *(As Alice lays the table.)* I say, what delicious-looking scones!

ALICE: They're Scotch scones.

JUNE: They're Childie's specialty. Copied from her grandmother's recipe.

MRS. CROFT: They look delish! May I try one?

ALICE: Help yourself. Here's the jam.

MRS. CROFT: They're what we used to call griddle scones—

JUNE: Or drop scones—

ALICE: It's important not to get the griddle too hot, or the outside of the scones will brown before the inside is cooked.

MRS. CROFT: They're a lovely even color . . .

ALICE: *(Very animated.)* I always cool them in a towel—

MRS. CROFT: Do you?

ALICE: Yes, and I wait till the bubbles rise to the surface before I turn them over—

MRS. CROFT: They're very successful.

ALICE: I use half a teaspoon of bicarbonate of soda—

MRS. CROFT: Now you're giving away trade secrets.

ALICE: And one level teaspoon of cream of tartar—

JUNE: *(Rising.)* Shut up!

(There is a moment's silence.)

ALICE: Eight ounces of flour—

JUNE: *(Exploding.)* Shut up!

ALICE: *(Softly.)* And one egg.

JUNE: Shut up! ! *(Hurls a cake in Alice's direction.)*

MRS. CROFT: *(Continuing to eat, unperturbed.)* Now then, girls—temper!

ALICE: She hates me to talk about food. *(Confidentially to Mrs. Croft.)* She's a wee bit overwrought—

JUNE: Overwrought, my arse!

ALICE: *(Chiding.)* Now, that wasn't nice—that was not a nice thing to say.

MRS. CROFT: *(Smiling indulgently.)* I expect she picked it up in the army.

ALICE: She swears like a trooper—

MRS. CROFT: But she has a heart of gold.

ALICE: One day, she got into such a temper, I wrote a poem about it.

JUNE: *(Bitterly.)* Yes, she fancies herself as a poetess. Goes to the City Lit. every Wednesday night, to learn about meter and things—

MRS. CROFT: What a nice hobby.

JUNE: As a poetess, she makes a good cook.

MRS. CROFT: It's still a question of mixing the right ingredients to make a tasty whole.

ALICE: That night she came back in a raging temper—

JUNE: Thank you very much, we don't want to hear anything about that—

ALICE: I wrote this poem. It began:
Fierce as the wind
Blows the rampaging termagant . . .

MRS. CROFT: Very expressive *(To June.)* And how did you like being compared to the wind?

ALICE: *(To Mrs. Croft.)* Slice of cake, Mrs. Croft?

MRS. CROFT: Just a teeny one. Mustn't be greedy.

JUNE: Her mother made it.

MRS. CROFT: You can always tell if it's home-baked; it tastes quite different.

JUNE: You'd be surprised if you knew what Mother McNaught put into it.

MRS. CROFT: I'm not even going to ask.

JUNE: I'm delighted to hear it! *(Laughs.)*

MRS. CROFT: *(Enjoying herself.)* Oh dear, this is just like a dormitory feast—all this girlish banter. *(To June.)* I bet your were a terror at school!

JUNE: I was captain of the hockey team and a keen disciplinarian—God help the girl I caught making me an apple-pie bed! *(She chuckles.)*

MRS. CROFT: Ah, there's Sister George again! It's wonderful how over the years the character *evolved* . . .

ALICE: Who first thought of putting her on a motorbike?

JUNE: That was because of sound effects. As long as I was on the old bike, listeners never knew whether I was static or mobile.

MRS. CROFT: A unique sound—Sister George on her motorbike, whizzing through the countryside, singing snatches of hymns—

JUNE: One day I got into trouble because I sang a hymn which sounded like "On the Good Ship Venus."

MRS. CROFT: A traditional air—?

JUNE: I've found it safer to stick to hymns. Once I tried a pop song, and d'you know, hundreds of letters came in protesting.

MRS. CROFT: We learn from experience . . . but we don't want Applehurst falling behind the times.

JUNE: No—no—of course not.

MRS. CROFT: But we must constantly examine criticism and if it's constructive, we must act on it. Ruthlessly.

JUNE: What sort of criticism?

MRS. CROFT: Oh, nothing in particular . . . at least . . .

JUNE: But what?

MRS. CROFT: Well, that brings me—I'm afraid—to the unpleasant part of my business . . .

ALICE: Oh dear—

MRS. CROFT: *(Rising.)* But first, would you show me to the little girls' room?

JUNE: Alice, show Mrs. Mercy to the . . .

ALICE: This way, Mrs. Mercy.

JUNE: —little—girls'—

(Mrs. Mercy exits, accompanied by Alice. June catches sight of her briefcase, look round furtively, and opens it as Alice returns.)

ALICE: *(Aghast.)* What are you doing?

JUNE: *(Rummaging in the case.)* Keep a lookout!

ALICE: You can't. You mustn't!

JUNE: *(Taking a folder.)* My personal file.

ALICE: *(In a hysterical whisper.)* Put it back!

JUNE: *(Perusing some papers.)* Quiet! *(She takes an envelope from the file. Reads.)* "Sister George. Confidential."

ALICE: She's coming.

JUNE: *(Quickly replaces the folder in the briefcase, realizes too late that she has still got the envelope in her hand puts it behind the nearest cushion.)* . . . So Emmeline said, "I don't want any griddle scones . . . thank you very much."

MRS. CROFT: *(Reentering.)* I got on the scales, to see if I've put on any weight.

JUNE: I don't suppose . . .

MRS. CROFT: *(Takes her briefcase, while June and Alice stand rigid with suspense.)* Now then . . .

ALICE: I'll make myself scarce . . . *(Goes into kitchen.)*

MRS. CROFT: Please sit down. *(June sits.)* You won't hold it against me if I speak plainly?

JUNE: Please do.

MRS. CROFT: It's my unpleasant duty to haul you over the coals, and administer a severe reprimand.

JUNE: Oh?

MRS. CROFT: Believe me, Sister George, I'd much rather let bygones by bygones—

JUNE: *(In a country accent.)* Let sleeping dogs lie—

MRS. CROFT: Precisely . . . But I must remind you of the little chat we had just about a year ago, after that unfortunate incident in the club . . . involving a lady colleague of mine.

JUNE: Let's not rake over old embers.

MRS. CROFT: I don't intend to. But in the light of recent events, it's difficult to forget an incident as vivid as the pouring of a glass of beer over the Assistant Head of Talks. I had hoped one black mark would have been enough for you, but this morning *(Takes a sheet of paper from the folder.)* I received this memo from the Director of Religious Broadcasting. *(She hands the paper to June.)* I should like to have your comments.

JUNE: *(Excitedly reads the paper, flushes, and jumps up violently.)* It's a lie! It's an utter, bloody lie!

MRS. CROFT: *(Firmly.)* Please calm yourself, Miss Buckridge. Kindly hand me back the paper. *(June hands over the paper.)* I take it you're not denying that you were drinking in the Coach and Horses on the night of the nineteenth?

JUNE: How the hell should I remember? *(Calling.)* Alice! Come here!

ALICE: *(Enters, wide-eyed and worried.)* You want me?

JUNE: Where was I on the night of the nineteenth?

MRS. CROFT: I'm sorry to involve you in this, Miss McNaught—

ALICE: *(Quietly.)* That was a Wednesday: I was at the City Lit.

JUNE: You bloody well would be. *(To Mrs. Croft.)* All right; it seems I was at the Coach and Horses on the night in question, having a drink with some of the boys. That's no crime.

MRS. CROFT: Miss Buckridge . . . according to this letter from the mother superior of the Convent of the Sacred Heart of Jesus, you boarded a taxi stopping at the traffic lights at Langham Place—

JUNE: I thought it was empty.

MRS. CROFT: *(Reading.)* A taxi bearing as passengers two novitiate nuns from Ireland who had just arrived at Kings Cross Station—

JUNE: How was I to know?

MRS. CROFT: You boarded this taxi in a state of advanced inebriation and *(Consulting the paper.)* proceeded to assault the two nuns, subjecting them to actual physical violence!

ALICE: *(To June.)* You didn't really!

JUNE: No, no, no. Of course not. I'd had a few pints . . . I saw this cab, took it to be empty, got in—and there were these two black things screaming blue murder!

MRS. CROFT: Why didn't you get out again!

JUNE: Well, I'd had a very nasty shock myself! What with their screaming and flapping about—I thought they were bats, you know, vampire bats! It was they who attacked me. I remember getting all entangled in their shirts and petticoats and things . . . the taxi driver had to pull me free . . .

MRS. CROFT: A deplorable anecdote. According to the mother superior, one of the nuns required medical treatment for shock, and is still under sedation. She thought it was the devil.

ALICE: George, how could you!

JUNE: Don't you start on me! *(Clapping her hands.)* Back to the kitchen! Washing up! Presto!

ALICE: *(Firmly.)* No, I'm staying. This concerns me, too.

JUNE: It was all a ghastly mistake.

MRS. CROFT: No doubt, but it'll take some explaining.

JUNE: Fancy informing the Director of Religious Broadcasting. What a nasty thing to do for a holy woman!

MRS. CROFT: The mother superior is responsible for the nuns in her charge—

JUNE: Then she should jolly well teach them how to behave in public! I got the fright of my life, in there! Those nuns were like *mice*—albino mice—with white faces and little red eyes. And they were vicious, too. They scratched and they bit! Look—you can still see the tooth marks—*(She points to her arm.)*—do you see that? I've a good mind to make a counter-complaint to the mother superior: They deserve to be scourged in their cells.

MRS. CROFT: *(Wearily.)* I can hardly put through a report to the Controller, informing him of your allegation that you were bitten by two nuns!

JUNE: No, well you could say—

MRS. CROFT: Let's be practical, Sister George—we're concerned with retaining the trust and respect of the public. Now, people understand perfectly well that artists frequently work under great emotional stress. We do all we can to gloss over the minor disciplinary offenses. But we simply cannot tolerate this sort of behavior. It's things like this which make people resent paying more for their wireless licenses! Thousands of pounds spent on public relations, and you jeopardize it all with your reckless and foolish actions. Really, Sister George, we have reason to be very, very angry with you.

JUNE: *(Beaten.)* What do you want me to do?

MRS. CROFT: You must write a letter immediately to the mother superior. You must sincerely apologize for your behavior and I suggest you offer a small donation for some charity connected with the convent. Then you must send a copy of your letter to the Director of Religious Broadcasting, with a covering note from you, couched in suitable terms.

JUNE: You mean humbling myself.

ALICE: Don't worry, Mrs. Mercy. I'll see she does it and I'll make quite sure she doesn't get into any mischief in the future.

MRS. CROFT: There speaks a true friend. *(To June.)* You're very lucky to have someone like Miss McNaught to rely on. Treasure her.

JUNE: *(Bitterly.)* I'll treasure her, all right!

ALICE: I'll see to it that the letters are written and sent off right away!

MRS. CROFT: *(Rising.)* Good. That's what I like to hear. *(To June.)* I'll leave you in Miss McNaught's expert charge.

JUNE: What about Applehurst?

MRS. CROFT: *(Noncommittally.)* That's another, rather more complex problem . . .

JUNE: But . . . has anything been decided about the future?

MRS. CROFT: I'm afraid I can't say anything about that at the moment.

JUNE: It comes as a bit of a shock to me, you know, all this.

MRS. CROFT: It comes as a bit of a shock to me too, I assure you— especially as I understand that you often open church bazaars—

ALICE: I'll look after her—I'll keep her away from convents.

MRS. CROFT: You keep her on a tight rein, and all will be well.

ALICE: Of course I will. Between us we'll keep her in order.

MRS. CROFT: She won't have a chance, will she?

JUNE: Look here—I'm sorry—you know—if I've been a bad boy.

MRS. CROFT: *(Turning to June and shaking hands.)* Well, good-bye, dear Sister George. Keep your chin up. Things are never as bad as they seem—

JUNE: *(Listlessly, in her country accent.)* Every cloud has a silver lining . . .

MRS. CROFT: That's the spirit! And *(Whispering confidentially)* no more walkouts at rehearsals, eh? If you have any complaints do come and see me about them.

JUNE: *(In her country accent.)* Well, it's the creaking gate that gets oiled . . .

MRS. CROFT: *(Reflecting for a moment.)* A somewhat unfortunate simile . . . *(To Alice.)* So nice to have met you—

ALICE: Nice to have met *you*, Mrs. Croft. What's the subject of your talk tomorrow? Is it a secret, or are you allowed to tell?

MRS. CROFT: *(Smiling graciously.)* It's family planning this week—and foundation garments next!

And Miss Reardon Drinks a Little

Paul Zindel
1970s

Scene: Anna, Catherine, and Ceil are sisters. Anna and Catherine still live together in a comfortable apartment. Ceil is married. They are teachers, and Anna has had a breakdown. While Anna is out of the room, Catherine sneaks mouthfuls of chopped beef (raw) that she has hidden in a Fanny Farmer candy box.

Anna, a teacher, vegetarian, has had a breakdown and is not teaching.

Ceil, on the Board of Education, married. Hasn't been over to the house in seven months, since their mother died.

Catherine, an assistant principal. Shares an apartment with Anna.

CEIL: Would you stop eating that?

CATHERINE: No. If I don't get some protein into me before Anna unsedates herself, I'm going to collapse.

CEIL: What the hell does Anna have to do with your eating that disgusting raw meat?

CATHERINE: Well, it's like this—ever since she broke down we're not allowed to eat flesh. You see, she's caressed vegetarianism. She made me throw out every piece of meat we had in the house. Even the bouillon cubes.

CEIL: You're joking.

CATHERINE: Yeah, I'm joking, but you'd better like zucchini because that's what you're getting for supper. Saturday we had sautéed zucchini, Sunday we had boiled zucchini, Monday night for variety we called it squash. I can't even cook a cod fish cake— "You've got no right to kill anything," she says. Monday night she rescued a cockroach out of the toilet bowl. It isn't bad enough we're paying over two hundred bucks a month for a co-op with cockroaches, I have to have a sister who acts as a life-guard for them.

CEIL: She's afraid of death . . . maybe the way Mama died . . .

CATHERINE: Oh, for Christ's sake, she's always been like that and you know it. Remember when Mama took us to St. Mary's Bazaar and we put her on that little Ferris wheel. There was only enough money for one, and Mama said she could go alone . . . remember?

CEIL: Yes.

CATHERINE: Jesus, I'll never forget her face when that motor started and she went up and up and up . . . *(Anna appears in the hall-way from the bedroom.)*

ANNA: And I told them to stop—stop the machine.

CEIL: Anna . . .

ANNA: Oh, Ceil, I didn't know you were coming.

CATHERINE: I told you nineteen times she was coming.

ANNA: I forgot. I must have forgotten. I'm so doped up on tranquil-izers and all those capsules. *(Beat.)* I'm sorry, Ceil . . . I'm so ashamed, so ashamed.

CATHERINE: If you'll excuse me I'll get dinner ready. I'm unsure of just how to peal a marinated zucchini. *(She exits to kitchen.)*

CEIL: Anna, stop crying. I want to talk to you.

ANNA: What did you come here for? She didn't even tell me you were coming.

CEIL: I was concerned about . . .

ANNA: Oh, my God—what a disgrace I've been to you, breaking down the way I did. I just couldn't give it back any more to all those snots.

CEIL: Anna—get a hold of yourself.

ANNA: *(Calling to offstage.)* Catherine! Did you ask her about the gun? Catherine, get back in here!

CEIL: What gun?

CATHERINE: *(Entering from the kitchen peeling a squash.)* I'll ask her now, and then you write it down so that tomorrow and all next week you don't keep asking me if I asked her. Ceil, when Mother died and you ramshackled this place for every piece of worthwhile silver, linen, and glassware you could lay your hands on, did you also suck up Mother's pistol? Because if you *did* suck up Mother's pistol I wish you'd give it back so I can melt it down in front of Anna so she stops driving me crazy! *(She exits.)*

CEIL: That old gun Mama used to keep in the phonograph?

ANNA: Yes. The one that would have frightened burglars and mashers away if we had ever gotten any.

CEIL: *(Yelling to offstage.)* Catherine! I resent the way you said that. I didn't ramshackle or suck up anything. I took a few of Mother's things just to save them. I just wanted to save them!

CATHERINE: *(Peeking her head in for just one remark.)* Bullshit!

ANNA: Well, did you take the gun or didn't you, because I don't want it in this house!

CEIL: *(Yelling to Catherine.)* You still have that same filthy mouth!

ANNA: Why can't you admit whether you have it or not?

CEIL: I don't have it!

ANNA: Then it's here. I knew it was still here and I'm afraid to have it in this house.

CEIL: Anna, the gun only had blanks in it.

ANNA: Blanks? That's all it had in it, but couldn't someone have gone right down the street to Morrison's Sport Shop and bought some real bullets for it? It could kill someone right this minute so I don't want it around, can't you get that through your skull?

CEIL: But nobody did buy real bullets for it.

ANNA: *(Searching through a desk and looking behind books in a bookcase.)* You tell me you know for sure someone didn't buy size 22 bullets for that gun—it could take size 22 real bullets, you know—you tell me you know for sure that right this minute that gun isn't in this house loaded and ready to kill and I'll call you a goddam liar! *(She throws a couple of books.)*

CEIL: What the hell are you afraid of?

ANNA: What am I afraid of?

CATHERINE: *(Entering with a pineapple on a plate that she sets as a centerpiece.)* We were going to have carrot and beet juice for the appetizer because they're supposed to be good for acne, boils, and carbuncles—but I assume none of us have acne, boils, and carbuncles so I thought crushed pineapple would be better. *(She exits.)*

ANNA: *(Continuing, to Ceil.)* I'm afraid of someone putting a bullet into my brain, that's what I'm afraid of. *(She throws another book.)*

CEIL: Stop throwing those books, please.

ANNA: And last week, just before I became officially debilitated, we were discussing death in the 105 Honors class, the one with all the brains—and I had them write all the ways of dying they could think of on the blackboards—fire, diphtheria, python constrictions, plane crashes, scurvy, decapitation—one kid remembered a little girl at Coney Island being run down by a miniature locomotive and getting a miniature death—and somebody else's uncle fell into a cement mixer in the Bronx and ended up as part of a bridge. By the end of the period we had the blackboards covered, crammed full of things—someone even thought of elephantiasis; we listed napalm and the bomb, and in the few seconds left to the class we all just sat back and wondered how the hell there was enough of us left alive to make up a class! *(She throws another book, then retrieves it.)*

CEIL: Stop it, Anna! *(Beat.)* Why did you save that one?

ANNA: It's Mother's Bible. She used to read it by proxy, remember? She'd have me read it when she was—atrophying—*(Her voice breaks.)*

CEIL: Anna, I came here tonight—I want you to know it's taken me a while to get used to Mama being gone, too.

ANNA: That's very comforting of you, Ceil. Very comforting. But you've got a husband and that helped you in your grief, I'm sure. I'll bet he's a pain in the ass, though. You must have loved him very much, Ceil—Havre de Grace, Maryland, wasn't it? Havre de Grace! Catherine and I would have loved to have come down for the wedding but I guess it was simply too precipitous. I know what it must have been like being swept away by Edward's impetuosity. *(Beat.)*

CEIL: Look, Anna . . .

ANNA: Ceil, dear, you didn't get stuck with Mama like I did—watching her dehydrate, bounce up and down while her throat was closing. Did Edward remind you of our father? You know I can't even remember what Papa looked like. I mean, I know his face from the pictures in the albums—did you suck those up, too?

CEIL: I didn't suck up anything!

ANNA: *(Opening an album.)* Oh, here it is, I mean, I was only three years old when he ran off to live with that skinny ostrich lady in Greenwich Village—123 Minetta Lane—but you and Catherine were nine, ten—remember? I couldn't go on the bus to see him at Christmas but you two could . . .

CEIL: *(Looking at a page from the album.)* I remember . . .

ANNA: Christmas. That was the only time you got to see him. All Mama would let me do is go along down to the bus stop and then you and Catherine would go and get all the gifts and money you could grab—and Mama told you to smile at him, smile at your father, smile big because then he'd give you more money and bigger dolls—and then she'd whisper sweetly—REMEMBER, GIRLS, DON'T MISS THE BUS BACK, AND DON'T GO WITH HIM IF HE TRIES TO TAKE YOU ANYWHERE, AND DON'T LET HIM TOUCH YOU BETWEEN YOUR LEGS, AND THEN AFTER YOU'VE FINISHED SMILING AND AFTER YOU'VE GRUBBED EVERYTHING YOU CAN GET, GET RIGHT BACK ON THE BUS AND ALL THE WAY HOME REMEMBER WHAT A BASTARD YOUR FATHER IS BECAUSE HE RAN AWAY WITH A SKINNY OSTRICH WOMAN FROM GREENWICH VILLAGE!

CEIL: *(Crying from a memory.)* Oh, Mama . . .

ANNA: *(Checking to see what picture Ceil is looking at.)* Oh, I think her nose is too big in that one. *(She turns to the last page in the album.)* I like this one. I took it three days before she died with a 3.5 lens opening and Tri-X film. I never thought it would come out there was so little light in the bedroom. She wanted me to tell her about the Visions of the Apocalypse that day and I figured by taking her picture I could make her forget because I was ruining my eyes from the little Biblical print. You need teensie eyes for that sort of thing. You know, if I hadn't bought *The Holy Bible in Brief*—that pocket edition put out by Mentor Books—*Mentor!*—

I swear to God words are weird!—if I hadn't bought it I would have gone blind. So I told her about this one vision with the horses, white, red, black, and pale horses coming out of the seals—Ceil! . . . the first four seals, *Ceil*, and I got tired of reading so I told her the end of Pinocchio—she liked that better than the horses. I don't even know what a pale horse is.

And Miss Reardon Drinks a Little

Paul Zindel
1970s

Scene: Anna, Catherine, and Ceil are sisters. Anna and Catherine still live together in a comfortable apartment. Ceil is married. They are teachers, and Anna has had a breakdown. The visit continues from the previous scene.

Anna, a teacher, vegetarian, has had a breakdown and is not teaching.

Ceil, on the Board of Education, married. Hasn't been over to the house in seven months, since their mother died.

Catherine, an assistant principal. Shares an apartment with Anna.

CEIL: *(Rises.)* Anna, go to your room and lie down.

ANNA: Go to your own room!

CEIL: *(To Catherine.)* Tell her to leave us alone.

CATHERINE: Now, sis, it is a bit tardy for disciplinary procedures.

CEIL: Catherine . . .

ANNA: Oh, Ceil . . . can't you remember all the fun when we were just getting started as teachers? How we'd all coming running home at three o'clock and Mama'd have the water boiling and some kind of pie made with Flako pie crust mix? and Mama'd be dying to know what happened in school all day and we'd be dying to tell her—and we'd sit around this same table and almost pass out laughing? We'd tell Mama what was going on in the schools and she wouldn't believe it. She'd say the whole world was going crazy. Remember when I told her about little Gracie Ratinski, that nutty kid with bugs in her hair at Jefferson who used to come into the cafeteria and sing her lunch order out at the top of her lungs?

(Catherine begins to laugh.) GIVE ME A PEANUT BUTTER SAND-

WICH, TRA LA. GIVE ME A PEANUT BUTTER SANDWICH, TRA LA. Don't you remember that? Don't you?

CATHERINE: *(Laughing harder, joining Anna at the table.)* I remember. I remember, all right. And remember how much Mama laughed when I told her about Rose Anadale the principal at P.S. 26 who kept the parakeet in her office . . .

ANNA: She used to talk about it on the P.A. system every morning after *The Star Spangled Banner* . . .

CATHERINE: *(Howling with Anna.)* She'd announce to the whole school, remember—GOOD MORNING, CHILDREN . . . GOOD MORNING, CHILDREN . . . LITTLE POLLY AND I HOPE YOU HAVE A WONDERFUL DAY.

ANNA: *(To Ceil.)* Don't you miss telling Mama those stories? Don't you miss it?

CEIL: *(To Catherine.)* Tell her to leave us alone.

CATHERINE: Look, Ceil, it's late—you probably have to get up early tomorrow and appoint a committee to study the salient factors of something or other.

CEIL: If that's the way you want it. *(She goes for her briefcase.)* I've made arrangements . . .

CATHERINE: *(Starting to clear the table.)* You don't say. They are floral, aren't then?

CEIL: She's going to a hospital.

CATHERINE: No kidding. Far way? Tudor or Swiss? Mountains and view of lake?

CEIL: *(Taking legal papers from the briefcase.)* It's only a two hour drive from here.

CATHERINE: No, don't tell me the best feature. It's state supported.

CEIL: *(Ordering.)* All you have to do is get her packed.

ANNA: She's the one who needs a rest, Catherine.

CEIL: *(Moving in with the papers.)* You're going to have to look at these, Catherine.

CATHERINE: *(Slamming a tray down on the buffet making a deafening noise. Then calmly:)* Don't tell me what I have to do. *(A long silence. Finally.)*

ANNA: Ceil, didn't you ever love us? Mama? Any of us?

CEIL: Our lives are not around this table anymore. *(She moves away from the table.)*

ANNA: Oh—I must have forgotten. This is all dead now, isn't it? Silent. The voices gone. Even the whispering forgotten: "Straighten up . . . careful your slip isn't showing . . skirt down . . . knees close together. Be careful if someone sits next to you . . . or across the way . . . beware of your eyes . . . he mustn't think you're looking at him. Even when you're . . . bleeding . . . he'll know . . . he'll try to find a way to force you apart . . . he'll want to hurt you . . . crush you . . . cut into you . . . "*(Anna rises— goes toward the bedroom hallway.)* And the sounds—you must have forgotten the sounds in the dark of our rooms . . . the quieting of the wounds by which we could be tracked. *(Anna reaches out to touch Ceil.)*

CEIL: Get your hands off me. *(Getting away from Anna and taking a seat at the table.)*

ANNA: Tell me, Ceil, when you're in bed—what does Edward manage to do? Does he actually get on top of you—mount you—and ride you like some blubbering old nag? *(In the middle of Anna's verbal assault. Ceil reaches for the Fanny Farmer box which falls from her hands. At Anna's last word she picks up the spilled meat and shoves it into Anna's face. Anna falls to her knees, senses the meat, and screams. She exits. Catherine goes after Anna.)*

CEIL: She can wash herself.

CATHERINE: Get out of my way.

CEIL: How the hell much longer did you think you could go on keeping her here?

CATHERINE: As long as I want, that's how long.

CEIL: Why? So you won't be alone? After all the filth and wisecracks are scraped off is that what's underneath? How pathetic you are!

CATHERINE: *(Ringing buffet bell.)* School's over. Everybody's dismissed *(Ceil yanks the bell out of Catherine's hand.)*

CEIL: Don't you think I need anything?

CATHERINE: I thought you always took everything you needed?

CEIL: Anything I did you made me do from the years of gnawing at me—you and her and Mama. The whole pack of you. For what? What was it you hated so much?

CATHERINE: *(Exploding.)* I'll tell you what and I'll tell you when! You see, there was this big hole in the ground with you on one side of it and me on the other—and we were watching them stick a coffin in the ground. But as it was going down I had to shut my eyes because I'll tell you all I could see: I saw you with a lawyer making sure the few bucks of a croaking old lady was transferred to your name. And I was admiring a casket you picked out that wouldn't waste a second getting her corpse back to ashes. And I remember when that imperfect gasping woman was dying how you made certain you didn't have to touch a penny in your bank account. *(She sits at the desk.)*

CEIL: That's not what you hated me for all your life! Anything you didn't like you could have done differently. Anything! You're not going to blame me for that or anything about your sick little life. You didn't have to follow me—let me do everything. I didn't bend anybody's arm. You could have lived your own lives you know. You didn't have to feed on me all the time!

CATHERINE: Get out of here.

CEIL: What is it deep down in your gut you so detest about me? That I haven't gone mad or become an obscene nasty witness? That's what you are, Catherine. *(There is a long pause. Then.)*

CATHERINE: You know, Ceil—the way you said that—I mean, you're louder and crueller—but there's a part of you that's just like Mama. I think that's the part of you I've always despised. *(Ceil get her coat from the closet and gathers up the papers, the gun and the album.)*

CEIL: I'll call you in the morning.

CATHERINE: *(Pouring a drink.)* Not in the morning, if you don't mind. You see, Miss Reardon drinks a little and she'll be sleeping off a colossal load.

CEIL: *(Throws album, gloves, and papers to the floor.)* Here! Here's everything. I'm not going to let you pin the rap on me or Mama or anybody anymore. Now it's up to you. For once in your life you pick up the pieces however the hell you want. But no matter what you do, let me tell you this—you're not going to drag me down. Not at this stage of the game, my sweet sisters. Not at this stage of the game. *(Ceil exits leaving Catherine sitting at the desk. Anna enters.)*

ANNA: You're worse than all of them. You never do anything to stop the destruction.

CATHERINE: I got rid of her. What else do you want from me?

ANNA: You're godless and you're killing all of us. Everything.

CATHERINE: Look, I'm warning you. I'm going shopping tomorrow and I'm buying a roast beef, frankfurters, liverwurst, knockwurst, brockwurst, and two pounds of Virginia ham. It may be primitive but it sure as hell's going to be delicious. *(Anna stops, slowly moves back to her place at the table.)*

ANNA: Catherine—sometimes . . . sometimes I see my reflection in a window . . . or look down at my hand resting in my lap and I see her. Mama. She's inside of me. She frightens me, Catherine. She makes me afraid. I look out the window . . . the telephone poles in the street . . . she makes me see them as dead trees . . . dead crucifixes. I'm losing my mind. I can't stop myself. She's at my throat now, Catherine, she's strangling me. Help me. Oh, God help me . . . *(Anna puts her head on the table. Slowly Catherine rises, turns off the floor lamp, goes to hall, turns off the foyer light. Only the table area is lighted.)*

CATHERINE: Everyone's going crazy, Anna, do you know that? The dentist—I went to the new dentist down the street—I went three weeks ago for my first appointment, and then last week, and then yesterday. He wears three wigs, Anna. On the first visit he was wearing a crew-cut wig. Last week he had a medium length wig. And yesterday he had this fuzzy llama-wool wig and he kept saying—"Dear me, oh, dear me—I've got to get a haircut . . ." And next week I know he'll have the crew-cut job on again. *(Catherine goes to Anna. It is the hardest journey she's every traveled—to reach out and touch Anna. Anna raises her head.)*

ANNA: Catherine—what world were we waiting for? *(Catherine and Anna are alone at the table as the Curtain Falls ending the play.)*

The Art of Dining

Tina Howe
1978

Scene: Time: The Present. Place: A small, elegant restaurant.

Of Note: Using real food will greatly enhance the humour in this scene. It is also very helpful for the actors to juggle the lines, the food and the movement when they have actual, edible food on the plates.

Herrick Simmons
Tony Stassio
Nessa Vox

HERRICK SIMMONS: You ought to taste this duck, it's heaven!

TONY STASSIO: I think I'm going to burst.

NESSA VOX: Tony, you haven't eaten anything!

HERRICK SIMMONS: *(Offering Tony a forkful of bass.)* Come on, try it . . .

TONY STASSIO: *(Shaking her head.)* Really, I'm . . .

NESSA VOX: *(Lays down her fork.)* I don't believe this!

HERRICK SIMMONS: *(Plows into her bass with renewed vigor.)* Well, you're missing something fabulous!

NESS VOX: *(To Herrick.)* She says she's finished . . .

HERRICK SIMMONS: Mmmmmm!

NESSA VOX: Look at her plate!

TONY STASSIO: Don't let me spoil your dinner just because I'm dieting . . .

HERRICK SIMMONS: Aaaaaaahhhhhhhh!

NESSA VOX: She hasn't touched it.

HERRICK SIMMONS: Nessa, you've got to try some of this duck. *(Offers her a forkful.)*

TONY STASSIO: You two just go right ahead . . .

NESSA VOX: Well if she's not going to eat, then neither am I!

HERRICK SIMMONS: *(Offering Nessa the duck more forcefully.)* Come on, it's sensational!

NESSA VOX: *(Tastes it.)* Mmmmmmmmmmmmm!

HERRICK SIMMONS: Isn't that something?

TONY STASSIO: *(Lifting up her plate.)* Would anyone like my bass?

HERRICK SIMMONS: *(Giving Nessa another bite.)* And not taste it with some of the peaches . .

NESSA VOX: *(Does.)* MY GOD!

HERRICK SIMMONS: Hmmmm?

NESSA VOX: *(Flutters.)*

TONY STASSIO: I've already lost four pounds this week!

NESSA VOX: TONY, YOU'VE GOT TO TRY THIS DUCK, YOU'LL DIE!

HERRICK SIMMONS: *(Reaching a forkful over to Tony.)* It's unbeliev-able . . .

NESSA VOX: It's the best duck I've ever . . .

HERRICK SIMMONS: Here, let me get you more sauce. *(She offers Tony a heaping spoonful.)*

NESSA VOX: You won't know what hit you!

TONY STASSIO: *(Shielding her mouth with her hand.)* No really, I couldn't . . .

NESSA VOX: *(To Herrick.)* Wouldn't you say that was the best duck you've ever . . .

TONY STASSIO: *(Trying to ward them off.)* Please . . .

HERRICK SIMMONS: *(More threatening with her fork.)* Just a little taste . . .!

NESSA VOX: Come on, it won't kill you!

HERRICK SIMMONS: Open!

NESSA VOX: *(Scoops some up with her fork and also menaces Tony with it.)* We insist!

HERRICK SIMMONS: It really is . . .

NESSA VOX: Quite . . .

TONY STASSIO: Please!

NESSA VOX: Wonderful.

TONY STASSIO: Don't . . .

HERRICK SIMMONS: You should . . .

TONY STASSIO: . . . force me!

HERRICK SIMMONS: . . . try it!

NESSA VOX: Come on, Tony! You promised . . .

HERRICK SIMMONS: Eat the duck!

NESSA VOX: You've hardly eaten anything.

TONY STASSIO: I've got to lose ten more pounds!

NESSA VOX: *(Dumps the duck off her fork and threatens Tony with some of her veal.)* At least try the veal!

TONY STASSIO: *(Slams down her fork.)* FUCK IT THEN. JUST FUCK IT! *(Silence.)*

HERRICK SIMMONS: *(Resumes eating her duck.)* Ignore her.

NESSA VOX: HOW CAN I IGNORE HER WHEN WE'RE SITTING AT THE SAME TABLE AND SHE REFUSES TO EAT?!

HERRICK SIMMONS: It's her problem. *(Offering Nessa another forkful of duck.)* Come on, help me with this duck.

TONY STASSIO: I'm fat.

NESSA VOX: She says she's fat!

HERRICK SIMMONS: *(Reaching across for a taste of Nessa's veal.)* How's your veal?

TONY STASSIO: *(Lifts up her arm, pulls the under part of it.)* Look at that!

NESSA VOX: That isn't fat! That's your arm!

HERRICK SIMMONS: *(Eating Nessa's veal.)* Mmmmmmmmm! Very nice!

TONY STASSIO: It's fat.

NESSA VOX: *(Lifts up her plate of veal and gives it to Herrick.)* Here, have it all, I don't want any.

HERRICK SIMMONS: Don't give it all to me!

TONY STASSIO: *(Gives Herrick her bass.)* You can have my bass too.

NESSA VOX: She ruined the whole meal.

HERRICK SIMMONS: I can't eat all of this! *(As she starts to do just that.)*

TONY STASSIO: *(Smiling, to Nessa.)* How was the veal?

NESSA VOX: You'd think I'd learn . . .

HERRICK SIMMONS: What's going on here?

TONY STASSIO: *(To Nessa, referring to the veal.)* It looks good.

NESSA VOX: She does it every time!

TONY STASSIO: *(To Herrick.)* And your bass looks really . . .

NESSA VOX: IT'S NOT AS IF SHE EVER STICKS TO ANY OF HER DIETS!

AS SOON AS SHE GETS HOME, SHE'LL OPEN UP THE REFRIGER-
ATOR AND HAVE HERSELF ONE WALLOPING ORGY . . . !

HERRICK SIMMONS: Take it easy . . .

NESSA VOX: SHE DENIES HERSELF IN FRONT OF US, BUT OH, WHEN
SHE GETS INTO THE PRIVACY OF HER OWN REFRIGERATOR . . .

TONY STASSIO: *(Hands over her ears.)* I don't know what she's talking about . . .

HERRICK SIMMONS: *(To Nessa.)* Come on . . .

NESSA VOX: DOES SHE EVER GO AT IT! I know her. *(To Herrick.)*
Would you like to hear?

HERRICK SIMMONS: Nessa, don't . . .

NESSA VOX: First . . . just to warm up, she wolfs down a Twin Pack
of Golden Ridges Potato Chips followed by a fistful of Nabisco
Nilla Wafers. Then, it's on to the freezer for the real stuff: Hungry
Man TV dinners flash-frozen by Swansons, Howard Johnson's,
Stouffers, Mortons, Mrs. Paul, Ronzoni, and Chun King! . . . But
. . . can she wait for them to heat up? . . . God knows, it's a long
wait for a Hungry Man TV dinner when you're languishing for it
. . . the piquant steak in onion gravy, the hashed brown potato
nuggets, the peas and carrots in seasoned sauce, and the delec-
table little serving of apple cake cobbler, pristine and golden in its
tidy aluminum compartment . . . So, while it's warming at 400
degrees, she'll help herself to some Pepperidge Farm corn
muffins, fully baked and ready to serve. Still frozen, mind you . . .
still frosted with a thin sheen of ice, but there's nothing wrong
with eating frozen corn muffins . . . especially if you turn out the
lights and eat them in the dark . . . lift them up to your mouth . . .
in the dark . . . roll your tongue over them . . . in . . .

HERRICK SIMMONS: NESSA, THAT'S ENOUGH! *(A silence.)*

TONY STASSIO: *(Trying to recover, in a quavering voice.)* Well, I wonder if it's warmed up at all outside . . . *(She wets her finger and
rubs it around the rim of her glass making eerie music. Another
silence.)*

HERRICK SIMMONS: *(Pushing her bass away.)* Well, I guess I'm done.
Anyone want the rest of this food?

TONY STASSIO: It's actually dangerous to go out on a night like this . . .
   (A silence.)
NESSA VOX: Well, if you two are finished, then so am I . . . *(Pushes her veal toward the center of the table.)*
HERRICK SIMMONS: . . . can't eat another bite!
TONY STASSIO: I don't know when I've been so full!
NESSA VOX: If I have one more taste, I'm going to explode!
HERRICK SIMMONS: You're going to explode! What about me? I won't be able to fit behind the wheel of the car to drive us home! *(This gets slower and slower.)*
TONY STASSIO: I can't go on . . .
NESSA VOX: I've had it . . .
HERRICK SIMMONS: I am stuffed!
TONY STASSIO: I can't move . . .
NESSA VOX: I'm in pain!
HERRICK SIMMONS: I feel sick . . .
TONY STASSIO: I'm . . . dying . . . *(The lights fade around them.)*

Crimes of the Heart

Beth Henley
1981

Scene: Babe has been arrested and is out on bail for shooting her husband. Meg has returned home from a less-than-glamorous attempt at a career in Hollywood and they are in the family home where Lenny still lives. It is Lenny's 30th birthday, which she has celebrated alone with a new box of candy she bought for herself.

Meg, late 20s.
Lenny, 30.
Babe, early 20s.

LENNY: I feel tired.

BABE: They say women need a lot of iron . . . so they won't feel tired.

LENNY: What's got iron in it? Liver?

BABE: Yeah, liver's got it. And vitamin pills.

>*(After a moment, Meg enters. She carries a bottle of bourbon that is already minus a few slugs, and a newspaper. She is wearing black boots, a dark dress, and a hat. The room goes silent.)*

MEG: Hello.

BABE: *(Fooling with her hair.)* Hi, Meg. *(Lenny quietly sips her coffee.)*

MEG: *(Handing the newspaper to Babe.)* Here's your paper.

BABE: Thanks. *(She opens it.)* Oh, here it is, right on the front page.
>*(Meg lights a cigarette.)*

BABE: Where's the scissors, Lenny?

LENNY: Look in there in the ribbon drawer.

BABE: Okay. *(She gets the scissors and glue out of the drawer and slowly begins cutting out the newspaper article.)*

MEG: *(After a few moments, filled only with the snipping of scissors.)* All right—I lied! I lied! I couldn't help it . . . these stories just came pouring out of my mouth! When I saw how tired and sick Old Granddaddy'd gotten—they just flew out! All I wanted was to see him smiling and happy. I just wasn't going to sit there and look at him all miserable and sick and sad! I just wasn't!

BABE: Oh, Meg, he is sick, isn't he—

MEG: Why, he's gotten all white and milky—he's almost evaporated!

LENNY: *(Gasping and turning to Meg.)* But still you shouldn't have lied! It just was wrong for you to tell such lies—

MEG: Well, I know that! Don't you think I know that? I hate myself when I lie for that old man. I feel so weak. And then I have to go and do at least three or four things that I know he'd despise just to get even with that miserable, old, bossy man!

LENNY: Oh, Meg, please don't talk so about Old Granddaddy! It sounds so ungrateful. Why, he went out of his way to make a home for us, to treat us like we were his very own children. All he ever wanted was the best for us. That's all he ever wanted.

MEG: Well, I guess it was; but sometimes I wonder what we wanted.

BABE: *(Taking the newspaper article and glue over to her suitcase.)* Well, one thing I wanted was a team of white horses to ride Mama's coffin to her grave. That's one thing I wanted. *(Lenny and Meg exchange looks.)* Lenny, did you remember to pack my photo album?

LENNY: It's down there at the bottom, under all that night stuff.

BABE: Oh, I found it.

LENNY: Really, Babe, I don't understand why you have to put in the articles that are about the unhappy things in your life. Why would you want to remember them?

BABE: *(Pasting the article in.)* I don't know. I just like to keep an accurate record, I suppose. There. *(She begins flipping through the book.)* Look, here's a picture of me when I got married.

MEG: Let's see. *(They all look at the photo album.)*

LENNY: My word, you look about twelve years old.

BABE: I was just eighteen.

MEG: You're smiling, Babe. Were you happy then?

BABE: *(Laughing.)* Well, I was drunk on champagne punch. I remember that! *(They turn the page.)*

LENNY: Oh, there's Meg singing at Greeny's!

BABE: Oooh, I wish you were still singing at Greeny's! I wish you were!

LENNY: You're so beautiful.

BABE: Yes, you are. You're beautiful.

MEG: Oh, stop! I'm not—

LENNY: Look, Meg's starting to cry.

BABE: Oh, Meg—

MEG: I'm not—

BABE: Quick, better turn the page; we don't want Meg crying—*(She flips the pages.)*

LENNY: Why, it's Daddy.

MEG: Where'd you get that picture, Babe? I thought she burned them all.

BABE: Ah, I just found it around.

LENNY: What does it say here? What's that inscription?

BABE: It says "Jimmy—clowning at the beach—1952."

LENNY: Well, will you look at that smile.

MEG: Jesus, those white teeth—turn the page, will you; we can't do any worse than this! *(They turn the page. The room goes silent.)*

BABE: It's Mama and the cat.

LENNY: Oh, turn the page—

BABE: That old yellow cat. You know, I bet if she hadn't of hung that cat along with her, she wouldn't have gotten all that national coverage.

MEG: *(After a moment, hopelessly.)* Why are we talking about this?

LENNY: Meg's right. It was so sad. It was awfully sad. I remember how we all three just sat up on the bed the day of the service all dressed up in our black velveteen suits crying the whole morning long.

BABE: We used up one whole big box of Kleenexes.

MEG: And then Old Granddaddy came in and said he was gonna take us out to breakfast. Remember, he told us not to cry anymore 'cause he was gonna take us out to get banana splits for breakfast.

BABE: That's right—banana splits for breakfast!

MEG: Why, Lenny was fourteen years old, and he thought that would make it all better—

BABE: Oh, I remember he said for us to eat all we wanted. I think I ate about five! He kept shoving them down us!

MEG: God, we were so sick!

LENNY: Oh, we were!

MEG: *(Laughing.)* Lenny's face turned green—

LENNY: I was just as sick as a dog!

BABE: Old Grandmama was furious!

LENNY: Oh, she was!

MEG: The thing about Old Granddaddy is, he keeps trying to make us happy, and we end up getting stomachaches and turning green and throwing up in the flower arrangements.

BABE: Oh, that was me! I threw up in the flowers! Oh, no! How embarrassing!

LENNY: *(Laughing.)* Oh, Babe—

BABE: *(Hugging her sisters.)* Oh, Lenny! Oh, Meg!

MEG: Oh, Babe! Oh, Lenny! It's so good to be home!

LENNY: Hey, I have an idea—

BABE: What?

LENNY: Let's play cards!!

BABE: Oh, let's do!

MEG: All right!

LENNY: Oh, good! It'll be just like when we used to sit around the table playing Hearts all night long.

BABE: I know! *(Getting up.)* I'll fix us up some popcorn and hot chocolate—

MEG: *(Getting up.)* Here, let me get out that old black popcorn pot.

LENNY: *(Getting up.)* Oh, yes! Now, let's see, I think I have a deck of cards around here somewhere.

BABE: Gosh, I hope I remember all the rules—Are hearts god or bad?

MEG: Bad, I think, Aren't they, Lenny?

LENNY: That's right. Hearts are bad, but the Black Sister is the worst of all—

MEG: Oh, that's right! And the Black Sister is the Queen of Spades.

BABE: *(Figuring it out.)* And spades are the black cards that aren't the puppy dog feet?

MEG: *(Thinking a moment.)* Right. And she counts a lot of points.

BABE: And points are bad?

MEG: Right. Here, I'll get some paper so we can keep score. *(The phone rings.)*

LENNY: Oh, here they are!

MEG: I'll get it—

LENNY: Why, look at these cards! They're years old!

BABE: Oh, let me see!

MEG: Hello . . . No, this is Meg McGrath . . . Doc. How are you? . . . Well, good . . . You're where? . . . Well, sure. Come on over . . . All right. 'Bye. *(She hangs up.)* That was Doc Porter. He's down the street at Al's Grill. He's gonna come on over.

LENNY: He is?

MEG: He said he wanted to come see me.

LENNY: Oh. *(After a pause.)* Well, do you still want to play?

MEG: No, I don't think so.

LENNY: All right. *(She starts to shuffle the cards, as Meg brushes her hair.)* You know, it's really not much fun playing Hearts with only two people.

MEG: I'm sorry; maybe after Doc leaves I'll join you.

LENNY: I know; maybe Doc'll want to play. Then we can have a game of bridge.

MEG: I don't think so. Doc never liked cards. Maybe we'll just go out somewhere.

LENNY: *(Putting down the cards. Babe picks them up.)* Meg—

MEG: What?

LENNY: Well, Doc's married now.

MEG: I know. You told me.

LENNY: Oh. Well, as long as you know that. *(Pause.)* As long as you know that.

The Cemetery Club

Ivan Menchell
1985

Scene: Ida's Apartment, in Queens, New York. The three friends, who
are widows, have tea before one of their regular visits to the
cemetery to visit the graves of their dead husbands.

Friends, widows:
Ida, Sweet-natured, homey.
Lucille, flambouyant and fun-loving.
Doris, serious, practical by nature.

*(As they laugh, Ida enters with the tea and a plate of cookies on
a tray.)*
IDA: So what are we talking? *(She sets the tray down on the coffee
table and hands out the cups.)*
LUCILLE: We're trying to figure out what the boys are doing right now.
IDA: Murry is easy. Right now he's sitting, smoking a cigar and any
minute his ash is going to fall and burn a small hole in the cloud.
LUCILLE: Let's see . . . Today's Sunday, so Harry'll go right for the
Manhattan real estate section then yell for half an hour how
thirty years ago he could've bought a brownstone on Park
Avenue for twenty-five thousand dollars.
DORIS: Abe is definitely out on a walk. Sunday was his day for walk-
ing, so wherever they walk up there, that's where he is.
IDA: Here's to the boys . . . wherever they are.
(They all raise their cups, toast, and drink.)
DORIS: Funny, you know, I was reading last week how this woman
contacts the dead through a . . . a what do you call it? You hold
hands in a circle around a big table. Like a seder.
LUCILLE: Séance.
DORIS: That's it. She says she actually talks to them. You have to put
something that belonged to the deceased on the table, or a picture.
LUCILLE: I don't believe in that.
IDA: I don't know. I've heard some pretty interesting things.

DORIS: I think one day I'm going to try it. Wouldn't it be something if I could contact Abe, if I could talk with him? Even if just for a few minutes.

IDA: I don't know if I'd want to contact Murry.

DORIS: Why not?

LUCILLE: Because it's unnatural. Your husband dies, that's it. The time for talking is finished.

DORIS: Unnatural is a man dying in his prime. You get married so you can spend the rest of your life with someone you love.

LUCILLE: You get married 'til "death do you part."

IDA: If I could contact Murry I'd like to ask him what he would've done, if I had gone first. I wonder if he would remarry.

DORIS: Abe, never.

IDA: I think Murry would. *(To Lucille.)* What about Harry, you think he would?

LUCILLE: I couldn't care less. The only thing I'd like to ask Harry is if maybe there's a bank account somewhere he forgot to tell me about. What difference does it make whether or not he'd remarry?

IDA: Oy, that reminds me. I completely forgot. I spoke to Selma this morning—

LUCILLE: No.

DORIS: Don't tell me.

IDA: She's getting married.

LUCILLE: I don't believe it.

DORIS: At her age.

IDA: Just goes to show you, you're never too old.

DORIS: *She's* too old.

IDA: She's the same age as I am.

DORIS: I rest my case.

IDA: Oh, you want to start talking age? After all, next month you're going to be—

DORIS: Don't you dare.

LUCILLE: It's like watching my two older sisters fight.

IDA: You keep out of this. You're only three days younger than dirt.

LUCILLE: Look who's talking. I was there when you celebrated your fiftieth birthday for the fourth time.

IDA: I did no such thing.

DORIS: Oh yes you did.

IDA: I am very proud of my age. I happen to think I look pretty terrific.

LUCILLE: You do. I hope *I* look as good as you do at your age.

IDA: You did.

DORIS: *(To Lucille.)* I just hope I *reach* your age.

LUCILLE: *(To Doris.)* You've been my age twice.

DORIS: *(To Lucille.)* And *you've* been your age since I've known you.

IDA: Can we call it a tie on this one?

DORIS: Fine.

LUCILLE: It's all right by me.

IDA: Now where was I?

LUCILLE: Selma's getting married.

IDA: So I told her we would all be there.

LUCILLE: Of course.

DORIS: We've never missed one of Selma's weddings.

IDA: That's what I figured. She also asked if we could be bridesmaids.

DORIS: You're kidding.

LUCILLE: I don't know her *that* well.

DORIS: What happened to the women she used last time?

IDA: She doesn't like to use the same bridesmaids for more than one wedding. It's bad luck. Why don't the two of you come over here? We'll change and all go together.

LUCILLE: Why not?

DORIS: Sure.

LUCILLE: When's the affair?

IDA: Month after next.

DORIS: So soon? She only met Arnold over the summer.

IDA: She's not marrying Arnold. She's marrying Ed.

DORIS and LUCILLE: Who's Ed?

IDA: Some man she met a couple of weeks ago on a singles weekend. She says they're madly in love. And are you ready for this? His name is Ed *Bonfigliano*.

DORIS and LUCILLE: Bonfigliano?

DORIS: That's not a Jewish name.

IDA: He's not a Jewish man.

DORIS: Selma *Bonfigliano* . . . What happened to Arnold?

IDA: He died.

LUCILLE: So Selma's marrying an Italian.

DORIS: Go figure.

IDA: Well, she never did like being alone. Selma always said she felt lonely being by herself in that house.

DORIS: If you don't like to be alone you get a dog not an Italian.

IDA: I don't know. Maybe she has the right idea.

LUCILLE: What are you talking about? The woman goes through husbands like I go through nylons.

IDA: Look who's talking.

LUCILLE: Dating is one thing. Marriage is something else.

DORIS: I have to agree there.

LUCILLE: So when are you going to start?

DORIS: Don't push it. I think it's time we should be going. I don't want to be late.

LUCILLE: What, if you're a little late he leaves?

(Doris gives her a look.)

LUCILLE: I'm sorry.

IDA: *(Puts the cups back on the tray and heads off to the kitchen. Offstage.)* It's cold out?

LUCILLE: A little chilly.

DORIS: It's perfect. The cemetery'll look gorgeous and if Abe's ivy is dead, heads are going to roll.

IDA: *(Re-entering.)* It'll be fine, I'm sure.

(They get their coats out of the closet, and put them on.)

LUCILLE: *(Showing off her coat.)* So Doris, what do you think of the coat?

DORIS: Gorgeous.

LUCILLE: Guess how much.

DORIS: For something like that, if it's second-hand and you got a good price, with a little haggling you should've paid maybe, what, nineteen hundred?

(Lucille, annoyed, opens the door and exits in a huff. Doris smiles at Ida as she picks up her folding stool. They exit with Ida closing the door behind them as the lights fade out.)

Camping

Jon Jory
1983

Scene: Three college girls are camping. It is around midnight. All that
is required are sleeping bags and an imaginary fire.

Marge
Jeannie
Ellen

MARGE: *(Reading a letter.)* "The subways aren't scary at all. Mind
you, nobody uses them after dark, except in groups, but I'm not
out that much in the evenings. I have been dating a terrific guy
on and off. I met him one night when I had standing room at the
Met. Now, don't be upset with me. He's married with three children, but the oldest girl is just wonderful. Some times we all do
things together, like the Zoo or Central Park. She's a couple of
years older than I am, so she's really showed me the ropes in the
city."
ELLEN: How old is he?
MARGE: *(Still reading.)* "I had to move out of that west side apartment because the girl from the roommate's service committed
suicide."
ELLEN: Suicide?
MARGE: "Well, I mean she didn't die, but she cut her wrists and it
kind of got me down a little." *(Marge looks up from the letter.)*
Got *her* down? *(She goes back to the letter.)* "No job in publishing yet, but I found some daytime work with a service called
Clean Jeans. It's a great idea. A lot of executives don't have time
to do their laundry so we go in twice a week and do it for them,
right at their apartment houses, and fold it and put it away and
everything. I love the girls I'm working with except for a couple
who are a little dikey, but that's not too big a hassle." *(She looks
up.)* You want to hear any more of this?
JEANNIE: Why not? It's real.

MARGE: *(Reading.)* "Give my love to Ellen and Jeannie and everybody. I'm keeping my fingers crossed that, come June, some of you will bust out and take a chew at the Big Apple. I do know some terrific bars where you can really get it on with some really smooth types. I notice advertising guys really put the moves on us cornfed Ohio girls. Love to all. Carol." *(A pause.)* Well, that was good reading. *(A long pause. She picks up her cup.)* There is dirt and sticks in my coffee. Crunchy coffee. *(A pause.)* So this is camping. Well, it could be worse. They could force me to be a vegetarian.

ELLEN: Or jogging.

MARGE: God, jogging! It can't be good for your brain, right? All that bouncing. All those little grey matters banging around. Cells jarred loose. After three of four years you probably end up as a Republican.

ELLEN: Hey, I am a Republican.

MARGE: How many miles do you do a day?

JEANNIE: Is the fire out?

ELLEN: Nearly.

MARGE: I thought that for all this physical discomfort you were supposed to get stars.

ELLEN: It's overcast.

MARGE: Oh, good, rain. Hey, Ellen, you're queen of the campfire. What do we do if it rains?

ELLEN: If you're a Catholic, you offer it up. The rest of us just get wet. Oh, I love being out here. No exams, no parents, no miserable, rotten, uncaring, insensitive fiancés, no impenetrable future, no declining job market, no sexists attitudes . . . just trees.

MARGE: Speaking of sexist attitudes, how's your rotten, uncaring, insensitive fiancé?

ELLEN: He bought me a Cuisinart.

MARGE: And an apron, right?

JEANNIE: You two are just awful. He's perfectly nice. Just a little nineteenth century.

MARGE: Look, do you realize the tidal wave's on the horizon: In the next year, it's out of the womb and into the world. We pick jobs, men, neighborhoods, brands of coffee. Gives me the shakes. *(She laughs.)* You know where my mother thinks I am tonight?

ELLEN: Staying over with your brother, locked in a night of sibling rivalry and good advice.

MARGE: Nope, with Ben.

JEANNIE: You're kidding? I thought sex before marriage gave her diarrhea.

MARGE: Nope. She hates Ben, and his music, and his "puke on the nukes" politics so much she decided the only remedy was for me to sleep with him 'til the magic was gone.

JEANNIE: And?

MARGE: She's dead right. He's a creep. He eats chocolate marshmallows, reads comic books, and blow-dries his hair.

ELLEN: Yuk.

MARGE: In any case, she would rather I was running through the Kama Sutra with Ben than thinking I was out with two helpless women providing a late night snack for the bears.

ELLEN: There no bears eight miles outside of Dayton. Tuesday nights they're all in town for their bowling league. Parents are a mess, aren't they? They have a view of women and roles that's a mile to the right of the V.F.W. I want a nontraditional wedding and they . . .

MARGE: There is no such thing as a nontraditional wedding. He gets a wife. You get a Cuisinart. That's how it always works out.

ELLEN: While you do what, Marge?

MARGE: Hey, don't get irritated.

ELLEN: No, really. While you do what?

MARGE: While I teach and write and get mildly famous and lunch with beautiful men who get high on my freedom and respect my person.

ELLEN: Right. There's no more powerful aphrodisiac than a public high-school teaching career. Of course, on that salary you can only afford one lunch a year, so I hope you make it count.

MARGE: But I will have a career instead of a liberal education.

ELLEN: On the other hand, I will have a home and children instead of a nondescript career in a counterproductive educational system.

JEANNIE: Anybody want a toke?

MARGE: Yeah, you'll have a home. It'll allow you the luxury of letting your brain atrophy in a traditional role.

ELLEN: That's really rotten!

JEANNIE: Hey, c'mon. Groove on nature. Be at one with the universe. Plus, I could use the sleep.

ELLEN: Sorry.

MARGE: Young women a little edgy. Young women a little nervous.

JEANNIE: Not me.

MARGE: Jeannie, you are drugged out.

JEANNIE: Maybe. I prefer to think I'm born to float.

MARGE: Born to float. You're so laid-back you're practically laid out.

JEANNIE: I tried last summer. It was terrific. Worked for three weeks, traveled three weeks, worked for three weeks, traveled for three weeks. Hit five states, lotta groovy people, filled up my head, changed, grew, took some risks. I loved it.

ELLEN: A cocktail waitress in five states. That's a lot of net stockings.

MARGE: Think it'll look as good at forty?

JEANNIE: Your cells turn over every seven years, that's three lifetimes from now.

MARGE: There's something in this damn sack.

ELLEN: Sh-h-h-h-h. Everybody will want one.

MARGE: I am so uncomfortable it is practically sensuous. *(A pause.)* Plus, I'm scared.

ELLEN: I said there are no bears.

MARGE: It's not bears. It's life.

ELLEN: Oh, life.

JEANNIE: You sure you don't want a toke?

MARGE: *(Picking up the letter.)* This is terrific, right? Carol got a Masters Degree in journalism and in eight months, she rocketed straight to the top as a laundress. *(A pause.)* Remember when you were little and you got scared?

JEANNIE: I always thought the furniture woke up when you went to sleep. I had this morbid fear of being eaten by chairs.

MARGE: Being little was terrific. Somebody could always make it better.

ELLEN: My dad and mom had a song. If I woke up or anything . . .
God, they'd run in, always both of them.

JEANNIE: That's great.

ELLEN: And they'd turn on the nightlight . . .

MARGE: God, nightlights!

ELLEN: It had a bear juggling.

MARGE: The nightlight?

ELLEN: Yeah.

MARGE: I slept with a cornhusk doll. You ever seen one? About this
big . . . I loved that doll right down to the dust.

ELLEN: After I yelled, or something, Mom and Dad would sit on each
side of me and sing this song. They'd just repeat it over and over.
I'd just drift off, you know.

MARGE: Music to soothe the savage chairs, eh, Jeannie?

JEANNIE: Too bad they didn't eat my mother. *(A pause.)*

ELLEN: We could all "Take a bite out of the Big Apple and meet some
real smooth advertising types who would really put the moves on
us corn-fed girls." (Jeannie *gets the giggles. It goes on. Then
silence.)*

MARGE: What was the song?

ELLEN: What song?

MARGE: The song your parents sang, nutsy.

ELLEN: Oh. Lemme see.
Rock-a-bye baby
The cradle is green
Daddy's a nobleman
Mother's a queen
Betty's a lady who wears a gold ring
And Jimmy's a drummer who drums for the King.
(Silence.)

MARGE: One more time.
*(Ellen begins again and they all join in going twice through as the
lights fade.)*

Heads

Jon Jory
1983

Scene: Three college women. A dormitory represented by usual col-
lege-room furniture. Kristen is packing and Margaret is studying
a script.

Margaret
Rose
Kristen

MARGARET: "Why look you now, how unworthy a thing you would
make of me! You would play upon me, you would seem to know
my stops, you would pluck out the heart of my mystery, you
would sound me from my lowest note to the top of my compass.
S'Blood, do you think I am easier to be played on than a pipe?"
KRISTEN: Hamlet, right?
MARGARET: Right.
KRISTEN: How come you always learn boys' parts?
MARGARET: 'Cause they've got all the best lines. You know what
women do in plays? Fall in love, get seduced, commit suicide, and
listen to the men say all the best lines. I can't believe you're going.
KRISTEN: I would have been the first one in my family to get a Masters.
MARGARET: You're really going to cut hair?
KRISTEN: Side by side with my daddy.
MARGARET: How come he won't stake you?
KRISTEN: Hasn't got it.
MARGARET: I thought all barbers were rich.
KRISTEN: Stylists are rich, barbers cut hair in Plenty Wood, Montana.
Invite me to the wedding, will you?
MARGARET: Cross my heart. *(They embrace.)*
KRISTEN: What's it going to be like?
MARGARET: The best you can get for under a hundred dollars.
KRISTEN: Day-old cake.
MARGARET: A double pop-top ceremony.

(The door opens and a third young woman, Rose, enters.)

MARGARET: Yikes.

ROSE: Sit down.

KRISTEN: Scared me to death! You're white as a sheet.

ROSE: Sit down. Shut up.

KRISTEN: Nice talk.

MARGARET: Your mother didn't tell you not to interrupt a conversation?

ROSE: I found a wallet.

MARGARET: Yeah?

KRISTEN: So?

ROSE: In the dorm parking lot.

MARGARET: Rose, you could make a sunny day sound like a clue in a Hardy Boys' mystery. You suffer from congenital implication.

ROSE: Have we got any beer left?

MARGARET: Over there.

ROSE: It was right by my car. Right by it. God meant us to have this wallet.

MARGARET: So what's to be so hyped up about?

KRISTEN: A lot of money? What?

ROSE: Sit.

KRISTEN: I have to pack.

ROSE: Sit!

MARGARET: I thought you didn't drink beer?

ROSE: This wallet belongs to Teddy Leonard.

KRISTEN: Who?

MARGARET: That little pip-squeak guy? The one who hangs around Pepito's by himself, reading Alfred North Whitehead so you'll know he's serious?

KRISTEN: From Joanie's class?

MARGARET: About this high. If you held him up to the light, he'd be transparent.

KRISTEN: The one she went out with that time? Splurged her to a fifty dollar French dinner, and then dragged her to some documentary film on laser technology?

ROSE: Right.

KRISTEN: Too shy to talk to her?

ROSE: That's the one.

KRISTEN: So?

ROSE: Read this. *(She pulls a clipping out of the wallet and hands it to Kristen. Rose goes to get another beer.)*

KRISTEN: *(Impressed.)* No damn kidding! *(She hands the clipping to Margaret.)*

MARGARET: So tell me?

ROSE: Read it!

MARGARET: *(Reading.)* This can't be right. The kid dresses like Lawrence Welk. I mean he's okay, but just kind of a nebbish. *(Kristen takes the clipping back.)*

KRISTEN: His daddy invented frozen orange juice.

ROSE: The nebbish is an only child. He's the heir to a couple of hundred million.

KRISTEN: *(Resuming her packing.)* Well, good for him. Maybe he'll be able to get a date.

ROSE: We're the only ones who know.

MARGARET: Listen, his secret is safe with me. Don't slurp the beer, okay? I have to study. *(She begins to read.)*

ROSE: Any one of us could have him.

MARGARET: I'm afraid I'd get cut by his braces.

ROSE: I'm not kidding.

KRISTEN: Kidding? Kidding? What is this, a movie about Nineteen Forties' chorus girls?

ROSE: Think about it. Don't put a label on it. Think about it.

MARGARET: So you're serious?

ROSE: Serious! The will's probably in probate. That means in maybe thirteen months he has two hundred million dollars. Have you ever watched him? Always alone, and doing what?

MARGARET: You writing a thesis on this guy?

ROSE: What does he do all the time? *All* the time?

KRISTEN: Wears herringbone sports coats.

ROSE: Stares at women. This kid is sexually desperate. He's twenty years old and he's been too shy all his life. One hundred to one he has never touched one. Worse than that, he wants one imponderable thing. He wants to be loved for himself. If anyone finds out he's rich, it will never, ever happen. He wants someone to love him for the nebbish he is.

MARGARET: Okay, so take him.

ROSE: I don't need him. I'll be a pediatric allergist, remember, a doctor. People marry *me* for money. Plus I have the trust fund. Plus I have doting parents. Plus I'm driving a Corvette.

MARGARET: Congratulations. You have just won our "Let them eat cake" award. Have another beer.

ROSE: I am giving him to you. Me. The goose who lays the golden eggs. Savvy? Blink your eyes twice if you catch my drift. *(They look at her.)* I ain't kidding, roomies. This is one of those moments that can change your life. We're the only ones who know. We call him up; he comes over; we're nice to him. He asks you out. You go. Again he asks. Again you go. You take your time. Maybe after two months you do some heavy petting. Instant marriage proposal!

MARGARET: Yuk, Rose, yuk.

KRISTEN: Deepest India. I mean, really. Listen, if he dies, do I have to throw myself on his funeral pyre?

ROSE: Two hundred million dollars. Two hundred million dollars. Stack it in tens it would fill the Astrodome. The interest income would be over two million a year. You want to be an actress? Produce the film. Hire Robert Redford. You want barbers: Buy a couple of hundred. Remember the law school you can't pay for? How about Harvard? Buy a house in Cambridge. Live-in help. Vacation in Tibet. Fly me in twice a week for tea and petit fours. Two hundred million dollars.

MARGARET: If I didn't know you were a paranoid schizophrenic, I would think you were a Tupperware salesman.

ROSE: *(To Kristen.)* You don't have your price?

KRISTEN: What a yucky thing to say.

ROSE: *(To Margaret.)* You don't have *your* price?

MARGARET: I'm engaged, nutso.

ROSE: Dump him.

MARGARET: Is this a joke, or what?

ROSE: Call it off.

MARGARET: I'm in love.

ROSE: You were in love last year.

MARGARET: That was different.

ROSE: Six times.

MARGARET: Okay, six times.

ROSE: And three weeks ago you went out with somebody else.

MARGARET: For coffee.

ROSE: Right. Coffee. Your first marriage, should it last more than two years, should be put in a natural history museum.

KRISTEN: Easy.

ROSE: You take him.

KRISTEN: I'm afraid I'm not that cynical.

ROSE: Want to end up in Plenty Wood?

KRISTEN: I won't.

ROSE: You don't have a dime, Kristen. Your family doesn't have a dime. You rode the scholarships 'til they gave out. You're going to end up being a dollar twenty-five barber.

KRISTEN: It's a little too late in the century to turn into a courtesan.

ROSE: It's a little too late in the century to turn into a barber.

KRISTEN: Knock it off.

ROSE: Take him. Get a divorce in two years. Settle for practically nothing, two million and the house. Be anything, marry anybody, go anywhere. Don't feed me this romantic, I'm-too-good-for-this, I'm-a-powerful-woman crap. This isn't another materialist, spiritual, self-expanding, liberated bull session. This is millions of dollars cold cash on the barrelhead. I already called him.

MARGARET: Teddy whatsis?

ROSE: Teddy whatsis. Be here in maybe five minutes. You don't have to invent the electric car, cure the cold, find yourself, none of it. It's gonna happen this once and never happen again. It's beyond cosmopolitan. Figure out who you are later. Figure out what you believe later. Sell out and praise the Lord. Don't tell me you're too damn dumb to figure this out.

MARGARET: Could you look at him in the morning?

ROSE: In the morning everybody looks terrible.

KRISTEN: What about him? What about his feelings?

ROSE: He'll love it. He's been waiting for it for years. Come on, look

it in the face. When it's over he'll kiss you good-bye and buy Jackie Kennedy.

MARGARET: You are really a monster.

ROSE: Don't kid me, ladies. We are born in America. We are middle-class down to our anklets and add-a-beads. We started learning this stuff with our Barbie dolls. And don't give me any "traditional rolls" stuff. You think guys wouldn't do this if you had the two hundred million. And if you don't do it, somebody else will. They will line up from here to Nome, Alaska. And what is your responsibility to yourself? Our responsibility is to our potential. Fifty percent of all American marriages end up in divorce anyway and you know what is given as chief cause? Financial problems. No kidding. And you are doing him a disservice? He's pining away out there. He sits with his back to the cafeteria wall drinking black coffee and wishing he wasn't alone. I mean you aren't hardened cases or something. You can't tell a book by its cover and all that. He's bright. He's a gentleman. Joanie says he practically threw *himself* over the puddles so she wouldn't get wet. I grant you he's short, shy and myopic, but listen, he is a man among men. What he can do for you, Superman can't do. And, by way of comparison, how hot is anything else we've gotten mixed up with? Your fiancé, Margaret, how many dawns and Bloody Marys have we shared while you agonized? I will, I won't, I will, I can't, I love him, I don't, we don't have the same interests, he's cute. Come on, face it. Prince Charles hasn't showed up. *(There is a knock at the door.)*

MARGARET: *(Mouthing the words and pointing to the door.)* Is that him? *(Rose nods.)*

ROSE: Your carriage waits without. No, no, don't push, don't shove. There's a way to settle this. I've got a quarter. You guys call it. *(There is a knock on the door.)* Bet it or regret it.

KRISTEN: I can't do this. How can I do this?

ROSE: One and only chance. *(Another knock. A pause.)*

KRISTEN: Tails.

MARGARET: Oh, what the hell. Heads. *(Rose flips the coin and holds it out for them to look at as the lights fade.)*

Three Tall Women

Edward Albee
1991

Scene: A wealthy bedroom, French in feeling.

A, avery old woman— thin, autocratic, proud, well-groomed.
B, looks as A would have at 52; plainly dressed.
C, looks as B would have at 26.

> *(At rise, A is in the stage left armchair, B is in the stage right one, C on the bed foot bench. It is afternoon.)*
> *(Some silence.)*

A: *(An announcement from nowhere; to no one in particular.)* I'm ninety-one.

B: *(Pause.)* Is that so?

A: *(Pause.)* Yes.

C: *(Small smile.)* You're ninety-*two*.

A: *(Longer pause; none too pleasant.)* Be that as it *may*.

B: *(To C.)* Is that so?

C: *(Shrugs: indicates papers.)* Says so here.

B: *(Pause, stretching.)* Well . . . what does it matter?

C: Vanity is amazing.

B: So's forgetting.

A: *(General.)* I'm ninety-one.

B: *(Accepting sigh.)* OK.

C: *(Smaller smile.)* You're ninety-*two*.

B: *(Unconcerned.)* Oh . . . let it alone.

C: No! It's important. Getting things . . .

B: It doesn't matter!

C: *(Sotto voce.)* It does to *me*.

A: *(Pause.)* I know because he says. "You're exactly thirty years older than I am; I know how old I am because I know how old *you* are, and if you ever forget how old you are ask me how old *I* am, and then you'll know." *(Pause.)* Oh, he's said that a lot.

C: What if he's wrong?

A: *(From a distance; curiously lighter, higher voice.)* What?

B: Let it *be*.

C: *(Still to A.)* What if he's wrong? What if he's not thirty years younger than you?

A: *(Oddly loud, tough.)* You'd think he'd know how old he is!

C: No. I mean . . . what if he's wrong about how old *you* are.

A: *(Pause.)* Don't be silly. How couldn't he be thirty years younger than me when I'm thirty years older than he is? He's said it over and over. *(Pause.)* Every time he comes to see me. What is today?

B: It's *(Whatever day it is in reality).*

A: You see?!

C: *(A bit as if to a child.)* Well, one of you might be wrong, and it might not be him.

B: *(Small sneer.)* He.

C: *(Quick smile.)* Yes; I know.

A: Don't be stupid. *What* is it? *What* day is it?

B: It's *(Same as above.)*

A: *(Shakes her head.)* No.

C: *(Interested.)* No what?

A: No it *isn't*.

B: OK.

C: *(To A.)* What day do you *think* it is?

A: *(Confusion.)* What day is it? What day do I . . .? *(Eyes narrowing.)* Why, it's today, of course. What day do you *think* it is?! *(Turns to B; cackles.)*

B: Right on girl!

C: *(Scoffs.)* What an answer! What a dumb . . .

A: Don't you talk to me that way!

C: *(Offended.)* Well! I'm sorry!

A: I pay you, don't I? You can't talk to me that way.

C: In a way.

A: *(A daring tone.)* What?!

C: Indirectly. You pay someone who pays me, someone who . . .

A: Well; there; you see? You can't talk to me that way.

B: She isn't talking to you that way.

A: What?

B: She isn't *talking* to you that way.

A: *(Dismissive laugh.)* I don't know what you're talking about. *(Pause.)* Besides.

> *(Silence; then she cries. They let her. It begins in self-pity, proceeds to crying for crying's sake, and concludes with rage and self-loathing at having to cry. It takes quite a while.)*

B: *(When it's over.)* There. Feel better?

C: *(Under her breath.)* Honestly.

B: *(To A.)* A good cry lets it all out.

A: *(Laughs; sly.)* What does a *bad* one do? *(Laughs again; B joins her.)*

C: *(Shakes her head in admiration.)* Sometimes you're so . . .

A: *(Ugly; suddenly.)* What?!

C: *(Tiny pause.)* Never *mind*. I was going to say something *nice*. Never *mind*.

A: *(To B.)* What did she say? She mumbles all the time.

C: I don't mumble! *(Annoyance at herself.)* Never mind!

A: How is anybody expected to hear what she says?

B: *(Placating.)* She didn't finish her sentence. It doesn't matter.

A: *(Small, smug triumph.)* I'll *bet* it doesn't.

C: *(Dogged, but not unpleasant.)* What I meant was you may have been incorrect about your age for so long—may have made up the fiction so many years ago, though why anyone would lie about one year . . .

B: *(Weary.)* Let her alone; let her have it if she wants to.

C: I will *not*.

A: Have what?

C: Why you would lie about one *year*? I can imagine taking off ten—or *trying* to. Though more probably seven, or five—good and tricky—but *one*?! Taking off *one year*? What kind of vanity is *that*?

B: *(Clucks.)* How you go *on*.

A: *(Imitation.)* How you go *on*.

C: *(Purrs.)* How I go on. So, I can understand ten, or five, or seven, but not one.

B: How you *do*.

A: *(To C.)* How you *do*. *(To B.)* How *what*?!

B: How she goes on.

A: *(Cheerful.)* Yes! How you go *on!*

C: *(Smiles.)* Yes; I do.

A: *(Suddenly, but not urgently.)* I want to go.

C: On?

A: *(More urgently.)* I want to go. I want to go.

B: You want to go? *(Rises.)* You want the pan? Is it number one? Do you want the pan?

A: *(Embarrassed to discuss it.)* No . . . Nooooo!

B: Ah. *(Moves to A.)* All right. Can you walk?

A: *(Weepy.)* I don't know!

B: Well, we'll try you. OK? *(Indicates walker.)* You want the walker?

A: *(Near tears.)* I want to walk! I don't know! Anything! I have to *go!* *(Starts to fret-weep.)*

B: All right! *(She moves A to a standing position. We discover A's left arm is in a sling, useless.)*

A You're hurting me! You're hurting me!

B: All right; I'm being careful!

A: No. you're *not!*

B: Yes, I am!

A: No you're *not!!!*

B: *(Angry.)* Yes, I *am.*

A: No. you're *not. (On her feet, weeping, shuffling with B's help, off.)* You're trying to hurt me; you know how I hurt!

B: *(To C, as they exit.)* Hold the fort.

C: I will. I will hold the fort. *(Muffled exchanges offstage. C looks toward them, shakes her head, looks back down.) (Both to herself and to be heard.)* I suppose one could lie about one year— some kind of one-upmanship, a private vengeance, perhaps, some tiny victory, maybe. *(Shrugs.)* I don't know, maybe these things get important. Why can't I be nice?

B: *(Re-enters.)* Made it that time. *(Signs.)* And so it goes.

C: Not always, eh?

B: In the morning, when she wakes up she wets—a kind of greeting to the day. I suppose: the sphincter and the cortex not in sync. Never during the *night* but *as* she wakes.

C: Good morning to the morning, eh?

B: Something to something.

C: Put a diaper on her.

B: *(Shakes her head.)* She won't have it. I'm working on it, but she won't have it.

C: Rubber sheet?

B: Won't have it. Get her up, put her in the chair and she does the other. Give her a cup of coffee . . .

C: Black.

B: *(Chuckles.)* Half cream and all that sugar! Three spoons! How has she lived this long? Give her a cup of coffee, put her in her chair, give her a cup of coffee, and place your bets.

C: *(Looks at the chair she is in.) What chair?! This chair?!*

B: *(Laughs.)* You got it. Don't worry.

C: It must be awful.

B: *(Deprecating.) For whom?*

C: *(Rising to it.)* For her! You're paid. It's probably awful for you, too, but you're paid.

B: As she never ceases to inform me . . . *and* you.

C: To begin to lose it, I mean—the control, the loss of dignity, the . . .

B: Oh, stop it! It's downhill from sixteen on! For all of *us!*

Shadow of a Man

Cherrie Moraga
1990

Scene: The home of the Rodriguez family in Los Angeles. In the kitchen Hortensia is baby-sitting her grandson.

Lupe, the daughter, age 12.
Hortensia, the mother, mid-forties.
Leticia, the older daughter, age 17.

(A Saturday afternoon. Hortensia is changing Rodrigo's baby on top of the kitchen table, making the usual exclamations a grandmother does over her first grandchild.)

HORTENSIA: Ah mi chulito! Riguito! Qué precioso!

LETICIA: *(Offstage.)* Mom, I got the car!

HORTENSIA: Is that you, hijas? *(Leticia and Lupe enter excitedly.)*

LUPE: It's so tough, Mami!

HORTENSIA: Miren lo que tengo aquí.

LETICIA: It's just an old jalopy, but I can fix it up.

LUPE: Hey! When'd Sean come?

HORTENSIA: Ay! don't call him tha'! It sounds like a girl's name.

LETICIA: That's what they called him.

HORTENSIA: Well, I call him Riguito . . . como su papá, not . . . Sean!

LETICIA: Yeah, well just don't try calling him that in front of Karen. What's he doing here anyway?

HORTENSIA: She left me the baby to watch. Qué milagro, eh?

LUPE: That's for sure.

HORTENSIA: Una 'mergency came up. She tole me would I mind watching the baby. I said a'course not, even though they only call me when they need me.

LETICIA: Where's Rigo?

HORTENSIA: He has the Army this weekend. Ay! You should of seen how handsome he look in that uniform! He remind me of your papá.

LETICIA: The entire Raza's on the streets protesting the war and my brother's got to be strutting around in a uniform.

HORTENSIA: Es mejor que he shoulda gone to Vietnam?

LETICIA: No, but he doesn't have to go around parading it. God, I hope nobody I know saw him.

HORTENSIA: No te entiedo.

LUPE: Lettie got the car, Mom.

HORTENSIA: I know, m'ija. *(To Leticia.)* But don' think this means you are free to go wherever you please now. Es para ir al trabajo, no más.

LETICIA: I paid for it.

HORTENSIA: And who's paid for you for the las' eighteen years of your life? *(She doesn't respond, takes out her keys and dangles them in front of the baby.)*

LETICIA: *(With a thick "chola" accent.)* Hey, little guy. You wannu go cruising with me, ése? *(Hortensia takes out a paper and powder, etc. from the diaper bag.)*

HORTENSIA: She brought enough things for a week. And she gave me along list of 'structions. *(Pulls out the list.)* You think I di'nt already have three babies of my own. *(To baby, changing the diaper.)* ¡Fuchi! Apesta. *(The baby sprays her.)* ¡Ay Dios! Miren. He soaked me. *(Wiping herself.)* No m'ijito, you haf' to learn not to shoot tu pajarito in the air. I forgot since I had you girls. Riguito use to do the same thing. I'd get it right in the face sometimes.

LUPE: Ugh!

HORTENSIA: They don't know yet to control their little peepees.

LUPE: Let me have the keys, Lettie. *(She gives them to her.)*

LETICIA: He is a little cutie, but I don't know about that blonde hair.

LUPE: *(Dangling the keys.)* The rest of him is brown.

HORTENSIA: Mi güerito. He's as purty as they get to be. *(Changing him.)* Miren, su pajarito es igual al de Rigo when he was a baby.

LETICIA: Please, spare me.

LUPE: *(Giggling.)* Really?

HORTENSIA: Igualito. *(To the baby.)* You got your papi's thing, mi Riguito. *(To her daughters.)* Dicen que esta parte siempre es la true color del hombre, el color de su . . . nature.

LETICIA: Does that make him a real Mexican then?

HORTENSIA: Mira, que lindo es . . . like a little jewel. Mi machito. Tha's one thing, you know, the men can never take from us. The birth of a son. Somos las creadoras. Without us women, they be not'ing but a dream.

LETICIA: Well, I don't see you getting so much credit.

HORTENSIA: But the woman knows. Tú no entiendes. Wail until you have your own son.

LETICIA: Who knows? Maybe I won't have kids.

HORTENSIA: Adió. Then you should of been born a man. *(Hortensia finishes changing the baby.)*

LETICIA: I'm gonna go wash the car. You want to help, Lupe?

LUPE: *(Dangling the keys above the baby.)* I'll be there in a second.

LETICIA: Well, give me the keys, then. *(She does. Leticia starts to exit.)*

HORTENSIA: When you're done, you can go pick up the panza from Pedro's Place. I want to make menudo for the morning.

LETICIA: All right. All right. *(She exits.)*

HORTENSIA: Ay! They grow up so fast, Lupita. In only minutes, los muchachitos are already standing at the toilet, their legs straight like a man's. I remember sometimes being in the kitchen and hearing little Riguito . . . he must have been only three or so, going to the toilet by himself. The toilet seat flipped back. Bang! it would go. Then the stream from his baby's body. But the sound was like a man's full . . . y fuerte. It gives you a kind of comfort, that sound. And I knew the time would fly so fast. In minutes, he would be a man. *(To the baby.)* You, too. ¿No, m'ijito? You got your papi's thing. El color de la tierra. A sleeping mountain, with a little worm of life in it. Una joya. *(Horstensia strokes the infant.)* Ya ya, duérmete, mi chulito.

LUPE: Duérmete. *(Fade out.)*

Zen Gravy

Sharon Bandy
1998

Scene: A kitchen in Suburbia. Thanksgiving Day. Grace is making
gravy. She has spent the bulk of her life trying to please her sister
and her late mother.

Margaret, mid-forties, wearing all black, exotic jewelry.
Grace, her sister—frumpier, wearing an apron, 30s.
Betsy, mid-thirties, Texas-southern. A neighbor.

MARGARET: Gravy is like a strange dog, Grace. It senses fear.

GRACE: Funny. *(Pause.)* I wish I could remember what Mama said to
do with the flour. Always pour it in before the drippings? Or
always put it in last? *Always* something.

MARGARET: You've either got the gravy gene or you don't. Mama
had. And I sure as hell don't. Give me that spoon. Forget the
spoon . . . *(Margaret digs through the kitchen drawer.)*

MARGARET: You should be using a whisk anyway. Do you even have
a goddamned whisk? I know Mama did.

GRACE: Margaret, SIT DOWN.

MARGARET: Well, I don't know why you've got to get so snippy all of
a sudden. I was just trying to help.

GRACE: Thank you, but I'm doing just fine.

MARGARET: What time did you tell Betsy to come over?

GRACE: Around two, I told her. She should be here shortly. She's
bringing rolls and pie. Such a sweet girl. Too bad about her and
Rick. I always thought they got on so well. Never heard any
yelling. Their lawn always looked so nice.

MARAGRET: What the hell does a nice lawn have to do with a happy
marriage?

GRACE: All I'm saying is that everything looked so perfect over there
. . . That's all I'm saying, Margaret. Can you try not to bite my
head off every time I open my mouth? It is Thanksgiving, after all!
(Throws big clump of flour in gravy pan.) Oh no, it's going to be

lumpy. All these lumps. Now I remember! Mama said "Always sprinkle the flour into the grease." Oh well—looks like we'll just have lumpy gravy.

MARGARET: You're fighting it too much, dear. Be one with the gravy.

GRACE: I really don't have time for your Zen-speak right now Margaret. If you haven't noticed, I'm trying to get Thanksgiving dinner on the table.

MARGARET: You really should try it. It might bring a little peace into your life. You're so angry. Back in my yoga days I could meditate for four hours straight without . . .

GRACE: If you will remember, your yoga days were followed by your physical-therapy-slash-chiropractor days, and you still walk with a limp, SO DON'T ZEN ME!

MARGARET: I just want you to relax a little Grace, dear. If you close your eyes while you stir you can feel the energy of the gravy. Be one with it.

GRACE: I am one with it Margaret *(Throws spoon to the floor)* I am lumpy, slowly thickening, and a blotchy shade of beige—I *AM* the God-damned gravy!

MARGARET: Sit down dear. You're taking this much too hard.

GRACE: Look at us Margaret. Here we are, two divorced women, waiting for a soon-to-be divorced third to join our club, for a pathetic Thanksgiving dinner. We're not even a family anymore. Can't you see that? This is all pretend. We have no kids, never had a father to speak of, and now we have no mother on top of it. All we have is each other. And we're so different, it's as if we're not related at all. I bet if we met each other, I mean, if we weren't sisters, we wouldn't want to spend a minute together. Not one minute . . .

(Doorbell rings.)

GRACE: Come on in Betsy. Door's open . . . *(Grace goes to stove to tend to gravy. Betsy enters briskly. She carries a basket of dinner rolls and a pastry box with a pie in it. She is Texas-southern, in her early 30s, perkily dressed with lots of makeup and well-tended hair.)*

BETSY: Oh my goodness, what a glorious smell. There's nothing quite like the smell of Thanksgiving turkey. I'm sorry I'm a little late. Did I miss anything? It really was so nice of you to invite me over. I think we're going to have a great time, don't you? I wasn't sure how I was going to feel about today, you know. What with Rick just two miles away at his folks' . . . without me. But I feel fine. Really, I feel just fine.

(Margaret looks at Betsy.)

BETSY: No, really . . .

MARGARET: Well great, then, We WILL have a good time. I think I'll put on some music.

BETSY: Oh, music sounds like a good idea. I've been listening to a lot more music. You know, since Rick left. The house just seems so empty, so quiet. I really am fond of the older stuff, the . .

(Margaret goes to the stereo and turns it on. Sitar music wafts painfully and loudly in the air, interrupting Betsy's rambling. Grace reacts by grabbing a bottle of aspirin and cupping her hand under the sink to catch water. Margaret reacts by going back to the stereo and turning the music off abruptly.)

GRACE: It really is nice of you to join us today. I imagine you're wishing you were down in Texas with your family?

BETSY: Oh, not really. We never celebrated Thanksgiving like y'all do. My Daddy'd usually barbecue up a big ol' batch of ribs and we'd stuff ourselves silly. Mama's a terrible cook, so she saved face by not having to cook a traditional dinner, and people thought we were eccentric—Mama likes that . . . people thinking she's eccentric.

GRACE: So does Margaret.

MARGARET: Humpff.

BETSY: Oh, I don't think you're eccentric at all Margaret. You dress a little different, sure, but you're really nice and you do normal things, drive a normal car, eat normal food I imagine, *(Nervous laugh.)* I guess I'll see soon enough . . .

GRACE: We're almost ready to eat. Margaret has set a lovely table, and I think the turkey is almost . . .

(Telephone rings. Margaret and Grace look at each other, as if to ask "Who could that be?" Grace moves to answer the phone.)

GRACE: I won't be a minute. *(On phone)* Hello. Yes, this is the Doyle residence, who is this? Yes, this is Grace. Who is this? *(Pause.)* Who? Oh my God.

(Grace drops the phone. Margaret picks it up.)

MARGARET: Hello, this is Margaret Doyle. May I help you? Who? No shit? *(Pause.)* Well, Mr. Doyle, it was kind of you to call after—let's see—how long has it been? Oh yes, thirty-five years, but we're not interested . . . Mother? She's not interested either . . . She's dead. *(Margaret slams down phone.)*

GRACE: You hung up on him? Did you get a number? I wanted to talk to him.

MARGARET: Oh sure, you really looked like you wanted to talk to him when you threw the phone down.

GRACE: I dropped it! It was a shock, that's all, and then you . . . you went and hung up on him. *(Close to tears.)*

BETSY: I'm afraid I'll have to agree with Grace here. She did drop the phone. Definitely a drop, not a throw. Shouldn't we begin eating soon?

MARGARET: What would you have to say to that man, Grace? What? Come on over? We're having a warm family Thanksgiving with turkey and stuffing and lumpy gravy—we're just missing a family? Love to have ya? Huh? Is that what you were going to say?

BETSY: Grace dear, don't cry, Margaret doesn't mean what she's saying. I'd guess you're both just a little shocked that's all.

GRACE: Margaret, calm down. We all should calm down. We've just got to think this through, that's all. What if he calls back? What'll we do? We need a plan.

MARGARET: What if he calls back? Are you serious?! Let's see . . . I'm forty-one now . . . carry the two . . . I'll be seventy-seven when he calls back. I'll worry about it then!

(Black out)

Barbies

Linnet Harlan
1998

Scene: The living room of Barbie's Dream House. Women's clothes, shoes, and accessories of all kinds are strewn about the room.

Of Note: The movements of the characters should be somewhat stiff to emulate Barbie movements. They only move at the shoulders and the hips.

Blonde Barbie, dressed in an elegant gown.
Brunette Barbie, in a teddy over which she will try on as many outfits as possible during the scene.
Bad Barbie, shorter than the others, dressed in black leather, wild hair.

BRUNETTE BARBIE: P-ss-ss-t! Blonde Barbie, is The Girl gone?
BLOND BARBIE: I think so.
>*(Both Barbies rise. Brunette Barbie slips into one of the party dresses. Blonde Barbie rummages around the room looking for something. Note: Whenever possible, Brunette Barbie is trying on clothes and admiring herself in a mirror.)*

BRUNETTE BARBIE: All I ever get to wear is uniforms. I hate being Waitress Barbie or Nurse Barbie.
BLONDE BARBIE: Have you seen my philosophy books?
BRUNETTE BARBIE: *(In an elegant gown.)* Will you zip me up?
BLONDE BARBIE: Better not let The Girl catch you wearing that.
BRUNETTE BARBIE: She never lets me wear any of the party dresses! Why does she hate me?
BLONDE BARBIE: She doesn't hate you. *(Blonde Barbie finds her books and sits down to study them. She pulls her long blonde hair back in a pony tail and puts on a pair of thick glasses.)*
BRUNETTE BARBIE: She has brown hair too.
BLONDE BARBIE: It's a cultural phenomenon. I studied it last year in sociology . . .
BRUNETTE BARBIE: You're not going to talk about sociology again . . .

BLONDE BARBIE: There's a cultural preference for lightness . . .

BRUNETTE BARBIE: I'm not listening.

BLONDE BARBIE: Some commentators believe it stems from notions of racial purity . .

BRUNETTE BARBIE: *(Singing.)* Ninety-nine bottles of beer on the wall, ninety-nine bottles of beer . . .

BLONDE BARBIE: While other commentators note that even as far back as the Renaissance . . .

BRUNETTE BARBIE: If one of those bottles should happen to fall . . .

BLONDE BARBIE: You do have a mind, you know.

BRUNETTE BARBIE: Sociology! Philosophy! If you're not careful, you're gong to end up like *(She whispers.)* Bad Barbie.
(At Bad Barbie's name, we hear a knock and Bad Barbie enters. She is dressed in a black leather jacket, a black tee shirt and black Levis. Her hair, styled in a slightly menacing manner, is at least two different colors, preferably neither of which occurs naturally in humans. She carries a cigarette and a bottle of beer.)

BAD BARBIE: Did I hear my name?

BLONDE BARBIE: Hey, B.B. Just the person I've been wanting to see. *(They exchange high fives.)*

BRUNETTE BARBIE: Oh, no, Bad Barbie—

BAD BARBIE: Bad Barbie!!?

BRUNETTE BARBIE: I mean Motorcycle Barbie. I mean Punk Barbie. I mean . . .

BAD BARBIE: Relax, kid. I like the name Bad Barbie. I earned it. So, what's the problem?

BRUNETTE BARBIE: Problem? There's no problem. Absolutely no—

BLONDE BARBIE: She doesn't like being a brunette.

BRUNETTE BARBIE: That's not it.

BLONDE BARBIE: You hold her hand, B.B. I've got to get some studying done. *(She exits.)*

BAD BARBIE: Tell Bad Barbie all about it.

BRUNETTE BARBIE: I never get to be Wedding Barbie.

BAD BARBIE: Jealous, huh, kid?

BRUNETTE BARBIE: No . . .

BAD BARBIE: It's not all it's cracked up to be.

BRUNETTE BARBIE: How would you know? You never spent time with Ken.

BAD BARBIE: Time? Babe, it felt like eternity!

BRUNETTE BARBIE: But he's so handsome in his tuxedo!

BAD BARBIE: The lights are on, but nobody's home.

BRUNETTE BARBIE: He's so romantic.

BAD BARBIE: Romantic? He spent less time with me than he did with his blow-drier.

BRUNETTE BARBIE: You never were Wedding Barbie.

BAD BARBIE: Kiddo, I did the whole nine yards—back before you were around. Wedding Barbie, the Tropical Honeymoon Resort. Ken. *(Slight pause.)* You know, it's only a bump.

BRUNETTE BARBIE: Huh? What are you talking . . . ? *(She gets it.)* Oh.

BAD BARBIE: Look, sweetie. If being Wedding Barbie were that great, I'd be blonde.

BRUNETTE BARBIE: But it's the perfect life. Clothes. Men . . .

BAD BARBIE: No men. Ken.

BRUNETTE BARBIE: Glamour. Attention.

BAD BARBIE: So, dye your hair.

BRUNETTE BARBIE: The Girl loves her more than she loves me.

BAD BARBIE: So get rid of her.

BRUNETTE BARBIE: How?

BAD BARBIE: *(Shrugs, takes a scarf that is lying nearby and winds one end around one hand, the other end around the other hand, making a garroting device. She snaps it taut.)* I learned a few things from G.I. Joe.

BRUNETTE BARBIE: We couldn't!

BAD BARBIE: Why not?

BRUNETTE BARBIE: The Girl wouldn't like it.

BAD BARBIE: Honey, you care way too much about what The Girl thinks. But okay. I'll talk to Blonde Barbie. *(She drains the remainder from the beer bottle.)* Tell her to come on in while you get me a refill.

BRUNETTE BARBIE: What if she doesn't want to come?

BAD BARBIE: Sugar, everybody wants to talk to B.B.

(Brunette Barbie exits. A few moments later, Blond Barbie enters.)

BLONDE BARBIE: You have my stuff? *(Bad Barbie pulls a plastic sack of pills from her jacket and hands it to Blonde Barbie who gives Bad Barbie some money.)* Finals are next week.

BAD BARBIE: Still hitting the books, huh?

BLONDE BARBIE: This is my last semester. Look, can you get me any of that human growth hormone?

BAD BARBIE: Blondie, you're not human.

BLONDE BARBIE: I'll never get a job! I'm only eleven-and-a-half inches tall!

BAD BARBIE: What about all this stuff around here? Doctor Barbie. Newscaster Barbie.

BLONDE BARBIE: I've checked. To be a medical student, you have to be human.

BAD BARBIE: But not to be a doctor. *(Blond Barbie shakes her head.)* TV news then. Most of them are plastic.

BLONDE BARBIE: I'm going into talk radio.

BAD BARBIE: You are definitely more human than Howard Stern.

BLONDE BARBIE: But I've got to grow another half inch! They've got standards!

BAD BARBIE: Not as long as Rush Limbaugh is on the air.

BLONDE BARBIE: They won't even consider anyone under a foot tall.

BAD BARBIE: I always thought they were just mental midgets.

BLONDE BARBIE: You've got to get me that human growth hormone.

BAD BARBIE: Slow down, babe. I don't "got" to do anything for you.

BLONDE BARBIE: You're forgetting what I know.

BAD BARBIE: What?

BLONDE BARBIE: You think I haven't seen you putting the moves on Brunette Barbie?

BAD BARBIE: It's nothing . . .

BLONDE BARBIE: You think I don't know about you before The Girl got you?

BAD BARBIE: That was a long time . . .

BLONDE BARBIE: Brunette Barbie asked me the other day why you were so short.

BAD BARBIE: Stop . . .

BLONDE BARBIE: What are your chances if she knows you aren't a Barbie at all, Skipper?

BAD BARBIE: There's nothing wrong with being a Skipper.

BLONDE BARBIE: Sure, that's why you call yourself "Bad Barbie."

BAD BARBIE: Skippers are great dolls.

BLONDE BARBIE: Name one thing a Skipper has that any Barbie would want.

BAD BARBIE: She likes me. She won't care.

BLONDE BARBIE: Then let's tell her right now. Bru . . .

(Bad Barbie puts her hand over Blonde Barbie's mouth.)

BAD BARBIE: Okay, okay. I'll get you the hormone.

BLONDE BARBIE: Very wise of you, B.B.

BAD BARBIE: But I need a favor.

BLONDE BARBIE: You're hardly in the position to ask for favors, Skipper.

BAD BARBIE: She wants to be Wedding Barbie.

BLONDE BARBIE: Haven't you told her about Ken? *(Bad Barbie shrugs.)* I get it—if she gets what she wants, you'll get . . . what you want? *(Bad Barbie says nothing.)* The Girl would . . . *(Slight pause.)* But I can handle The Girl.

BAD BARBIE: Thanks . . .

BLONDE BARBIE: But I don't disappear until I have that hormone in my hand.

BAD BARBIE: I'll get right on it. *(She begins to exit.)*

(Brunette Barbie enters, carrying a bottle of beer.)

BAD BARBIE: Sorry, kid, I got to split. But that thing we were talking about *(She nods her head toward Blonde Barbie)*, I think I've got it taken care of.

BRUNETTE BARBIE: Really? *(She rushes over and gives* Bad Barbie *a kiss on the cheek.)* How can I ever thank you? *(Blonde Barbie and Bad Barbie exchange a look.)*

BAD BARBIE: See ya tomorrow, kiddo. *(She ruffles Brunette Barbie's hair and exits.)*

BRUNETTE BARBIE: Don't you just love her?

BLONDE BARBIE: The question is "Do you?"

BRUNETTE BARBIE: I'm not going to discuss silly sociology. I've got a wedding to plan.

(Blonde Barbie shrugs and begins to hum "Skip to My Lou," while she measures a half inch above her head on the wall and tries to stretch herself to be that tall. Brunette Barbie ignores her and Blonde Barbie begins to sing, heavily emphasizing each "Skip." As the lights fade, Brunette Barbie begins to try on a wedding dress and veil while Blonde Barbie swallows one of her pills, assisted by a swig of beer.)
(Curtain.)

Ladies in Retirement

Edward Percy and Reginald Denham
1939

Scene: At the living room window, late afternoon sun pours in. Louisa is gazing through a telescope at the marshes visible through the window. Ellen enters from the kitchen, as Louisa spots her sister Emily returning home. Louisa naively believes that this house belongs to Ellen and not Leonora and that her visit here is actually permanent.

Louisa, elderly, simple-witted and frail, fluttering, fretful, childlike.

Ellen, Louisa's younger sister—housekeeper to Leonora, a strong, clearheaded woman.

Leonora, 60s, Roman Catholic, energetic and good-hearted, retired.

ELLEN: You oughtn't to be standing by that window, darling. The wind's turning quite cold.

LOUISA: *(Rather fearfully.)* Don't be cross with me. Ellen. I'm so happy—looking.

ELLEN: *(Taking up* Louisa's *shawl and arranging it tenderly round her shoulders.)* Well, put your shawl on, then.

LOUISA: Oh, but I'm strong. Much stronger than when I came. *(Looking through the telescope.)* It must be quite rough on the river. Do you see the waves? They're like little white feathers blowing about.

ELLEN: Is that Emily coming over the marsh?

LOUISA: *(Altering the direction of the telescope.)* Yes. Her apron's loaded. I wonder what she's picked up this time. Oh, Ellen! Isn't is exciting? She brings in such pretty things. I wish I were brave like Emily. I should like to take long walks, too, and pick up things and bring them home. Perhaps I shall be able to when I've stayed here longer.

ELLEN: I'm sure you will, darling

LOUISA: *(Anxiously.)* I shall be staying here, shan't I? You're not planning to send me away, are you Ellen?

ELLEN: No, of course I'm not.

LOUISA: This is what you always promised us. A little house in the country and the three of us being in it together. You and Emily and me.

ELLEN: Yes, dear. That's the one thing I've schemed for—ever since we had to give up the old house.

LOUISA: I wonder who's living there now. I often think of the rhododendron hedge and the flag irises down by the river. And our copper beech tree! Do you remember how we three planted it, Ellen—with father looking on and laughing at us?

ELLEN: I expect Richmond's changed—like everything else.

LOUISA: Of course this could never be like Richmond! But it's nice here.

ELLEN: And Miss Fiske's been very kind to us.

LOUISA: And Miss Fiske . . . May I tell you something, Ellen? Just one of my secrets?

ELLEN: Of course, darling.

LOUISA: I don't like Miss Fiske. I don't like her religion. Can't we send her away? Then it would be really just the three of us.

ELLEN: But I keep telling you, Louisa—it's her house.

LOUISA: *(Shaking her head.)* Oh, no. You'll never make me believe that. You've always had your own house. This is yours. Here are your things. You've always had your own house, Ellen, haven't you? You're the clever one. And you'll always keep me near you, won't you? I don't want to be sent back to Kennington. To those awful ugly streets. Nothing to look at from the window.

ELLEN: Darling, I've promised you. I won't send you back.

LOUISA: I think Miss Fiske wants me to go. She wants us both to go— Emily and me. I think so.

ELLEN: You're just imagining it.

LOUISA: No, I'm not, Ellen. I'm not imagining it.

ELLEN: But, darling, I'm sure I can persuade her to let you stay.

LOUISA: Yes, Ellen. I'm sure you can. You can do anything. *(She has wandered across the room and stands looking at the statue of the Virgin with wondering disapproval.)* I wish you'd take this away. It isn't right to worship idols, is it?

ELLEN: We can't take it away. It doesn't belong to us.

LOUISA: Father always said that Roman Catholics aren't saved. I don't trust people who aren't saved.

(The front door opens and Leonora sails in. She is carrying a basket of ripe William pears. This time she is dressed in a gay blue gown. She is kind and charming to her guests, but you can see that they have begun to get badly on her nerves.)

LEONORA: *(Brightly.)* I've just been down to the Priory. Look what the Reverend Mother's given me.

ELLEN: Oh, what lovely pears! Look, Louisa.

LEONORA: Yes. They're Williams. Have one, dear.

ELLEN: *(Taking one.)* May I?

LEONORA: Won't you·have one, Miss Louisa?

LOUISA: Did you say they came from the convent?

LEONORA: Yes.

LOUISA: *(Shrinking a little.)* Oh . . . I don't think I . . .

ELLEN: *(It is almost a command)* Do, dear.

LOUISA: *(Taking one.)* Thank you. May I eat it later?

LEONORA: Of course.

ELLEN: *(As though to cover Louisia's ungraciousness.)* I think I'll keep mine till supper, too.

LEONORA: *(Sitting at the table)* Well, I'm going to eat one now.

(Ellen goes to the dresser and fetches a dessert plate and silver knife and fork which she sets before Leonora. She has laid her own and Louisa's pear on a plate on the dresser.)

ELLEN: They're beautiful pears.

LEONORA: They're from that tree by the pond.

ELLEN: The one that looks so lovely in spring?

LEONORA: Yes.

LOUISA: *(Almost clapping her hands.)* Oh, I shall like to see that!

LEONORA: *(Dryly.)* I wish you could. What have you been doing all today?

LOUISA: I've been resting. And looking at things.

ELLEN: She's been watching the sailing barges going up and down the Thames.

LOUISA: There've been some big steamers passing, too. It's been the turn of the tide. They've been going up and down. I do think people are brave to go on the water in boats.

LEONORA: *(Beginning on the pear.)* It doesn't strike me as particularly brave. No braver than living in a city where you might be run over or have a chimney-pot blow down on your head.

LOUISA: But I don't like living in a city. Just for that reason. And I don't care to go out. I'm not very brave. I don't go out in the streets. That's why I like being here. It's so lovely—so safe.

LEONORA: I don't know what you'll do when you go back to London, then!

LOUISA: *(Like a sly child.)* Ah, but I'm not going back to London.

LEONORA: Aren't you?

ELLEN: That's just Louisa's way of telling you how much she's enjoying it here.

LOUISA: Yes, I am enjoying it.

ELLEN: That telescope's been such a pleasure to her. She's never had much opportunity of using it before.
(Louisa fetches her telescope and exhibits it to Leonora while she eats. Leonora eyes it with no particular pleasure.)

LOUISA: Yes. It's a beautiful instrument, isn't it? I keep it beautifully polished, don't I? It belonged to the man I was going to marry. He was the captain of a sailing ship. It was lost in a typhoon in the Indian Ocean. They were sailing from Madagascar with a cargo of raffia grass. You know, it's the thing they tie up plants with in gardens. Fancy a boatload of something you tie up plants with in gardens! Funny, isn't it? They were all drowned. He hadn't taken this with him on his last voyage. His sister gave it me. I've kept it ever since.

LEONORA: Oh dear! What's a tragic story!

LOUISA: It doesn't seem tragic to me now. You see, I've no picture of him, and it's so long ago I've almost forgotten what he looked like.
(She takes the telescope back to the window. Leonora rises, thankful to escape.)

LEONORA: How sticky these pears make one! I must go and dip my fingers.

(She goes out through the kitchen door. Louisa picks up her workbag and slips the two pears Leonora gave them into it.)

ELLEN: *(Sharply.)* What are you doing? You mustn't do that!

LOUISA: *(In a whisper.)* I'll burn them. Before I go to bed. In the stove in the kitchen. I'll slip in when no one's there.

ELLEN: Give them to me at once!

LOUISA: *(Handing them over like a naughty child.)* You mustn't be cross with me, Ellen. They come from the nuns.

ELEN: *(Putting them back on the dresser.)* The nuns didn't make the tree, Louisa.

LOUISA: No. I suppose they didn't. I see *(Nodding.)* Yes. Yes, I was wrong.

PART THREE:

SCENES FOR TWO MEN AND ONE WOMAN

Oedipus at Colonus

Sophokles
405 B.C.

Scene: Colonus in Greece, where the oracle prophesied that Oedipus
would die. Early afternoon on an outcropping of rocks.

Oedipus, 20 years after being banished, blind, aged, ragged but car-
rying himself with pride.
Antigonê, his daughter.
A stranger

OEDIPUS: Child of the blind old man, daughter, Antigonê,
  What land have we come to now, what town?
  Who will give scanty courtesy today
  To wandering old Oedipus? I ask but little,
  And receive still less; and yet I'm satisfied.
  Suffering and time, vast time, have taught me acceptance
  Of life's adversities, as has nobility of birth.
  But now, child, tell me, is there a place
  Where we might find a seat—
  On public ground or sacred?
  (Extending his hands to her.)
  Give me your arm; lead me there.
  And when I'm seated, we'll inquire where we have come to;
  As strangers we must learn from the local people
  And do as they do.
  (Antigonê looks off to the right in the direction of Athens.)
ANTIGONÊ: Father, poor, tired, wandering old Oedipus—
  The towers that crown the city are a long way off.
  As for this place, it is surely sacred ground—
  You can sense it: heavy with olive, laurel and vine:
  A haven for the song and flutter of nightingales.
  *(She leads him to a natural stone seat resembling a throne within
  the confines of the grove.)*
  There now, rest a while on this rough stone.

You've come a long road for a man of your years.

OEDIPUS: Help me sit; care for the blind old man.

ANTIGONÊ: Time has taught me some things, too, father. *(She backs him onto the stone seat, then arranges his clothes, perhaps placing his walking stick at his feet.)*

OEDIPUS: Can you tell me what place this is?

ANTIGONÊ: The city off there is Athens.

Here, I don't know.

OEDIPUS: We learned as much from travelers!

ANTIGONÊ: Shall I go ask its name?

OEDIPUS: Yes, child; and if anyone lives here.

ANTIGONÊ: Oh, that they do! But no need to leave.

There's a man not far off: I can see him.

OEDIPUS: Is he coming in our direction?

(A Citizen of Colonos enters right and approaches them while also remaining outside the Sacred Precinct.)

ANTIGONÊ: He's here already.

Say what you think right;

He's by our side.

OEDIPUS: Stranger—my daughter, whose eyes serve us both,

Tells me of our good fortune in meeting you here.

I think that you have come to learn who we are,

And perhaps can shed some light on—

CITIZEN: No, no questions! Not yet!

First you must leave that seat at once!

The ground you stand on is sacred;

It mustn't be touched!

Leave it now, please.

OEDIPUS: What ground is this?

What god does it honor?

CITIZEN: It mustn't be violated; no one may live here:

The Terrible Goddesses hold it in power:

Daughters of the Earth, Daughters of Darkness.

OEDIPUS: Tell me, sir, by what dread name are they known,

So that I may do them honor.

CITIZEN: We here call them the Gentle All-Seeing Ones;

Though elsewhere they are honored by other names.

OEDIPUS: May they receive me gently, then,
    For I will never leave this refuge.

CITIZEN: What are you saying?

OEDIPUS: My destiny is here.

CITIZEN: Well, if that's true, I don't dare turn you out;
    Not without word first from the city;
    Not before I report to them what you're doing.

OEDIPUS: In god's name, stranger, don't refuse
    A poor wanderer the knowledge that he seeks.

CITIZEN: Ask me what you want; I'll answer.

OEDIPUS: Tell me, what is this place we have come to?

CITIZEN: I'm glad to tell you whatever I know.
    Everything you see, the country round you,
    Is holy ground, held in protective power
    By mighty Poseidon; but the fire-wielding Titan
    Prometheus is honored here as well.
    The ground you rest on there is known by all
    As the Brazen-Floored Threshold of Earth, bulwark
    Of Athens. And the neighboring fields and the people
    Are known by the name of our founding father,
    The horseman Kolonos, whose statue you see there.
    This land of ours may not be honored in legend,
    But it has a place in the hearts of those that love it.

OEDIPUS: The people really live on their lands?

CITIZEN: Indeed they do; and named for their hero.

OEDIPUS: Who rules the people? A king or themselves?

CITIZEN: The King of Athens. He lives in the city.

OEDIPUS: Who is this king who holds the power?

CITIZEN: Thêseus, the son of King Aigeus before him.

OEDIPUS: Could someone be sent to him with a message?

CITIZEN: To deliver one or to call him here?

OEDIPUS: A small favor brings him great gain.

CITIZEN: What is to be gained from a man without eyes?

OEDIPUS: My every word will radiate light!

CITIZEN: Listen, stranger, I'm trying to help you here.

I can see that you are of noble birth,
Despite your luck.
Stay where you are, right there,
Don't move, and I'll go tell the people who live here.
It is theirs to decide whether you leave or stay.
(He goes off right.) (Silence.)
OEDIPUS: Child, Antigonê, has the stranger gone yet?
ANTIGONÊ: He has; you may speak freely now; we're alone.
(Oedipus rises from his seat and approaches the altar. Antigonê assists him. Once he is at the altar, facing outward, he shakes her hands from him imperiously and, bracing himself on the stone of the altar, slowly and painfully lowers himself to his knees. Antigonê retreats and, finally, kneels at a distance.)
(Silence.)
OEDIPUS: Dread Goddesses, you whose eyes are terrible,
It is here on this seat in your Sacred Grove
That I first find rest in this land.
Be gracious to Apollo and to me:
For when he cried aloud those prophesies of evil
That would afflict my life, he also spoke
Of this resting place to crown long years of suffering:
A land at journey's end where I should find
A seat belonging to the Awful Goddesses.
And there, too, he said, I would find a home
To round out the days of my miserable being:
Conferring on them who received me a great benefit;
A curse on those who rejected me.

Man's Disobedience—The York Pageant of the Coopers

Anonymous
1500s

Scene: The Garden of Eden. The recounting of the Temptation of Adam.

Satan, the fallen angel.
Eve
Adam

SATAN: For woe my wits are in a whirl here!
　　　This moves me greatly in my mind:
　　　That Godhead whom I saw so clear
　　　I perceived that He would take his nature
　　　From a being of a kind
　　　That he had wrought, and I was angered
　　　That these not angels were to be!
　　　For we were fair and bright
　　　And therefore thought that He
　　　Our nature take he might
　　　Yet He disdained me.

　　　The nature of *man* He thought to take
　　　And thereat had I great envy.
　　　But He has made to man a mate,
　　　So fast to her I will haste
　　　That ready way,
　　　With purpose fixed to put by
　　　And try to steal from God that prey.
　　　My labor were well set
　　　Might I him so betray,
　　　And from him this mankind get,
　　　And this soon I shall essay.

Scene 2

(In Paradise, Satan appears in the shape of a "worm" —that is, a serpent.)

SATAN: In a worm's likeness I will wend
   And attempt to feign a rousing lie:
   Eve! Eve!

EVE: Who is there?

SATAN: I! A Friend!
   And for thy good is the journey
   I hither sought.
   Of all the fruit that you see high
   In Paradise, why eat you nought?

EVE: We may of them take
   All that good is in our thought
   Save one tree, lest we mistake
   And to harm be brought.

SATAN: And why *that tree*—that would I wit—
   Any more than any other nigh?

EVE: For our Lord God forbids to try
   The fruit thereof. Adam and I
   May not come near
   For if we did both should die,
   He said, and lose our solace here.

SATAN: Yea, Eve, attend to my intent
   Take heed and you shall hear
   What all this matter meant
   That he moved you to fear.

   To eat thereof he did forbid,
   I know it well. This is his will
   Because he would that none should know
   The great virtues that are hid
   Therein. For thou wilt see
   That who eats this fruit of good and ill
   Shall be as knowing as is He.

EVE: Why, what thing art thou

That tells this tale to me?
SATAN: A worm that knoweth well how
    Ye both may worshipped be.
EVE: What worship should we win thereby?
    To eat thereof it needs us nought—
    We have lordship to make mastery
    Of all things that in earth are wrought.
SATAN: Woman, away!
    To a *greater* state ye may be brought
    If ye will do as I shall say.
EVE: To do this we are loath
    For this would our God dismay.
SATAN: Nay, certain, it will bring no hurt,
    Eat it safely ye may.

    For peril none therein lies
    But advantage and a great winning.
    For right as God ye shall be wise,
    And peer to Him in everything.
    Ay, gods shall ye be,
    Of ill and good you will have knowing,
    And be as wise as is he.
EVE: Is this truth that thou says?
SATAN: Yea, why believest thou not me?
    I would by no kind of ways
    Tell nought but truth to thee.
EVE: Then will I to thy teaching trust,
    And take this fruit unto our food.
    (And then she must take the apple.)
SATAN: Bite on boldly, be not abashed.
    And make Adam too amend his mood
    And enlarge his bliss
    (Then Satan retires.)
EVE: Adam, have here of fruit full good!
ADAM: Alas, woman, why took'st thou this?
    Our Lord commanded us both

To beware this tree of his.
Thy work will make him wroth:
Alas, thou hast done amiss!
EVE: Nay, Adam, grieve thee not at it,
And I shall tell the reason why:
A worm has given me to wit
We shall be as gods, thou and I,
If that we eat
Here of this tree. Adam, thereby,
Fail not this worship so to get,
For we shall be as wise
As God that is so great,
And also of the same great price.
Therefore, eat of this meat.
ADAM: To eat it I would not eschew
Might I be sure of thy sayings.
EVE: Bite on boldly, for it is true:
We shall be gods and know all things.
ADAM: To win that name,
I shall taste it at thy teaching.
(He takes and eats. Instantly, he is seized with remorse.)
Alas, what have I done? For Shame!
I'll counsel, woe worth thee!
Ah, Eve, thou art to blame,
To this hast thou enticed me.—
And my body now fills me with shame,
(Looking at himself.)
For I am naked, as I think—
EVE: Alas, Adam, right so am I!
ADAM: And for sorrow sere why might we not sink?
For we have grieved God Almighty
That made me man,
Broken His bidding bitterly,
Alas, that ever we began!
This work, Eve, hast thou wrought,
And made this bad bargain.

EVE: Nay, Adam, blame me nought.
ADAM: Away, dear Eve, whom then?
EVE: The worm to blame well worthy were:
    With tales untrue we were betrayed.
ADAM: Alas that I listened to thy lore,
    Or trusted the trifles thou to me said,
    So may I bid,
    For I may curse that bitter braid
    And dreary thing that I did.
    And our shape, with shame it grieves—
    Wherewith shall our bodies be hid?
    (Eve picks up some leaves, twines them together, and starts to cover herself, and gives Adam some leaves too.)
EVE: Let us take this fig-leaf
    Since now befalls us this grief.
ADAM: Right as thou say'st so shall it be,
    For we are naked and all bare.
    Full wondrous fain would I hide me
    From the Lord's sight, if I wist where;
    Where, I would care nought!

Fifteen Strings of Cash

Shih Wi Kuan

Scene: Yu Hu-lu has received money from his sister-in-law to revive his business, but he returns home and scares his daughter with a cruel trick.

Yu Hu-lu, a failed businessman, drunk, owns a pork shop.
Ch'in Ki-Hsin, his old friend, owns an oil and salt shop.
Su Hsü-Chaün, Yu Hu-lu's daughter, teens–20s.

Of Note: The main stage is curtained off, leaving a performing area front stage. Yu Hu-lu enters left of the audience. He is drunk and staggers in his steps, which nevertheless are performed with the formalized patterns of movement common to traditional acting. The foot movement used is known as yun-pu and is carried out by placing the left foot apart, dragging it up obliquely to the right foot three times in succession, and then repeating the sequence with the right foot in the other direction. This gait can be alternated with a similar pattern of steps in which one foot is crossed over the other each time the body sways drunkenly but rhythmically. Over his left shoulder Yu Hu-lu carries the fifteen strings of cash, copper coins pierced through their centers and threaded on strings in the old Chinese fashion. He heaves the coins with a jingle as he drunkenly addresses the audience.

YU HU-LU: A-ah! What a weight!
(He begins to sing in the Liu Yao Ling modal pattern.)
The more wine I drink, the better I'll be;
The more money I spend, the less I'll keep.
I was sad in heart so long without trade.
To secure a loan, I've run around everywhere.
(He relapses into monologue before the audience.)
Consider me, Yu Hu-lu. Since I closed down my pork shop, I've had to rely on pawning and borrowing to keep going. Every day I've been distracted with the thought of it. My late wife's sister

lives at Kaoch'iao. She's a faithful, affectionate soul, and today she invited me to drink a couple of jugs of wine and lent me these fifteen strings of cash to go into business again. I'm feeling very happy indeed.

(He begins singing again.)

Sister's heart is full of true kindness;

Those who help the poor and needy are rare in this world.

I left her house as dusk fell.

The watch is on his round already and my journey's done.

(He relapses into monologue again.)

Before, when I bought a pig, I relied entirely on my old friend Ch'in to help me. I'm going to buy a pig tomorrow, so now I'll just go and see if he'll help. *(Crosses the stage to stand left of the audience.)* This is his door. *(Shouting.)* Hey, Ch'in, old friend, are you home? Ch'in!

CH'IN KU-HSIN: *(Behind the curtain.)* Who's that outside?

YU HU-LU: *(Feigning a girlish voice.)* It's me.

(He makes an ugly face. Ch'in' Ku-hsin comes on.)

CH'IN KU-HSIN: So it's friend Yu! It's too late to play jokes like this. What do you want?

YU HU-LU: Look at this, my old friend. *(He holds up the cash.)*

CH'IN KU-HSIN: *(His face expressing astonishment.)* Where did all that money come from?

YU HU-LU: *(Heaving the cash to the floor with a jangle and then straightening himself to speak.)* Picked it up on the street!

CH'IN KI-HSIN: You're joking again! *(He is standing to the right of Yu, right arm behind his back and left hand raised to chest height as he speaks.)*

YU HU-LU: *(Leans backward, laughing uproariously, and gesticulates with his right hand.)* I'll deceive you no more. My sister-in-law at Kaoch'iao lent me these fifteen strings of cash to go into business again. *(He stoops to pick up the cash and slings them over his shoulder again.)*

CH'IN KU-HSIN: *(Emphasizing his words with his right hand.)* Good, good! Now you've got some capital, you can open up your shop again with no more financial worries. It'll be to my advantage too; my oil and wine sales will go up. If you like, tomorrow we'll go together and buy a pig.

YU HU-LU: Thanks very much, old friend.

CH'IN KU-HSIN: But I'm afraid you're so drunk you'll forget. I'll come and call for you.

YU HU-LU: *(Stands swaying slightly and answers in a convivial tone)* Thanks very much indeed!

CH'IN KU-HSIN: See you tomorrow. *(He goes off stage to the left.)*

YU HU-LU: *(Walking unsteadily to front stage center.)* Leaving Ch'in's oil and salt store, I arrive at my own pork shop. *(He faces the curtain and calls out loudly while miming knocking at the door, coordinating voice and gesture.)* Open the door! Open the door! Open the door!

(The curtain is opened to show the interior of Yu Hu-lu's pork shop, the second acting area. The use of curtains in this way has become customary since 1949, allowing for greater use of stage settings and the disappearance from view of the old stage assistant. The stage is carpeted, as always in the Chinese theatre.

Against the curtain backdrop two rectangular panels nine feet high are placed to represent the walls of the shop. The back one, flush with the rear curtain, is painted to represent plaster and brick and has a sign suspended in the top right-hand corner. On the sign are painted Chinese characters which read "Yu's Butcher Shop." At the front of this panel and to the left, almost at center stage, is Yu Hu-lu's bed. This is a rectangular construction, a low dais painted to represent wooden planking, with a bamboo pole at each corner and crosspieces supporting an embroidered curtain looped back in front of the bed. The second wall of the shop, placed to make a wide angle with the first, to the right of the stage from the audience, is painted to represent wooden planking, against which two meat hooks hang from a wooden support. In front of this wall stands a four-legged butcher's wooden chopping block, on which a large axe is placed. This set is a concession to the naturalism that increasingly dominates the Chinese Communist stage. In the old days a simple, small wooden table with bamboo poles and curtains would have

*sufficed for the bed and that would have been all. In the context
of the highly formalized mime and movement of traditional acting, this preoccupation with set details serves little dramatic func-
tion except to emphasize the obvious. On hearing her father's
voice, Su Hsü-chüan appears to the left of the stage to the audience. She calls out on making her entry.)*

SU HSÜ-CHÜAN: I'm coming.

*(She then crosses the stage to open the door, a traditional mime
described in the previous play. As his daughter mimes opening
the door, Yu Hu-lu stands parallel to it, facing the left side of the
stage to the audience, as though listening to the bolts being shot.
After opening the door, Su Hsü-chüan leans forward, head and
shoulders tilted to the right, and placing her hands beneath her
father's right arm, is about to help him indoors.)* Oh, there you
are, Father.

YU HU-LU: Here I am.

SU HSÜ-CHÜAN: *(Looking at the string of cash on his shoulder.)*
Wherever did you get so much money?

YU HU-LU: *(His voice heavy with wine.)* Guess where I got it!

SU HSÜ-CHÜAN: Did you borrow it?

YU HU-LU: Where is there anybody kind enough to lend me so much?

SU HSÜ-CHÜAN: Then where did you get it? *(Yu Hu-lu raises his right
arm to address her, and as he speaks, punctuates his words with
his first and middle fingers together and extended, the thumb,
fourth finger, and little finger touching at the tips. His voice, still
thick with wine, is bantering in tone.)*

YU HU-LU: Ai, it's no good hiding it from you; it's come to this now.
When I went out this morning, I happened to meet old mother
Chiang, the go-between. She told me Wang Yuan-wai's daughter is going to be married and is short of a slave girl in her dowry.
So I sold you to her for fifteen strings of cash. *(Su Hsü-chüan
starts back in alarm at hearing her father's words. Her right arm,
bent at the elbow, is placed against her right breast, hand curved
back, fingers crooked. The left arm is thrust forward at a slightly
lower level, though with the elbow still half bent. The middle finger and thumb are placed together in each hand. The left shoulder*

is raised a little higher than the right and her head tilted slightly downwards. She holds herself at a little distance from her father and steps back two paces at his final words.)

SU HSÜ-CHÜAN: Are you really telling the truth?

YU HU-LU: *(Wagging his fingers at her.)* They want you to go early tomorrow morning. You'd better get your things together quickly and be ready. *(Su Hsü-chüan gives a loud wail of grief, the traditional high crescendo of sound that drops away in a drawn-out cadence, as she quickly makes her exit to the right of the stage to the audience.)*

SU HSÜ-CHÜAN: Aiya! Oh, Mother!

YU HU-LU: *(Pvercome with drunken laughter and addressing the audience.)* What a joke! She really believes it. We'll tease her for tonight and tell her the truth tomorrow morning. *(He turns away as though pondering for a moment, facing left stage from the audience. His right leg is forward and slightly bent; his left hand is raised to caress his beard. His right arm, elbow bent, is raised a little above face level; the water sleeve hangs down. In this position, he turns around as though peering into the lamplight and goes towards the bed.)* I'll put the money safely away, and then I shall sleep well. *(He puts the string of cash beneath the hard, round pillow at the head of the bed, but the cash is only half hidden and hangs down over the edge of the bed, nearly touching the floor. He then gets onto the bed and composes himself for sleep beneath the curtains, his head on the pillow, his arms folded over his chest, and his left leg crossed over the knee of his bent right leg. This is a typical sleeping posture on the traditional Chinese stage, particularly when a scene of action or violence is to follow. Su Hsü-chüan enters left of the stage to the audience. She is in distress and begins to sing in the Shang P'o Yang modal pattern. As she sings, she walks slowly, pausing for each line, with one leg slightly bent and poised on the toes placed just behind the heel of the forward foot, which is squarely on the floor. She emphasizes her lines with her raised hands, first the right hand, then the left. The fingers are delicately curved in the traditional position for female roles: the thumb and middle finger are held together in a curve, the index finger is extended, the fourth finger is crooked slightly above the center of the middle finger, and the little finger is curved above the center of the fourth finger.)*

SU HSÜ-CHÜAN: My heart is sad, my tears drop down.
I am like a frail boat on the boundless ocean,
Tossed by the breakers and unable to reach the peaceful shore.
I will plead with him, for my dead mother's sake.
To reconsider selling the body of his lonely child,
Like goods for cash.

(She has approached the bed at this point and stands looking down on the sleeping man. Her right arm is bent at a right angle across her waist, the hand raised toward the left arm, which is extended at waist height. Her head is slightly inclined, and her body faces toward the right of the stage to the audience. She cries out.)

Father, Father!

(But Yu Hu-lu is fast asleep and Su–Hsü-chüan begins to sing again.)

I am not his own child,
So he sold me with a smile
Just as though I were a stranger.
How can I make him take pity on me?
I fear it is difficult to persuade him
To change his mind.
It's worse than boiling in oil.
I implore the heavens ten million times.
It's as though my heart were pierced with arrows.
I call upon my mother, call until my lips are dry!

(As she sings, her steps have taken her toward the butcher's block, on which lies the axe. The thought enters her mind to die. She stands posing for a moment. Her body is inclined toward the block; her head is turned away over her left shoulder. Her right arm is across her body with her left hand resting lightly on her right forearm above the wrist. The third and middle fingers only lightly touch the sleeve, while the index and little fingers are del-

icately poised. She picks up the axe, holding it at chest height and away from the body, and turns toward the audience. The left arm still supports the right arm. The index finger of the right hand is extended behind the blade of the axe; the remaining fingers grasp the handle. Su Hsü-chüan stares fixedly at the axe, then puts it down on the block again as she changes her mind.)

But wait! I remember my aunt Kaoch'iao once telling me that if I was ever in difficulty to go to her. Things have reached such a dreadful pass, the best plan would be to do that first.

(Sings in the Ma Shang Shui Hung Ling modal pattern)

If only my aunt can save me from all this trouble!

I'll take this opportunity while he is in drunken sleep

To go to my relative without delay.

(She moves to center front stage, mimes opening the shop door but does not close it, steps hastily through, pauses, then runs offstage to the right of the audience.)

Peter Quill's Shenanigans

Anonymous
1485

Scene: The Quill's house. Peter feigns illness to escape paying his debt to Joss for the yards of cloth he took home with him earlier. Joss believes he's to be paid after dinner and he arrives at the house with an appetite.

Joss, a cloth merchant.
Madge, a housewife.
Peter, her husband, a clever fellow.

JOSS: Anybody home? Mr. Quill!

MADGE: *(Letting him in.)* Silence, for heaven's sake! If you have anything to say, say it softly.

JOSS: Good afternoon, Mrs. Quill.

MADGE: Softer!

JOSS: What's that?

MADGE: I'm telling you—

JOSS: Where is he?

MADGE: Oh god, where should he be?

JOSS: Where should who be?

MADGE: It isn't kind of you to ask, dear Mr. Joss. The poor wretch is where he's been these eleven weeks without stirring.

JOSS: Who are you—

MADGE: Excuse me if I don't talk any louder. I think he's resting a bit. Oh Jesus, you should see how low he is!

JOSS: Who?

MADGE: My husband, Peter.

JOSS: Who are you talking about? Didn't he pick up six yards of cloth in my store just now?

MADGE: Who? Peter?

JOSS: Two hours ago! One hour ago! Don't keep me standing here; I haven't got all day. Stop this fiddle-faddle and give me my money.

MADGE: This is no time for joking, Mr. Joss.

JOSS: My money! Have you gone mad? My thirty-nine dollars!

MADGE: Mr. Joss, you're not in a lunatic asylum. Why don't you go and entertain your cronies instead of pestering me?

JOSS: I'll curse God if I don't get my thirty-nine dollars!

MADGE: I'm sorry, but we don't all feel like fooling around.

JOSS: Mrs. Quill, stop this nonsense and call Mr. Quill.

MADGE: Is this going to go on all day?

JOSS: Am I or am I not in Mr. Quill's house?

MADGE: I hope you drop dead if you don't lower your voice!

JOSS: What's that? Can't I even ask for him?

MADGE: Quiet, you'll wake him.

JOSS: What is it you want? Am I supposed to whisper in your ear or talk from the cellar or from the bottom of a well?

MADGE: I guess God made you a loudmouth and there's no help for it.

JOSS: Devils in hell! All right, I'll keep my voice down. I'm not used to this kind of squabbling. All right. Mr. Quill made off today with six yards of my cloth.

MADGE: What? What's that? Made off, made off? I hope they hang the liar that said it! Oh my poor husband! Eleven weeks in a coma and I have to listen to this slop! Clear out of here, stop torment- ing a helpless woman!

JOSS: You told me to keep my voice down. Who's shouting now?

MADGE: You're looking for a fight, aren't you?

JOSS: Well, if you want me to leave the house, hand me—

MADGE: Softer!

JOSS: You're the one who'll wake him up! Your voice is ten times louder than mine. Come on, Mrs. Quill, don't keep me waiting any longer.

MADGE: I see it now: You're drunk.

JOSS: Drunk? Me? God punish you!

MADGE: Not so loud!

JOSS: Madam, I demand, for six yards of cloth—

MADGE: The cloth again! Who did you give it to?

JOSS: To *him*!

MADGE: Is he fit for a piece of cloth? He can't even lift an arm. The only cloth he'll ever see will be white, and it'll be wrapped around him when he leaves this house feet first.

JOSS: All this must have just happened, because I talked to him today.

MADGE: Down with your voice!

JOSS: It's you, devils in hell, you, blood and damnation! Pay me and I'll go! *(Aside.)* This is what happens every time I'm fool enough to give credit.

PETER: *(From his curtained four-poster.)* Madge! The smelling salts. Prop me up a bit . . Put a pillow under me . . . Water! Who am I talking to? Somebody please rub the soles of my feet.

JOSS: That's his voice.

MADGE: Sure.

PETER: Come here, you trollop. Didn't I tell you to open the windows? Cover me up. Drive these black people away! Marmara! Carimara! Carimara!

MADGE: What's the matter? Look at the way you're tossing about! Are you crazy?

PETER: You can't see what I see! There's a witch flying in the room! Catch her! There's a black cat! Look at it going up!

MADGE: Stop tossing! Aren't you ashamed of yourself?

PETER: These doctors are killing me with their drugs. And a man can't argue with them. We're all putty in their hands.

MADGE: Poor man! *(To Joss.)* Go on, take a look at him, see how sick he is.

JOSS: Did he really become ill after returning from my shop?

MADGE: Your shop?

JOSS: Yes, that's where he was, I think. The cloth I lent you, Mr. Quill, I have to have the money for it.

PETER: Oh doctor, today in my stool there were two small pellets, each one black and round and hard as a stone. Should I take another enema?

JOSS: How do I know? I want my thirty-nine dollars.

PETER: What about these three sharp objects you gave me, doctor, do you call those pills? They nearly broke my jaws. Don't make me take them anymore, for pity's sake. They were so bitter I threw them up.

JOSS: Why don't you throw up my thirty-nine dollars?

MADGE: People like you should be strung up! Get out of here!

JOSS: Not before I get my cloth or my money.

PETER: And what about my urine? Does it look fatal? Dear God, don't let me die, no matter how long I have to suffer!

MADGE: *(To Joss.)* Go away! You should be ashamed to be making him delirious.

JOSS: Am I supposed to forget about my six yards of cloth? You tell me—is that fair?

PETER: Couldn't you take a look at my feces, doctor? They're so hard, I don't know how I'm surviving, it hurts so much when I push.

JOSS: I want my money!

MADGE: Oh Jesus, how can you go on tormenting the poor man? Can't you see he's mistaken you for the doctor? Eleven weeks in bed, poor Christian, without a break.

JOSS: But how could this have happened to him? He came to see me today and we made a deal, or so I thought, I don't know what's what anymore.

MADGE: Your mind is a little shaky, Mr. Joss. Take my advice, really, go home and lie down. People might think that you came here for my sake. And the doctors will be here in a minute.

JOSS: I don't care what dirty people think as long as I'm not thinking any dirt. *(Aside.)* Damnation, has it come to that? *(To Madge.)* Look here, I thought—

MADGE: Still at it?

JOSS: Aren't you roasting a duck?

MADGE: What a question! Roast duck for a sick man? Go on, eat your own ducks and don't come here with your blabber. Can't you see you're intruding?

JOSS: I don't mean to offend you, but it was my impression—

MADGE: Again?

JOSS: God damn you both and good-bye? *(He goes outside.)* Devils in hell, I know he took six yards all in one piece, but this woman has managed to muddle my brain. I know he took them. No he didn't. It doesn't make sense. I saw him in the grip of death. Or was he faking? Damn it, he did take six yards, he stuck the bolt under his arm, I saw it. Or did I? Maybe I'm dreaming. Since when do I give my goods away on credit? Which means he hasn't got the cloth. Yes he has. No he hasn't. Has. Hasn't. I'm going mad. I don't know who's right. It's a bottomless pit. *(Exit.)*

PETER: Is he gone?

MADGE: Be still; I'm listening. He's going off mumbling and grumbling God knows what.

PETER: I might as well get out of bed.

MADGE: No, don't! He could be back any moment, and if he finds you up we'll both be hanged.

PETER: Oh Jesus, how we baited that suspicious dunderhead! A dunce cap on Bill Joss would look better than a crucifix in church.

MADGE: And serves him right—a pennypincher who leaves a shirt button in the collection plate on Sundays. Oh Lord oh Lord!

PETER: Hush, don't laugh, for God's sake. I'm sure he's coming back.

MADGE: I can't stop.

JOSS: *(In his shop.)* Yes, by the holy shining sun, I'm going back to that shyster's house whether he likes it or not. I know his kind—he'd put his own mother behind bars for an IOU. The rascal has my cloth, I gave it to him here, on this very spot.

MADGE: When I think of the face he made when he looked at you, oh I've got to laugh! Give me my money! Six yards!

PETER: Stop laughing, I tell you. If he comes back and hears you, that's it; we'll have to beat it out of town.

JOSS: *(In the street.)* That courthouse parasite, does he think we're all cretins? I'll have him strung up on a tree. He's got my cloth and he's trying to skin me. God strike me dead if he isn't. *(He returns to Quill's house.)* Laughter! Open the door!

MADGE: *(Low.)* Oh God, he heard me!

PETER: *(Low.)* I'll pretend I'm delirious. Go on.

MADGE: *(Opening the door.)* What's all the shouting about?

JOSS: So you're laughing, are you? Good enough. Hand over my money.

MADGE: Merciful heavens, I was laughing? At what? I'm in agony. He's sinking fast. You never heard such a storm and frenzy. He's raving, singing, and jabbering away in a dozen languages—he'll be gone in half an hour, and that's why I'm laughing and crying all at the same time.

JOSS: I don't know about laughing and crying, but, to make a long story short, I want my money.

MADGE: Are we starting all over again?

JOSS: I'm a businessman, I'm used to straightforward talk. Do you think I can't tell a bull from a cow?

PETER: Up, Madge, up! It's the Queen of Mandolina! Let her come in! I know she's been delivered of twenty-four tiny Mandolinnies, the bishop is their daddy and I'm requested to be the godfather.

MADGE: Alas, alas, set your mind on God the Father, my dear Peter, and not on Mandolinnies.

JOSS: What in hell does this drivel mean? Money! I want my money!

MADGE: Stop harassing my poor husband! But when I look at your face I realize you're insane. If only I had somebody to help, I'd have you tied up, you're a raving lunatic.

JOSS: I take a solemn oath that if I ever give credit again, I'll renounce God and deliver my soul to the devil.

PETER: Mon Dieu! Holy Virgin! Take me to la mer! Je suis tu suis il suis! Ding dong, frère Jacques, ding dong, ring ze bell mam'selle, but don't talk about ze money! *(To Joss.)* Get it, brother?

MADGE: That was mostly French. One of his uncles, actually the brother of his uncle's wife, was a Frenchman.

JOSS: Nevertheless, he finagled me out of my cloth.

PETER: Herein, bitte, schöne Damen! Wer sind diese ugly toads? Teufelsdreck, heraus! Mach schnell, ich will bekommen ein priest! Why is the priest laughing, der Hund, mach ihm singen his Mass!

MADGE: Oh God have mercy on his soul, the time for the last sacrament is at hand.

JOSS: Wasn't that German he was talking just now?

MADGE: His mother was German, that's why?

PETER: Pépé, olé! I entiendo you, madre de Dios, it's good to see you as hermoso as ever, José! Let me pour you a leetle glass of tequila, no agua in it, no? Cheers! bottoms up! Qué tal? Oh I want to confess!

JOSS: How many languages does he speak? If he'd only give me a small installment on his debt, I'd gladly leave.

MADGE: How can you be so stubborn? Oh I'm so unhappy!

PETER: Why dontcha talka to me, Giuseppe? My povero stomacco, ai ai ai, she hurta so much, she busta my culo, oh sole mio, pasta asciutta! Belle signorine, catcha this fly before she stinga me, per favore!

JOSS: Where does he find the strength to talk so much? *(Quill does a death rattle.)* He's going mad!

MADGE: It's the end. His schoolteacher came from Italy, and now with his last breath he remembers him.

JOSS: This is the strangest day of my life. I could have sworn he was in my store today, but I guess I was mistaken.

PETER: Et bona dies sit vobis, magister amantissime, pater reverendissime.

MADGE: Latin! He's really dying. His last words show his veneration for God. And I'm going to be left a widow without a penny.

JOSS: *(Aside.)* I'd better get out of here. *(To Madge.)* Your husband may have a few secrets to impart to you before he gives up the ghost, so I'll be going. Please forgive me. I really thought he had my cloth. Forgive me in God's name.

MADGE: A poor afflicted widow blesses you.

JOSS: *(Aside.)* What a day! The devil must have disguised himself as Mr. Quill and stolen my cloth in order to lead me into temptation. Let him keep it and leave me in peace.
(Exit.)

PETER: *(Jumping out of bed.)* I did it! And away he goes, handsome Joss, his mind in a whirl, and tonight the nightmares will gripe him!

MADGE: God, how we fuddled him! Didn't I perform like a star?

PETER: You did, my pigeon, and I'm proud of you. Where's the cloth? Look at it, enough for two new wardrobes!

Clizia

Nicolo Machiavelli
1524

Scene: Outside their home. Clizia, adopted as a young girl, is loved
by all the men. Sofronia is disgusted by her husband's behavior.

Nicomaco, a wealthy Florentine businessman, in love with his ward,
Clizia.
Cleandro, his son, 22, also in love with Clizia.
Sofronia, Nicomoco's wife.

NICOMACO: Cleandro, if you want this family to survive, go find your
mother, and tell her what's what! She's still in the church; go talk
to her. I'll wait here at home. And if you see that rascal Eustachio,
tell him I want to see him, post haste and double pronto! Or he'll
be more than sorry! Go on! Good-bye! *Au revoir! Ciao!*

CLEANDRO: *(Starting off to town)* I'm on my way . . . *(Nicomaco exits
to the house; Cleandro halts, remains onstage.)* Oh the misery of
love! All I do is go from one torment to another! I know that anyone in love with a beautiful girl like Clizia is going to have rivals,
but . . . my own father! I've never heard of anything like this!
Fathers are supposed to help their sons, not compete against
them! Mother's on my side—but more because she wants Dad to
lose than for me to win! I can't even tell her my plans: She'll think
I'm pushing Eustachio's suit for the same reason Dad's pushing
Pirro's: She'll think we're pimping for ourselves, and she'll give up
on both of us. I'm going to go kill myself! No, wait, there's
Mother now, coming out of church. Let me see: Maybe she's
come up with some way to foul up the old man's scheme!
(Sofronia enters from the town.) Momma!

SOFRONIA: Ah, Cleandro! Have you just come from the house?

CLEANDRO: Yes . . .

SOFRONIA: You've been there since I left?

CLEANDRO: Yes . . .

SOFRONIA: Where's your father?

CLEANDRO: He's home.

SOFRONIA: Doing what?—He's with Clizia, God knows! Like a boy let loose in a candy shop, I'll bet. Did he say anything to you?

CLEANDRO: Oh, he's gone sky high this time; the Devil's in him for sure! Let's see: He's going to have Eustachio and me thrown in jail, he's going to give you back your dowry and send you home to your father, and he's going to burn down the house: All this if we don't agree to Clizia marrying Pirro! He's sent me to convince you to go along with this, "or else!"

SOFRONIA: And you said . . .?

CLEANDRO: What could I say? I love Clizia like a sister, and I can't stand the thought of Pirro getting his dirty hands on her.

SOFRONIA: Like a sister? I hope so: I'm not interested in getting her out of Nicomaco's bed just to put her in yours. But Eustachio loves her himself; he can marry her, and then we'll find you another wife who'll make you forget all about Clizia.

CLEANDRO: Great! Sure! Yes! Just make sure this marriage with Pirro never takes place! Marry here off to Eustachio if you have to! Or, maybe you could let her stay single for a while longer: She's still young, there's plenty of time! I mean, suppose her parents show up after all this: How do you think they'd feel, knowing we married her off to a servant? From the country?

SOFRONIA: You're right. I've thought of that, but your father's going crazy. We have to do something. Let me think some more: I'll work this out. There, look; there's your father waiting for me by the door. I'll go see him; you go to the church and get Eustachio. Tell him to come home and not be afraid . . .

CLEANDRO: Done!

(Cleandro exits toward town, Sofronia following a step with him. Nicomaco enters from the house.)

NICOMACO: *(Aside.)* Well, Sofronia's returned. I think I'll try a little sweet talk; women like that sort of thing. *(Aloud.)* Darling! Awwww, Whatsa' matta', sweety-bird, puddy-twos, you look so boo-boo-eyes today? Gimme' li'l kissy-wissy . . .

SOFRONIA: Let go of me!

NICOMACO: Awww . . . come back to Nico-micko . . .

SOFRONIA: No! What, have you gone completely out of your mind????

NICOMACO: Then I'm coming after youzy-wouzy . . .!

SOFRONIA: Are you crazy?

NICOMACO: Cwazy for you, Cwazy wiv desire . . .

SOFRONIA: Well, I don't desire your desire!

NICOMACO: I can't help myself!

SOFRONIA: I'd die first! You're disgusting!

NICOMACO: You don't mean that . . .

SOFRONIA: Better believe it!

NICOMACO: My love! Just look at me!

SOFRONIA: I'm looking at you, all right, and smelling you too! What, are you wearing perfume, now?

NICOMACO: *(Aside.)* Dammit! She noticed; I knew I shouldn't have put this on!

SOFRONIA: *(Sniffs.)* Ah, Eau de Whorehouse! You crazy old fool!

NICOMACO: A traveling salesman . . . he bumped into me . . . one of his perfume bottles broke . . .

SOFRONIA: What a lie! Listen, you've been fooling around this whole year, drinking, whoring, gambling, spending recklessly: What kind of example is this for Cleandro? It's like father, like son right? What kind of husband is HE going to make?

NICOMACO: Look, don't throw the whole book at me today! You won't have anything left to accuse me of tomorrow! Ha ha ha! But really, Sofronia, my pet, doesn't it make more sense for a wife to obey her husband than the other way around?

SOFRONIA: It might, if the husband were an honorable man.

NICOMACO: Well, isn't it honorable to have our young girl married off?

SOFRONIA: Yes, to a decent husband.

NICOMACO: And isn't Pirro decent?

SOFRONIA: No!

NICOMACO: Why not?

SOFRONIA: I've already told you!

NICOMACO: I think I know a bit more about these things than you do. Anyway, I'm about to talk to Eustachio; when I'm through, he won't even want her anymore.

SOFRONIA: Go ahead! But I'm going to talk to Pirro, and, believe me, when I'm through HE won't want her either!

NICOMACO: All right, you're on! And let the best man win!

Ralph Roister Doister

Nicholas Udall
1566

Scene: Ralph is madly in love with the widow Custance. Ralph and
Merrygreek have gone to Dame Custance's home. Ralph has had
a scriver write her a love letter but it is misread by Merrygreek and
creates an opposite effect.

Ralph Roister Doister
Mathew Merrygreek, a friend to Ralph but in truth a parasite.
Dame Christian Custance, a wealthy widow.

(Merrygreek and Ralph Roister Doister. Enter Dame Custance.)
DAME CUSTANCE: What gauding and fooling is this afore my door?
MERRYGREEK: May not folks be honest, pray you, though they be
poor?
DAME CUSTANCE: As that thing may be true, so rich folks may be
fools.
ROISTER DOISTER: Her talk is as fine as she had learned in schools.
MERRYGREEK: Look partly toward her, and draw a little near.
DAME CUSTANCE: Get ye home, idle folks!
MERRYGREEK: Why, may not we be here?
Nay, and ye will haze, haze; otherwise, I tell you plain.
And ye will not haze, then give us our gear again.
DAME CUSTANCE: Indeed I have of yours much gay things, God save all.
ROISTER DOISTER: Speak gently to her, and let her take all.
MERRYGREEK: Ye are too tender-hearted; shall she make us daws?
Nay, dame, I will be plain with you in my friend's cause.
ROISTER DOISTER: Let all this pass, sweetheart, and accept my ser-
vice!
DAME CUSTANCE: I will not be served with a fool, in no wise;
When I choose an husband, I hope to take a man.
MERRYGREEK: And where will ye find one which can do that he can?
Now this man toward you being so kind
You not to make him an answer somewhat to his mind!

DAME CUSTANCE: I sent him a full answer by you, did I not?

MERRYGREEK: And I reported it.

DAME CUSTANCE: Nay, I must speak it again.

ROISTER DOISTER: No, no! he told it all.

MERRYGREEK: Was I not meetly plain?

ROISTER DOISTER: Yes.

MERRYGREEK: But I would not tell all; for faith, if I had,
    With you, Dame Custance, ere this hour it had been bad,
    And not without cause, for this goodly personage
    Meant no less than to join with you in marriage.

DAME CUSTANCE: Let him waste no more labour nor suit about me.

MERRYGREEK: Ye know not where your preferment lieth, I see,
    He sending you such a token, ring and letter.

DAME CUSTANCE: Marry, here it is; ye never saw a better! *(She holds
    out a letter.)*

MERRYGREEK: Let us see your letter.

DAME CUSTANCE: Hold, read it, if ye can.
    And see what letter it is to win a woman!

MERRYGREEK: "To mine own dear coney, bird, sweetheart, and pigsny,
    Good Mistress Custance, present these by and by."
    Of this superscription do ye blame the style?

DAME CUSTANCE: With the rest as good stuff as ye read a great
    while!

MERRYGREEK: *(Reading.)* "Sweet mistress, whereas I love you noth-
    ing at all,
    Regarding your substance and riches chief of all,
    For your personage, beauty, demeanour and wit
    I commend me unto you never a whit.
    Sorry to hear report of your good welfare.
    For *(as I hear say)* such your conditions are
    That ye be worthy favour of no living man;
    To be abhorred of every honest man;
    To be taken for a woman inclined to vice;
    Nothing at all to virtue giving her due price.
    Wherefore concerning marriage, ye are thought
    Such a fine paragon, as ne'er honest man bought.

And now by these presents I do you advertise
That I am minded to marry you in no wise.
For your goods and substance, I could be content
To take you as ye are. If ye mind to be my wife,
Ye shall be assured for the time of my life
I will keep you right well from good raiment and fare;
Ye shall not be kept but in sorrow and care.
Ye shall in no wise live at your own liberty;
Do and say what ye lust, ye shall never please me;
But when ye are merry, I will be all sad,
When ye are sorry, I will be very glad;
When ye seek your heart's ease, I will be unkind;
At no time, in me shall ye much gentleness find.
But all things contrary to your will and mind
Shall be done: otherwise I will not be behind
To speak. And as for all them that would do you wrong.
I will so help and maintain, ye shall not live long.
Nor any foolish dolt shall cumber you but I.
I, whoe'er say nay, will stick by you till I die.
Thus, good mistress Custance, the Lord you save and keep
From me Roister Doister, whether I wake or sleep.
Who favoureth you no less *(ye may be bold)*
Than this letter purporteth, which ye have unfold."
DAME CUSTANCE: How by this letter of love? is it not fine?
ROISTER DOISTER: By the arms of Calais, it is none of mine?
MERRYGREEK: Fie, you are foul to blame! this is your own hand!
DAME CUSTANCE: *(Sarcastically.)* Might not a woman be proud of
such an husband?
MERRYGREEK: Ah, that ye would in a letter show such despite!
ROISTER DOISTER: Oh, I would I had him here the which did it endite.
MERRYGREEK: Why, we made it yourself, ye told me by this light.
ROISTER DOISTER: Yea, I meant I wrote it mine own self, yesternight.
DAME CUSTANCE: Iwis, sir, I would not have sent you such a mock.
ROISTER DOISTER: Ye may so take it, but I meant it not so, by Cock.
MERRYGREEK: Who can blame this woman to fume, and fret, and
rage?

Tut, tut! yourself now have marred your own marriage.
Well, yet, mistress Custance, if ye can this remit,
This gentleman otherwise may your love requit.
DAME CUSTANCE: No! God be with you both, and seek no more to
me. *(She leaves in a huff.)*
ROISTER DOISTER: Wough! she is gone for ever! I shall her no more
see!
MERRYGREEK: What, weep? fie, for shame! and blubber? For man-
hood's sake,
Never let your foe so much pleasure of you take!
Rather play the man's part, and do love refrain.
If she despise you, e'en despise ye her again!
ROISTER DOISTER: By Goss, and for thy sake I defy her indeed!
MERRYGREEK: Yea, and perchance that way ye shall much sooner speed;
For one mad property these women have, in fey:
When ye will, they will not; will not ye, then will they.
Ah, foolish woman! Ah, most unlucky Custance!
Ah, unfortunate woman! Ah, peevish Custance!
Art thou to thine harms so obstinately bent
That thou canst not see where lieth thine high preferment?
Canst thou not lub dis man, which could lub dee so well?
Art thou so much thine own foe?
ROISTER DOISTER: Thou dost the truth tell.
MERRYGREEK: Well, I lament.
ROISTER DOISTER: So do I.
MERRYGREEK: Wherefore?
ROISTER DOISTER: For this thing. Because she is gone.
MERRYGREEK: I mourn for another thing.
ROISTER DOISTER: What is it, Merrygreek, wherefore thou dost grief
take?
MERRYGREEK: That I am not a woman myself for your sake,
I would have you myself, and a straw for yond Gill!
And mock much of you, though it were against my will.
I would not, I warrant you, fall in such a rage
As so to refuse such a goodly personage.
ROISTER DOISTER: In faith, I heartily thank thee, Merrygreek.

MERRYGREEK: An I were a woman——

ROISTER DOISTER: Thou wouldest to me seek.

MERRYGREEK: For, though I say it a goodly person ye be.

ROISTER DOISTER: No, no.

MERRYGREEK: Yes, a goodly man as e'er I did see.

ROISTER DOISTER: No, I am a poor homely man, as God made me.

MERRYGREEK: By the faith that I owe to God, sir, but ye be!
 Would I might, for your sake, spend a thousand pound land.

ROISTER DOISTER: I dare say thou wouldest have me to thy husband.

MERRYGREEK: Yea; an I were the fairest lady in the shire,
 And knew you as I know you, and see you now here—
 Well, I say no more!

ROISTER DOISTER: Gramercies, with all my heart!

MERRYGREEK: But since that cannot be, will ye play a wise part?

ROISTER DOISTER: How should I?

MERRYGREEK: Refrain from Custance a while now,
 And I warrant her soon right glad to seek you.
 Ye shall see her anon come on her knees creeping,
 And pray you to be good to her, salt tears weeping.

ROISTER DOISTER: But what an she come not?

MERRYGREEK: In faith, then, farewell she!
 Or else if ye be wroth, ye may avenged be.

ROISTER DOISTER: By Cock's precious potstick, and e'en so I shall!
 I will utterly destroy her, and house and all!
 But I would be avenged in the mean space,
 On that vile scribbler, that did my wooing disgrace.

MERRYGREEK: "Scribbler," ko you? indeed, he is worthy no less.
 I will call him to you, and ye bid me, doubtless.

ROISTER DOISTER: Yes, for although he had as many lives,
 As a thousand widows, and a thousand wives,
 As a thousand lions, and a thousand rats,
 A thousand wolves, and a thousand cats,
 A thousand bulls, and a thousand calves,
 And a thousand legions divided in halves,
 He shall never 'scape death on my sword's point—
 Though I should be torn therefore joint by joint!

MERRYGREEK: Nay, if ye will kill him, I will not fetch him;
　　I will not in so much extremity set him.
　　He may yet amend, sir, and be an honest man.
　　Therefore pardon him, good soul, as much as ye can.
ROISTER DOISTER: Well, for thy sake, this once with his life he shall pass.
　　But I will hew him all to pieces, by the Mass!
MERRYGREEK: Nay, faith, ye shall promise that he shall not harm have.
　　Else I will not fetch him.
ROISTER DOISTER: I shall, so God me save!
　　But I may chide him a good?
MERRYGREEK: Yea, that do hardily.
ROISTER DOISTER: Go, then.
MERRYGREEK: I return, and bring him to you by-and-by.
　　(Exit, leaving Roister Doister alone on the stage.)

Twelfth Night

William Shakespeare

Scene: Olivia's House. Olivia is mourning the death of her brother. She sends her maid Maria down to tell her guests, Andrew and Sir Toby, to stop drinking and carousing.

Sir Toby Belch, fat, jolly, a guest of Lady Olivia in Illyria.
Maria, Lady Olivia's maid.
Sir Andrew Aguecheek, awkward, inept, wants to woo Lady Olivia.

SIR TOBY: What a plague means my niece, to take the death of her brother thus? I am sure care's an enemy to life.

MARIA: By my troth, Sir Toby, you must come in earlier o' nights: your cousin, my lady, takes great exception to your ill hours.

SIR TOBY: Why, let her except before excepted.

MARIA: Ay, but you must confine yourself within the modest limits of order.

SIR TOBY: Confine! I'll confine myself no finer than I am. These clothes are good enough to drink in, and so be these boots too: an they be not, let them hang themselves in their own straps.

MARIA: That quaffing and drinking will undo you: I heard my lady talk of it yesterday; and of a foolish knight that you brought in one night here to be her wooer.

SIR TOBY: Who? Sir Andrew Aguecheek?

MARIA: Ay, he.

SIR TOBY: He's as tall a man as any's in Illyria.

MARIA: What's that to the purpose?

SIR TOBY: Why, he has three thousand ducats a year.

MARIA: Ay, but he'll have but a year in all these ducats: he's a very fool and a prodigal.

SIR TOBY: Fie, that you'll say so! He plays o' the viol-de-gamboys, and speaks three or four languages word for word without book, and hath all the good gifts of nature.

MARIA: He hath indeed, almost natural; for, besides that he's a fool, he's a great quarreller; and but that he hath the gift of a coward to allay the gust he hath in quarrelling, 'tis thought among the prudent we would quickly have the gift of a grave.

SIR TOBY: By this hand, they are scoundrels and substractors that say so of him. Who are they?

MARIA: They that add, moreover, he's drunk nightly in your company.

SIR TOBY: With drinking healths to my niece. I'll drink to her as long as there is a passage in my throat and drink in Illyria. He's a coward and a coystril, that will not drink to my niece till his brains turn o' the toe like a parish-top. What, wench! Castiliano vulgo! for here comes Sir Andrew Agueface.

(Enter Sir Andrew Aguecheek)

SIR ANDREW: Sir Toby Belch! How now, Sir Toby Belch!

SIR TOBY: Sweet Sir Andrew!

SIR ANDREW: Bless you, fair shrew.

MARIA: And you too, sir.

SIR TOBY: Accost, Sir Andrew, accost.

SIR ANDREW: What's that?

SIR TOBY: My niece's chambermaid.

SIR ANDREW: Good Mistress Accost, I desire better acquaintance.

MARIA: My name is Mary, sir.

SIR ANDREW: Good Mistress Mary Accost,—

SIR TOBY: You mistake, knight: "accost" is, front her, board her, woo her, assail her.

SIR ANDREW: By my troth, I would not undertake her in this company. Is that the meaning of "accost"?

MARIA: Fare you well, gentlemen.

SIR TOBY: An thou let her part so, Sir Andrew, would thou mightst never draw sword again!

SIR ANDREW: An you part so, mistress, I would I might never draw sword again. Fair lady, do you think you have fools in hand?

MARIA: Sir, I have not you by the hand.

SIR ANDREW: Marry, but you shall have; and here's my hand.

MARIA: Now, sir, "thought is free": I pray you, bring your hand to the buttery-bar and let it drink.

SIR ANDREW: Wherefore, sweetheart? What's your metaphor?

MARIA: It's dry, sir.

SIR ANDREW: Why, I think so: I am not such as ass but I can keep my hand dry. But what's your jest?

MARIA: A dry jest, sir.

SIR ANDREW: Are you full of them?

MARIA: Ay, sir, I have them at my fingers' ends: marry, now I let go your hand, I am barren. *(Exi.)*

SIR TOBY: O knight! thou lackest a cup of canary: when did I see thee so put down?

SIR ANDREW: Never in your life, I think; unless you see canary put me down. Methinks sometimes I have no more wit than a Christian or an ordinary man has; but I am a great eater of beef, and I believe that does harm to my wit.

SIR TOBY: No question.

SIR ANDREW: An I thought that, I'd forswear it. I'll ride home to-morrow, Sir Toby.

SIR TOBY: Pourquoi, my dear knight?

SIR ANDREW: What is "pourquoi"? Do or not do? I would I had bestowed that time in the tongues that I have in fencing, dancing, and bear-baiting. O! had I but followed the arts!

SIR TOBY: Then hadst thou had an excellent head of hair.

SIR ANDREW: Why, would that have mended my hair?

SIR TOBY: Past question; for thou seest it will not curl by nature.

SIR ANDREW: But it becomes me will enough, does't not?

SIR TOBY: Excellent; it hangs like flax on a distaff, and I hope to see a housewife take thee between her legs, and spin it off.

SIR ANDREW: Faith, I'll home to-morrow, Sir Toby: your niece will not be seen; or if she be, it's four to one she'll none of me. The count himself here hard by woos her.

SIR TOBY: She'll none o' the count; she'll not match above her degree, neither in estate, years, nor wit; I have heard her swear it. Tut, there's life in 't, man.

SIR ANDREW: I'll stay a month longer. I am a fellow o' the strangest mind i' the world; I delight in masques and revels sometimes altogether.

SIR TOBY: Art thou good at these kickchawses, knight?

SIR ANDREW: As any man in Illyria, whatsoever he be, under the degree of my betters: and yet I will not compare with an old man.

SIR TOBY: What is they excellence in a galliard, knight?

SIR ANDREW: Faith, I can cut a caper.

SIR TOBY: And I can cut the mutton to 't.

SIR ANDREW: And I think I have the back-trick simply as strong as any man in Illyria.

SIR TOBY: Wherefore are these things hid? Wherefore have these gifts a curtain before 'em? Are they like to take dust, like Mistress Mall's picture? Why dost thou not go to church in a galliard, and come home in a coranto? My very walk should be a jig: I would not so much as make water but in a sink-a-pace. What dost thou mean? Is it a world to hide virtues in? I did think, by the excellent constitution of thy leg, it was formed under the star of a galliard.

SIR ANDREW: Ay, 'tis strong, and it does indifferent well in a flame-coloured stock. Shall we set about some revels?

SIR TOBY: What shall we do else? Were we not born under Taurus?

SIR ANDREW: Taurus! that's sides and heart.

SIR TOBY: No, sir, it is legs and thighs. Let me see thee caper. Ha! higher: ha, ha! excellent!

(Exeunt.)

The Taming of the Shrew

William Shakespeare

Scene: Act Three Scene One, Padua. A room in Batista's House. Both
young men have come to court Bianca. Hortensio intends to woo
with his music, Lucentio with his Latin skills.

Bianca, a young lady, sister to Katharine who is to be wed.
Hortensio, in love with Bianca.
Lucentio, also in love with Bianca.
Brief entrance of Servant.

LUCENTIO: Fiddler, forbear; you grow too forward, sir:
    Have you so soon forgot the entertainment
    Her sister Katharine welcom'd you withal?
HORTENSIO: But, wrangling pendant, this is
    The patroness of heavenly harmony:
    Then give me leave to have prerogative;
    And when in music we have spent an hour,
    Your lecture shall have leisure for as much.
LUCENTIO: Preposterous ass, that never read so far
    To know the cause why music was ordain'd!
    Was it not to refresh the mind of man
    After his studies or his usual pain?
    Then give me leave to read philosophy,
    And while I pause, serve in your harmony.
HORTENSIO: Sirrah, I will not bear these braves of thine.
BIANCA: Why, gentlemen, you do me double wrong.
    To strive for that which resteth in my choice.
    I am no breeching scholar in the schools;
    I'll not be tied to hours nor 'pointed times,
    But learn my lessons as I please myself.
    And, to cut off all strife, here sit we down:
    Take you your instrument, play you the whiles;
    His lecture will be done ere you have tun'd.
HORTENSIO: You'll leave his lecture when I am in tune?

(Retires.)

LUCENTIO: That will be never: tune your instrument.

BIANCA: Where left we last?

LUCENTIO: Here, madam:—

> Hic ibat Simois; hic est Sigeia tellus;
> Hic steterat Priami regia celsa senis.

BIANCA: Construe them.

LUCENTIO: 'Hic ibat,' as I told you before, 'Simois,' I am
Lucentio, 'hic est,' son unto Vincentio of Pisa, 'Siegeia
tellus,' disguised thus to get your love; 'Hic steterat,' and
that Lucentio that comes a-wooing, 'Priami,' is my man
Tranio, 'regia,' bearing my port, 'celsa senis,' that we
might beguile the old pantaloon.

HORTENSIO: *(Returning.)* Madam, my instrument's in tune.

BIANCA: Let's hear.— *(Hortensio plays.)* O fie! the treble jars.

LUCENTIO: Spit in the hole, man, and tune again.

BIANCA: Now let me see if I can construe it: 'Hic ibat Simois,' I know you not, 'hic est Sigeia tellus,' I trust you
not; 'Hic steterat Priami,' take heed he hear us not, 'regia,'
presume not; 'celsa senis,' despair not.

HORTENSIO: Madam, 'tis now in tune.

LUCENTIO: All but the base.

HORTENSIO: The base is right; 'tis the base knave that jars.
How fiery and forward our pedant is!
(Aside.) Now, for my life, the knave doth court my love:
Pedascule, I'll watch you better yet.

BIANCA: In time I may believe, yet I mistrust.

LUCENTIO: Mistrust it not; for, sure Æacides
Was Ajax, call'd so from his grandfather.

BIANCA: I must believe my master; else, I promise you,
I should be arguing still upon that doubt:
But let it rest. Now, Licio, to you.
Good masters, take it not unkindly, pray,
That I have been thus pleasant with you both.

HORTENSIO: *(To Lucentio.)* You may go walk, and give me leave a while:
My lessons make no music in three parts,

LUCENTIO: Are you so formal, sir? *(Aside)* Well, I must wait,
  And watch withal; for, but I be deceiv'd,
  Our fine musician groweth amorous.
HORTENSIO: Madam, before you touch the instrument,
  To learn the order of my fingering,
  I must begin with rudiments of art;
  To teach you gamut in a briefer sort,

  More pleasant, pithy, and effectual,
  Than hath been taught by any of my trade:
  And there it is in writing, fairly drawn.
BIANCA: Why, I am past my gamut long ago.
HORTENSIO: Yet read the gamut of Hortensio.
BIANCA: "Gamut" I am, the ground of all accord,
  "Are," to plead Hortensio's passion;
  "B mi," Bianca, take him for thy lord,
  "C fa ut," that loves with all affection:
  "D sol re" one clef, two notes have I;
  "E la mi," show pity, or I die."
  Call you this gamut? Tut, I like it not:
  Old fashions please me best; I am not so nice,
  To change true rules for odd inventions.
  (Enter a Servant.)
SERVANT: Mistress, your father prays you leave your books,
  And help to dress your sister's chamber up:
  You know to-morrow is the wedding-day.
BIANCA: Farewell, sweet masters both: I must be gone.
  (Exeunt Bianca and Servant.)
LUCENTIO: Faith, mistress, then I have no cause to stay. *(Exit.)*
HORTENSIO: But I have cause to pry into this pedant:
  Methinks he looks as though he were in love.
  Yet if thy thoughts, Bianca, be so humble
  To cast thy wandering eyes on every stale,
  Seize thee that list: if once I find thee ranging,
  Hortensio will be quit with thee by changing.
  (Exit.)

The Lady of Pleasure

James Shirly
1637

Scene: Lady Aretina, loathing life in the country, has convinced her
husband to come to London.

Aretina, Sir Thomas Bornwell's Lady.
Steward, to Lady Bornwell.
Bornwell, a country gentleman.

STEWARD: Be patient, Madam, you may have your pleasure.
ARTENIA: Tis that I came to towne for, I wo'd not
    Endure againe the countrey conversation,
    To be the Lady of sixe shires! The men
    So neare the Primitive making, they retaine
    A sence of nothing but the earth, their braines
    And barren heads standing as much in want
    Of plowing as their ground. To heare a fellow
    Make himselfe merry—and his horse—with whisteling
    Sellingers round! To observe with what solemnitie
    They keep their Wakes, and throw for pewter Candlestickes!
    How they become the Morris! with whose bells
    They ring all into Whitson Ales, and sweate
    Through twenty Scarffes and Napkins, till the Hobbyhorse
    Tire, and the maide Marrian, dissolv'd to a gelly,
    Be kept for spoone meate.
STEWARD: These—with your pardon—are no Argument
    To make the country life appeare so hatefull,
    At least to your particular, who enjoy'd
    A blessing in the calme, would you be pleasd
    To thinke so, and the pleasure of a kingdome;
    While your owne will commanded what should move
    Delights, your husbands love and power joyned
    To give your life more harmony; you liv'd there
    Secure and innocent, beloved of all,

Praisd for your hospitality, and praid for;
You might be envied, but malice knew
Not where you dwelt. I wo'd not prophecy
But leave to your owne apprehension
What may suceede your change.
ARETINA: You doe imagine,
No doubt, you have talk'd wisely, and confuted
London past all defence; your Master should
Doe well to send you backe into the countrie,
With title of Superintendent Baylie.
STEWARD: How, Madam?
ARETINA: Even so, sir.
STEWARD: I am a Gentleman,
Though now your servant.
ARETINA: A country gentleman,
By your affection to converse with stuble;
His tenants will advance your wit, and plumpe it so
With beefe and bag-pudding.
STEWARD: You may say your pleasure,
It becomes not me dispute.
ARETINA: Complaine to
The Lord of the soyle, your master.
STEWARD: Y'are a woman
Of an ungovern'd passion, and I pity you.
(Enter Sir Thomas Bornwell.)
BORNWELL: How, how? Whats the matter?
STEWARD: Nothing. Sir.
(Exit.)
BORNWELL: Angry, sweet heart?
ARETINA: I am angry with my selfe,
To be so miserably restrained in things,
Wherein it doth concerne your love and honour
To see me satisfied.
BORNWELL: In what, Aretina,
Dost you accuse me? Have I not obeyed
All thy desires? Against mine owne opinion

Quitted the countrie, and removed the hope
Of our returne, by sale of that faire Lordship
We liv'd in? Chang'd a calme and retire[d] life
For this wild towne, composd of noise and charge.

ARETINA: What charge more than is necessarie
For a Lady of my birth and education?

BORNWELL: I am not ignorant, how much Nobilitie
Flowes in your bloud, your kinsmen great and powerful
I'th State; but with this lose not your memory
Of being my wife. I shall be studious,
Madam, to give the dignitie of your birth
All the best ornaments which become my fortune,
But would not flatter it, to ruine both,
And be the fable of the towne, to teach
Other men losse of wit by mine, emploid
To serve your vaste expences.

ARETINA: Am I then
Brought in the balance? So, Sir.

BORNWELL: Though you weigh
Me in a partial scale my heart is honest,
And must take libertie to thinke you have
Obeyed no modest counsell to [a]ffect,
Nay, study wayes of pride and costly ceremony;
Your change of gaudy furniture and pictures,
Of this Italian Master, and that Dutchmans;
Your mighty looking-glasses, like Artillery
Brought [home] on Engins; the superfluous plate,
Anticke and novell; vanities of tires;
Fourescore pound suppers for my Lord your kinsman;
Banquets for tother Lady, aunt, and cozens;
And perfumes that exceede all; traine of servants
To strife us at home and shew abroad
More motley than the French, or the Venetian,
About your Coach, whose rude Postillion
Must pester every narrow lane, till passengers
And tradsmen curse your choaking up their stalls,

And common cries pursue your Ladiship
For hindring o' their market.

ARETINA: Have you done sir?

BORNWELL: I would accuse the gayetie of your wardrobe,
And prodigall embroderies, under which
Rich Sattens, Plushes, cloath of Silver, dare
Now shew their owne complexions; your jewells,
Abel to burne out the Spectators eyes,
And shew like Bonfires on you by the tapers.
Something might here be spar'd, [with safety] of
Your birth and honour, since the truest wealth
Shines from the soule, and drawes up just admirers.
I could urge something more:—

ARETINA: Pray doe; I like
Your homilie of thrifte.

BORNWELL: I could wish, Madam,
You would not game so much.

ARETINA: A gamster too?

BORNWELL: But are not come to that repentance yet,
Should teach you skill enough to raise your profit;
You looke not through the subtiltie of Cards,
And mysteries of Dice; nor can you save
Charge with the boxe, buy petticotes and purles,
And keepe your familie by the precious income;
Nor doe I wish you should,—my poorest servant
Shall not upbraid my tables, nor his hire
Purchasd beneath my honour. You may play
Not a Pastime but a tyrannie, and vexe
Your selfe and my estate by't.

ARETINA: Good, proceed!

The Man of Mode; or Sir Fopling Flutter

Sir George Etherege
1676

Scene: London. A street. News of a beautiful woman reaches Dorimant.

Dorimant, a man-about-town.
Medley, his friend—also a man-about-town.
Orange Woman, (Foggy Nan) a fruit peddlar and gossip.
Handy, accompanies Dorimant (may be eliminated from the scene).

OR.WOM: Well, on my conscience, there never was the like of you!
God's my life, I had almost forgot to tell you there is a young gentlewoman lately come to town with her mother, that is so taken
with you.

DOR: Is she handsome?

OR. WOM: Nay, gad, there are few finer women, I tell you but so, and
a hugeous fortune, they say. Here, eat this peach. It comes from
the stone; 'tis better than any Newington y'have tasted.

DOR: *(Taking the peach.)* This fine woman, I'll lay my life, is some
awkward, ill-fashioned country toad who, not having above four
dozen of black hairs on her head, has adorned her baldness with
a large, white fruz, that she may look sparkishly in the forefront
of the King's box at an old play.

OR. WOM: Gad, you'd change your note quickly if you did but see
her.

DOR: How came she to know me?

OR WOM: She saw you yesterday at the Change; she told me you
came and fooled with the woman at the next shop.

DOR: I remember there was a mask observed me, indeed. Fooled, did
she say?

OR. WOM: Ay; I vow she told me twenty things you said, too, and
acted with head and with her body so like you—
(Enter Medley.)

MED: Dorimant, my life, my joy, my darling sin! how dost thou?

OR. WOM: Lord, what a filthy trick these men have got of kissing one another!

(She spits.)

MED: Why do you suffer this cartload of scandal to come near you and make your neighbors think you so improvident to need a bawd?

OR. WOM: Good, now! we shall have it you did but want him to help you! Come, pay me for my fruit.

MED: Make us thankful for it, huswife, bawds are as much out of fashion as gentlemen-ushers; none but old formal ladies use the one, and none but foppish old stagers employ the other. Go! You are an insignificant brandy bottle.

DOR: Nay, there you wrong her; three quarts of Canary is her business.

OR. WOM: What you please, gentlemen.

DOR: To him! give him as good as he brings.

OR. WOM: Hang him, there is not such another heathen in the town again, except it be the shoemaker without.

MED: I shall see you hold up your hand at the bar next sessions for murder, huswife; that shoemaker can take his oath you are in fee with the doctors to sell green fruit to the gentry that the crudities may breed diseases.

OR. WOM: Pray, give me my money.

DOR: Not a penny! When you bring the gentlewoman hither you spoke of, you shall be paid.

OR. WOM: The gentlewoman! the gentlewoman may be as honest as your sisters for aught as I know. Pray, pay me, Mr. Dorimant, and do not abuse me so; I have an honester way of living—you know it.

MED: Was there ever such a resty bawd?

DOR: Some jade's tricks she has, but she makes amends when she's in good humour.— Come, tell me the lady's name and Handy shall pay you.

OR. WOM: I must not; she forbid me.

DOR: That's a sure sign she would have you.

MED: Where does she live?

OR. WOM: They lodge at my house.

MED: Nay, then she's in a hopeful way.

OR. WOM: Good Mr. Medley, say your pleasure of me, but take heed how you affront my house! God's my life!—"in a hopeful way"!

DOR: Prithee, peace! What kind of woman's the mother?

OR WOM: A goodly grave gentlewoman. Lord, how she talks against the wild young men o' the town! As for your part, she thinks you an arrant devil; should she see you, onr my conscience she would look if you had a cloven foot.

DOR: Does she know me?

OR. WOM: Only by hearsay; a thousand horrid stories have been told her of you, and she believes 'em all.

MED: By the character this should be the famous Lady Woodvill and her daughter Harriet.

OR. WOM: The devil's in him for guessing, I think.

DOR: Do you know 'em?

MED: Both very well; the mother's a great admirer of the forms and civility of the last age.

DOR: An antiquated beauty may be allowed to be out of humour at the freedoms of the present. This is a good account of the mother; pray, what is the daughter?

MED: Why, first, she's an heiress—vastly rich.

DOR: And handsome?

MED: What alteration a twelvemonth may have bred in her I know not, but a year ago she was the most beautifullest creature I ever saw: a fine, easy, clean shape; light brown hair in abundance; her features regular; her complexion clear and lively; large, wanton eyes; but above all, a mouth that has made me kiss it a thousand times in imagination; teeth white and even, and pretty, pouting lips, with a little moisture ever hanging on them, that look like the Provins rose fresh on the bush, ere the morning sun has quite drawn up the dew.

DOR: Rapture! mere rapture!

OR. WOM: Nay, gad, he tells you true; she's a delicate creature.

DOR: Has she wit?

MED: More than is usual in her sex, and as much malice. Then, she's as wild as you would wish her, and has a demureness in her looks that makes it so surprising.

DOR: Flesh and blood cannot hear this and not long to know her.

MED: I wonder what makes her mother bring her up to town; an old doting keeper cannot be more jealous of his mistress.

OR. WOM: She made me laugh yesterday; there was a judge came to visit 'em, and the old man, she told me, did so stare upon her, and when he saluted her smacked so heartily. Who would think it of 'em?

MED: God-a-mercy, judge!

DOR: Do 'em right; the gentlemen of the long robe have not been wanting by their good examples to countenance the crying sin o' the nation.

MED: Come, on with your trappings; 'tis later than you imagine.

DOR: Call in the shoemaker, Handy.

OR. WOM: Good Mr. Dorimant, pay me. Gad, I had rather give you my fruit than stay to be abused by that foul-mouthed rogue; what you gentlemen say, it matters not much, but such a dirty fellow does one more disgrace.

DOR: Give her ten shillings, and be sure you tell the young gentlewoman I must be acquainted with her.

OR. WOM: Now do you long to be tempting this pretty creature. Well, heavens mend you!

MED: Farewell, bog! *(Exit Orange Woman and Handy.)* Dorimant, when did you see your *pisaller*, as you call her, Mrs. Loveit?

DOR: Not these two days.

MED: And how stand affairs between you?

DOR: There has been great patching of late, much ado; we make a shift to hang together.

MED: I wonder how her mighty spirit bears it.

DOR: Ill enough, on all conscience; I never knew so violent a creature.

MED: She's the most passionate in her love and the most extravagant in her jealousy of any woman I ever heard of. What note is that?

DOR: An excuse I am going to send her for the neglect I am guilty of.

MED: Prithee, read it.

DOR: No; but if you will take the pains, you may.

MED: *(Reads.)* I never was a lover of business, but now I have just reason to hate it, since it has kept me these days from seeing you. I intend to wait upon you in the afternoon, and in the pleasure of your conversation forget all I have suffered during this tedious absence.

This business of yours, Dorimant, has been with a vizard at the playhouse; I have had an eye on you. If some malicious body should betray you, this kind note would hardly make your peace with her.

DOR: I desire no better.

MED: Why, would her knowledge of it oblige you?

DOR: Most infinitely; next to the coming to a good understanding with a new mistress, I love a quarrel with an old one. But the devil's in't, there has been such a calm in my affairs of late, I have not had the pleasure of making a woman so much as break her fan, to be sullen, or forswear herself, these three days.

MED: A very great misfortune. Let me see; I love mischief well enough to forward this business myself. I'll about it presently, and though I know the truth of what y'ave done will set her a-raving, I'll heighten it a little with invention, leave her in a fit o' the mother, and be here again before y'are ready.

DOR: Pray, stay; you may spare yourself the labour. The business is undertaken already by one who will manage it with as much address, and I think with a little more malice, than you can.

MED: Who i'the devil's name can this be!

DOR: Why, the vizard—that very vizard you saw me with

MED: Does she love mischief so well as to betray herself to spite another?

DOR: Not so neither, Medley. I will make you comprehend the mystery: this mask, for a farther confirmation of what I have been these two days swearing to her, made me yesterday at the playhouse make her a promise before her face utterly to break off with Loveit, and, because she tenders my reputation and would not have me do a barbarous thing, has contrived a way to give me a handsome occasion.

MED: Very good.

DOR: She intends about an hour before me, this afternoon, to make Loveit a visit, and, having the privilege, by reason of a professed friendship between 'em, to talk of her concerns—

MED: Is she a friend?

DOR: Oh, an intimate friend!

MED: Better and better; pray, proceed.

DOR: She means insensibly to insinuate a discourse of me and artificially raise her jealousy to such a height that, transported with the first motions of her passion, she shall fly upon me with all the fury imaginable as soon as ever I enter; the quarrel being thus happily begun, I am to play my part, confess and justify all my roguery, swear her impertinence and ill-humour makes her intolerable, tax her with the next fop that comes into my head, and in a huff march away, slight her, and leave her to be taken by whosoever thinks it worth his time to lie down before her.

MED: This vizard is a spark and has a genius that makes her worthy of yourself, Dorimant.

Hernani

Victor Hugo
1830

Scene: In Doña Sol's chambers. Night. Don Carlos, hearing of her
betrothal to the old uncle has come to claim her, but hides in a
closet because he has heard that she is in love with a young man
who comes nightly to her room. Hernani arrives.

Doña Sol, a beautiful young woman engaged to her old uncle, the
Duke de Pastrana.
Hernani, a young man, in love with Doña Sol.
Don Carlos, also in love with Doña Sol.

HERNANI: *(Not hearing her.)* So the duke is away from the castle . . .
DOÑA SOL: *(Smilingly.)* How tall you are!
HERNANI: He is gone awhile—
DOÑA SOL: Dear Hernani, let us not think about the duke.
HERNANI: But we must think about him! That old man loves you, and
will marry you . . . He took a kiss from you the other day—not
think about him!
DOÑA SOL: *(Laughing.)* Is that what's thrown you into such despair?
An uncle's kiss—and on the brow besides! Almost a fatherly
caress . . .
HERNANI: No; a lover's kiss, a husband's—the kiss of a jealous man.
Oh, my lady, you will soon belong to him! Do you realize that?
The foolish, stooped old man, he needs a wife to end his journey
and complete his day—and so the chilly specter takes himself a
young girl! The mad old man! Does he not see that while he marries you with one hand, death weds him by the other? He comes
so heedlessly to thrust himself into our love—when he should
instead be measuring himself for the gravedigger! Doña Sol, who
made this match? You were forced to it, I hope?
DOÑA SOL: The king desires it, they say.
HERNANI: The king! the king! My father died upon the gallows, condemned by his! And though we have grown older since that day,

my hatred is still fresh toward the old king's ghost, his widow, and his son—toward all his flesh. He is dead, he counts no more; but when I was a child I made a vow to avenge my father on his son. Carlos, king of the Castiles—I have sought you everywhere, for the loathing between our houses does not die! Our fathers struggled without pity or remorse for thirty years; now, with our fathers dead, nothing has changed. They died in vain, for their enmity lives on; peace has not yet come to them, for their sons still stand, and still pursue the duel. So it is you, Carlos, who made this shameful match! So much the better. I sought for you, and here you are astride my path.

DOÑA SOL: You frighten me.

HERNANI: I have sworn to carry out a curse, and I must frighten even myself. Listen. The man they have betrothed you to, Don Ruy de Silva, is duke of Pastraña; he is a nobleman of Aragon, a count and grandee of Castile. He cannot give you youth, my sweet young girl; but in its place he offers you such gold, such jewels and gems that your brow will shine among the glittering crowns of royalty. His duchess will hold such power and pride, splendor and wealth, that many a queen could envy her. Such is the duke. While I—I am poor; as a child I had nothing but the forests where I roamed barefoot. I too may own some glowing coat of arms, hid now by clotted blood; I too may have rights that now are cloaked in the folds and shadows of a black gallows-cloth; unless my waiting be in vain, perhaps one day those rights will flash out from this sheath again as I draw my sword. Meanwhile, a jealous heaven has granted me nothing but air, and light and water—no more than the dowry it offers every man. Let me free you now from one of us, the duke or me. You must choose between us: marry him, or come with me.

DOÑA SOL: I shall go with you.

HERNANI: To live among my rough companions? They are outlaws, whose names the hangman already knows, men whose blades never grow blunt, nor their hearts tender—each of them with some blood vengeance that whips him on. Would you come and be the queen of such a band? For I never told you this—I am an outlaw! When I was hunted through the land of Spain, only old Catalonia welcomed me like a mother into her forests, her harsh mountains, her rough rocks where only the soaring eagle peers. Among her highlanders, her solemn, poor, free men, I grew to manhood; and tomorrow if I sound this horn, three thousand of them will come . . . You shiver—think again. Would you follow me into the trees, over the hills, along the river's edge? To the land of men who look like the devils in your dreams? And live in doubt, suspecting everything—eyes, voices, footfalls, rustlings—and sleep on the bare grass, and drink from the stream; and as you nurse some waking child at night, to hear musket balls go hissing by your ear?

Would you be an outlawed wanderer with me, and if need be, follow me to where I shall follow my father—onto the scaffold?

DOÑA SOL: I will follow you.

HERNANI: The duke is prosperous and powerful—his life is good. There is no stain on his old family name. The duke can do what he will. He offers you not just his hand, but treasure, titles, and contentment.

DOÑA SOL: We will leave tomorrow. Hernani, do not condemn me for my new boldness. Are you my demon or my angel? I cannot tell—but I am your slave. Wherever you go I will go. Stay, or depart—I belong to you. Why? I cannot say. I need to see you, and must have you near, and have you all the time. When the sound of your step fades, then I think that my heart has stopped its beat; you are gone, and I am gone from myself. But no sooner does that beloved footfall sound in my ear again, than I remember life and feel my soul come back to me!

HERNANI: *(Taking her in his arms.)* My love!

DOÑA SOL: At midnight, then, tomorrow. Bring your men to my window, and clap your hands three times. You will see—I will be strong and brave.

HERNANI: Do you realize now what I am?

DOÑA SOL: My lord, what does it matter? I am going with you.

HERNANI: No—since you want to follow me, impulsive woman, you must learn what name, what rank, what soul, what destiny is hidden in rough Hernani. You would take a brigand; but would you have a banished man?

DON CARLOS: *(Clattering the cupboard door open.)* Will you never finish telling her your tale? Do you suppose it's pleasant, cramped into this closet?

(Hernani starts back, astonished. Doña Sol cries out and flies into his arms, staring fearfully at Don Carlos.)

HERNANI: *(His hand on his sword hilt.)* Who is this man?

DOÑA SOL: Great heavens! Help! Help, guards!

HERNANI: Quiet, Doña Sol! You'll waken angry eyes! When I am with you, please, whatever comes, never call for any hand but mine to aid you. *(To Don Carlos.)* What were you doing there?

DON CAROLS: I can hardly claim I was out for a gallop through the woods.

HERNANI: When a man banters after he offends, only his heir is likely to enjoy the joke.

DON CARLOS: One good line deserves another. Sir, let us speak frankly. You love this lady; you come to watch your eyes in hers each night: very good. I love her too, and want to know who it is I have seen so often entering by the window while I stay at the door.

HERNANI: I swear you shall leave the way I enter, sir.

DON CARLOS: We shall see. So then, I offer my lady my love too. Let us share her, shall we? I've seen such goodness in her soul, so much tender feeling, that I should think she had enough for two lovers. And so, tonight, I thought to bring my plans to fruit. I was mistaken for you, and slipped in by surprise; I hid, I listened—you see how frank I am—but in this slot I hardly heard a word, and nearly suffocated. Besides my French vest was crumbling badly. I am coming out.

HERNANI: My dagger is uneasy in its hiding place too, and eager to come out.

DON CARLOS: *(Acknowledging the challenge.)* As you like, sir.

HERNANI: *(Drawing his sword.)* En garde!

(Don Carlos draws his own.)

DOÑA SOL: *(Throwing herself between them.)* Hernani! No!

DON CARLOS: Peace, señora.

HERNANI: Tell me your name.

DON CARLOS: Tell me your own!

HERNANI: I am keeping it a deadly secret for another man—one day he will lie beneath my conquering knee and feel my name in his ear, and my knife at his heart.

DON CARLOS: Then what is that man's name?

HERNANI: What can it mean to you? On guard! Defend yourself!

(They cross swords. Doña Sol falls trembling onto a chair. Knocking at the main door.)

DOÑA SOL: *(Rising in alarm.)* Someone is at the door!

Ruddigore or The Witch's Curse

Gilbert and Sullivan

1887

Scene: The fishing village of Rederring in Cornwall. Richard has just married Rose. Robin has been in love with her for a long while and was too shy to tell her. Richard has stolen her away.

Robin, Sir Rutheven Murgatroyd, a handsome young man, shy.
Rose, a lovely young maiden.
Richard, a sailor, friend to Robin.

RICH: What could I do? I'm bound to obey my heart's dictates.

ROB: Of course—no doubt. It's quite right—I don't mind—that is, not particularly—only it's—it *is* disappointing, you know.

ROSE: *(To Robin.)* Oh, but, sir I knew not that thou didst seek me in wedlock, or in very truth I should not have hearkened unto this man, for behold, he is but a lowly mariner, and very poor withal, whereas thou art a tiller of the land, and thou hast fat oxen, and many sheep and swine, a considerable dairy farm and much corn and oil!

RICH: That's true, my lass, but it's done now, ain't it, Rob?

ROSE: Still it may be that I should not be happy in thy love. I am passing young and little able to judge. Moreover, as to thy character I know naught!

ROB: Nay, Rose, I'll answer for that. Dick has won thy love fairly. Broken-hearted as I am, I'll stand up for Dick through thick and thin!

RICH: *(With emotion.)* Thankye, messmate! that's well said. That's spoken honest. Thankye, Rob! *(Grasps his hand.)*

ROSE: Yet methinks I have heard that sailors are but worldly men, and little prone to lead serious and thoughtful lives!

ROB: And what then? Admit that Dick is *not* a steady character, and that when he's excited he uses language that would make your hair curl. Grant that—he does. It's the truth, and I'm not going to deny it. But look at his *good* qualities. He's as nimble as a pony, and his hornpipe is the talk of the Fleet!

RICH: Thankye, Rob! That's well spoken. Thankye, Rob!

ROSE: But it may be that he drinketh strong waters which do bemuse a man, and make him even as the wild beasts of the desert!

ROB: Well, suppose he does, and I don't say he don't, for rum's his bane, and ever has been He *does* drink—I won't deny it. But what of that? Look at his arms—tattooed to the shoulder! *(Rich rolls up his sleeves.)* No, no—I won't hear a word against Dick!

ROSE: But they say that mariners are but rarely true to those whom they profess to love!

ROB: Granted—granted—and I don't say that Dick isn't as bad as any of 'em. *(Rich chuckles.)* You are, you know you are, you dog! a devil of a fellow—a regular out-and-out Lothario! But what then? You can't have everything, and a better hand at turning-in a dead-eye don't walk a deck! And what an accomplishment *that* is in a family man! No, no—not a word against Dick. I'll stick up for him through thick and thin!

RICH: Thankye, Rob, thankye. You're a true friend. I've acted accordin' to my heart's dictates, and such orders as them no man should disobey.

ENSEMBLE—RICHARD, ROBIN, ROSE:
> In sailing o'er life's ocean wide
> Your heart should be your only guide;
> With summer sea and favouring wind,
> Yourself in port you'll surely find.

SOLO—RICHARD:
> *My* heart says, "To this maiden strike—
> She's captured you.
> She's just the sort of girl you like—
> You know you do.
> If other man her heart should gain,
> I shall resign."

That's what it says to me quite plain,
This heart of mine.

SOLO—ROBIN:
My heart says, "You've a prosperous lot,
With acres wide;
You mean to settle all you've got
Upon your bride."

It don't pretend to shape my acts
By work or sign;
It merely states these simple facts,
This heart of mine!

SOLO—ROSE:
Ten minutes since my heart said "white"—
It now says "black".
It then said "left"—it now says "right"—
Hearts often tack.
I must obey its latest strain—
You tell me so *(To Richard.)*
But should it change its mind again,
I'll let you know.
(Turning from Richard to Robin, who embraces her.)

Ghosts

Henrik Ibsen
1881

Scene: In the large, comfortable home of Mrs. Alving on one of the large fiords in western Norway. Manders is visiting to arrange for an endowment to the new orphanage in town. They are discussing the fate of Regina Engstrand, a servant in Mrs. Alving's home.

Manders, a pastor, conservative and cautious by nature.
Mrs. Helen Alving, widow of Capt. Alving, late Chamberlain to the King of Norway.
Osvald Alving, her son—an artist who has recently returned from living in Europe.

PASTOR MANDERS: Remember that he is her father, no matter what.
MRS. ALVING: And I know just exactly the kind of father he's been to her. No, she'll never get my consent to go back with him.
PASTOR MANDERS: *(Rising.)* My dear lady, don't take it so violently. I'm sorry to see you midjudge Jakob Engstrand so completely. It's almost as if you were frightened—
MRS. ALVING: *(More calmly.)* Never mind. I have taken Regina into my house, and she'll stay in my house. *(Listens.)* Shh, Pastor Manders, let's not talk about this any more. *(Joy lights up her face.)* Listen! Osvald's coming downstairs. Now we'll concentrate on him.
   (Osvald Alving, in a light overcoat, hat in hand and smoking a large meerschaum pipe, enters through the door, left.)
OSVALD: *(Remains standing in the doorway.)* Oh, excuse me, I thought you were in the study. *(Comes forward.)* Good morning.
PASTOR MANDERS: *(Staring.)* That's extraordinary!
MRS. ALVING: Yes, what do you have to say about him now, Pastor Manders?
PASTOR MANDERS: I'd say—I'd say—but is it really—?
OSVALD: Yes, it really is the Prodigal Son, Pastor.
PASTOR MANDERS: My dear young friend—

OSVALD: Well, the homecoming son, then.

MRS. ALVING: Osvald remembers when you had so much against his becoming a painter.

PASTOR MANDERS: To mortal eyes, many a step can well seem perilous that later—ah, welcome, welcome home! Really, my dear Osvald—I suppose I may still use your first name?

OSVALD: Of course, what else would you call me?

PASTOR MANDERS: Good. What I meant was—my dear Osvald—you mustn't think that I condemn everything artists stand for. I assume there must be quite a few who can preserve their inner selves unstained in that way of life.

OSVALD: Let's hope so.

MRS. ALVING: *(Beginning with pleasure.)* I know one who has preserved an unstained self both inside and out. All you have to do is look at him, Pastor.

OSVALD: *(Pacing up and down.)* Yes, yes Mother—that's enough.

PASTOR MANDERS: Without a doubt, there's no denying it. And you've already begun to make a name for yourself. The papers have mentioned you quite a bit, and always in glowing terms. Although I have to say that lately there hasn't been as much.

OSVALD: *(Near the conservatory.)* I haven't been painting much recently.

MRS. ALVING: A painter needs to rest now and then, like everyone else.

PASTOR MANDERS: Yes, I understand—to prepare himself, to gather strength for some really big project.

OSVALD: Yes. Mother, are we eating soon?

MRS. ALVING: In half an hour. He's got a good appetite, thank God.

PASTOR MANDERS: And a taste for tobacco, too.

OSVALD: I found Father's pipe upstairs in the bedroom, so—

PASTOR MANDERS: Aha! That's it then.

MRS. ALVING: What?

PASTOR MANDERS: When Osvald came through that door there with the pipe in his mouth, it was as if I saw his father alive again.

OSVALD: Really?

MRS. ALVING: How can you say that? Osvald takes after me.

PASTOR MANDERS: Yes, but there's a line there, around the corner of the mouth, something about the lips, that brings Alving back to mind—at least when he's smoking.

MRS. ALVING: No, absolutely not. I think Osvald's mouth reminds me more of a priest's

PASTOR MANDERS: Yes, yes, many of my colleagues have a similar expression.

MRS. ALVING: Put the pipe down now—I don't want smoking in here.

OSVALD: *(Does so.)* Gladly. I just wanted to try it—because I smoked it once before, as a child.

MRS. ALVING: You did?

OSVALD: Yes. I was very small at the time. And I remember I came up to Father's room one evening when he was feeling happy and good.

MRS. ALVING: Oh, you don't remember anything from those years.

OSVALD: Oh yes—I remember it clearly. He took me and sat me on his knee and let me smoke his pipe. "Smoke it, boy," he said— "smoke it down deep, boy." And I smoked as much as I could, until I felt myself going pale and my forehead broke out in huge drops of sweat. Then he laughed so uproariously—

PASTOR MANDERS: Extraordinary.

MRS. ALVING: It's just something he dreamt.

OSVALD: No, Mother, I definitely didn't dream it. Don't you remember? You came in then and carried me to the nursery. I got sick, and I saw you were crying. Did father often play jokes like that?

PASTOR MANDERS: As a young man he was so full of the joy of life.

OSVALD: And yet he was able to accomplish so much in the world— so much that was good and useful, even dying as young as he did.

PASTOR MANDERS: Yes, it's a fact that you've inherited the name of an energetic and worthy man, Osvald Alving. Let's hope it will be an inspiration to you—

OSVALD: It ought to be.

PASTOR MANDERS: It was nice of you to come home for these celebrations in his honor.

OSVALD: It's the least I can do for Father.

MRS. ALVING: And the nicest thing of all is how long I'll get to keep him.

PASTOR MANDERS: Yes, I hear you'll be staying all winter.

OSVALD: I'll be staying indefinitely, Pastor. Oh, it's wonderful to come home again.

MRS. ALVING: *(Beaming.)* Yes, isn't that true?

PASTOR MANDERS: *(Looking at him sympathetically.)* You went out into the world very early, Osvald.

OSVALD: Yes, I did. I wonder sometimes if it wasn't too early.

MRS. ALVING: Not at all. It's good for a bright boy. Especially when he's an only child. He shouldn't be kept at home to be spoiled by his mother and father.

PASTOR MANDERS: That's a highly debatable point, Mrs. Alving. The ancestral home is and always will remain a child's rightful place.

OSVALD: Now I'm in total agreement with the Pastor.

PASTOR MANDERS: Just look at your own son. Yes, we can talk about this in front of him. What has the result been for him? He's twenty-six or twenty-seven and he's never had the chance to see what a respectable home is like.

OSVALD: I beg your pardon, Pastor, but you're quite mistaken about that.

PASTOR MANDERS: Really? I thought you lived almost exclusively among artists.

OSVALD: I did, yes.

PASTOR MANDERS: Mostly among younger artists.

OSVALD: Yes, that's right.

PASTOR MANDERS: But I thought most of those people didn't have the means to support a home and family.

OSVALD: Many of them lack the means to get married, Pastor.

PASTOR MANDERS: That's what I'm saying.

OSVALD: But they can still have a home. And one or two do—very respectable, very pleasant homes. *(Mrs. Alving, following closely, nods but says nothing.)*

PASTOR MANDERS: I'm not talking about bachelor's houses. When I say home, I mean a real family home where a man lives with his wife and his children.

OSVALD: Yes, or with his children and the mother.

PASTOR MANDERS: *(Startled, claps his hands.)* But merciful—!

OSVALD: Well?

PASTOR MANDERS: Lives with—his children's mother?

OSVALD: Yes. What should he do—abandon her?

PASTOR MANDERS: So you're talking about illicit relationships! About those irresponsible, so-called "free marriages"!

OSVALD: I've never noticed anything especially irresponsible about the way these people live together.

PASTOR MANDERS: But how is it possible that young men and women of even moderately decent upbringing can bring themselves to live like that—in the public eye.

OSVALD: What should they do instead? A poor young artist—a poor young girl—getting married costs money. What should they do?

PASTOR MANDERS: What should they do? Well, Mr. Alving, I'll tell you what they should do. They should stay away from each other from the beginning, that's what they should do.

OSVALD: That kind of advice wouldn't get you very far with young, warm-blooded people in love.

MRS. ALVING: No, not too far.

PASTOR MANDERS *(Persisting.)* And the authorities tolerate such things! It goes on openly, no one stops it! *(Facing Mrs. Alving.)* Didn't I have good reason to be worried about your son? Moving in circles where blatant immorality is the custom—where it's even claimed as a right?

OSVALD: Let me tell you something, Pastor. I've been a regular Sunday guest in some of these unconventional homes—

PASTOR MANDERS: On Sundays, no less!

OSVALD: Yes, when people should be enjoying themselves. And never once have I heard an offensive word, much less witnessed anything that could be called immoral. But do you know where I *have* encountered immorality among the artists?

PASTOR MANDERS: No, praise God!

OSVALD: Then I think I should enlighten you: I run into it whenever one of our exemplary husbands and fathers comes down there to get a close look at the other side of life—so they do us artists the honor of paying a visit to our humble cafés. What an education we're treated to then! Those gentlemen can teach us about places and things we never even dreamed of.

PASTOR MANDERS: What? You're claiming that respectable men from here at home would—?

OSVALD: Haven't you ever—when these respectable men come home again—haven't you heard them screaming about the rampant epidemic of immorality abroad?

PASTOR MANDERS: Naturally, of course—

MRS. ALVING: I've heard it too.

OSVALD: Well, they know what they're talking about. There are connoisseurs among them. *(Clutching his head.)* Ah!—this beautiful, glorious, free life out there—polluted like that!

MRS. ALVING: You mustn't excite yourself, Osvald, it's not good for you.

OSVALD: No, Mother, you're right. It's not healthy. It's this damn fatigue. I'll go for a little walk before we eat. I'm sorry, Pastor—I know you can't bring yourself to see that. But it just suddenly came over me and I had to say it. *(He goes out through the second door, right.)*

MRS. ALVING: My poor boy.

PASTOR MANDERS: Yes, you might well say that. So this is what's become of him. *(Mrs. Alving looks at him silently. Manders walks up and down.)* He called himself the Prodigal Son. Alas, how true—how true. So what do you think of all this?

MRS. ALVING: I think every word Osvald said was right.

The Bear

Anton Chekhov
1888

Scene: The drawing room of Popova's country home. She is in deep
mourning. Smirnov claims the widow owes him money and he
will not leave until he is paid. She refuses, claiming that she is too
grief-stricken to deal with this.

Elena Ivanova Popova, a widow—young, a landowner.
Smirnov, her neighbor and a landowner, middle-aged.
Luka, her trusty servant, elderly.

SMIRNOV: *(With a contemptuous laugh.)* Widow's weeds! . . . I don't
understand, what do you take me for, anyway? As if I didn't
know why you walk around in this getup and bury yourself alive!
Oh, please! It's so alluring, so poetic! Some young officer happens to wander past the estate, or some crackpot poet, say, and
he looks up at the window and he thinks: "There dwells the mys-
terious Tamara, our dark lady of Lermontov, who out of love for
a man has enterred herself twixt these four walls!" We all know
that story!
POPOVA: *(Incensed.)* What! How dare you say such things to me?
SMIRNOV: You've buried yourself alive, and yet you haven't forgotten
to powder your nose!
POPOVA: How dare you speak to me in such a manner!
SMIRNOV: Will you stop shouting at me, please, I'm not your stew-
ard! And let's call things by their proper names here, shall we? I
am not a woman, I'm accustomed to speaking my mind plainly!
So will you kindly stop shouting!
POPOVA: I'm not shouting, you're shouting! And you can kindly leave
me in peace!
SMIRNOV: Pay me my money, and I'll go away.
POPOVA: I am not giving you any money!
SMIRNOV: Oh yes you will, give it to me!

POPOVA: You're not getting a single kopek, that'll serve you right! So you can kindly leave me in peace!

SMIRNOV: I do not have the pleasure of being either your husband or your fiancé, so let's not make a scene here, thank you very much. *(Sits down.)* I don't like it.

POPOVA: *(Choking with rage.)* So you've taken a seat?

SMIRNOV: Yes, I have.

POPOVA: I am asking you to go away!

SMIRNOV: Give me my money . . . *(Aside.)* What a rage I'm in! What a rage!

POOPOVA: I have no desire to converse with insolent individuals! Will you kindly get out of here! *(Pause.)* So are you going? Yes or no?

SMIRNOV: No.

POPOVA: No?

SMIRNOV: No.

POPOVA: Very well, then! *(Rings.)*

(Enter Luka.)

POPPVA: Luka, please show this gentlemen out!

LUKA: *(Goes up to Smirnov.)* Sir, please, if you're told to go, then go! And let's not have any discussion about it . . .

SMIRNOV: *(Jumping up.)* Will you shut up! Who do you think you're talking to? I'll make a salad out of you!

LUKA: *(Clutching his heart.)* Oh good heavens! . . . Saints above! . . . *(Collapses into an armchair.)* I feel faint! I feel faint! I can't breathe!

POPOVA: Where is Dasha? Dasha? Dasha? *(Shouts.)* Dasha! Pelegea! Dasha! *(Rings the bell.)*

LUKA: Ach! They're all out picking berries . . . There's no one home . . . I feel faint! Water!

POPOVA: Will you please get out of here!

SMIRNOV: Would you mind putting it more politely?

POPOVA: *(Clenching her fists and stamping her feet.)* Peasant! Boor! Bear! Lout! Monster!

SMIRNOV: What? What did you say?

POPOVA: I said you're a bear, a monster!

SMIRNOV: *(Advances toward her.)* Excuse me, but what right do you have to insult me in this way?

POPOVA: That's right, I'm insulting you . . . so what? You think I'm afraid of you? Is that it?

SMIRNOV: And you think that just because you're a woman, you have the right to insult me with impunity? Is that what you think? I challenge you to a duel!

LUKA: Oh good heavens! . . . Saints above! . . . Water!

SMIRNOV: Bring out the pistol!

POPOVA: Just because you can clench your fists and bellow like a bull, you think I'm afraid of you? Eh? You boor!

SMIRNOV: A duel! I will not tolerate an insult! Never mind that you're a member of the weaker sex!

POPOVA: *(Trying to outshout him.)* Bear! Bear! Bear!

SMIRNOV: Why is it only men who must pay for their insults! The dark ages are over! You want equality, you'll get equality, goddammit! Choose your weapons!

POPOVA: You want a duel? You've got a duel! Be my guest!

SMIRNOVE: This very minute!

POPOVA: This very minute! My husband left a pair of pistols . . . I'll bring them right away . . . *(Rushes out and stops for a moment.)* What a pleasure it will be to blow your brains out! Damn you to hell! *(Exits.)*

SMIRNOV: I'll wing her like a chicken! I'm no sissy, no simpering, sentimental little puppy, there's no such thing as the weaker sex, not as far as I'm concerned, there isn't!

LUKA: Dear sir! . . . *(Gets on his knees.)* Have mercy on me, pity an old man, go away from here! First you frighten me to death, and now you're getting ready to fight a duel!

SMIRNOV: *(Not hearing him.)* A duel, now there's equality, there's emancipation for you! Parity of the sexes! I'll shoot her out of principle! But what sort of woman is this *(Mimics.)* "Damn you to hell . . . I'll blow your brains out . . . " What sort of woman? Her face was flushed, her eyes were shining . . . She rose to the challenge! I swear, I've never seen such a woman before in my entire life . . .

LUKA: Go away, sir! and I'll pray for you for the rest of my days!

SMIRNOV: Now this is what a woman is! This I understand! A real woman! This is not a whiner, this is not a wimp, this is a fireball, a rocket, this is gunpowder! A shame to have to kill her, though!

LUKA: *(Weeping.)* Sir . . . dear sir, go away!

SMIRNOV: I positively like her! Positively! Yes, she's got dimples, and I like her anyway! Forget the debt . . . I'm not even angry any more . . . What an astonishing woman!

(Enters Popova with the pistols.)

POPOVA: Here they are, the pistols . . . But before we fight, if you don't mind please, show me how to shoot . . . I've never held a pistol before in my life.

LUKA: Heavenly father, have mercy upon us . . . I'll go and get the gardener and the coachman . . . Why has this calamity befallen us! . . . *(Exits.)*

SMIRNOV: *(Looking the pistols over.)* All right, now you see, there are several different types of pistols . . . There's a special Mortimer percussion cap dueling pistol, for example. But what you've got here is a Smith and Wesson revolver, triple action with extractor, central firing mechanism . . . Marvelous firing pistols! . . . Cost you at least ninety rubles a pair . . . So, you hold the revolver like this . . . *(Aside.)* Those eyes, those eyes! The woman is on fire!

POPOVA: Like this?

SMIRNOV: That's right, like this . . . Next, you cock the pistol . . . then you aim . . . Head back just a little bit! Extend your arm "so" . . . Like that, right . . . Next, you squeeze this little gadget with your finger—and that's all there is to it . . . Only remember this golden rule: Don't get excited, and don't be in a rush to take aim . . . Try to keep your arm steady.

POPOVA: Very good . . . It's awkward shooting indoors, let's go outside.

SMIRNOV: Fine, let's go. Only I warn you, I shall shoot in the air.

POPOVA: This is the last straw! Why?

SMIRNOV: Because . . . Because . . . That's my business, why!

POPOVA: So, you're afraid, are you? Really? Ah ha-a-a-a! No, sir, you can't get out of this one! Follow me, please! I won't have satisfaction until I put a hole in your head . . . that head which I so deeply despise! Afraid, eh?

SMIRNOV: Yes, I'm afraid.

POPOVA: Liar! Why don't you want to fight?

SMIRNOV: Because . . . because . . . I think I've taken a liking to you.

How He Lied to Her Husband

George Bernard Shaw
1904

Scene: Time 8 P.M. The Bompas home. Apjohn's love letters to Aurora have been lost and Aurora fears that her sister-in-law Georgina may have shown them to Teddy. The illicit lovers had been planning to attend the theater but have been arguing. Suddenly Aurora hears a sound and rushes to the door.

He, Apjohn.
She, Aurora Bompas, 37, spoiled, elegant, dressed for the theater.
The husband, Mr. Bompas (Teddy), a bit older.

HE: What is it?

SHE: *(White with apprehension.)* It's Teddy: I hear him tapping the new barometer. He can't have anything serious on his mind or he wouldn't do that. Perhaps Georgina hasn't said anything *(She steals back to the hearth.)* Try and look as if there was nothing the matter. Give me my gloves quick. *(He hands them to her. She pulls on one hastily and begins buttoning it with ostentatious unconcern.)* Go further away from me, quick. *(He walks doggedly away from her until the piano prevents his going farther.)* If I button my glove, and you were to hum a tune, don't you think that—

HE: The tableau would be complete in its guiltiness. For Heaven's sake, Mrs. Bompas, let that glove alone: You look like a pickpocket.

(Her husband comes in: a robust, thick-necked, well-groomed city man, with a strong chin but a blithering eye and credulous mouth. He has a momentous air, but shews no sign of displeasure: rather the contrary.)

HER HUSBAND: Hallo! I thought you two were at the theatre.

SHE: I felt anxious about you, Teddy. Why didn't you come home to dinner?

HER HUSBAND: I got a message from Georgina. She wanted me to go to her.

SHE: Poor dear Georgina! I'm sorry I haven't been able to call on her last week. I hope there's nothing the matter with her.

HER HUSBAND: Nothing, except anxiety for my welfare—and yours. *(She steals a terrified look at Henry.)* By the way, Apjohn, I should like a word with you this evening, if Aurora can spare you a moment.

HE: *(Formally.)* I am at your service.

HER HUSBAND: No hurry. After the theatre will do.

HE: We have decided not to go.

HER HUSBAND: Indeed! Well, then, shall we adjourn to my snuggery?

SHE: You needn't move. I shall go and lock up my diamonds since I'm not going to the theatre. Give me my things.

HER HUSBAND: *(As he hands her the cloud and the mirror.)* Well, we shall have more room here.

HE: *(Looking about him and shaking his shoulders loose.)* I think I should prefer plenty of room.

HER HUSBAND: So, if it's not disturbing you, Rory—?

SHE: Not at all. *(She goes out.)*

(When the two men are alone together Bompas deliberately takes the poems from his breast pocket; looks at them reflectively; then looks at Henry, mutely inviting his attention. Henry refuses to understand, doing his best to look unconcerned.)

HER HUSBAND: Do these manuscripts seem at all familiar to you, may I ask?

HE: Manuscripts?

HER HUSBAND: Yes. Would you like to look at them a little closer? *(He proffers them under Henry's nose.)*

HE: *(As with a sudden illumination of glad surprise.)* Why, these are my poems!

HER HUSBAND: So I gather.

HE: What a shame! Mrs. Bompas has shewn them to you! You must think me an utter ass. I wrote them years ago after reading Swinburne's *Songs Before Sunrise*. Nothing would do me then but I must reel off a set of Songs to the Sunrise. Aurora, you know: the rosy fingered Aurora. They're all about Aurora. When Mrs. Bompas told me her name was Aurora, I couldn't resist the temptation to lend them to her to read. But I didn't bargain for your unsympathetic eyes.

HER HUSBAND: *(Grinning.)* Apjohn: that's really very ready of you. You are cut out for literature; and the day will come when Rory and I will be proud to have you about the house. I have heard far thinner stories from much older men.

HE: *(With an air of great surprise.)* Do you mean to imply that you don't believe me?

HER HUSBAND: Do you expect me to believe you?

HE: Why not? I don't understand.

HER HUSBAND: Come! Don't underrate your own cleverness, Apjohn. I think you understand pretty well.

HE: I assure you I am quite at a loss. Can you not be a little more explicit?

HER HUSBAND: Don't overdo it, old chap. However, I will just be so far explicit as to say that if you think these poems read as if they were addressed, not to a live woman, but to a shivering cold time of day at which you were never out of bed in your life, you hardly do justice to your own literary powers—which I admire and appreciate, mind you, as much as any man. Come! own up. You wrote those poems to my wife (*An internal struggle prevents Henry from answering.*) Of course you did. (*He throws the poems on the table; and goes to the hearth rug, where he plants himself solidly, chuckling a little and waiting for the next move.*)

HE: *(Formally and carefully.)* Mr. Bompas: I pledge you my word you are mistaken. I need not tell you that Mrs. Bompas is a lady of stainless honor, who has never cast an unworthy thought on me. The fact that she has shewn you my poems—

HER HUSBAND: That's not a fact. I came by them without her knowledge. She didn't shew them to me.

HE: Does not that prove their perfect innocence? She would have shewn them to you at once if she had taken your quite unfounded view of them.

HER HUSBAND: *(Shaken.)* Apjohn: play fair. Don't abuse your intellectual gifts. Do you really mean that I am making a fool of myself?

HE: *(Earnestly.)* Believe me, you are. I assure you, on my honor as a gentlemen, that I have never had the slightest feeling for Mrs. Bompas beyond the ordinary esteem and regard of a pleasant acquaintance.

HER HUSBAND: *(Shortly, shewing ill humor for the first time.)* Oh! Indeed! *(He leaves his hearth and begins to approach Henry slowly, looking him up and down with growing resentment.)*

HE: *(Hastening to improve the impression made by his mendacity.)* I should never have dreamt of writing poems to her. The thing is absurd.

HER HUSBAND: *(Reddening ominously.)* Why is it absurd?

HE: *(Shrugging his shoulders.)* Well, it happens that I do not admire Mrs. Bompas—in that way.

HER HUSBAND: *(Breaking out in Henry's face.)* Let me tell you that Mrs. Bompas has been admired by better men than you, you soapy-headed little puppy, you.

HE: *(Much taken aback.)* There is no need to insult me like this. I assure you, on my honor as a—

HER HUSBAND: *(Too angry to tolerate a reply, and boring Henry more and more towards the piano.)* You don't admire Mrs. Bompas! You would never dream of writing poems to Mrs. Bompas! My wife's not good enough for you, isn't she! *(Fiercely.)* Who are you, pray, that you should be so jolly superior?

HE: Mr. Bompas: I can make allowances for your jealousy—

HER HUSBAND: Jealousy! do you suppose I'm jealous of you? No, nor of ten like you. But if you think I'll stand here and let you insult my wife in her own house, you're mistaken.

HE: *(Very uncomfortable with his back against the piano and Teddy standing over him threateningly.)* How can I convince you? Be reasonable. I tell you my relations with Mrs. Bompas are relations of perfect coldness—of indifference—

HER HUSBAND: *(Scornfully.)* Say it again: say it again. You're proud of it, aren't you? Yah! you're not worth kicking. *(Henry suddenly executes the feat known to pugilists as slipping, and changes sides with Teddy, who is now between Henry and the piano.)*

HE: Look here: I'm not going to stand this.

HER HUSBAND: Oh, you have some blood in your body after all! Good job!

HE: This is ridiculous. I assure you Mrs. Bompas is quite—

HER HUSBAND: What is Mrs. Bompas to you, I'd like to know. I'll tell you what Mrs. Bompas is. She's the smartest woman in the smartest set in South Kensington, and the handsomest, and the cleverest, and the most fetching to experienced men who know a good thing when they see it, whatever she may be to conceited penny-a-lining puppies who think nothing good enough for them. It's admitted by the best people; and not to know it argues yourself unknown. Three of our first actor-managers have offered her a hundred a week if she'll go on the stage when they start a repertory theatre; and I think they know what they're about as well as you. The only member of the present Cabinet that you might call a handsome man has neglected the business of the country to dance with her, though he don't belong to our set as a regular thing. One of the first professional poets in Bedford Park wrote a sonnet to her, worth all your amateur trash. At Ascot last season the eldest son of a duke excused himself from calling on me on the ground that his feelings for Mrs. Bompas were not consistent with his duty to me as host; and it did him honor and me too. But *(With gathering fury.)* she isn't good enough for you, it seems. You regard her with coldness, with indifference; and you have the cool cheek to tell me so to my face. For two pins I'd flatten your nose in to teach you manners. Introducing a fine woman to you is casting pearls before swine *(Yelling at him.)* before SWINE! d'ye hear?

HE: *(With a deplorable lack of polish.)* You call me a swine again and I'll land you one on the chin that'll make your head sing for a week.

HER HUSBAND: *(Exploding.)* What! *(He charges at Henry with bull-like fury. Henry places himself on guard in the manner of a well taught boxer, and gets away smartly, but unfortunately forgets the stool which is just behind him. He falls backwards over it, unintentionally pushing it against the shins of Bompas, who falls forward over it. Mrs. Bompas, with a scream, rushes into the room between the sprawling champions, and sits down on the floor in order to get her right arm around her husband's neck.)*

SHE: You shant, Teddy: You shant. You will be killed: he is a prize-fighter.

HER HUSBAND: *(Vengefully.)* I'll prize-fight him. *(He struggles vainly to free himself from her embrace.)*

SHE: Henry: Don't let him fight you. Promise me that you won't.

HE: *(Ruefully.)* I have got a most frightful bump on the back of my head. *(He tries to rise.)*

SHE: *(Reaching out her left hand to seize his coat tail, and pulling him down again, whilst keeping fast hold of Teddy with the other hand)* Not until you have promised: not until you both have promised. *(Teddy tries to rise: she pulls him back again.)* Teddy: you promise, don't you? Yes, yes. Be good you promise.

HER HUSBAND: I won't, unless he takes it back.

SHE: He will: he does. You take it back, Henry?—yes.

HE: *(Savagely.)* Yes. I take it back. *(She lets go his coat. He gets up. So does Teddy.)* I take it all back, all, without reserve.

SHE: *(On the carpet.)* Is nobody going to help me up? *(They each take a hand and pull her up.)* Now won't you shake hands and be good?

HE: *(Recklessly.)* I shall do nothing of the sort. I have steeped myself in lies for your sake; and the only reward I get is a lump on the back of my head the size of an apple. Now I will go back to the straight path.

SHE: Henry: for Heaven's sake—

HE: It's no use. Your husband is a fool and a brute—

HER HUSBAND: What's that you say?

HE: I say you are a fool and a brute; and if you'll step outside with me I'll say it again. *(Teddy begins to take off his coat for combat.)* Those poems were written to your wife, every word of them, and to nobody else. *(The scowl clears away from Bompas's countenance. Radiant, he replaces his coat.)* I wrote them because I loved her. I thought her the most beautiful woman in the world, and I told her so over and over again. I adored her: Do you hear? I told her that you were a sordid commercial chump, utterly unworthy of her; and so you are.

HER HUSBAND: *(So gratified, he can hardly believe his ears.)* You don't mean it!

HE: Yes, I do mean it, and a lot more too. I asked Mrs. Bompas to walk out of the house with me—to leave you—to get divorced from you and marry me. I begged and implored her to do it this very night. It was her refusal that ended everything between us. *(Looking very disparagingly at him.)* What she can see in you, goodness only knows!

HER HUSBAND: *(Beaming with remorse.)* My dear chap, why didn't you say so before? I apologize. Come! don't bear malice: shake hands. Make him shake hands, Rory.

SHE: For my sake, Henry. After all, he's my husband. Forgive him. Take his hand. *(Henry, dazed, lets her take his hand and place it in Teddy's.)*

HER HUSBAND: *(Shaking it heartil.y)* You've got to own that none of your literary heroines can touch my Rory. *(He turns to her and clasps her with fond pride on the shoulders.)* Eh, Rory? They can't resist you: none of em. Never knew a man yet that could hold out three days.

SHE: Don't be foolish, Teddy. I hope you were not really hurt, Henry. *(She feels the back of his head. He flinches.)* Oh, poor boy, what a bump! I must get some vinegar and brown paper. *(She goes to the bell and rings.)*

HER HUSBAND: Will you do me a great favor, Apjohn. I hardly like to ask; but it would be a real kindness to us both.

HE: What can I do?

HER HUSBAND: *(Taking up the poems.)* Well, may I get these printed? It shall be done in the best style. The finest paper, sumptuous binding, everything first class. There're beautiful poems. I should like to shew them about a bit.

SHE: *(Running back from the bell, delighted with the idea and coming between them.)* Oh Henry, if you wouldn't mind?

HE: Oh, *I* don't mind. I am past minding anything.

HER HUSBAND: What shall we call the volume? *To Aurora,* or something like that, eh?

HE: I should call it *How He Lied to Her Husband.*

Genius and Culture

Umberto Boccioni
1915

Scene: In the center of the stage is a costly dressing table with a mirror. The woman is finishing putting on her makeup. At the right, the critic is sitting at a table brimming over with books and papers. He has a large, shiny paper knife of no particular style. The artist sits on a cushion on the floor searching through a large file.

Of Note: This is a complete play of the Italian Futurist movement. Brevity and compression were hallmarks of this style.

The Woman, elegant.
The Critic, neither this or that; rather neutral.
The Artist, an elegant youth.

THE ARTIST: *(Leaving the file, and with his head between his hands)* It's terrible! *(Pause.)* I must get out of here! To be renewed! *(He gets up, tearing the abstract designs from the file with convulsive hands.)* Liberation!! These empty forms, worn out. Everything is fragmentary, weak! Oh! Art! . . . who, who will help me!? *(He looks around; continues to tear up the designs with sorrowful and convulsive motions.)*
(The Woman is very near him, but doesn't hear him. The Critic becomes annoyed, but not very, and going near her, takes a book with a yellow jacket.)
THE CRITIC: *(Half-asking the Woman, and half-talking to himself.)* But what's the matter with the clown that he acts and shouts that way?
THE WOMAN: *(Without looking.)* Oh well, he is an artist . . . he wants to renew himself, and he hasn't a cent!
THE CRITIC: *(Bewildered.)* Strange! An artist! Impossible! For twenty years I have profoundly studied this marvelous phenomenon, but I can't recognize it. *(Obviously with archeological curiosity.)* That

one is crazy! Or a protester! He wants to change! But creation is a serene thing. A work of art is done naturally, in silence, and in recollection, like a nightingale sings . . . Spirit, in the sense that Hegel means spirit . . .

THE WOMEN: *(Intrigued.)* and if you know how it is done, why don't you tell him? Poor thing! He is distressed . . .

THE CRITIC: *(Strutting.)* For centuries, the critic has told the artist how to make a work of art . . . since ethics and aesthetics are functions of the spirit . . .

THE WOMAN: But you, you've never made any?

THE CRITIC: *(Nonplussed.)* Me? . . . Not me!

THE WOMAN: *(Laughing with malice.)* Well, then, you know how to do it, but you don't do it. You are neutral. How boring you must be in bed! *(She continues putting on her rouge.)*

THE ARTIST: *(Always walking back and forth sorrowfully, wringing his hands.)* Glory! Ah! Glory! *(Tightening his fists.)* I am strong! I am young! I can face anything! Oh! Divine electric lights . . . sun . . . To electrify the crowds . . . Burn them! Dominate them!

THE WOMAN: *(Looking at him with sympathy and compassion.)* Poor thing! Without any money . . .

THE ARTIST: *(Struck.)* Ah! I am wounded! I can't resist any longer! *(Toward the Woman, who doesn't hear him.)* Oh! A woman! *(Toward the Critic, who has already taken and returned a good many books, and who leafs through them and cuts them.)* You! You, sir, who are a man, listen . . . Help me!

THE CRITIC: Calm down . . . let's realize the differences. I am not a man, I am a critic. I am a man of culture. The artist is a man, a slave, a baby, therefore, he makes mistakes. I don't see myself as being like him. In him nature is chaos. The critic and history are between nature and the artist. History is history, in other words subjective fact, that is to say fact, in other words history. Anyway it is itself objective.

(At these words, the Artist, who has listened in a stupor, falls on the cushions as if struck by lightning. The Critic, unaware of this, turns, and goes slowly to the table to consult his books.)

THE WOMAN: *(Getting up dumbfounded.)* My God! That poor youth is dying! *(She kneels in front of the Artist and caresses him kindly.)*

THE ARTIST: *(Reviving.)* Oh! Signora! Thank you! Oh! Love . . . maybe love . . . *(Revives more and more.)* How beautiful you are! Listen . . . Listen to me . . . If you know what a terrible thing the struggle is without love! I want to love, understand?

THE WOMAN: *(Pulling away from him.)* My friend, I understand you . . . but now I haven't time. I must go out . . . I am expected by my friend. It is dangerous . . . He is a man . . . that is to say, he has a secure position . . .

THE CRITIC: *(Very embarrassed.)* What's going on? I don't understand anything . . .

THE WOMAN: *(Irritated.)* Shut up, idiot! You don't understand anything . . . Come! Help me to lift him! We must cut this knot that is choking his throat!

THE CRITIC: *(Very embarrassed.)* Just a minute . . . *(He carefully lays down the books and puts the others aside on the chair.)* Hegel . . . Kant . . . Hartmann . . . Spinoza.

THE WOMAN: *(Goes near the youth, crying irritably.)* Run! . . . come here help me to unfasten it.

THE CRITIC: *(Nonplussed.)* What are you saying?

THE WOMAN: Come over here! Are you afraid! Hurry . . . back here there is an artist who is dying because of an ideal.

THE CRITIC: *(Coming closer with extreme prudence.)* But one never knows! An impulse . . . a passion . . . without control . . . without culture . . . in short, I prefer him dead. The artist must be . . . *(He stumbles, and falls clumsily on the Artist, stabbing his neck with the paper knife.*

THE WOMAN: *(Screaming and getting up.)* Idiot! Assassin! You have killed him. You are red with blood!

THE CRITIC: *(Getting up, still more clumsily.)* I, Signora? How? I don't understand . . . Red? Red? Yours is a case of color blindness.

THE WOMAN: Enough! Enough! *(Returns to her dressing table.)* It is late. I must go! *(Leaving.)* Poor youth! He was different and likable! *(Exits.)*

THE CRITIC: I can't find my bearings! *(Looks attentively and long at the dead Artist.)* Oh my God! He is dead! *(Going over to look at him.)* The artist is really dead! Ah . . . he is breathing. I will make a monograph. *(He goes slowly to his table. From a case, he takes a beard a meter long and applies it to his chin. He puts on his glasses, takes paper and pencil, then looks among his books without finding anything. He is irritated for the first time and pounds his fists, shouting.)* Aesthetics! Aesthetics! Where is Aesthetics? *(Finding it, he passionately holds a large volume to his chest.)* Ah! Here it is! *(Skipping, he goes to crouch like a raven near the dead Artist. He looks at the dead body, and writes, talking in a loud voice.)* Toward 1915, a marvelous artist blossomed . . . *(He takes a tape measure from his pocket and measures the body.)* Like all the great ones, he was 1.68 [meters] tall, and his width . . . *(While he talks, the curtain falls.)*

Thunder on Sycamore Street

Reginald Rose
1954

Scene: 1950s Suburbia. Inside one of the homes on Sycamore Street. A plot has been hatching among all the families on Sycamore Street to form a mob and demonstrate in front of the home of the newest residents. Arthur is the one male on the block with serious reservations about this lynch mob mentality.

Mr. Harkness, retired.
Phyllis, his daughter, with whom he lives, 30s.
Arthur, her husband, 30s–40s.

MR. HARKNESS: Hello, Arthur. *(Calling off.)* Here he is, Phyllis. *(To Arthur.)* Little bit late, aren't you? *(Arthur is hanging up his coat. He is obviously worried. His face shows concern. His entire manner is subdued. He speaks quietly, even for Arthur.)*
ARTHUR: No. Usual time. *(Mr. Harkness takes out a pocket watch, looks at it, shakes it.)*
MR. HARKNESS: Mmm. Must be fast. *(He goes back to his newspaper. Arthur walks into the living room tiredly.)*
ARTHUR: *(Not caring.)* How's your cough?
MR. HARKNESS: *(Reading.)* Still got it. I guess I must've swigged enough cough syrup to float a rowboat today. Waste of time and money!
(Phyllis enters from kitchen as Arthur goes over to phonograph from which the dance music is blasting. He is just ready to turn it off as she enters.)
MR. HARKNESS: Cough'll go away by itself like it always does.
PHYLLIS: *(Brightly.)* Hello, darling. Ah . . . don't turn if off. *(He turns as she walks over to him. She kisses him possessively and leads him away from the phonograph. The music continues.)*
PHYLLIS: How did it go today, dear?
ARTHUR: All right, Nothing special.
PHYLLIS: What about the Franklin closing?

ARTHUR: It's called off till tomorrow.

PHYLLIS: How come?

ARTHUR: I didn't ask them.

PHYLLIS: Well, you'd think they'd at least give you a reason. You should've asked. I don't like it when people push you around like that. *(Arthur goes over to the chair without answering. A pipe is on an end table next to the chair. He begins to fill it. Phyllis goes to a small bar on which is a cocktail shaker and one glass. She picks up the shaker.)*

ARTHUR: What's that?

PHYLLIS: I made you a drink.

ARTHUR: No. No thanks. I don't want a drink now.

PHYLLIS: Oh, Artie! I made it specially for you. You look tired. Come on, it'll do you good. *(She begins to pour the drink.)* Sit down, dear. I'll bring it over to you. *(Arthur sits down. Phyllis finishes pouring the drink and brings it to him. He takes it. She waits, smiling, for him to drink it.)*

ARTHUR: How come you made me a drink tonight?

PHYLLIS: Just for luck. Taste it. *(She sits on the arm of the chair. He tastes it slowly. She puts her arm around him.)* Good?

ARTHUR: *(Slowly.)* It's good.

PHYLLIS: I thought you'd like it.

ARTHUR: Where's Billy?

PHYLLIS: Asleep.

ARTHUR: Isn't it kind of early?

PHYLLIS: He didn't get much of a nap today. The poor baby couldn't keep his eyes open. Artie, he's getting to be such a devil. You should've seen him this afternoon. He got into my bag and took my lipstick. If I only could've taken a picture of his face. He walked into the kitchen and I swear I almost screamed. You never saw anything so red in your life. Drink your drink, darling. It took me ten minutes to scrub it off. *(Obediently, Arthur sips his drink.)*

ARTHUR: *(Mildly.)* I'd like to have seen him before he went to bed.

PHYLLIS: Now you know I had to get finished early tonight, Artie. *(She gets up and goes toward the kitchen.)* We're eating in a few minutes. I'm just making melted cheese sandwiches. We can have a snack later if you're hungry.

ARTHUR: Later?

PHYLLIS: *(Looking at him oddly.)* Yes, later. When we get back.
(Arthur puts his drink down. All of his movements are slow, almost mechanical, as if he has that day aged twenty years. Phyllis goes into the kitchen. He takes off his glasses and begins polishing them.)

MR. HARKNESS: Melted cheese sandwiches.

ARTHUR: *(Not hearing.)* What?

MR. HARKNESS: I said melted cheese sandwiches. That gluey cheese. Do you like it?

ARTHUR: No.

MR. HARKNESS: Me neither. Never did. *(He goes back to his paper. Arthur gets up and goes to phonograph. He stands over it, listening. Phyllis comes in carrying a tray on which are three glasses of tomato juice. She gives it to Arthur.)*

PHYLLIS: Put these on the table like a good boy. *(He takes it and looks at her strangely.)* What's the matter with you, Artie? You've hardly said a word since you got home . . . and you keep looking at me. Are you sick, or something?

ARTHUR: No. I'm not sick.

PHYLLIS: Here, let me feel your head. *(She does so.)* No, you feel all right. What is it?

ARTHUR: Nothing. I'm just tired, I guess.

PHYLLIS: Well, I hope you perk up a little.
(She goes off into kitchen. Arthur goes slowly to dining table which is set in the same spot as the Morrison dining table. He puts the glasses on it, and sets the tray on the end table. He takes a sip of his drink. Phyllis comes in from the kitchen carrying a platter of melted cheese sandwiches. She goes to the table, puts in down.)

PHYLLIS: Dinner. Come on, Dad, while they're hot. Artie . . .

ARTHUR: You go ahead. I'm not hungry.

PHYLLIS: Oh, now, let's not start that. You have to eat. Try one. They're nice and runny.

ARTHUR: Really, I'm not hungry.

PHYLLIS: Well, you can at least sit with us. I haven't seen you since half-past eight this morning.

(Arthur goes slowly over to the table and sits down, Mr. Harkness ambles over.)

MR. HARKNESS: Well, I'm good and hungry. Tell you that. Got any pickles?

PHYLLIS: No pickles. You know they give you heartburn.

MR. HARKNESS: Haven't had heartburn in a long time. Wouldn't mind a slight case if it came from pickles.

(They are all seated now, Phyllis facing the window. Arthur sits quietly. Mr. Harkness busies himself drinking water while Phyllis serves the sandwiches, potato salad, etc.)

PHYLLIS: Artie . . . potato salad?

ARTHUR: No. Look, Phyllis . . .

PHYLLIS: Just a little. *(She puts a spoonful on a heavily loaded plate and passes it to him. He takes it. Now she serves her father.)*

PHYLLIS: Potato salad, Dad?

MR. HARKNESS: I'll help myself. *(She puts the bowl down and helps herself as does Mr. Harkness.)*

PHYLLIS: *(Brightly.)* What happened at the office, dear? Anything new?

ARTHUR: No. It was quiet.

PHYLLIS: Did you hear about the Walkers wanting to sell their house?

ARTHUR: No.

PHYLLIS: You know, for a real-estate man you hear less about real estate than anyone I ever saw. I spoke to Margie Walker this morning. I just got to her in time. You're going to handle the sale. She told me she hadn't even thought of you till I called. Why is that, dear?

ARTHUR: I don't know why it is.

PHYLLIS: Well, anyway, she's expecting you to call her tomorrow. It ought to be a very nice sale for you, dear.

(Arthur nods and looks down at his plate. There is silence for a moment.)

MR. HARKNESS: *(Chewing.)* This stuff gets under my teeth.

PHYLLIS: Dad!

MR. HARKNESS: Well, I can't help it, can I?

(They eat for a moment and then Phyllis, looking out the window, sees movement in the house next door, the Blake house. She can no longer hold back the topic she's been trying not to discuss in front of Arthur.)

PHYLLIS: Look at them. Every shade in the house is down. *(She looks at her watch.)* There isn't much more time. I wonder if they know. Do you think they do, Artie?

ARTHUR: *(Tired.)* I don't know.

PHYLLIS: They must. You can't keep a thing like this a secret. I wonder how they feel. *(She looks at Arthur.)* Artie, aren't you going to eat your dinner?

ARTHUR: *(Slowly.)* How can you talk about them and my dinner in the same breath?

PHYLLIS: For Heaven's sake . . . I don't know what's the matter with you tonight.

ARTHUR: *(Quietly.)* You don't, do you?

MR. HARKNESS: What'd you suppose is gonna happen over there? Boy, wouldn't I like to go along tonight.

PHYLLIS: *(Looking at Arthur.)* Dad, will you please stop.

MR. HARKNESS: Well, I would! How do you think it feels to be sixty-two years old and baby-sitting when there's real action going on right under your nose? Something a man wants to get into.

ARTHUR: *(Turning.)* Be quiet!

MR. HARKNESS: Now listen here—

ARTHUR: I said be quiet! *(He takes off his glasses and walks over to the table.)*

PHYLLIS: Artie, stop it! There's no need for you to raise your voice like that. *(Arthur speaks more quietly now, feeling perhaps that he has gone too far.)*

ARTHUR: Then tell your father to keep his ideas to himself!

MR. HARKNESS: *(Angrily.)* Wait a minute!

(Phyllis in the ensuing argument, is quiet, calm, convincing, never losing her temper, always trying to soothe Arthur, to sweeten the ugly things she says by saying them gently.)

PHYLLIS: Dad, be quiet. Listen, Artie, I know you're tired, darling, but there's something we might as well face. In about fifteen or twenty minutes you and I and a group of our friends and neighbors are going to be marching on that house next door. Maybe it's not such a pleasant thing to look forward to, but something has to be done. You know that, Artie. You agreed to it with all the others.

ARTHUR: I didn't agree to anything. You agreed for the Hayes household. Remember?

PHYLLIS: All right, I agreed. I didn't hear you disagreeing. Oh, what's the difference, darling? You've been acting like there's a ten-ton weight on your back ever since you heard about it. And there's no point to it. It's all decided.

ARTHUR: All decided. What right have we got to decide?

PHYLLIS: It's not a question of right. Artie. Don't you see? It's something we have to do, right or wrong. Do you want them to live next door to you? Do you really want them?

ARTHUR: I always thought a man was supposed to be able to live anywhere he chooses no matter what anyone else wants.

PHYLLIS: But, dear, this isn't anywhere. This is Sycamore Street. It's not some back alley in a slum! This is a respectable neighborhood. Artie, let's be realistic. That's one of the few things we can really say we have. We're respectable. Do you remember how hard we worked to get that way?

ARTHUR: Respectable! Phyllis, for Heaven's sakes. We're talking about throwing a man out of his own home. What is the man? He's not a monster. He's a quiet guy who minds his own business. How does that destroy our respectability?

PHYLLIS: *(Hard.)* He got out of prison two months ago. He's a common hoodlum.

ARTHURS: We don't know for sure.

PHYLLIS: We know. Charlie Denton doesn't lie. He saw the man's picture in the Rockville papers just fifty miles from here the day he got out. Tell me, what does he do for a living? Where did he get the money to buy that house?

ARTHUR: I don't think that's any of your business.

PHYLLIS: But, Artie, the man was in jail for four years. That's our business! How do you know what he did? How do you know he won't do it again?

ARTHUR: We have police.

PHYLLIS: Police! Will the police stop his child from playing with Billy? What kind of a child must that be? Think about it. Her father is an ex-convict. That's a lovely thing to tell our friends. Why yes . . . you know Billy's little friend Judy. Of course you do. Her father spent a great deal of time in prison. Charming people. It's beautiful for the neighborhood, isn't it, Artie? It makes real-estate prices just skyrocket up. Tell me, who do you think'll be moving in next . . . and where'll we go?

(Arthur doesn't answer. He sits down in a chair, troubled, trying to find an argument. Phyllis watches him closely.)

MR. HARKNESS: Listen, Artie—

(But Phyllis puts her hand on his arm to shut him up. Arthur is thinking and she wants to see if her argument has worked.)

ARTHUR: Look, Phyllis, this is a mob we're getting together. We're going to order this man out of his house . . . or we're going to throw him out. What right have we got to do it? Maybe most of us'd rather not have him as a neighbor, but, Phyllis, the man is a human being, not an old dog. This is an ugly thing we're doing.

PHYLLIS: We've got to do something to keep our homes decent. There's no other way. Somebody's always got to lose, Artie. Why should it be all of us when there's only one of him?

ARTHUR: I . . . I don't know. *(Arthur suddenly gets up and goes toward the front door as if going out. He buttons his jacket. Phyllis gets up, concerned.)*

PHYLLIS: Where are you going?

ARTHUR: I'm going to talk to Frank Morrison.

PHYLLIS: All right. Maybe Frank'll make sense to you. *(Calling)* Wear your coat.

(But Arthur has opened the door and intends to go out without it. Phyllis looks at her watch.)

PHYLLIS: Arthur, it's freezing out! *(He is outside the door now.)* You'll catch cold. *(The door closes. She stands watching after him, obviously* upset. *Her father resumes his eating. She looks at the door for a long time. Then, without looking around.)* Dad . . .

MR. HARKNESS: Mmmm?

PHYLLIS: What do you think he'll do?

MR. HARKNESS: Well . . . I don't know. You got any more of these melted cheese businesses? I'm hungry.

PHYLLIS: No. *(She goes to the window and looks out.)*

MR. HARKNESS: Why don't you sit down. Phyl? He'll be all right.

PHYLLIS: What do you mean all right? Look at him. He's standing in front of Frank's house afraid to ring the bell.

MR. HARKNESS: He'll calm down. Come away from that window and sit down. Have some coffee. *(She moves away from window and sits at table.)*

PHYLLIS: I've never seen him like this before.

MR. HARKNESS: Well, what are you worried about? Tell you what. I'll go along with you. Boy, wouldn't I like to be in on a thing like this once. Let Artie stay home and mind the baby if that's how he feels.

(Phyllis turns on her father violently and for the first time we see how much Arthur's decision means to her.)

PHYLLIS: *(Fiercely.)* He's got to go! Don't you understand?

Take a Giant Step

Louis Peterson
1954

Scene: 1950s New England. Typical middle-class neighborhood. Spence has been suspended for two weeks for sassing the history teacher about blacks during the Civil War period. He refers to the history teacher as "the fruitcake."

Spencer Scott (Spence), 17, black, a high school senior.
Tony, his friend, Italian.
Grandma, a semi-invalid, proud, outspoken, usually rises to Spence's defense.

SPENCE: You mean that I shouldn't have gotten sassy with the fruit cake.

GRANDMA: Spencer, I'm not going to say one more word to you if you don't stop using that language like that—and put that stick down.

SPENCE: *(Gets up, throwing the stake on the floor.)* God—you're getting to be a crumb—just like the rest of the whole crummy world.

GRANDMA: Where are you going?

SPENCE: No place. Where in hell is there to go?

GRANDMA: You ought to be thrashed with a stick for using that kind of language to me.

SPENCE: Listen—are you my friend or not? *(Crosses back to Grandma.)*

GRANDMA: No—I'm not—when you talk like that.

SPENCE: *(Closer to Grandma.)* Well—thanks for that. Thanks. You're a real cool Joe. You're a psalm singer—just like the rest of them. Gram. Love me when I'm good—hate me when I'm bad. Thanks. *(Crosses Right.)*

GRANDMA: Don't mention it.

SPENCE: You're welcome. *(Sits in armchair Right.)*

GRANDMA: The pleasure was all mine.

SPENCE: For an old lady—you can sure be plenty sarcastic when you want to be.

(Pause.)

GRANDMA: These will be exactly the last words I will say to you today, Master Scott.

(From outside a Voice begins calling Spence. Softly at first and then more loudly.)

TONY: Spence.

GRANDMA: Who's that calling you?

SPENCE: Tony.

TONY: Hey—Spence!

GRANDMA: Well—what does he want?

SPENCE: I don't know, Gram. I haven't asked him yet.

TONY: Spencer!

GRANDMA: Well, why don't you answer him?

SPENCE: Let him wait—let him wait—it won't hurt him. He likes to holler like that anyway—he has to use his voice some place. No one could ever accuse him of speaking up while he's in school. *(Rises.)*

TONY: Spencer!

GRANDMA: *(Gets up.)* Spencer Scott—if you don't answer him—I will.

SPENCE: All right, all right. *(He starts for the door and opens it.)* What're you doing there? *(Tony bounces in. He is a young Italian boy.)* Rehearsing for the Metropolitan or something? Come on in *(Crosses to Grandma Left.)*

TONY: *(Crosses to center.)* Hi, Spence. Hello, Mrs. Scott.

GRANDMA: Tony—since the first day you could talk—*(Sits.)* I've told you that I'm not Mrs. Scott. I'm Mrs. Martin. How long are you going to keep doing that?

TONY: I forget, Mrs. Martin. *(Front of sofa.)*

SPENCE: You forget lots of things—don't you, pal. *(Pause. Back to chair.)* Well—you got a week's vacation so it certainly can't be because you want me to help you with your algebra—besides I won't be doing algebra for a while. I got the heave-ho as you well know.

TONY: Thrown out?

SPENCE: Yep.

TONY: For how long? *(Crosses to Right.)*

SPENCE: Not counting vacation—for a week.

TONY: Gee!

SPENCE: You can say that again. *(Crosses to below table Left.)*

TONY: Gee!

SPENCE: Well—you said it. Thanks, pal. *(Pause. Sits Left of the table.)* Well, Tony—what little favor can I do you?

TONY: Gee, Spence. I'm sure sorry. All the guys were talking about it on the way home from school.

SPENCE: Yeh! Yeh! I know. I caught their sympathy when Miss Crowley was bitching me out.

GRANDMA: I'm going to tell your mother.

SPENCE: *(Looking at Grandma.)* Gram.

TONY: That's not the way it was at all. *(Pause.)* What could we say?

SPENCE: Exactly what you did. It was fine. What'd I call you when you came in—a pal? That's what you all were. *(Grandma goes into kitchen.)* Two hundred carat, solid gold plate pals. *(To piano. Sits.)*

TONY: *(Crosses Right.)* Geeze—Spence—I'm sorry you feel that way about it.

SPENCE: *(Gets up.)* Ah! You're scratching my back with a rake, Tony. Remember the time the cop had you for stealing apples down at Markman's?

TONY: Sure I remember.

SPENCE: Did I or did I not shoot him with my slingshot? Remember the time Mrs. Donahue comes out of her house and calls you a dirty wop?

TONY: Well, hell, this was in school.

(Grandma crosses to sink with glass.)

SPENCE: Did I stand there and let her get away with it? I did not. That night, as nice as you please, I throw a nest of caterpillars through her window.

TONY: *(To Center.)* Yeah! And when she found out who did it—I cut your telephone wires for three nights running so she couldn't get to your mother.

GRANDMA: *(Enters room.)* I think I should warn you both now—that

everything you're saying is going to be used against you—
because I'm going to tell all of it.

SPENCE: *(Crossing to Grandma.)* Oh! No, you won't. If you so much
as open your craw, Gram, I'll spill everything—and I'll really spill.
I'm desperate. *(Crosses to Tony.)* So there's a big difference about
whether it's in school or not. Has that ever made any difference
to me?

TONY: Naw!

SPENCE: Naw! Is that all you've got to say?

TONY: No—it isn't

SPENCE: You're a crumb, Tony—just like the rest of them. *(Crosses to
Right.)* And another thing—I dunno—maybe I'm getting deaf
and need a hearing aid or something, but I don't hear you guys
calling me for school any more in the morning.

TONY: *(Crosses to Spence.)* Ah, Spence—how many times do I have
to tell you. I'm taking Marguerite to school in the morning.

SPENCE: And where are you taking her at night when you mosey past
the house with her curled around your arm like a snake?

TONY: We're doing our homework together.

SPENCE: It's a little dark up in the park for homework.

TONY: Spence—cut it out—your grandmother.

SPENCE: My grandmother knows what the score is. She's been knowing it an awful long time now. She's going on eighty-three years
old. You can talk freely in front of her.

TONY: Lay off—will you?

SPENCE: I'll lay off, Tony. I'll lay off plenty. You and that Marguerite
Wandalowski. Two crumbs together. That don't even make a
damn Saltine.

TONY: *(Close to Spence.)* It's not her fault. I told you before. *(Spence
crosses to Center.)* She likes you. She thinks you're a nice kid.
(Crosses; sits on ottoman.) It's her father—he—well he just doesn't
like colored people. I'm sorry, Mrs. Martin. But that's the damn
truth, Spence—he just doesn't like them. *(Spence goes to piano.)*

GRANDMA: Well I don't like Polish people either. Never have—never
will. They come over here—haven't been over, mind you, long

enough to know "and" from "but"—and that's the first thing they learn. Sometimes I think Hitler was right—

SPENCE: *(Down two steps.)* You're talking off the top of your head, Gram. You know he wasn't right. What've you got to say that for?

GRANDMA: I don't care—I don't like them. Never have—never will.

SPENCE: *(Crosses to Grandma.)* You say "them" as though it was some kind of bug or something. *Will* you do me a favor like a real pal, Gram? Quit trying to mix in things that you don't understand. *(To Tony.)* O.K., Friend—you've said your piece—what did you come over for? *(Crosses down to Tony.)*

TONY: Nothing—I didn't want nothing.

SPENCE: Aw—cut the bull, Tony. You must've come over here for something. You just don't come here for nothing any more. What to you *want?*

Tiny Alice

Edward Albee
1964

Scene: Miss Alice's room. Feminine but not frilly. The butler has just
ushered brother Julian and the lawyer into her presence. Brother
Julian has arrived representing the Cardinal to receive Miss Alice's
$100 million dollar-per-year grant to the church.

Julian, a lay brother in the church, secretary to the Cardinal.
Lawyer, tough, sarcastic, rose from a poor childhood.
Miss Alice, white-haired, a withered crone (for a while), enormously
wealthy.

LAWYER: *(After Butler exits, chuckles.)* What is it the nouveaux riches
are always saying? "You can't get good servants nowadays"?
JULIAN: He seems . . .
LAWYER: *(Curt.)* He is very good. *(Turns to the chair.)* Miss Alice, our
Brother Julian is here. *(Repeats it, louder.)* Our Brother Julian is
here. *(To Julian)* She's terribly hard of hearing. *(To Miss Alice.)* Do
you want to see him? *(To Julian.)* I think she's responding.
Sometimes . . . well, at her age and condition . . . twenty minutes
can go by . . . for her to assimilate a sentence and reply to it.
JULIAN: But I thought . . . His Eminence said she was . . . young.
LAWYER: Shhhhhhhhh! She's moving. *(Miss Alice slowly rises from
her chair and comes around it. He face is that of a withered
crone, her hair gray and white and matted; she is bent; she
moves with two canes.)*
MISS ALICE: *(Finally, with a cracked and ancient voice, to Julian.)* Hello
there, young man.
LAWYER: *(As Julian takes a step forward.)* Hah! Don't come too close,
you'll unnerve her.
JULIAN: But I'm terribly puzzled. I was led to believe that she was a
young woman, and . . .
MISS ALICE: Hello there, young man.
LAWYER: Speak to her.

JULIAN: Miss . . . Miss Alice, how do you do?

LAWYER: Louder.

JULIAN: How do you do?

MISS ALICE: *(To Lawyer.)* How do I do *what*?

LAWYER: It's a formality.

MISS ALICE: What!?

LAWYER: It is a formality, an opening gambit.

MISS ALICE: Oh. *(To Julian.)* How do *you* do?

JULIAN: Very well . . . thank you.

MISS ALICE: What!?

JULIAN: Very well, thank you.

MISS ALICE: Don't you scream at me!

JULIAN: *(Mumbled.)* Sorry.

MISS ALICE: What!?

JULIAN: Sorry!

MISS ALICE: *(Almost a pout.)*

LAWYER: *(Who has enjoyed this.)* Well, I think I'll leave you two now . . . for your business. I'm sure you'll have a . . .

JULIAN: *(An attempted urgent aside to the Lawyer.)* Do you think you . . . shouldn't you be here? You've . . . you've had more experience with her, and . . .

LAWYER: *(Laughing.)* No, no, you'll get along fine. *(To Miss Alice.)* I'll leave you two together now. *(Miss Alice nods vigorously.)* His name is Brother Julian, and there are six years missing from his life. *(She nods again.)* I'll be downstairs. *(Begins to leave.)*

MISS ALICE: *(When the Lawyer is at the door.)* Don't steal anything.

LAWYER: *(Exiting.)* All right!

JULIAN: *(After a pause, begins bravely, taking a step forward.)* Perhaps you should sit down. Let me . . .

MISS ALICE: What!?

JULIAN: Perhaps you should sit down!

MISS ALICE: *(Not fear; malevolence.)* Keep away from me!

JULIAN: Sorry. *(To himself.)* Oh, really, this is impossible.

MISS ALICE: What!?

JULIAN: I said this was impossible.

MISS ALICE: *(Thinks about that for a moment, then.)* If you're a defrocked priest, what're you doing in all that? *(Pointing to Julian's garb.)*

JULIAN: I am not a defrocked priest, I am a Lay Brother. I have never been a priest.

MISS ALICE: What did you drink downstairs?

JULIAN: I had a glass of port . . . port!

MISS ALICE: *(A spoiled, crafty child.)* You didn't bring *me* one.

JULIAN: I had no idea you . . .

MISS ALICE: What!?

JULIAN: Shall I get you a glass?

MISS ALICE: A glass of *what.*

JULIAN: Port. A glass of port.

MISS ALICE: *(As if he were crazy.)* What for?

JULIAN: Because you . . . *(To himself again.)* Really, this *won't* do.

MISS ALICE: *(Straightening up, ridding herself of the canes, assuming a normal voice.)* I agree with you, it won't do, really.

JULIAN: *(Astonishment.)* I beg your pardon?

MISS ALICE: I said it won't do at all. *(She unfastens and removes her wig, unties and takes off her mask, becomes herself, as Julian watches, openmouthed.)* There. Is that better? And you needn't yell at me any more; if anything, my hearing is *too* good.

JULIAN: I . . . I don't understand.

MISS ALICE: Are you annoyed?

JULIAN: I suspect I will be . . . might be . . . after the surprise leaves me.

MISS ALICE: *(Smiling.)* Don't be; it's only a little game.

The Waste Disposal Unit

Bridget Brophy
1964

Scene: An Italian palazzo. Hot. Summer. The rooms are empty save for two window seats. There is a crate of Coca-Cola on the floor.

Homer Knockerbicker, a plump, rumpled American.
Virgil Knockerbicker, dresses all in black, Hamlet-like, Homer's younger brother.
Merry, cute, flirtatious, married to Homer.

HOMER: Virgil?

VIRGIL: *(Without looking up from his reading.)* Homer?

HOMER: Virgil, you planning on lying around all day today, the way you did yesterday?

VIRGIL: Mm-hm. *(Virgil thinks he has now disposed of the subject.)*

HOMER: This heat's murder. Merry says it isn't any worse than Southern California, but I tell her it is, it carries a higher degree of humidity. Southern California, you get the ocean. *(After a pause.)* Gee, it's hot. It's hot as hell.

VIRGIL: Maybe you should relax more.

HOMER: I guess one in the family is enough.

VIRGIL: One what?

HOMER: Oh, you know. You know what I mean, Virgil. It's hot enough so it even mists up my lenses. You're lucky you don't have to wear glasses. This heat, you wouldn't be able to see to write.

VIRGIL: I'm not writing. I'm reading back what I already did.

HOME: That reminds me, sometime I got to talk with you—you want a drink, Virgil?

VIRGIL: Mm-hm. Whisky sour.

HOMER: I didn't mean hard liquor.

VIRGIL: Oh. No thanks.

HOMER: I wish we had a water cooler in this place. Guess I'll have myself a Coke. I wonder if Merry could use a Coke. You think

Merry could use a Coke, Virgil? *(Homer alludes to the door at the left.)*

VIRGIL: How would I know? Go on in and ask her.

HOMER: Oh, I can't go in there right now. She isn't through fixing her face.

VIRGIL: Oh. Well yell.

HOMER: *(As he helps himself to a bottle of Coca-Cola and removes the cap.)* What?

VIRGIL: Yell. Ask her through the bedroom door.

HOMER: Heh, I might *do* that. *(He drinks deep, directly from the bottle.)* I might *do* that. Sure.

VIRGIL: Well go ahead.

HOMER: Sure.

MERRY: *(Offstage, calling cooingly in a pretty, tinkling voice.)* Ho-mer!

HOMER: *(Calling hastily back, towards the door at the left.)* I'll be right in, honey. I just grabbed myself a Coke. I just gotta find some place to put it down. *(He crams it into the crate and runs over to the door at the left; but as his hand turns the knob.)*

MERRY: Oh, don't come *in*, Homer. *(Homer shuts the door hastily.)*

HOMER: I certainly am sorry, Merry.

MERRY: Why, that's perfectly all right, Homer, think no more of it. Homer?

HOMER: Yes, Merry?

MERRY: Would you take a look round the *palazzo* to see if I left my Kleenex some place.

HOMER: Sure, Merry *(Homer returns to the middle of the room.)* I don't see too well, my lenses got misted up again. *(Calling.)* I don't see them any place, honey, but I'll keep right on searching. Virgil, you see them?

VIRGIL: See what?

HOMER: Merry's Kleenex.

VIRGIL: Sure. *(Virgil pulls out a box from behind his back.)*

HOMER: Now why in the world would you want to do that?

VIRGIL: This window seat isn't too soft, Homer.

HOMER: If you wouldn't lie around all day—

VIRGIL: Don't you want them?

HOMERS; What?

VIRGIL: Merry's Kleenex.

HOMER: Wait a moment, can't you, I got to wipe off these lenses again.

VIRGIL: Don't *you* get steamed up, too.

HOMER: I'm not getting steamed up, but you don't seem to understand, I got to get those Kleenex to Merry. Give here. *(He takes the box from Virgil.)* Why, Virgil, you crushed in one whole side of the pack. I don't know how Merry's going to—

VIRGIL: Yeh, well, these sharp-angled packs aren't really any more comfortable than marble. I guess I really took Merry's Kleenex more as a kind of talisman. You know, like a chicken sits on a china egg. To inspire my work.

HOMER: Now that's something I have to talk with you about, Virgil. I'll just go give these to Merry. I'll be right back. *(Approaching the door at the left and calling.)* Merry! I found them, honey. But I'm afraid the pack didn't stand up too well—

MERRY: Now isn't that just too bad of me, Homer. I was just going to call out I didn't need them any more.

HOMER: Oh.

MERRY: Homer, don't be sore. I found another pack right in here.

HOMER: Oh, I'm not sore, Merry. I'm certainly glad you found another pack. That's swell. You through yet, honey?

MERRY: Not yet, Homer.

HOMER: Oh. OK.

VIRGIL: *(As, without looking away from his book, he reaches a hand out towards the Kleenex.)* Give here.

HOMER: What?

VIRGIL: If Merry doesn't want them, I may as well sit on them a while longer. You never know what might hatch. I'll take a look around later, see if I can find a pack that isn't crushed. You don't have any scatter cushions round the place, Homer, I guess you don't have the domesticated touch, but you have to hand it to Merry, she certainly does have scatter Kleenex.

HOMER: Now see here, Virgil—

MERRY: *(Offstage.)* I don't hear you too well but you boys sound to be having a lot of fun out there. I'll be right along.

HOMER: That's swell, honey.

VIRGIL: I don't figure how it takes a woman that long to make up like she was twenty-five when she *is* twenty-five.

HOMER: Now wait a moment, Virgil—

VIRGIL: Mm-hm?

HOMER: Merry's a lovely person.

VIRGIL: Sure. Sure, Homer. Merry's just great. She's great material.

HOMER: What do you mean, "material"?

VIRGIL: You know how it is, Homer. I guess I have a professional attitude, that's all. I'm certainly glad you married Merry.

HOMER: *(Not sure whether to be angered.)* I don't know just how you mean that, Virgil. Do you mean you're glad on account of your work?

VIRGIL: Oh, I don't separate my work from my life.

HOMER: Now that's something we have to talk about. I'll just have myself that Coke . . .

VIRGIL: In fact, I don't separate my work from *your* life. *(Homer puts the bottle abruptly back into the crate, and prepares to be angry.)*

HOMER: I didn't hear you too well, Virgil, I was kind of swallowing, but did you say "my life" or "my wife"?

VIRGIL: I, I wouldn't dare—

HOMER: Let's leave Merry out of this, Virgil. I want to talk with you.

VIRGIL: Mm-hm?

HOMER: Don't you ever look up from that book?

VIRGIL: I'm told I have very remarkable concentration.

HOMER: I guess you wouldn't break your concentration no matter what happened.

VIRGIL: Nothing does happen.

HOMER: Maybe not, but most of the time it sounds like it did. Know what I think, Virgil? I think Italy's the noisiest country I was ever in.

VIRGIL: It's no worse than Southern California.

HOMER: It is *so* worse than Southern California. Out here you got the cicadas. It it isn't the cicadas, it's the lambrettas. If it isn't the lambrettas, it's the doves. If it isn't the doves, it's those goddam chickens out there in the yard.

VIRGIL: I don't mind the chickens in the *yard* too much.

HOMER: Now see h—

VIRGIL: Cool off, Homer.

HOMER: How can I cool off, in this heat? We ought to have drapes at those windows, cut out the sun, but I don't know the Italian for drapes, anyway Merry likes looking out the window . . . I'm worried, Virgil. I don't know how Merry's going to take this kind of climatic conditions.

VIRGIL: Relax, Homer. Merry doesn't feel it at all.

HOMER: You don't know how Merry feels. Merry is a very delicate character. I don't see how I can ask Merry to live in a climate like this.

VIRGIL: You didn't ask her. It was Merry's idea.

HOMER: You know what I *mean*, Virgil. You know how it is. A guy has to look out for his wife, he has to make provision. If I'd have known there wouldn't even have been a shower in the *palazzo*—

VIRGIL: You had one fixed.

HOMER: Sure I had one fixed, I'm going to have plenty else fixed, I'm going to make this old *palazzo* like so it won't know itself . . . But Merry's a very sensitive person. She's delicate, Virgil, even though she doesn't make any song and dance—

MERRY: *(Calling musically from the next room.)* Ho-mer!

HOMER: Yes, honey?

MERRY: Could you step in here for a moment, Homer?

HOMER: Sure, Merry. I'll be right in. You through now? *(A bell rings loudly.)*

HOMER: I'll get it. *(He stops making towards the door at the left, and sets out for the door at the right; checks himself; executes a step-dance of hesitation; and finally calls, in a despairing flurry, toward the door on the left.)* I'll be right back, Merry. I just got to see to the front door bell.

VIRGIL: Let Lia-Pia get it.

HOMER: How can I let Lia-Pia get it? She doesn't speak English.

VIRGIL: So she doesn't speak English. Maybe it was an Italian dropped by.

HOMER: Are you crazy? How would an Italian drop by?

VIRGIL: Well, we're in Italy.

HOMER: Sure, I *know* we're in Italy, but—

MERRY: Ho-mer! Would you step along to the front door. The bell just rang.

HOMER: Sure, Merry, sure. I'll get it. *(As Homer leaves by the door at the right, Merry trips in by the door at the left. She tiptoes on her sneakers across the room, comes up behind Virgil as he reads, and places her hands as a blindfold over his eyes.)*

MERRY: Morning, Virgil. Guess who?

VIRGIL: *(Sourly.)* Merry.

MERRY: *(Releasing his eyes)* You're a good guesser, Virgil.

VIRGIL: *(Craning round and looking at her.)* Mm-hm, Merry. Just like I thought. Morning, Merry. You look cute.

MERRY: *(Dropping him a mock curtsey.)* Why, thank you, Virgil.

VIRGIL: *(Looking her up and down.)* Sure, cute. Little pony tail, all done up in a tartan bow, and those long white kneehose, and our Bermuda shorts, and that cute little—what you call it?

MERRY: Shirtwaister?

VIRGIL: Sure, shirtwaister. Oh, you look cute, Merry. You look like all the college girls in Southern California rolled into one.

MERRY: Why, Virgil, that's the darlingest thing you ever said to me, I guess you must be becoming a better integrated personality. I'm going to give you a little kiss on your brow, just for saying that. *(She bends over and neatly deposits the kiss.)*

VIRGIL: Oh, don't take any account of me, Merry, I'm just apple-polishing. There's something I want you to tell me.

MERRY: Well, I'll certainly tell you anything I can, Virgil, but Homer says you already know 'most everything. I'm going to just curl up alongside of you on this lovely *Renaissance* window seat, and then you can ask me anything you want. *(Doing so.)* I guess wherever I am I find myself some corner I can curl up in. There now, Virgil. What's your problem? You know, Virgil, Homer has a very, very high regard for your intellectural integrity.

VIRGIL: Now how would he be able to judge, I wonder?

MERRY: Now, Virgil, Homer's—

VIRGIL: Oh sure, Homer's a lovely person.

MERRY: *(Subsiding.)* I'm certainly glad you appreciate it. Now what is it I can tell you?

VIRGIL: Why don't you let your husband in your bedroom, Merry?

MERRY: *(Rising in fury.)* Virgil Knockerbicker, how can you make such an absolutely awful insinuation? If you dare imply for one moment—

VIRGIL: Merry, I only asked—

MERRY: Virgil Knockerbicker, I'm going right back in the bou*doir* until Homer returns. *(She turns her back on Virgil.)*

VIRGIL: Merry, what did I do?

MERRY: *(Swinging on him.)* What did you *do!* You were insinuating that my relationship with Homer is not perfectly adjusted on the physical side.

VIRGIL: Merry, I only—

MERRY: You as good as called me a frigid wife!

VIRGIL: Merry, I—

MERRY: *(Stamping.)* I do so let him in my bedroom!

VIRGIL: He told me a while back he couldn't go in there.

MERRY: *(Losing all her anger, now the trouble is explained.)* Oh sure, but that was in the morning.

VIRGIL: What's the difference?

Friends

Kobo Abe
1969

Scene: A public park with several benches. Elder son has arrived to ingratiate himself with the Man's fiancée and cause a rift between them. His family has completely overtaken the Man's apartment, edging him out. No one believes him and now they are trying to get to his fiancée.

Elder son, 20s, representative of his family of eight who have invaded the Man's life and home.
Fiancée, 20s, a young lady of quality.
Man, 20s, a young man whose life has been invaded by strangers.

ELDER SON: *(With a slight bow of the head.)* Excuse me. *(He starts to seat himself beside Fiancé, indifferent to her reactions.)*
FIANCÉE: I'm sorry, but I'm waiting for somebody.
ELDER SON: Oh, I see. *(He decides not to sit, but shows no sign of going away. He continues to stare boldly at the woman.)* I was impressed even by your picture, but you're far more charming in the flesh. Oh, you've changed the way you do your hair, haven't you? A natural effect looks better on you than fancy styling. That only goes to show how good the foundations are.
FIANCÉE: I don't think we've met . . . *(Her expression reveals mingled caution and curiosity.)*
ELDER SON: But I know all about you . . . Of course, you make such an impression that nobody who ever saw you once could forget you the second time. It's only natural, I suppose.
FIANCÉE: I wonder where I've had the pleasure . . ?
ELDER SON: Last night, in the drawer of your Fiancée's desk.
FIANCÉE: *(At last catching on.)* Then it was you last night . . .
ELDER SON: *(Nods.)* Yes, it was. Against my own inclinations I interrupted you in the midst of your telephone call.
FIANCÉE: *(Sharply.)* Have you come as his stand-in?
ELDER SON: Heaven forbid! I wouldn't do such a thing even if he

asked me. To tell the truth, he and I have had a slight difference of opinion concerning what happened last night.

FIANCÉE: And you've come to tell on him?

ELDER SON: How severe you are! I wonder what he could've told you about us? I gather from your tone he hasn't been too friendly. I suppose he's trying to clean up the mess he left behind by shifting the blame onto us for that telephone call.

FIANCÉE: What happened anyway?

ELDER SON: How can I answer unless I know the nature of his explanation?

FIANCÉE: *(Finally induced to discuss the matter on his terms.)* I couldn't make the least sense out of him. He was so vague that I . . .

ELDER SON: *(With a suppressed laugh that does not seem malicious.)* I can well imagine . . . I wonder if the problem is that he's timid, or clumsy at expressing himself, or can never get to the point, or that he's too earnest or too good natured or too inflexible, or that he's stubborn or an introvert or self-centered . . .

FIANCÉE: *(Mustering her courage.)* Were there also women present?

ELDER SON: Yes, four—no, five.

FIANCÉE: Five!

ELDER SON: But there were men there, too—three of us, besides him.

FIANCÉE: What were you all doing, so many of you?

ELDER SON: It's a little hard to explain.

FIANCÉE: *(Rather irritated)* But generally speaking, when people have gathered together for a purpose there's some sort of name for their activity. Would you describe it as a meeting, or a card game, or a drinking party? Is there anything that can't be given a name?

ELDER SON: That's the crux of the problem. *(He takes out a comb and smoothes his hair.)* I'd really be most interested to hear how *he* would answer that question. *(He puts away the comb.)* But I've really been making a great nuisance of myself when you've more important things on your mind. *(He bows and starts to leave.)*

FIANCÉE: *(Standing before she realizes.)* Wait a moment! What is it you came to tell me, anyway? You and he make a good pair—one's just as vague as the other. I don't suppose you could have come for the express purpose of mystifying me.

ELDER SON: *(Sanctimoniously, his eyes lowered.)* Of course not. But when I meet you face-to-face this way I suddenly lose my courage.

FIANCÉE: Go ahead. You're not bothering me.

ELDER SON: *(Lighting a cigarette; slowly.)* To be perfectly honest, I don't really understand his feelings . . . Correct me if I'm wrong, but I gather he's engaged to you and has been planning to hold the wedding in the near future.

FIANCÉE: Yes, he only recently managed at last to rent that apartment. It's more than he could afford, but we needed it to get married.

ELDER SON: In other words, he and you are already as good as married. Right? Why, then, should he have had to keep things a secret from you, of all people, in such a furtive way? If I may cite a rather vulgar example, you often see in the advice to the lovelorn column how a man is extremely reluctant to introduce the girl he's interested in to his parents or his family . . . In such cases is it not fair to assume in general that the man's sincerity is to be doubted?

FIANCÉE: You mean you and your family are in that relationship with him?

ELDER SON: Of course, I don't know how he would answer you.

FIANCÉE: *(Reduced to supplication.)* For heaven's sake, please tell me! Who are you all and what is your connection with him.

ELDER SON: *(Avoiding the issue.)* Oh, yes. I've just remembered. It was something he let slip in the course of the conversation last night, but I wonder if it doesn't give us a clue to his intentions. He seems to hold extremely prejudiced views against any form of communal living, and even with respect to family life he seems to be feeling something close to dread.

FIANCÉE: I can't believe that.

ELDER SON: He went so far as to say that it actually refreshed him to be all alone in a crowd of total strangers.

FIANCÉE: But he's even made arrangements with the movers to have my furniture taken to his place at the end of the month.

ELDER SON: I'd like to believe that he got carried away by his own words. Or maybe he was just bluffing . . . After all, with such a pretty girl like you . . .

FIANCÉE: You still haven't answered my question.

ELDER SON: Oh—you mean our relationship with him? I wonder if it wouldn't be better, though, for you to get him to verify it with his own mouth. I wouldn't want my words to have the effect of implanting any preconceptions . . . It's not that I'm trying to pretend to be more of a gentleman than I am, but I just wouldn't want to make a sneak attack, or anything like that . . . I realize that it must be hard for you to understand, but basically speaking, we're closer to him than blood relations.

FIANCÉE: You must have known him a long time, then?

ELDER SON: (Calmly.) We don't set too much store by the past. The same holds true of marriage, doesn't it? The real problems are always in the future.

FIANCÉE: (Again withdrawing into her shell.) Then was it something like a political meeting?

ELDER SON: (Looking at his watch.) I'm sure he has no intention of trying to strengthen his position by lying to you . . . He may in fact be planning to use this opportunity to reveal to you his true feelings. Anyway, I advise you to sound him out. Maybe we'll meet again, depending on how your interview turns out.

FIANCÉE: (Looking stage left.) Oh, there he is now.

ELDER SON: (Showing no special embarrassment.) I hope and pray that all goes well. But I suppose I'm also half hoping that things don't go well. In that case I'll get to see you again. (Suddenly, as if he had remembered something urgent.) Excuse me, but would you mind sitting there again? Just the way you were before . . . Hurry! (Fiancée, overcome by his urgency, sits as requested.)

ELDER SON: (With a conspiratorial smile.) That's right. Now I can see the dimples in your knees . . . Aren't they sweet? I could eat them up, those dimples. (Fiancée, flustered brings together the hems of her coat. At the same moment Man hurriedly enters from stage left. He catches sight of Elder Son, and stops in his tracks with an expression of amazement. Fiancé, noticing Man, stands and turns *toward him as he speaks. In other words, her actions should not start after* Man's *dialogue begins.)*

MAN: *(To Elder Son, sharply.)* What are *you* doing here

(Elder Son turns to Man as if having become aware of his presence only then. Far from showing any embarrassment, he smiles broadly, as if greeting an old friend.)

ELDER SON: Late, aren't you? This will never do!

(Man looks from Fiancée to Elder Son and back, then steps forward aggressively.)

MAN: What's the meaning of this, anyway?

FIANCÉE: *(Unable to hide her guilty conscience.)* It was a complete coincidence.

ELDER SON: But as far as I'm concerned, an accidental meeting that only a marvelous necessity could have brought about.

MAN: *(Angrily.)* I don't know what mischief you've been up to, but you're to get the hell out of here, right now.

ELDER SON: *(Still smiling.)* Don't be uncouth. Well, I'll be saying goodbye. *(He winks secretly at Fiancée.)* Go to it now, the both of you. *(He makes a clownish gesture with his hand, then saunters off to stage left. The couple stands for a time in silence, still looking off in the direction Elder Son has gone. They slowly turn and exchange glances, only to avert their eyes. Fiancée sits down on the bench, and Man then also sits. Each occupies an end of the bench.)*

MAN: *(Gloomily.)* What was he filing your ear with?

FIANCÉE: *(Looking at Man reproachfully.)* Before we go into that, it seems to me you have a lot of explaining to do.

MAN: Explaining? There's nothing worth explaining. It's just as I told you on the phone this morning. I'm the victim. I'm sorry I worried you with that call last night. But even that was their fault, if you get right down to it.

FIANCÉE: So it would seem. It's pretty hard to keep someone from guessing, even over the phone, when you have eight people in the room with you. But tell me, why was it necessary for you to act so secretly, as if you were playing hide-and-seek with me?

MAN: I thought I'd told you. I couldn't think of any way of explaining in an intelligible manner who those people were or what they were doing.

FIANCÉE: And you're going to explain now, is that it?

MAN: Unfortunately, I still don't know what happened, even now.

FIANCÉE: *(A little defiantly.)* But I thought you asked me here in order to explain.

MAN: *(Bearing up under the confusion.)* Yes, that's so . . . But my real purpose was not so much to explain as to get you to understand how difficult it is to make an explanation. Maybe I won't succeed in making you understand . . . How could you understand an outfit like that? I suppose that if it happened that I had been on the receiving end of this story, I wouldn't have been able to believe it either . . . I don't know where to start. The only way to describe what happened is to say it was plain crazy.

FIANCÉE: *(Losing her temper.)* That certainly doesn't seem to be an explanation of anything.

MAN: But have you ever heard anything like it—a bunch of complete strangers, suddenly march in on me without warning, and install themselves in my apartment, exactly as if it were their natural right?

FIANCÉE: *(Coldly.)* It *is* a little unusual.

MAN: It certainly is. As a matter of fact, even the policemen who came after I called refused to take it seriously. *(His voice becomes more emphatic.)* But I assure you, it happened. This impossible thing has befallen me.

FIANCÉE: That man who was just here also thought it was strange. He couldn't figure out what your motive was in keeping their presence such a secret.

MAN: A secret? It's simply that I couldn't think how to explain, don't you see? So he encouraged you to act suspicious. But you're carrying your foolishness too far. Tell me, what possible advantage could there be in it for me to cover up for that bunch of parasites?

God's Favorite

Neil Simon
1975

Scene: The scene is the palatial home of the Benjamin family. Darkness. Midnight. The clock strikes twelve. Winter night. A shadowy figure is seen on the portico. Then the burglar alarm goes off and the figure disappears. As the alarm blares, Ben, Joe and Sarah run into the living room dressed in their nightclothes.

Of Note: Sarah and Ben are described as twenty-four-year-olds with an IQ of 160—between them.

Joe Benjamin, a wealthy businessman.
Sarah Benjamin, his daughter.
Ben Benjamin, his son and Sarah's twin brother.

BEN: What is it Dad? What happened?

JOE: I don't know.

SARAH: What happened, Dad? What is it?

JOE: I said I don't know.

SARAH: We heard the alarm go off, Dad?

BEN: Did you hear the alarm go off, Dad?

JOE: Certainly I heard it go off. That's why I'm down here. *(To Sarah.)* Close your bathrobe. *(Sarah can never keep her robe tied. She closes it.)*

SARAH: My God, it was really the alarm.

BEN: *(Points.)* The French door is open. Look!

SARAH: It's open, Dad. The French door. Look!

JOE: I can see it's open. Stop repeating everything. *(The telephone rings.)*

BEN: It's the phone, Dad.

SARAH: Dad, it's the phone. *(It rings again.)*

JOE: I can hear it. Close your bathrobe. Ben, answer the phone.

SARAH: Answer the phone, Ben.

JOE: I'm going to look outside.

SARAH: Suppose someone's out there?

JOE: That's why I'm looking. That's the whole point of it. Close your robe. *(The phone rings again.)* Answer that. *(Joe goes out to the portico, and Ben picks up the phone.)*

BEN: *(Into the phone.)* Hello? . . . Yes?

SARAH: Who is it?

BEN: The burglar alarm company.

SARAH: Daddy, it's the burglar alarm company.

BEN: *(Into the phone.)* Yes, we just heard it.

SARAH: Ben said we just heard it.

JOE: *(From out on the portico, yells.)* Close your bathrobe!

BEN: *(Into the phone.)* We found the living-room French door open. My father's checking now.

SARAH: What do they think?

BEN: *(Into the phone.)* What do you think?

JOE: *(Coming back into the room.)* I think someone tried to break in.

BEN: *(Into the phone.)* My father thinks someone tried to break in.

JOE: I found footprints in the snow.

BEN: *(Into the phone.)* He found footprints in the snow.

SARAH: My God, footprints in the snow.

JOE: Close your robe, you want to catch cold? Go to bed. Look at you shivering.

SARAH: I'm not cold. I'm scared. My God, someone tried to break in.

JOE: Stop using God's name in vain.

SARAH: It's not in vain. I'm really scared.

BEN: *(Into the phone.)* One second, please. *(To Joe.)* They want to know if they should send somebody.

JOE: No one got into the house.

BEN: How can you tell?

JOE: There's snow outside. There would be footprints on the rug.

SARAH: There *are* footprints *(Points.)* Right there!

JOE: *Those are mine!* Wasn't I just in the snow?

BEN: Suppose he wore galoshes and left them outside?

JOE: What kind of a robber wears galoshes? No one got in. Tell them never mind. Everything's all right. I'm going to look around again. *(He goes back out on the portico.)*

BEN: *(Into the phone.)* Hello? No one got in . . . Never mind, please. Everything's all right. My father's going to look around again . . . Thank you. We will. *(He hangs up.)* Close your bathrobe.

JOE: *(Comes back in.)* Someone was here. He dropped these outside. *(He holds up a pair of steel-rimmed glasses.)*

BEN: Eyeglasses!

SARAH: Look, Daddy, it's a pair of eyeglasses!

JOE: *Didn't I just find them?* I can see they're glasses. Well, whoever dropped them won't get far without them. They're a half-inch thick—I can't see two feet through them.

SARAH: A half-blind burglar, my God, it gives me the creeps. *(She shivers.)*

JOE: I'm not going to tell you about God's name or your bathrobe again . . . I wouldn't be surprised if he broke both his legs. There are no footprints going down the stairs, so he must have just jumped off the balcony.

BEN: Jumped off the balcony? Forty feet? He'd break both his legs.

SARAH: Oh God, a crippled blind burglar . . .

BEN: Why don't we call the police? A crippled blind burglar shouldn't be too hard to find.

JOE: First of all, he isn't a burglar because he didn't steal anything. And second of all, I don't want any police around here with your mother in the house. You know how frightened she is.

BEN: But whoever it was could still be out there. He could be a dangerous lunatic.

SARAH: He could be a rapist! . . . A *sexual* rapist! *(She closes her robe, which always falls open.)*

BEN: *All* rapists are sexual.

JOE: *(Looks at her.)* He can't see two feet ahead of him, who's he going to find to rape?

SARAH: He could feel his way into the house.

BEN: Not if has two broken legs.

SARAH: He could *crawl* and feel his way into the house.

JOE: *(Yells.)* People don't break into houses if they have to crawl and feel around . . . How would they ever get away?

SARAH: A girl in my college was attacked by a man with one arm and one leg . . . They still can't figure out how he held her down.

JOE: A nineteen-room house with priceless paintings, irreplaceable antiques, and a half a million dollars in jewelry, who's going to stop for a rape? He's got other things on his mind.

SARAH: What if rape was the thing he had on his mind?

JOE: Will you stop talking about rape and close your bathrobe? Ben, take her upstairs. Go to bed, the both of you.

SARAH: Yes, Daddy. Good night, Daddy.

BEN: Good night, Dad.

JOE: Wait a minute! Did you just hear something? . . . Listen! *(We hear a door screech open, then shut. They all look at each other.)*

JOE: It's in the house.

BEN: Someone's in the house!

SARAH: Oh God, the rapist!

JOE: *(Whispers.)* Be quiet! Listen . . . footsteps!

SARAH: Coming this way!

BEN: Out in the hall!

SARAH: Give them what they want, Daddy, don't let them do you-know-what.

JOE: Get back, both of you. Near the wall! *(They all move back and pin themselves against the wall.)*

BEN: The burglar alarm is off. We forgot to reset it.

JOE: It's too late now.

BEN: I could call them. What's the number?

JOE: How should I know the number?

BEN: Should I call information?

JOE: Will you get back against the wall?

SARAH: Oh God, I can just feel his hands on me now, his clammy hands rubbing all over me, up and down, up and down—

JOE: No one's going to rub you up and down! Stop it! Grab something! *(They each pick up a vase.)* The minute I hit him, call the police! Stand back! Here he comes . . . Close your bathrobe! *(They all stand behind the door, and raise the vases over their heads, poised for action—and then the phone rings. They all turn and look at it.)* Now? Now the phone rings?

BEN: What a time for the phone to ring.

JOE: Answer it! Answer it! *(Ben runs over on tiptoe and answers the phone, still speaking in a soft voice.)*

BEN: Hello? . . . Yes? . . . Yes, this is the Benjamin residence—

JOE: Who is it?

BEN: *(Hand over the receiver, to Joe.)* It's a woman. She's asking for Sidney.

JOE: Sidney who? *(The vase is still poised over his head.)*

BEN: *(Into the phone)* Sidney who, please? *(He nods. To Joe.)* Sidney Lipton.

JOE: There's no Sidney Lipton here. She's got the wrong number.

BEN: *(Into the phone.)* There's no Sidney Lipton here, madam. You've got the wrong number.

SARAH: Hang up! Stop talking before the rapist goes away.

BEN: *(Into the phone.)* Just a minute. *(To Joe.)* She says she's *Mrs.* Lipton. Her husband had an appointment here tonight . . . with you. *(Joe shakes his head "No" and shrugs. Ben, back into the phone.)* My father doesn't know anything about it . . . Listen, Mrs. Lipton, this is a bad time for us to talk . . . We're expecting someone . . . Yes, I will . . . Thank you. *(He hangs up carefully, then rushes back to his spot against the wall. He doesn't say anything. Joe stares at him.)*

JOE: Yes, you will what?

BEN: Tell Sidney that his wife called.

SARAH: Here he comes!

Golden Accord

Wole Soyinka

Scene: Time: 1980. Setting—the living room. The Lonestones have just won the title of Mr. and Mrs. Golden Accord on a television game show.

Lonestone
Annabelle, his wife.
Sergeant, police guard for the Lonestones.

LONESTONE: Well, spell it out man. What is it? You want my autograph?

SERGEANT: No, though I wouldn't mind that too. But . . . if you wouldn't mind, could you . . . open . . . while I'm here. *(Pointing to the box.)* I've never seen a hundred-and-fifty-thousand dollars in real life, much less handled it.

LONESTONE: *(A slow grin spreading over his face, erupts suddenly in a thigh-slapping roar of laughter.)* Well I'll be damned . . . if you only knew what had been going through my mind! As soon as you left I was going to open up that golden box, strip stark naked and scrub myself from head to crotch with those stacks of bills. *(Excitement mounting.)* Come on, get the damned thing out in the open air. Must be getting suffocated in there. Wait a minute, wait a minute, this needs some champagne. There must be a couple of bottles in the fridge. You get to work on the wrapping while I hunt down the champagne!

ANNABELLE: *(Appears in the bedroom doorway.)* Do you mind? The children are trying to sleep.

LONESTONE: To hell with that. Tell them to come out and celebrate. Christ! Is this a night for sleeping?

ANNABELLE: What are they supposed to celebrate, Lonestone?

LONESTONE: *(Hesitates. They hold each other's gaze for a moment.)* Oh get back to sleep Mrs. Wet Blanket 1980. *(He dashes towards the refrigerator, rummages within and hauls out one, then two bottles of champagne.)*

SERGEANT: Perhaps I ought to go. I could come back later.

LONESTONE: Nonsense. Take off the wrapping. When she sets her eyes on those hundred-dollar bills she'll feel different. Wait, something is missing. Music. We should have some music.
(Annabelle turns back into the bedroom. Sergeant hesitates, then begins feverishly to unwrap the box.)

LONESTONE: Now what would be appropriate for an occasion like this? A hundred-and-fifty-thousand-dollar composition. Do you enjoy classical music, officer? *(He is shoving aside one disc after another as he talks.)* Damn! I used to have Tchaikovsky's 1812 in my collection. All those cannon booms and church bells—Ah-ha, this will do I think. What do you think of the sound track to that fantastic space film—2001? Yeah, absolutely perfect. It's like being launched in space you know—spaced out—Man, with a hundred and fifty thousand sitting in my living room, who needs drugs?

SERGEANT: *(Has untied the strings and removed the wrappers. The strains of Strauss's* Thus Spake Zarathustra *envelop the scene. He steps back from the table.)* Undo the clasp please, Mr. Lonestone. *(Lonestone, still on his knees by the record player, turns toward the table. His eyes light on the shiny metallic box sitting in a cloud of chiffon paper wrappings. Picking up the champagne bottle, He begins to crawl towards the table on both knees.)*

LONESTONE: I did it. Oh my God, you mean, I actually did it?

SERGEANT: Oh yes Mr. Lonestone, it took guts but you did it. You and your wife.

LONESTONE: Just look at it. I call that poetry. Music.

SERGEANT: Lonestone.

LONESTONE: The clasp. Oh yes, in a minute. *(He eases the cork off the champagne bottle, pops it, and sprays the frothing liquid all over the box. With his other hand he quickly releases the clasp of the box. The vertical lid falls slowly down, revealing a concertina-like interior from which stacks of dollar bills fan outwards.)*

SERGEANT: Style. If there is one thing that program has, it is—style.

LONESTONE: *(Gently plucking out a stack of notes. Holds it up and raises the champagne bottle.)* To the sweet notes of the Golden Accord. *(Drinks and passes the bottle to the Sergeant.)*

(Annabelle re-enters, takes in the scene, then comes forward to the table so that she is standing behind it, overlooking both the box and Lonestone on the down side of the table.)

ANNABELLE: *(Quietly.)* The children just woke up.

LONESTONE: *(His gaze does not swerve from the box.)* I said bring them out to join the fun.

ANNABELLE: I don't think they want to join the fun.

LONESTONE: Why the hell not?

ANNABELLE: They watched the program.

LONESTONE: Then they must know that their father is one-hundred-and-fifty-thousand, seven-hundred-and-fifty dollars richer than he was when he left the house this evening.

ANNABELLE: Yes. They heard their father's answer to the questions: What is the most shameful secret your wife ever confided in you? *(A brief silence. Lonestone raises his head to meet his wife's unsmiling face. The policemen takes a step away from the table, turning his head away. He moves progressively farther as if trying to place himself out of earshot.)*

LONESTONE: Well, then they must also have heard their mother confirm the story when it came to her turn.

ANNABELLE: Would there have been any point in denying it?

LONESTONE: We agreed before we set out—no lies. Wasn't that the deal?

ANNABELLE: Oh yes. Does your husband snore in bed? Who does the washing up in your home? Is your wife a slob around the house? That sort of question was all we had in mind. You are not an honest man if you claim otherwise, Lonestone. What is the most shameful secret your wife ever confided in you—and you told.

LONESTONE: A deal is a deal. What are you beefing about anyway? That was the jackpot question. We were way up in front of the other couples—what was the point throwing it all away on account of some silly sensitivity?

ANNABELLE: No one ever told you that secrets of the bedroom are as sacred as those of the confessional?

LONESTONE: Yeah? What century are you thinking of? Come off it woman.

ANNABELLE: Well, to tell the truth, I had this same century in mind.

You know, this same one from which you received twelve years of my life, of my body. Twelve years nursing your frustrations, your miseries, and weaknesses in the privacy of my strength, and bearing you three children.

LONESTONE: *(Getting up.)* Look, you keep your mind on the money . . .

ANNABELLE: I do have my mind on the money.

LONESTONE: Good. I mean, what else could have been on it when it came to your turn? Damnit, you got the same question didn't you? What is the most shameful secret you ever confided in your husband—eh?—Mrs. Lonestone? And you told.

ANNABELLE: I saw your face. It was there. The whole studio reeked of it. The other couples in the competition, the studio audience, even the ones I couldn't see, the millions of strangers wallowing in the secret mess I thought I had buried safely with you. Yes, I thought then of the money . . .

LONESTONE: Who cares when you thought of it? You backed up the truth, we qualified for the Perfect Accord between husband and wife and here we are—overnight celebrities, a hundred and fifty grand richer, so cut out the bellyaching!

ANNABELLE: Have you ever watched yourself die, Lonestone?

LONESTONE: What's that?

ANNABELLE: Because that was what happened to me tonight. After I read my betrayal on your face, those studio lights burnt right through into my brain, and I felt myself shrivel and die. Do you know what that is like?

LONESTONE: *(Offhand.)* No, tell me.

ANNABELLE: Actually I don't believe you are listening to me, Lonestone.

LONESTONE: Sure I am. You said you watched yourself shrivel and die—okay? *(He gathers up a fistful of notes and thrusts them under her nose.)* Get a whiff of that. Nothing like it for reviving the dead.

ANNABELLE: *(Produces a gun from her pocket and levels it at him.)* I have thought about this all evening: I wasn't sure I could bring myself to do it but . . . now I think I shall actually enjoy it.

LONESTONE: *(His eyes incredulous on the gun.)* What . . . what is that for?

SERGEANT: *(Turns, hand to his holster.)* For God's sake Mrs. Lonestone!

ANNABELLE: Do what you like Sergeant. As long as you know I'm making sure of him.

LONESTONE: *(Backing off.)* Now wait Annabelle, just wait a minute . . .

ANNABELLE: Don't move one step further Lonestone.

LONESTONE: *(Stops dead.)* No, I'm not moving, I'm not moving Annabelle. Just listen to me a minute.

ANNABELLE: You are alone with your death, Lonestone. Just you and your death. It is rather late in the day but maybe you now understand what a private moment means . . . just you, and your death. Try and savor it—if you can.

SERGEANT: Mrs. Lonestone, please don't make me draw. Put down the gun.

LONESTONE: You can have all the money, Annabelle. I'll sign it over to you. It's all yours . . . everything . . . the Sergeant can witness it . . .

ANNABELLE: What money? It's all gone on legal defense. The jury will be sympathetic but lawyers still cost money.

SERGEANT: I'm warning you Mrs. Lonestone. If you don't put that thing down . . .

ANNABELLE: Don't be a fool, officer. My husband taught me how to use this gun.

LONESTONE: Think of the children for God's sake! Look, I'll leave the house tonight, never come back. Anything you want . . .

ANNABELLE: Good-bye Lonestone.

(She presses the trigger. There is a click but no explosion. Lonestone raises his arms instinctively to ward off impact. The Sergeant draws his gun and covers Annabelle.)

SERGEANT: Drop it!

ANNABELLE: *(Let's the gun dangle from a finger, lowers her arm.)* It's empty. I unloaded it myself. *(She replaces the gun in her pocket, moves toward the bedroom. Stops and turns to the Sergeant.)* Remember to take that—*(Indicating her husband.)* thing with you when you leave.

Cover

Jeffrey Sweet

Scene: A high-rise office building with a great view. Scene is in Frank's office where Marty has told Diane to meet him so they can all go to dinner. However, Marty has arrived early to beseech Frank to lie for him about his whereabouts the previous evening. He has asked Frank to say that they were out together, to cover for having been out with another woman.

Marty
Frank
Diane

> All in their 20s or 30s. Diane and Marty are a couple. Frank is their friend.

FRANK: Look, I don't want to lie to her.
MARTY: I'm not asking you to *want* to.
FRANK: You're just asking me to do it.
MARTY: Yes, as a favor to a friend.
FRANK: No, I don't want to.
MARTY: You do lots of things you don't want to do. Everybody does.
FRANK: The things that I sometimes do that I don't want to do are things that I have to do. I don't have to do this. I don't have to break that trust.
MARTY: No, and we don't have to be friends, either.
FRANK: Oh, come on. Are you saying if I won't lie for you we won't be friends any more?
MARTY: Of course not. I'm just asking you for a favor.
FRANK: I can't do it.
MARTY: Can't means won't.
FRANK: Can't means can't.
MARTY: Can't means won't.
FRANK: Can't means can't.
MARTY: No, you could.
FRANK: I couldn't

MARTY: You *could*.

FRANK: I couldn't.

MARTY: Your mouth could say the words. Physically, your mouth could say the words.

FRANK: I couldn't do it.

MARTY: Of course you could.

FRANK: No, I couldn't

MARTY: You could, but what you're saying is you won't.

FRANK: I'm saying I can't

MARTY: You're saying you won't.

FRANK: I'm saying . . . OK, I'm saying I won't because I can't.

MARTY: But you *could*.

FRANK: I wouldn't if I could, but I can't so I won't. Anyway, you don't want me to lie for you.

MARTY: Yes, I do.

FRANK: I'm a terrible liar. She'd see right through me.

MARTY: How do you know until you try?

FRANK: Look, I'm not going to tell her where you were. I mean, I couldn't because I don't know.

MARTY: I was at Marvin Gardens. That's on the West Side.

FRANK: I don't want to know. Don't tell me any more.

MARTY: Barbara Schaeffer.

FRANK: I don't want to know who.

MARTY: Barbara Schaeffer.

FRANK: Barbara Schaeffer?

MARTY: See, now you know.

FRANK: I wish you hadn't told me.

MARTY: But you know, and if you don't tell Diane that means you've already lied. Passive-shmassive, it's a lie, and you've gone that far, why not go a little farther for a friend?

FRANK: Look, you can argue rings around me, but I'm not going to.

MARTY: OK, sorry I asked.

FRANK: I wish you'd understand.

MARTY: It really is a hell of a nice office. You should be very proud. *(A beat. Diane enters.)*

DIANE: I've found you at last.

FRANK: You have trouble?

DIANE: You could've at least left a trail of breadcrumbs. So, you guys ready to go?

FRANK: In a second.

DIANE: Hey, nice view.

FRANK: You like it?

DIANE: That's Jersey, isn't it?

MARTY: You can see thunderstorms, Franks says.

DIANE: Oh really? That must be exciting.

FRANK: What, I don't get a kiss?

DIANE: Absolutely! *(She kisses Frank.)*

FRANK: Hey, you look swell.

DIANE: In contrast to . . . ?

FRANK: No, of course not.

DIANE: Thank you.

FRANK: That's a nice outfit.

DIANE: I'm glad you like it.

FRANK: It really is. I really do. *(Frank goes offstage with a file.)*

DIANE: *(To Marty.)* So, how was your day?

MARTY: Fine.

DIANE: You and Jacobs get that thing cleared up?

MARTY: No big problem.

DIANE: I thought you were worried.

MARTY: No seriously. We sat down, we talked.

DIANE: You compromised.

MARTY: I didn't have to.

DIANE: It must be a relief.

MARTY: And your interview?

DIANE: Nothing definite.

MARTY: But there's interest?

DIANE: They didn't say no.

MARTY: That's half the battle.

DIANE: Yeah.

MARTY: Fingers crossed. *(Frank returns.)*

DIANE: You got here early, huh?

MARTY: Just a few minutes ago.

DIANE: You've got a lot of papers on your desk, Frank. You must work awfully hard.

FRANK: It just looks that way. Gives the impression I'm earning my money, which of course, I'm not.

DIANE: Oh, no, I know you. Industrious. Kind, loyal, honest, brave. You're the only person I know who lives up to . . . what is it?

MARTY: *(A little dig.)* The Boy Scout code.

DIANE: *(An immediate echo.)* The Boy Scout code.

FRANK: I wouldn't know. I wasn't a Scout.

DIANE: I can see you loaded down with merit badges.

FRANK: Yes, well now, *Touch of Evil* starts at 7:10 at the museum, so that means we should figure out what restaurant in the area . . .

MARTY: We should be pushing along, right.

FRANK: There's not a big hurry, but if we want to have a few drinks first . . .

DIANE: *(To Marty.)* Hey . . .

MARTY: How are ya?

DIANE: What are you doing?

MARTY: Just saying hi to you. *(A beat.)*

DIANE: We have to be at the museum at what?

FRANK: Well, by seven at least.

DIANE: So, where shall be eat?

FRANK: How does Italian sound, or are you on a diet and don't want that, or what? Chinese?

DIANE: Do you think I should be on a diet?

FRANK: Women always seem to be on diets. Men, too. People in general.

DIANE: Women aren't always on diets. Some women diet. The heavy variety. They tend to diet.

FRANK: I can remember you being on some pretty screwy diets.

DIANE: You think I'm screwy?

FRANK: No, of course not. I didn't say that.

DIANE: I'm sorry. I'm a little weird tonight. The ozone or something

FRANK: Sure, I mean, air quality does . . .

DIANE: *(Interrupting to Marty.)* You didn't get home till really late last night.

MARTY: I know.

DIANE: I wasn't even awake when you got home.

MARTY: I know. I didn't want to disturb you.

DIANE: Listen to the man! My favorite thing in the world is to wrap my arms around him in bed and he says he doesn't want to disturb me. And you got up and left early this morning, too.

MARTY: I know. I had to get out.

DIANE: Away from me?

MARTY: No, no, of course not. I just had to leave.

DIANE: Why?

MARTY: I had someplace to be.

DIANE: Oh.

MARTY: Preparing for the Jacobs thing, you know.

DIANE: Yeah.

FRANK: Do you want me to leave? Would you rather be alone or . . .?

DIANE: *(Interrupting.)* I promised myself I wasn't going to ask this question. I mean, I was in the bathroom and I combed my hair and I looked in the mirror and I said to myself, "You're looking good, Diane. You're looking very good."

FRANK: You look terrific.

DIANE: *(Quiet, intense.)* Where were you last night? Where were you till so late?

MARTY: *(A beat, then—)* I was with Frank all night long. Isn't that right, Frank? *(A beat.)*

FRANK: Yeah, that's right. He was. With me. We were . . .

DIANE: With Frank?

MARTY: Yes. Is that what you were so worried about?

DIANE: Yes, I'm sorry. It's stupid.

FRANK: We were playing . . .

MARTY: Playing . . .

FRANK: Poker.

MARTY: Cards. I didn't want to tell you because, well, I know you don't like be gambling.

DIANE: No.

MARTY: And I lost a little last night.

FRANK: Yeah, I zapped him for a little.

DIANE: How much?

FRANK: Forty-something. He made me promise not to tell.

DIANE: I see. Well . . .

FRANK: Tell you what, dinner's on me tonight, OK?

DIANE: *(She knows they've been lying now. She looks at Frank very directly and says—)* Why not? *(A beat.)*

MARTY: I guess we'd better get going hunh?

(Diane nods. She exits first. Frank and Marty exchange a look before exiting. Lights fade out.)

Death and the Maiden

Ariel Dorfman
1991

Scene: Roberto is bound and gagged in a chair. Paulina has done this
    to him because she firmly believes, based on hearing his voice,
    that he was her torturer during the years of fascist dictatorship.
    Her husband does not know whether to believe her or not.

Paulina, about 40, a victim of torture during the previous fascist
    regime in an unspecified South American country.
Gerardo, 40s, her husband, a lawyer and defender of the oppressed.
Roberto, 40s–50s, a gentleman whose car has broken down near the
    home of Paulina and Gerardo.

(The sound of a car outside. Then a car door opening and closing. Paulina goes to the table and takes the gun in her hand.
Gerardo enters.)

PAULINA: How did it go? Was the flat easy to fix?

GERADO: Paulina, you are going to listen to me.

PAULINA: Of course I'm going to listen to you. Haven't I always lis-
    tened to you?

GERARDO: I want you to sit down and I want you to really listen to
    me. *(Paulina sits down.)* You know that I have spent a good part
    of my life defending the law. If there was one thing that revolted
    me in the past regime—

PAULINA: You can call them fascists .. .

GERARDO: Don't interrupt. If something revolted me about them it
    was that they accused so many men and women, that they
    forged evidence and ignored evidence and did not give the
    accused any chance of defending themselves, so even if this man
    committed genocide on a daily basis, he has the right to defend
    himself.

PAULINA: But I have no intention of denying him that right Gerardo.
    I'll give you all the time you need to speak to your client, in pri-
    vate. I was just waiting for you to come back, that's all, so we

could begin this in an orderly official fashion. *(She gestures to Gerardo, who takes the gag off Roberto. Then she indicates the cassette recorder.)* You should know, Doctor, that everything you say will be recorded here.

GERARDO: My God, Paulina, shut up! Let him say what he . . .

(Brief pause. Paulina switches on the recorder.)

ROBERTO: *(Coughs, then in a rough, hoarse voice.)* Water.

GERARDO: What?

PAULINE: He wants water, Gerardo.

(Gerardo rushes to fill a glass with water and brings it to Roberto, giving it to him to drink. Roberto drinks it down noisily . . .

PAULINA: Nothing like good fresh water, eh, Doctor? Beats drinking your own piss.

ROBERTO: Escobar. This is inexcusable. I will never forgive you as long as I live.

PAULINA: Hold on, hold on. Stop right there, Doctor. Let's see if this thing is working.

(She presses some buttons and them we hear Roberto's voice.)

ROBERTO'S VOICE FROM THE CASSETTE: Escobar. This is inexcusable. I will never for give you as long as I live.

PAULINA'S VOICE FROM THE CASSETTE: Hold on, hold on. Stop right there, Doctor. Let's see.

(Paulina stops the recorder.)

PAULINA: Ready. It's recording everything marvellously. We already have a statement about forgiveness. It is Doctor Miranda's opinion that it is inexcusable—that he could never forgive as long as he lives—tying someone up for a few hours, holding that person without the right to speak for a few hours. Agreed. More? *(She presses another button.)*

ROBERTO: I do not know you, madam. I have never seen you before in my life. But I can tell you this: You are extremely ill, almost prototypically schizoid. But you, Escobar, you, sir, are not ill. You're a lawyer, a defender of human rights, a man who has been persecuted by the former military government, as I was myself, and your case is different, you are responsible for what you do and what you must do is untie me immediately. And I want you to know that every minute that passes makes you more of an accomplice to this abuse and that you will therefore have to pay the consequences of—

PAULINA: *(Puts the gun to his temple.)* Who are you threatening?

ROBERTO: I wasn't—

PAULINA: Threatening, yes you were. Let's get this clear, Doctor. Threat time is over. Out there you bastards may still give the orders, but in here, for now, I'm in command. Now is that clear?

ROBERTO: I've got to go to the bathroom.

PAULINA: Piss or shit?

GERARDO: My God, Paulina! Doctor Miranda, she has never spoken like this in her life.

PAULINA: The Doctor's used to this sort of language . . . Come on, Doctor. Front or rear?

ROBERTO: Standing up.

PAULINA: Untie his legs, Gerardo, I'll take him.

GERARDO: Of course not. I'll take him.

PAULINA: I'll do it. Don't look at me like that. It's not as if it's the first time he's going to take his—instrument out in front of me, Gerardo. Come on, Doctor. Stand up. I don't want you pissing all over my rug.

(Gerardo unties the legs. Slowly, painfully, Roberto limps toward the bathroom, with Paulina sticking the gun in his back. Gerardo turns off the cassette recorder. Paulina goes out with Roberto. After a few instants, we can hear the sounds of urination and then flushing. Meanwhile, Gerardo has been pacing nervously. Paulina returns with Roberto.)

PAULINA: Tie him up again. *(Gerardo begins to tie up Roberto's legs.)* Tighter, Gerardo!

GERARDO: Paulina, this in intolerable. I must talk with you.

PAULINA: And who's stopping you?

GERARDO: Alone.

PAULINA: Why? The doctor used to discuss everything in my presence, they—

GERARDO: Dear, dear Paulie, please, don't be so difficult. I want to talk to you where we have some privacy. *(Gerardo and Paulina go* out onto the terrace. During their conversation, Roberto slowly manages to loosen his leg bonds.) What are you trying to do? What are you trying to do, woman, with these insane acts?

PAULINA: I already told you—put him on trial.

GERARDO: Put him on trial, what does that mean, put him on trial? We can't use their methods. We're different. To seek vengeance in this fashion is not—

PAULINA: This is not vengeance. I'm giving him all the guarantees he never gave me. Not one, him and his—colleagues.

GERARDO: And his—colleagues—are you going to kidnap them and bring them here and tie them up and . . .

PAULINA: I'd have to know their names for that, wouldn't I?

GERARDO: —and then you're going to . . .

PAULINA: Kill them? Kill them? As he didn't kill me, I think it wouldn't be fair to—

GERARDO: It's good to know that, Paulina, because you would have to kill me too, I'm warning you that if you intend to kill him, you're going to have to kill me first.

Poetry Reading

John Chandler

1995

Scene: A street person in a long coat suspiciously like a religious man is sitting against a building. Sarah and Byron are on date and have repeatedly tried to avoid Putzman who claims Sarah is his wife. Byron and Sarah met at one of Putzman's poetry readings and he has been haunting them ever since.

Putzman the Poet, disguised as a street person and then as an ice cream vendor, an "interactive poet" in love with Sarah.

Sarah, a thirty-something neurotic starting a promising love affair with Byron.

Byron, a graduate student and fledgling poet.

STREET PERSON (PUTZMAN): Spare seventy-nine cents for a can of dog food?

BYRON: What?

STREET PERSON (PUTZMAN): Dog food.

BYRON: *(Suspiciously and somewhat defiantly.)* Well . . . where's your dog?

STREET PERSON (PUTZMAN): Whaddya mean? *I'm* the dog.

BYRON: Well . . . Look, I don't want to give you money if you're just going to spend it on alcohol.

STREET PERSON (PUTZMAN): So let me know when you've reached a decision.

BYRON: *(To Sarah, privately.)* I never know what to do with these situations. He doesn't *look* drunk.

SARAH: *(to Street Person [Putzman])* How do we know you're not lying?

STREET PERSON (PUTZMAN): Seventy-nine cents is the special price. Pedigree beef chunks. I coulda ast you for ninety-eight cents. You'd a never known the difference, that's the regular price. But I bargain shop. And I pass the savings along to the supplier. You.

(From one pocket produces a can opener. From another a spoon.) There . . . is that enough?

BYRON: *(Shaken.)* Does, does it taste all right?

STREET PERSON (PUTZMAN): Are you kidding? It's terrible. What do you think 'For the dogs' means? But you can't always get what you want. It gives me all the vitamins I need. *(To Sarah, flirtatiously.)* And it keeps my coat shiny.

BYRON: Here, here's a dollar.

STREET PERSON (PUTZMAN): I got change.

BYRON: No, no, I want you to keep the change. Buy a Big Mac. They're on sale for ninety-nine cents.

STREET PERSON (PUTZMAN): I like Pedigree better. I don't like feasts, they give me false expectations. *(Comes up with change.)* The fourteen ounce size sets me up for the day.

BYRON: No, no, please keep it. I want you to keep it. What about sales tax?

STREET PERSON (PUTZMAN): Sales tax? There's no tax on food.

BYRON: Yes, there is, there is. There's a tax on dog food.

STREET PERSON (PUTZMAN): Not for me. I'm a person.

BYRON: It doesn't work that way.

STREET PERSON (PUTZMAN): Don't tell me my business. For me it does.

BYRON: Well . . . how?

STREET PERSON (PUTZMAN): *(Pulling out his spoon and can opener again.)* I open it and begin eating. No tax. Here, take the change. This is a matter of honor. Honor. You know what that word means?

BYRON: But I want to help.

STREET PERSON (PUTZMAN): *I'm* the one who says what help is. *(Begins to growl.)*

SARAH: *(As growling gets louder.)* Take the money. Let's get out of here. *(Byron accepts money. Street person's growl intensifies. He gets up onto all fours, begins to bark. Byron and Sarah continue, looking over their shoulders as Sarah continues to talk. Street person runs offstage on all fours in opposite direction.)*

SARAH: Look, forget it. You did fine. He's probably on some drug. That new one, Agony, the ultimate downer.

BYRON: Agony?

SARAH: You think we got a lot of patients on Ecstacy. That was nothing.

BYRON: *(Looks at the change still in his hand.)* So I was okay.

SARAH: You were great. Hey, here we are.

(They are walking near a small window like those motel windows that are bullet proof and have only a small opening to hand through change or credit cards. A crude drawing of an ice cream cone is on it, and above the window of the store, The Emperor of Ice Cream. While Sarah stands back a few feet Byron walks up to the small opening and bending down slightly speaks, slowly and forcefully.)

BYRON: *(Forcefully.)* We would like two single-scoop vanilla cones, sugar cones.

VOICE INSIDE: Are you kidding?

BYRON: I've never been more serious in my life.

VOICE: Live a little. The nonfat, low-cal garlic walnut crunch is getting rave reviews.

BYRON: Vanilla.

VOICE: A favorite is the Double Funky Chunky Chocolate Run-Amok.

BYRON: We don't want that. We want what we want.

VOICE: How can you know what you want unless you've heard what the choices are? There's Tummy Tickle Butter Brickle Rum and Raisin Resolution. There's our sin and Thin-No Repentance Ollaliberry Mousse Truffle Royale, there's Praline Chocoholic Madness . . .

BYRON: *(Fiercely.)* We are interested in one thing and one thing only. We do not need suggestions, however helpful your intention may be. We have come here sure of what we want. We are not interested in what other people have thought of; other choices. Our tastes are not dictated by some marketing psychologist's ploys. We have made our choice and nothing you have to suggest will sway us from that choice. We want vanilla. A single scoop in a

sugar cone. If that's something you cannot supply, we'll go somewhere else. It's just as simple as that.

VOICE: Okay, okay, I was just trying to be helpful. *(The cones appear.
Byron hands Sarah one, licks his.)*

VOICE: This choice of yours, it isn't very imaginative. It's the kind of
ice cream people who haven't thought their choices through
make. I thought . . .

BYRON: *(Leaning into the small window opening.)* Thank you, but I
hope you won't be offended if I offer *you* a suggestion. Things
don't have to be complex. Sometimes the simple pleasures are
the most intense. I think we've come way too far in trying to con-
coct intricate combinations. I think that instead of trying to sell
these fancy creations you should ask yourself the question,
"What happened to vanilla? Why did we give up on it so easily?"

VOICE: *(After some delay.)* I see. I see your point. I have been in this
business for twenty years. I've had a kind of feeling that things
were slipping away, but you know, you're a businessman, you
adapt. But you know, the other day I said to my wife, I remember it now, I said ice cream is not what it was. She said, What are
you talking about, marbling, double chocolate fudge, it's better
than it ever was. I didn't have an answer. Well, you can bet she'll
get an earful when I get home. Sure it's new, I'll tell her, but does
it improve your life? Hey, those cones are on me.

SARAH: *(To Byron.)* I *love* this cone. It's just . . . itself. I mean, you and
this cone, you're like scotch together. Only I don't feel I need to
be in a bubble. I feel like this world is my bubble.

BYRON: It's like poetry, just itself. You don't have to try to interpret it.
You just taste it.

SARAH: Oh, I can feel I'm ready. I'm ready for Putzman.

BYRON: *(Back to the ice cream voice.)* You won't be sorry. Talking to
your wife. Some things need talking out.

Parcheesied

John Howie Patterson
1994

Scene: The dining area of a small apartment. A table and three chairs. The three are playing Parcheesi. Time: The present. Evening.

Darryl, 20s.
Dad, 50s–60s.
Sylvia, 20s, Darryl's girlfriend.

> *(Three people are sitting around the table, playing Parcheesi. Dad is a man in his sixties. His son Darryl is a man in his twenties. Darryl's girlfriend Sylvia is a woman in her twenties. Dad taunts Darryl shaking his dice cup at him.)*

DARRYL: Just roll Dad. Roll

DAD: *(Whispering to his dice.)* I need a one. C'mon give me a one.

DARRYL: Dad.

DAD: Hey, can't a guy talk to his dice?

DARRYL: Like they're listening Dad. Roll.

DAD: Okay, okay, okay, pipe down. This is an important roll—all right? The game's on the line here. Right Sylvia?

SYLVIA: Right Mr. Perkins. Whatever you say.

DAD: *(To Darryl.)* Don't rush me. Gotta build a little heat up in these babies before I can—

DARRYL: You see me taking five minutes to roll? Jesus Christ—

DAD: There's nothing in the rules that says I can't take as much time as I want. Nothing. No time limit. If you'd just relax and shut up maybe we could get on with this thing.

DARRYL: Fine.

> *(Dad breathes on his dice and whispers a secret message to them.)*

DARRYL: *(Crossing his fingers.)* No one. No one. No one—

DAD: *(Stopping, glaring at Darryl.)* Now how am I supposed to roll with you putting a hex on me huh? How am I supposed—

DARRYL: You put a spell on my dice don't you. Aren't I entitled to—

SYLVIA: C'mon you guys, it's just a game. We were having a perfectly wonderful evening. Let's just get on with the game okay? It's supposed to be fun right?

DAD: What's not fun about it? I enjoy seeing your boyfriend here get all flustered. Takes things too seriously doesn't he?

DARRYL: You're one to talk Dad. If you world just roll—

DAD: All right, all right, I'll roll. You want me to roll, I'll roll. I'll roll so fast you won't have time to cast a counter spell. *(Dad dumps his dice onto the board.)*

DAD: A one and a five. It worked. It worked, it worked, it worked.

DARRYL: Shit.

DAD: *(To Darryl.)* Now let's see, as much as I hate to, I'll use the one to send you home. And this five—

(Darryl hits the table with his hand.)

DAD: Oh now, you're not going to flip over the board are you? *(To Sylvia.)* He's got that tendency you know. All through childhood. Monopoly, chess, checkers, you name it. And this baseball game they used to play with dice. Yes, my Darryl was always a board flipper—

DARRYL: Okay, all right, gloat away. Just gloat your heart out. I don't care. But remember this, I'm right behind you Dad, right behind. And what goes around, comes around.

DAD: On, c'mon Darryl. It's just a game. Isn't that right Sylvia, that's what you said?

SYLVIA: Yes that's what I said.

DARRYL: Finish your move Dad, it's Sylvia's turn.

DAD: Yes sir. *(Dad finishes his turn.)*

DARRYL: *(To Sylvia.)* Get him. You need a four or a five. Both would be even better.

SYLVIA: Shall I pray?

DAD: Nah, don't bother. If you don't have that relationship with your dice, like I have with mine, it won't do a thing. You gotta live with the dice, be close to the dice. Like me, I keep 'em right by the bed when I—

DARRYL: Just roll Sylvia. *(She rolls.)*

DAD: Damn—a four and a three.

DARRYL: Yes honey. Yes. Oooooh it feels so good. Victory. *(He gives her a kiss on the cheek.)* Thank you Sylvia. You have done a great service to humanity.

DAD: She was lucky, that's all. I don't hold it against her.

SYLVIA: *(To Darryl.)* So what do I do now?

DARRYL: What do you mean what you do now? You send him back. Move your guy four and send him back. Here, I'll do—
(Sylvia slaps his hand away.)

SYLVIA: I'll move my own pieces thank you.

DAD: I believe that is within her right.

DARRYL: She's just learning Dad. Remember? This is her first game. She's never played before. I'm just trying to speed things up. *(to Sylvia)* Move the piece four honey.

SYLVIA: Which one?

DARRYL: *(Pointing.)* That one.

SYLVIA: But I don' have to, do I? I could move the other four right? And move the other three—

DARRYL: Yeah but, you don't want to do that.

DAD: How do you know? Maybe she does.

DARRYL: You want to send him back. Move that one four, that one three. You want to win don't you?

SYLVIA: I don't really care actually. I'm so far behind at this point.

DARRYL: Honey, what are you saying? You're not gonna—

DAD: Let her do what she wants Darryl.

DARRYL: You're not going to send him back? You're not going to—

SYLVIA: What if I don't?

DARRYL: Sylvia, what is wrong with you? Send him back for crying out loud. You're supposed to. That's the whole point of—

DAD: Don't you tell her what to do. Let her make up her own—

DARRYL: Sylvia—you want to help him? Is that what you're saying? You're going to let him win? *(Darryl points to his father.)* The monster? This monster who—

SYLVIA: I didn't say I was going to. I just wanted to know what would happen if I did. And I think I have my answer. *(She moves her pieces.)*

DARRYL: *(Smiling incredulously.)* You're not going to send me home.

My own girlfriend betrays me, the woman I've spent the last two years with, getting to know, caring for—

SYLVIA: With the way you've been acting Darryl, I think I'm doing you a favor.

DAD: You're talking sense Sylvie, you're talking sense.

SYLVIA: *(To Darryl.)* Maybe you need to learn a thing or two about sportsmanship.

DAD: You tell him Sylvie—

SYLVIA: *(To Dad.)* It's Sylvia Mr. Perkins.

DAD: Sylvia.

SYLVIA: Your turn Darryl.

DARRYL: I'm not going to forget this. Sylvie.

SYLVIA: Darryl. Give it a rest okay? It's just a game. *(Darryl taunts them with his dice cup, then rolls.)*

DARRYL: Yes. Yes. Yes. Double-fives. That'll bring me out. *(He moves a piece.)* And with doubles I can move another nine—

DAD: Hold it. Hold it right there. *(Dad picks up the box top.)* You can't do that.

DARRYL: Why the hell not? It's doubles. I used the five to get out and I've got nine left to use as I please. You count what's on the bottom of the dice too, remember?
(Dad studies the rules.)

DAD: Says here, and I quote, "After all of his four pawns have been entered, a player throwing doublets—

DARRYL: I know the rule Dad.

DAD: —a player throwing doublets may count the numbers on both top and bottom of the dice—"

DARRYL: Which I did, so what's the problem?

DAD: All your pawns weren't entered. You can't use the doublet. You can use the five to get out. But you can't use the rest of it.

DARRYL: Oh, come on Dad. We've been through this time and time again. Remember when we decided that was a vague rule?

SYLVIA: Oh my God, you two make me sick.

DAD: I don't recall that Darryl.

SYLVIA: Can we finish this up please before midnight? Before you guys kill each other?

DARRYL: *(To Dad.)* Last Thanksgiving. The big blowup. Uncle Jerry? Remember?

DAD: Nope. Can't say I do.

DARRYL: We finally decided that when you roll double fives with just one player left on start and the rest on home, you can use the top and the bottom. So it is a legal move. *(beat)* And—I get to roll again. *(Dad fumes. Darryl rolls and moves his pieces in silence.)*

DAD: *(Whispering to dice.)* Double-six baby, double-six— *(Darryl crosses his fingers.)*

DARRYL: No. sixes. No sixes. No sixes—

DAD: *(Whispering.)* Give me a fix, double-six. *(Dad rolls.)*

DAD: a lousy one and a useless two.

DARRYL: Praise the lord. There is a God after all.

SYLVIA: Yeah and I wish he would hurry up and end this game.

DARRYL: What's the matter Sylvie, aren't you having fun?

SYLVIA: It's Sylvia. Please. I don't call you Darrylie do I?

DAD: *(To himself.)* Now wait a minute here Bill, things aren't so bad. *(He moves his pieces)* I can keep the blockade.

DARRYL: You're keeping the blockade?

DAD: Why shouldn't I?

DARRYL: You are trying to win aren't you? You've had that blockade forever. Sylvia's no threat to you. Why don't you let her through?

DAD: Don't know. Just don't feel like it I guess. *(He looks at Sylvia)* Or do I? Yes, I guess, maybe I do. She did do me a good turn once after all, didn't she? I think it's time to return the favor. *(Dad moves his pieces.)*

SYLVIA: Thank you Mr. Perkins. You're such a gentlemen. *(Looks at Darryl.)* Unlike some people I know. *(Sylvia rolls.)*

DAD: Well how about that. The double-sixes I ask for she gets. *(Dad shouts into his dice cup. To dice.)* What are ya deaf? I said double-sixes. *(To Sylvia.)* Your dice must a heard. Best hearing on a pair dice I've ever seen. Better hold onto those.

SYLVIA: *(Studying the board.)* I plan to Mr. Perkins. *(She looks up at Darryl.)* That is, if Darryl will let me. *(Darryl studies the board nervously.)*

DARRYL: Aren't you gonna move your pieces honey?

SYLVIA: I thought I'd take my time. Or maybe I'm just waiting for you to tell me what to do.

DARRYL: You might want to concentrate on that piece you've got back near start. Move that fourteen—

DAD: Darryl, you think she can't see it? You think she doesn't know? come on Darryl, we're both sunk and you know it. *(Sylvia begins to move her pieces.)*

SYLVIA: Let's see. Six here— *(To Dad.)* That puts one of yours back to start. Sorry Mr. Perkins.

DAD: Quite all right Sylvia, I'll just get started on the dishes. *(Dad starts to get up.)*

DARRYL: It's not over yet Dad. Sit down.

DAD: May as well be. May as well be. I'm tired anyway. Let her win. *(Dad exits to the kitchen.)*

DARRYL: It's not over.

SYLVIA: Now let's see, where was I? That gives me another twenty to play with, in addition to the other six and the two on the other side. Let's see, one, two, three, four, five, six, oh and that sends another of poor Mr. Perkin's back. Gives me another twenty. That's forty-two all together now. *(Beat.)* Yes, this is working out very well. *(Her hand hovers over the board.)* Now, I wonder, should I leave this last little piece here, just to keep it interesting? You are dangerously close—

DARRYL: *(Fuming.)* You told me you didn't know how to play Parcheesi. Where'd you learn?

SYLVIA: No, I don't think so. Better move this one along. *(Sylvia makes her final move.)*

DARRYL: Where'd you learn?

SYLVIA: Well isn't it obvious, I learned from watching you two. *(Darryl looks homicidal.)*

DARRYL: Oh yeah? *(Beat.)* Well I quit. *(He flips the board onto the floor. Dad returns from the kitchen.)*

SYLVIA: Mr. Perkins, why does Parcheesi always bring out the worst in people?

DAD: I don't have any idea Sylvie. But if I did, I don't think I'd want to play anymore.

SYLVIA: Why's that?
DAD: It would take all the fun out of it.
  (Blackout.)

PART FOUR:

SCENES FOR TWO WOMEN AND ONE MAN

Prometheus Bound

Aeschylus
460 B.C.

Scene: The daughters of Oceanus come upon Prometheus, chained
to a huge boulder on a craggy mountainside in European Scythia.
It is cold and raw. It is as though it were the end of the known
world.

Prometheus, a Titan, from the race of Giants, has stolen fire and given
it to mankind despite the Olympian Gods warning against it.
Chorus, daughters of Oceanus, the Father of the Sea, (divided into
two voices), bird-like creatures representing nature.

PROMETHEUS: Hark, again! I hear the whirring
As of winged birds approaching;
With the light strokes of their pinions
Ether pipes ill-boding whispers!—
Alas! alas! that I should fear
Each breath that nears me.
(The Oceanides approach, borne through the air in a winged car.)

STROPHE I:
CHORUS: Fear nothing; for a friendly band approaches;
Fleet rivalry of wings
Oar'd us to this far height, with hard consent
Wrung from our careful sire
The winds swift-sweeping bore me: for I heard
The harsh hammer's note deep deep in ocean caves,
And, throwing virgin shame aside, unshod
The winged car I mounted.
PROM: Ah! ah!
Daughters of prolific Tethys,
And of ancient father Ocean,
With his sleepless current whirling
Round the firm ball of the globe.

Look! with rueful eyes behold me
Nailed by adamantine rivets,
Keeping weary watch unenvied
On this tempest-rifted rock!

ANTISTROPHE I.
CHORUS: I look, Prometheus; and a tearful cloud
My woeful sight bedims,
To see they goodliest form with insult chained,
In adamantine bonds,
To this bare crag, where pinching airs shall blast thee.
New gods now hold the helm of Heaven; new laws
Mark Jove's unrighteous rule; the giant trace
Of Titan times hath vanished.
PROM: Deep in death-receiving Hades
Had he bound me, had he whelmed me
In Tartarean pit, unfathomed,
Fettered with unyielding bonds!
Then nor god nor man had feasted
Eyes of triumph on my wrongs,
Nor I, thus swung in middle ether,
Moved the laughter of my foes.

STROPHE II.
CHORUS: Which of the gods hath heart so hard
To mock thy woes? Who will withhold
The fellow-feeling and the tear,
Save only Jove. But he doth nurse
Strong wrath within his stubborn breast,
And holds all Heaven in awe.
Nor will he cease till his hot rage is glutted,
Or some new venture shakes his stable throne.
PROM: By my Titan soul, I swear it!
Though with harsh chains now he mocks me,
Even now the hour is ripening,
When this haughty lord of Heaven

Shall embrace my knees, beseeching
Me to unveil the new-forged counsels
That shall hurl him from his throne.
But no honey-tongued persuasion,
No smooth words of artful charming,
No stout threats shall loose my tongue,
Till he loose these bonds of insult,
And himself make just atonement
For injustice done to me.

ANTISTROPHE II.
CHORUS: Thou art a bold man, and defiest
    The keenest pangs to force they will.
    With a most unreined tongue thou speakest;
    But me—sharp fear hath pierced my heart.
    I fear for thee: and of thy woes
    The distant, doubtful end
    I see not. O, 'tis hard, most hard to reach
    The heart of Jove! prayer beats his ear in vain.
PROM: Harsh is Jove, I know—he frameth
    Justice for himself; but soon,
    When the destined arm o'ertakes him,
    He shall tremble as a child.
    He shall smooth his bristling anger,
    Courting friendship shunned before,
    More importunate to unbind me
    Than impatient I of bonds.
CHORUS: Speak now, and let us know the whole offence
    Jove charges thee withal; for which he seized,
    And with dishonor and dire insult loads thee.
    Unfold the tale; unless, perhaps, such sorrow
    Irks thee to tell.
PROM: To tell or not to tell
    Irks me the same; which way I turn is pain.
    When first the gods their fatal strife began,
    And insurrection raged in Heaven—some striving

To cast old Kronos from his hoary throne,
That Jove might reign, and others to crush i' the bud
His swelling mastery—I wise counsel gave
To Titans, sons of primal Heaven and Earth;
But gave in vain. Their dauntless stubborn souls
Spurned gentle ways, and patient-working wiles,
Weening swift triumph with a blow. But me,
My mother Themis, not once but oft, and Earth
(One shape of various names), prophetic told
That violence and rude strength in such a strife
Were vain—craft haply might prevail. This lesson
 I taught the haughty Titans, but they deigned
Scarce with contempt to hear my prudent words.
Thus baffled in my plans, I deemed it best,
As things then were, leagued with my mother Themis
To accept Jove's proffered friendship. By my counsels
From his primeval throne was Kronos hurled
Into the pit Tartarean, dark, profound,
With all his troop of friends. Such was the kindness
From me received by him who now doth hold
The masterdom of Heaven; these the rewards
Of my great zeal: for so it hath been ever.
Suspicion's a disease that cleaves to tyrants,
And they who love most are the first suspected.
As for your question, for what present fault
I beat the wrong that now afflicts me, hear.
Soon as he sat on his ancestral throne
He called the gods together, and assigned
To each his fair allotment, and his sphere
Of sway supreme; but, ah! for wretched man!
To him nor part nor portion fell: Jove vowed
To blot his memory from the Earth, and mould
The race anew. I only of the gods
Thwarted his will; and, but for my strong aid,
Hades had whelmed, and hopeless ruin swamped
All men that breathe. Such were my crimes: these pains

Grievous to suffer, pitiful to behold,
Were purchased thus; and mercy's now denied
To him whose crime was mercy to mankind:
And here I lie, in cunning torment stretched,
A spectacle inglorious to Jove.
CHORUS: An iron-heart were his, and flinty hard,
Who on thy woes could look without a tear,
Prometheus; I had liefer not so seen thee,
And seeing thee fain would call mine eyesight liar.
PROM: Certes no sight am I for friends to look on.
CHORUS: Was this thy sole offence?
PROM: I taught weak mortals
Not to foresee harm, and forestall the Fates.
CHORUS: A sore disease to anticipate mischance:
How didst thou cure it?
PROM: In their dark breasts.
CHORUS: That was a boon indeed,
To ephemeral man.
PROM: Nay more, I gave them fire.
CHORUS: And flame-faced fire is now enjoyed by mortals?
PROM: Enjoyed, and of all arts the destined mother.
CHORUS: And is this all the roll of thy offendings
That he should rage so fierce? Hath he not set
Bounds to his vengeance?
PROM: None, but his own pleasure.
CHORUS: And when shall he please? Vain the hope; thou see'st
That thou hast erred; and that thou hast to us
No pleasure brings, to thee excess of pain.
Of this enough. Seek now to sure the evil.
PROM: 'Tis a light thing for him whose foot's unwarped
By misadventure's meshes to advise
And counsel the unfortunate. But I
Foreknew my fate, and if I erred, I erred
With conscious purpose, purchasing man's weal
With mine own grief. I knew I should offend
The Thunderer, though deeming not that he

Would perch me thus to pine 'twixt Earth and Sky,
Of this wild wintry waste sole habitant.
But cease to weep for ills that weeping mends not;
Descend, and I'll discourse to thee at length
Of chances yet to come. Nay, do not doubt;
But leave thy car, nor be ashamed to share
The afflictions of the afflicted; for Mishap,
Of things that lawless wander, wanders most;
With me today it is with you tomorrow.
CHORUS: Not to sluggish ears, Prometheus,
Hast thou spoken thy desire;
From our breeze-borne car descending,
With light foot we greet the ground.
Leaving ether chaste, smooth pathway
Of the gently-winnowing wing,
On this craggy rock I stand,
To hear the tale, while thou mayst tell it,
Of thy sorrows to the end.

The Haunted House

Plautus

200 B.C.

Scene: In front of Theopropides House. Scapha has brought out a dressing table and cosmetics and Philematium has begun to primp. Philolaches is off to one side observing her.

Philematium, a beautiful woman, a courtesan.
Scapha, her servant.
Philolaches, in love with Philematium.

PHILEMATIUM: *(Stretching luxuriously.)* Scapha, I haven't enjoyed a bath so much in ages. And I don't know when I've felt cleaner.

SCAPHA: *(Indulgently.)* Wait until you see how things turn out, I always say. For example, this year the harvest turned out fine.

PHILEMATIUM: *(Puzzled.)* And just what does the harvest have to do with my bath?

SCAPHA: *(Pointedly.)* No more or less than your bath has to do with *your* harvest.

PHILOLACHES: *(Watching the two unobserved, aside.)* O my lovely, lovely beloved! *(To the audience.)* There's the windstorm that raised the roof with my will power. And then love and passion poured into my breast, and I'll never be able to make any repairs. The walls of my heart are drenched. My whole house is a ruin.

PHILEMATIUM: *(Worriedly.)* Scapha dear, do you think this dress is becoming? I want to be sure Philolaches likes the way I look. *(Rapturously.)* He's my darling; I owe everything to him.

SCAPHA: You're such a nice girl, why not make do with your nice sweet ways to set off? Lovers aren't in love with a woman's clothes but with what's in them.

PHILOLACHES: *(Aside.)* So help me, that was very nicely said, Scapha. The old witch knows a thing or two. She has a nice idea of the way lovers feel.

PHILEMATIUM: Well, what about it?

SCAPHA: What about what?

PHILEMATIUM: What about looking at me and telling me if this becomes me?

SCAPHA: You're so pretty that whatever you wear becomes you.

PHILOLACHES: *(Aside.)* Scapha, for saying that you get a gift from me today. I can't let you give compliments to the girl I love and not get something for it.

PHILEMATIUM: *(Impatiently.)* Now, don't just yes me.

SCAPHA: *(Indulgently.)* You're such a silly girl. What do you prefer? That I tell lies and run you down or tell the truth and compliment you? Lord knows *I'd* much rather have people lie to pay me a compliment than tell the truth and find fault or poke fun at my looks.

PHILEMATIUM: *(Passionately.)* I love the truth. I *want* people to tell me the truth. I hate lies.

SCAPHA: All right. *(With mock solemnity.)* I swear, by your love for me and Philolaches' for you, you're a lovely girl.

PHILOLACHES: *(Aside.)* What's that, you old witch? How did you swear? By my love for her? What's the matter with adding by her love for me? That settles you. That gift I promised you is all off. You've just lost it.

SCAPHA: *(Shaking her head disapprovingly.)* It amazes me that such a smart, sensible, and well-trained girl like you can do such silly things.

PHILEMATIUM: Please, you must warn me if I'm making any mistakes.

SCAPHA: *(Vehemently.)* You're certainly making a mistake in having eyes for just one man, and giving yourself all to him and forgetting about the others. *(Scornfully.)* Devoting yourself to one lover! That's being a married woman, not a mistress.

PHILOLACHES: *(Stunned, aside.)* God in heaven! What sort of plague is this upon my house? I'll be damned if I don't kill that old hag. I'll starve her; I'll let her freeze to death!

PHILEMATIUM: *(Sharply.)* Scapha, I don't want any wrong ideas from you.

SCAPHA: *(Scornfully.)* You *are* a silly girl. What do you expect? That he'll be your loving friend forever? I'm warning you: You'll get older, he'll get colder—and then he'll leave you.

PHILEMATIUM: *(Worriedly.)* I hope not.

SCAPHA: *(Bitterly.)* What you don't hope for happens more often than what you do. All right. If my saying so won't make you believe the truth, maybe some facts will. Compare what I am now with what I used to be. Men once fell in love with me just as much as they do with you. I went ahead and gave myself to one man. And, god help me, as soon as these hairs turned gray, he left me in the lurch. If you ask me, the same thing will happen to you.

PHILOLACHES: *(Beside himself, aside.)* I can't hold myself back—I'll scratch that bitch's eyes out.

PHILEMATIUM: *(Firmly.)* He paid the price from his own pocket to free me—me and only me—to be his alone. So I feel I owe it to him to devote myself to him, to be his alone.

PHILOLACHES: *(Rapturously, aside.)* So help me, there's a fine girl, one with real character. By god, I did the right thing: I'm glad I spent every cent I had for her sake.

SCAPHA: *(Witheringly.)* God, what a fool you are!

PHILEMATIUM: Why?

SCAPHA: Because you care about his being in love with you.

PHILEMATIUM: *(With asperity.)* And why shouldn't I care?

SCAPHA: You've already got your freedom. At this very moment you have what you were after. But he—if he doesn't keep on loving you, he's thrown away every penny he paid for you.

PHILOLACHES: *(Raging, aside.)* God damn it, I'll murder that hag! That filthy tongue of hers is corrupting the girl. That old woman's a bawd, that's what she is.

PHILEMATIUM: *(With conviction.)* I'll never be able to give him the thanks he deserves from me, never! *(Sharply.)* Scapha! Stop trying to make me think any less of him.

SCAPHA: Just remember one thing: If you're going to devote yourself to him alone, now when you're lovely and young, you'll be sorry when you're old.

PHILOLACHES: *(As before.)* God, I wish I could turn myself into a case of lockjaw. I'd close that foul mouth. I'd kill that blasted bitch.

PHILEMATIUM: *(Resolutely.)* Now that I have what I wanted, I ought to act toward him just as I did before he gave in—when I was doing all I could to be sweet to him.

PHILOLACHES: *(Aside.)* So help me, for those words I'm ready to pay what I did all over again—and murder Scapha in cold blood.

SCAPHA: *(Ironically.)* Well, if you've got it in writing that he'll provide for you forever, that he's going to be your own true love till the end of your days, then I suppose you should devote yourself entirely to him—and start dressing like a wife.

PHILEMATIUM: *(Loftily.)* A good name is money. It I keep mine, I'll be rich enough.

PHILOLACHES: *(Rapturously, aside.)* So help me, even if I have to sell my own father, I'll do it before I'll ever let that girl be in need as long as I'm alive.

SCAPHA: What's going to happen to all the others who were in love with you?

PHILEMATIUM: They'll be even more in love with me when they see the gratitude I show to someone who's earned it.

PHILOLACHES: *(As before.)* I wish I'd be given the news right now that my father's dead— I'd disinherit myself and turn the whole estate over to her.

SCAPHA: He'll go through every cent he has before long. Drinks and parties all day and all night, nobody trying to save a penny, nothing but eat, eat, eat . . .

PHILOLACHES: *(Between his teeth, aside.)* All right, damn you I'll find out how economically I can live—and I'll start with you: You're not going to eat or drink a thing in my house for ten days in a row.

PHILEMATIUM: *(Sharply.)* If you have anything nice to say about him, you can say it. But if you're simply going to run him down, believe me, I'll give you a beating.

PHILOLACHES: *(Exultantly, aside.)* I couldn't have spent the money I paid for her any better if I had put it on the altar for god almighty himself. You see how she loves me? From the bottom of her heart. Pretty smart of me: I paid to set her free—and got a defense attorney for my money.

SCAPHA: *(Grumbling.)* All right, all right. I can see that, for you, no other man in the world can compare with Philolaches. So I'll just say yes; I don't want any beatings on his account.

PHILEMATIUM: Scapha, quick, the mirror and my jewel box. I want to be all ready when my sweetheart comes.

SCAPHA: *(Handing her the mirror and box.)* It's the woman who has to worry about her looks and her age that needs a mirror. But what do you need one for? You're a mirror of beauty yourself.

PHILOLACHES: *(Aside.)* Scapha, I must reward a compliment as pretty as that. So today I'll give a special present—to Philematium.

PHILEMATIUM: Is everything in place? How's my hairdo? Is it attractive?

SCAPHA: On an attractive girl like you, how could it help but be attractive?

PHILOLACHES: *(Aside.)* Did you ever hear of anything worse than that old woman? All she could say before was no; now it's nothing but yes.

PHILEMATIUM: My powder, please.

SCAPHA: What in the world do you want with powder?

PHILEMATIUM: For my cheeks.

SCAPHA: You might just as well try to make ivory shine by putting soot on it.

PHILOLACHES: *(Aside.)* Make ivory shine with soot? That's not bad. Good for you, Scapha.

PHILEMATIUM: Then give me my lipstick.

SCAPHA: No, I won't. You *are* a silly girl. What do you want to do? Mess up a beautiful work of art with some splashes of fresh paint? At your age you don't need any makeup—no rouge, no powder, none of that junk.

PHILEMATIUM: All right, then, take the mirror. *(Before handing it over she takes a last look and, pleased with what she sees, kisses it.)*

PHILOLACHES: *(Writhing, aside.)* Oh, god, oh, god! She's kissed the mirror! If I only had a stone to smash that thing into bits!

SCAPHA: *(Handing her a towel.)* Now take this towel and wipe your hands.

PHILEMATIUM: What for?

SCAPHA: You held the mirror. I'm afraid your hands'll smell of the silver. We don't want Philolaches to suspect that silver's ever crossed your palm.

PHILOLACHES: *(Shaking his head in reluctant admiration, aside.)* I don't know where I've ever seen a wiser old bawd than that filthy-minded hag. That's a pretty good idea she had about the mirror.

PHILEMATIUM: Don't you think I need some perfume?

SCAPHA: Absolutely not.

PHILEMATIUM: Why?

SCAPHA: Because the right smell for a woman is no smell at all. You know those patched-up, toothless old crones who drench themselves with perfume and cover up their ugly spots with makeup? Well, once sweat starts mixing in with all that, they begin to smell like some sauce a cook's concocted: You don't know what the smell is from, but you do know it's pretty bad.

PHILOLACHES: *(Again shaking his head admiringly, aside.)* Clever old crone—you'll never see one smarter. *(To the audience.)* It's the truth and most of you know it, you fellows with old hags at home who bought you with their dowries.

PHILEMATIUM: Look at my jewelry and my dress. Are they becoming?

SCAPHA: *I* don't have to bother about them.

PHILEMATIUM: Then who should?

SCAPHA: I'll tell you: Philolaches—so he'll buy you only what he thinks you'll like. You see, a lover just uses jewelry and clothes to buy himself a mistress; he's not interested in those things himself. So why go to the trouble of parading them before him? Anyway, jewelry's for an ugly woman and gowns are for an old one to hide her age. A good-looking girl is better in the nude than in a gorgeous gown. Good looks are ornament enough.

PHILOLACHES: *(Aside.)* And I've held back long enough. *(Stepping out of his hiding place, to Philematium.)* Well, what are you doing?

PHILEMATIUM: Trying to look my best to please you.

PHILOLACHES: You look fine as is. *(To Scapha, gesturing toward the toilet articles.)* Get inside and take all this stuff with you. *(To Philematium.)* Philematium, sweetheart, let's have a drink together.

PHILEMATIUM: *(Tenderly.)* Yes, lets. Anything you want I want too, sweetheart.

PHILOLACHES: *(Exulting.)* It's cheap at ten thousand dollars to hear you talk that way.

PHILEMATIUM: *(Caressing him.)* Oh, make it five; I want to give you a bargain, when I hear *you* talk that way.

Dulcitius

Hrotsvitha
900 A.D.

Scene: Time: circa 290 A.D. Setting: The apartment where the girls, along with a third young woman, Chionia, are being held captive. They have refused to give up their belief in Christianity.

Of Note: The name *Agape* means love, *Irena* means peace, and *Chionia* means purity. This play is based on the legend of the martyrdom of the three women during the reign of Diocletian.

Agape, young woman.
Irena, young woman.
Chionia, young woman. (Brief appearance.)
Diocletian, Emperor of Rome.

DIOCLETIAN: The renown of your illustrious family, your noble birth, and the brilliance of your beauty demand that you be united in marriage to the highest rank in our court. This we will not oppose, if, at our command, you will deny Christ and offer sacrifice to our gods.

AGAPE: Be not concerned with us, nor with the preparations for our marriage, for nothing in the world can force us to renounce a Name that we are called upon to defend, nor to sully our virginal purity.

DIOCLETIAN: What does this mean, this folly which impels you?

AGAPE: What sign of folly do you detect in us?

DIOCLETIAN: A sign clearly evident.

AGAPE: In what manner?

DIOCLETIAN: Is it not folly for you to renounce the practice of our ancient religion and follow this new Christian superstition?

AGAPE: You rashly attack the majesty of Almighty God. That is dangerous.

DIOCLETIAN: Dangerous! To whom?

AGAPE: To you and to the state which you govern.

DIOCLETIAN: She is mad. Take her away.

CHIONIA: My sister is not mad but justly reproves your folly.

DIOCLETIAN: This girl raves more violently than the first; remove her likewise from our presence, and we will question the third.

IRENA: You will find the third equally rebellious to your orders and ready to resist you.

DIOCLETIAN: Irena, since you are the youngest, show yourself the eldest in dignity.

IRENA: Show me how, I beg of you.

DIOCLETIAN: Bow your head to the gods; and in this deference, be an example to your sisters that they may be freed.

IRENA: Let those who wish to incur the wrath of the Most High bow before idols; as for me, I will not dishonor my head, which has been anointed with kingly oil, by abasing myself at the feet of idols.

DIOCLETIAN: The worship of the gods brings no dishonor; on the contrary, it brings the greatest honor.

IRENA: What baser shame, what greater disgrace to venerate slaves as if they were princes or lords?

DIOCLETIAN: I do not ask you to venerate slaves but the gods of the leaders and princes.

IRENA: Is not that which can be purchased cheap in the marketplace a slave?

DIOCLETIAN: Enough of this presumptuous talk; let these girls be taken away and put to the tortures.

IRENA: That is what we most desire: to bear the cruelest torture for the love of Christ.

DIOCLETIAN: Let these stubborn girls who defy our orders be bound with chains, be cast into a prison, and be examined by Governor Dulcitius.

The Washtub

Anonymous
circa 1400

Scene: Jack's house. Jack is upset.

Jack
His wife
Her mother

JACK: It was the devil himself who made me get married. I've had
    nothing but tempests, storms, worry, and grief. My wife carries
    on like a beast, and her mother never fails to back her up. There's
    not a moment's peace, happiness, or relief for me. My brain feels
    as if pebbles were rolling around in it. The one yells, the other
    grumbles; one swears, the other rages at me. And that's the way
    I live weekdays and Sundays, with nothing else for entertainment.
    However, I swear by the blood of Christ who made me that I'll
    become master in my house the moment I make up my mind.
WIFE: Always complaining about something or other! If you know
    what's good for you, you'll keep your mouth shut.
MOTHER: What's the matter with him?
WIFE: How do I know? I have to mend whatever he touches, and
    besides he pays no attention to our household needs.
MOTHER: Why are you so unreasonable, Jack? My lord in heaven! A
    good husband ought to obey his wife. And if she decides to give
    you a hiding because you failed in your duties—
JACK: Ha! That'll be the day!
MOTHER: Why not? Goodness gracious! If she chastises you and tries
    to improve you now and then with a slap or two, do you think it's
    out of malice? Not in the least. A sign of love is what it is.
JACK: Very eloquent, mother dear. But why don't you tell me in plain
    words what's on your mind instead of beating around the bush?
MOTHER: All I meant is—this is only your first year of marriage, dear
    mousy.
JACK: What's that? My name isn't mousy; it's Jack, and don't forget it.

MOTHER: Of course not, sweetheart. Jack the married man.

JACK: That I am; mauled and married.

MOTHER: Nonsense; you were never so well off.

JACK: Well off? I'll be damned! I'd be better off with my throat cut! Oh God! Well off!

MOTHER: Just listen to your wife whenever she gives you an order.

JACK: I get too many orders from her as it is; that's the very trouble.

MOTHER: Well, to keep them all in your head, you should make a list. Write all your duties down on a sheet of paper.

JACK: Why not? Go ahead. I'm writing.

WIFE: Write clearly, do you hear? Put down that you'll always obey me, never disobey me, and do everything I ask.

JACK: Nothing doing. Itemize, and I'll agree to what's reasonable.

WIFE: Let's get to the point. Put down, if you want to keep me happy, that you'll always get up first in the morning.

JACK: I object to that article! Get up first? What for?

WIFE: To warm my clothes by the fire.

JACK: Is that the custom?

WIFE: It is. Apparently you need a lesson in customs.

MOTHER: Write!

WIFE: Write, Jackie!

JACK: Don't rush me. I'm still at the first word.

WIFE: At night, if the baby wakes up—and he does all the time—it's your duty to get out of bed to rock him and carry him and walk up and down the room no matter how late it is.

JACK: But that's not fair!

WIFE: Write!

JACK: The sheet is full already. Where am I supposed to write?

WIFE: My palm is itching.

JACK: I guess there's room on the other side.

MOTHER: After that, Jackie boy, you'll have to run to the store for bread and milk.

WIFE: Also feed the cat, wash the clothes, and then hang them up to dry.

MOTHER: Come and go, hop, skip, and run, and sweat like Lucifer.

WIFE: Make the coffee.

MOTHER: Serve her breakfast.

WIFE: Then, to avoid a drubbing, make the bed.

MOTHER: Get lunch started and clean out the kitchen.

JACK: Wait, wait! If you want all this written down, you'll have to dictate word by word.

MOTHER: We don't mind. Let's start off: Buy the bread.

WIFE: And the milk.

MOTHER: Do the laundry.

WIFE: Make the coffee.

MOTHER: Serve her breakfast.

WIFE: Wash up.

JACK: Wash up what?

MOTHER: The pots and pans.

JACK: Slowly, slowly. Pots and pans.

WIFE: And all the dishes.

JACK: Damnation, I'm not bright enough to remember all this.

WIFE: Keep writing so you won't forget. Do you hear me? That's an order.

JACK: All right. Wash the—

WIFE: Baby's dirty diapers.

JACK: That does it! I won't put it down. Dirty diapers isn't decent.

WIFE: Put it down, ninny. What's there to be ashamed of?

JACK: I won't, I swear I won't

WIFE: I can see I'll have to knock the lesson into your brain.

JACK: I'll put it down. Who am I to object? Forget I opened my mouth.

WIFE: The only item left is that you'll straighten out the house. And right now, quick as a rabbit, you'll help me wring the linen dry over the washtub.

JACK: It's all down.

MOTHER: One more article. Now and then you'll steal a moment to give her a bit of you know what.

JACK: I'll let her have a sample in two weeks or a month.

WIFE: Oh yes? Every day five or six times. At least! That's an order too.

JACK: I refuse, by the living God! Five or six times! All the saints help me! Neither five or six nor two or three. I'm not playing.

WIFE: Milksop, weakling, killjoy!

JACK: Jesus Christ, I'm an idiot to allow myself to be led by the nose. How can a man find a moment's rest in this house if he's kept busy with your list?

MOTHER: Don't forget the last article. Hurry up and sign.

JACK: Here, I've signed it. Keep it and don't lose it. From this moment on, I've sworn to do nothing except what's written down on that sheet, not even if it's to save myself from the hangman's noose.

MOTHER: *(To the wife.)* Here, you keep it.

WIFE: Good-bye for now, mother dear.

(The mother leaves.)

WIFE: On with the job. I want to see you sweat a little. Help me stretch these sheets out. It's one of the articles in your contract.

JACK: What's that she's saying? I don't understand.

WIFE: I'll give you the back of my hand in a minute. I'm talking about the wash, you clown!

JACK: It's not in the list.

WIFE: It is too.

JACK: It's not.

WIFE: Oh no? Here it is, if you please. I hope it burns your hand.

JACK: All right, all right, I was wrong, it's in the list; I'll know better next time.

WIFE: There. Hold this end. Pull, pull hard.

JACK: God, is this sheet foul and smelly!

WIFE: The only foul thing around here is your mouth. Come on, do it nicely like me.

JACK: But it's disgusting I tell you! God what a household!

WIFE: I'll throw it all in your face, and don't think I'm joking.

JACK: No you won't, devils in hell.

WIFE: I won't? Here, fool.

JACK: Damnation, you've ruined my clothes!

WIFE: Nothing but alibis for not doing your work. Hold this end. And I hope you choke to death! *(She falls into the tub.)* Oh God, have mercy on me, look down on me, help me out of here or I'll die a shameful death! Jackie, save your wife! Pull her out of this tub!

JACK: It's not in the list.

WIFE: This tub is my death! Oh I'm so miserable! Help me out of here for God's sake!

JACK: Just turn up your backside, you drunken sack.

WIFE: Dearest, sweetest love, save my life! I'm dying. Give me your hand for one little second.

JACK: It's not in my list. Down to hell you go.

WIFE: Somebody help me before I drown!

JACK: *(Reading from the list.)* Buy the bread, make the coffee, serve breakfast, wash the pot and pans.

WIFE: I'm turning blue. I'm breathing my last.

JACK: Knock you up five times a day.

WIFE: Help. Help.

JACK: Come and go, hop, skip, and run.

WIFW: My last hour has struck.

JACK: Heat your clothes over the fire.

WIFE: Your hand, quick! This is the end.

JACK: Walk the baby.

WIFE: You're a dog.

JACK: Make up the bed in the morning.

WIFE: You think this is a laughing matter!

JACK: Hang up the laundry.

WIFE: Mother! Where's mother?

JACK: And keep the kitchen clean.

WIFE: Call a priest.

JACK: I'm scrutinizing this paper, but I have to inform you that it's not in the list.

WIFE: Why didn't you write it in?

JACK: Because you didn't make me. Save yourself any way you can. As far as I'm concerned you're staying where you are.

WIFE: At least go find a policeman to help me.

JACK: It's not in the list.

WIFE: Won't you give me your hand, dearest? I'm ever so weak.

JACK: Dearest is it? I'm the enemy, drop dead!

(The mother knocks at the door.)

MOTHER: Open up!

JACK: Who's knocking?

MOTHER: It's me. I've come to see how you are.

JACK: I'm fine, my wife is dead. Now I'm happy and rich.

MOTHER: What, my daughter is dead?

JACK: Drowned in the wash.

MOTHER: What's that? Murderer!

JACK: I pray to God in Paradise and their worships the saints in heaven to let the devil puncture her guts before the soul comes out.

MOTHER: Is my daughter dead?

JACK: While she was wringing a sheet it fell out of her hands, she bent over the tub and fell in.

WIFE: Mother, I'm dead if you don't rescue your daughter.

MOTHER: Of course I will. Jack, give me a hand.

JACK: It's not in the list.

MOTHER: Is that a nice thing to say?

WIFE: Help!

MOTHER: Miserable cur, are you going to let her die?

JACK: As far as I'm concerned, yes. I don't want to be her flunky anymore.

WIFE: Help me.

JACK: It's not in the list. Can't find if anywhere.

MOTHER: Stop this nonsense at once, Jack, and help me get your wife out.

JACK: I swear I won't, unless I first receive a pledge that I'm to be master of the house.

WIFE: With all my heart, I promise, if only you'll pull me out of here.

JACK: And what do you promise to do?

WIFE: I'll do all the chores, I'll never bother you, and never give you an order unless it's absolutely necessary.

JACK: That's good. Now I'll pull you out. But you'd better keep your promise, by God.

WIFE: I will, and I'll never break it, dear.

JACK: Well then, it looks as if I'll be in charge from now on, since my wife says so.

MOTHER: A rotten business is strife
Between husband and his wife.

JACK: Then let the world be told

A wife should never scold
Nor make her man a slave
Though he be fool or knave.
WIFE: I've learned my lesson too.
I'll never be a shrew.
With diligence and zeal
On my two knees I'll kneel
To scrape and scrub the floor
Under the husband I adore.
Because the rule must be obeyed:
He's my master, I'm his maid.
JACK: Always please me, always mind me,
Always walk two steps behind me,
And I will love you, sweet,
Provided you don't cheat.
From this day on I'll live in clover.
Adieu, my friends, the play is over.

Gammer Gurton's Needle

Mr. S.

circa 1559

Scene: Gammer Gurton has lost her needle and goes, with Hodge, to
Dame Chat's house. She accuses Dame Chat of taking her needle.

Gammer Gurton, an old crone.
Dame Chat, another old crone and a neighbor.
Hodge, Gammer Gurton's Servant.

(Gammer and Hodge; Dame Chat, inside her house.)
GAMMER: Dame Chat, chould pray thee fair, let me have that is
    mine!
    Chill not his twenty years take one fart that is thine;
    Therefore give me mine own, and let me live beside thee.
CHAT: Why art thou crept from home higher, to mine own doors to
    chide me?
    Hence, doting drab, avaunt, or I shall set thee further!
    Intends thou and that knave me in my house to murther?
GAMMER: Tush, gape not so on me, woman! Shalt not yet eat me!
    Nor all the friends thou hast in this shall not entreat me!
    Mine own goods I will have, and ask thee no by-leave,
    What woman! Poor folks must have right, though the thing you
    aggrieve.
CHAT: Give thee thy right, and hang thee up, with all thy beggar's
    brood!
    What, wilt thou make me a thief, and say I stole thy good?
GAMMER: Chill say nothing, ich warrant thee, but that ich can prove
    it well.
    Thou fetched my good even from my door, cham able this to tell!
CHAT: Did I, old witch, steal oft was thine?
    How should that thing be known?
GAMMER: Ich can no tell; but up thou tookst it as though it has been
    thine own,
CHAT: Marry, fie on thee, thou old gib, with all my very heart!

GAMMER: Nay, fie on thee, thou ramp, thou rig, with all that take any part!

CHAT: A vengeance on those lips that layeth such things to my charge!

GAMMER: A vengeance on those callet's hips, whose conscience is so large!

CHAT: Come out, hog!

GAMMER: Come out, hog, and let have me right!

CHAT: *(Coming out.)* Thou arrant witch!

GAMMER: Thou bawdy bitch, chill make thee curse this night!

CHAT: A bag and a wallet!

GAMMER: A cart for a callet!

CHAT: Why, weenest thou thus to prevail?
I hold thee a groat I shall patch thy coat!

GAMMER: Thou wert as good kiss my tail!
Thou slut, thou cut, thou rakes, thou jakes!
Will not shame make thee hide thee?

CHAT: Thou scald, thou bald, thou rotten, thou glutton!
I will not longer chide thee,
But I will teach thee to keep home.

GAMMER: Wilt thou, drunken beast?

HODGE: Stick to her, Gammer!
Take her by the head, chill warrant you this feast!
Smite, I say, Gammer! Bite, I say, Gammer!
I trow ye will be keen!
Where be your nails?
Claw her by the jaws, pull me out both her eyne
Gogs' bones, Gammer, hold up your head!

CHAT: I trow, drab, I shall dress thee.
Tarry, thou knave, I hold thee a groat I shall make these hands bless thee!
Take thou this, old whore, for amends, and learn thy tongue well to tame,
And say thou met at this bickering, not thy fellow but thy dame!

HODGE: Where is the strong-stewed whore?
Chill gear a whore's mark!
Stand out one's way, that ich kill none in the dark!

Up, Gammer, an ye be alive! Chill fight now for us both.
Come no near me, thou scald callet! To kill thee ich were loth.
CHAT: Art here again, thou hoddy peak? What, Doll! Bring me out my
spite.
HODGE: Chill broach thee with this, by'm father's soul, chill conjure
that foul sprite!
(To Cock within the Gammer's house.)
Let door stand, Cock! Why comes, indeed?
Keep door, thou whoreson boy!
CHAT: Stand to it, thou dastard, for thine ears, ise teach thee, a slut-
tish toy!
HODGE: Gog's wounds, whore, chill make the avaunt!
Take head, Cock, pull in the latch!
CHAT: I'faith, sir Loose-breech, had ye tarried, ye should have found
your match!
GAMMER: *(Knocking her down from behind.)*
Now 'ware thy throat, losel, thouse pay for all!
HODGE: Well said, Gammer, by my soul.
House her, souse her, bounce her, trounce her, pull out her throat-
bowl!
CHAT: Comest behind me, thou withered witch? An I get once on foot
Thouse pay for all thou old tarleather! *(Picking herself up.)*
I'll teach thee what 'longs to't!
Take thee this to make up thy mouth, till time thou come by
more!
(She knocks Gammer Gurton down and runs away.)
HODGE: Up, Gammer, stand on your feet; where is the old whore?
Faith, would chad her by the face, chould crack her callet crown!
GAMMER: *(Rising.)* Ah, Hodge, Hodge, where was thy help, when
vixen had me down?
HODGE: By the Mass, Gammer, but for my staff Chat had gone nigh
to spill you!
Ich think the harlot had not cared an chad not come, to kill you.
But shall we lose our neele thus?
GAMMER: No, Hodge, chware loth do so,
Thinkest thou chill take that at her hand?

No Hodge, ich tell thee no!

HODGE: Chould yet this fray were well take up, and our neele at home.
'Twill be my chance else some to kill, wherever it be or whom!

GAMMER: We have a parson, Hodge, thou knows, a man esteemèd wise,
Mast Doctor Rat; chill for him send, and let me hear his advise
He will her shrive for all this gear, and give her penance strait;
Wese have our neele, else Dame Chat comes ne'er within heaven
gate.

HODGE: Yea, marry, Gammer, that ich think best; will you now for
him send?
The sooner Doctor Rat be here, the sooner wese ha an end,
And hear, Gammer! Diccon's devil, as ich remember well,
Of cat, and Chat, and Doctor Rat, a felonous tale did tell.
Chold you forty pound, that is the way your neele to get again.

The Cave of Salamanca

Miguel Cervantes
1615

Scene: Pancracio's house which is two stories high. Pancracio is leaving to attend his sister's wedding. His wife seems distraught at his leaving.

Pancracio
Leonarda, his wife.
Christina, her maid.

PANCRACIO: Sweet wife and Madam, dry those tears; cease your sad weeping! Just remember it is but short four days that I'll be absent from you—not for eternity. On the fifth, at the very latest, I'll return, my pretty turtle dove—if the good Lord gives me life. Oh, oh, I'm so sorry to see you grieving. Perhaps . . . perhaps, just not to see those shimmering pearls in your eyes—I'd better break my word and give up this journey. My sister can enter solemn matrimony without me, I'm certain.

LEONARDA: Ah, no, my most agreeable Pancracio, most perfect of husbands, I'd not have you seem discourteous for my sake for anything in the world. Go, in God's name, my noble master, and fulfill your solemn, and serious, and worthy obligation. I shall control my uncontrollable grief and spend the lonely hours of your absence thinking of you. There is but one plea I have: Do not stay a moment longer than you say, for if you do . . . I couldn't . . . Lord . . . Cristina . . . hold me . . . my heart is falling . . . from grief . . *(She faints.)*

PANCRACIO: Lord! Water! A glass! Cristina, child . . . for her face. But hold! I know a few little words of magic . . . that cure fainting. *(He whispers into her ear and she recovers.)*

LEONARDA: Ah! Oh! Enough. That is a potent spell. What must be, must be. I shall have patience, balm of my heart. Go quickly. The longer you tarry, the longer must my misery last. Leoniso, your friend, must surely be waiting for you at the coach. God be with you and may he direct your steps homeward as speedily and happily as I desire.

PANCRACIO: My adorable angel! Say but the word, and I shall be immovable as a statue riveted to this spot.

LEONARDA: No, my eternal love. Your wish is my command, and now I wish you to go, rather than stay. You gave your word of honor and your honor is mine as well.

CRISTINA: O model of perfect wifehood! On my word, were all wives as loving and as true to their husbands as my mistress Leonarda, this world would be a paradise.

LEONARDA: Come, Cristina, and get me my cloak. I would accompany my sweet husband to the coach.

PANCRACIO: No, not that. On my life that is thoughtfulness! All for my sake. Stay here, sweet—embrace me just once again. Cristina, dear, take care of your mistress. If you do, I shall bring you a pair of fine stockings when I return—just the kind you've been wishing for.

CRISTINA: Go along, good master, and don't worry about my mistress. I'll see to it that she doesn't grieve too much. I'll persuade her to have a little pleasure once in a while, so she won't think too often of your absence.

LEONARDA: I enjoy myself while my husband is away! Little do you understand my nature, child. Separated from the heart of my life's body no joy or pleasure can be mine, only pain and sorrow.

PANCRACIO: Lord! I can't stand this any longer. Farewell, happy light of my eyes, which henceforth shall see no light until they see you once again. *(He runs out overpowered by sorrow.)*

LEONARDA: Go! and may lightning take you at the house of your sister, the Diaz! Go! and may you never return. By God! this time neither bragging nor avowals, neither cleverness nor watchfulness will help you.

CRISTINA: I was in terrible fear a thousand times that your protestings and weepings would prevent his going and our joys.

LEONARDA: Cristina, will they whose happy coming we long for be here this evening?

CRISTINA: Of course. I sent the good word long ago, and they were so overjoyed at the news they couldn't wait for evening to show it. This very afternoon, in full daylight, they sent by our washer-woman, whom you know we can trust, a load full of finest meats and wines and gifts, hidden in a basket of linen. It's a very trea-sure! It looks like the fruit baskets our good King gives to the poor on Holy Thursday, only it doesn't smack of Lent; rather of Easter: filled with meat pies, cold cuts, delicate fricassees and two capons which have not been even plucked. Besides there is every fruit you can think of. And best of all, there is a little skin of wine, pure, and clear, and with a rare bouquet.

LEONARDA: Just like Reponce. Always considerate and thoughtful— the sacristan of my soul.

CRISTINA: And what's wrong with my Nicolas, the barber of my heart and the shearer of my sorrows? No sooner am I in his presence than he clips and shears all unhappiness from me as if it had never existed.

LEONARDA: Did you hide the basket?

CRISTINA: I put it in the kitchen near the clothes hamper and covered it with old linen.

(There is a knocking at the door.)

LEONARDA: Cristina, look and see who is knocking.

As You Like It

William Shakespeare

Scene: The new Duke, knowing that Rosalind is beloved by the people, decides to banish her. Celia and Rosalind are in the palace. Rosalind has fallen in love with Orlando, youngest son of Sir Rowland de Boys.

Rosalind, daughter to the Banished Duke.
Celia, her cousin and dear friend, daughter of Duke Frederick.
Duke Frederick, (accompanied by Lords, who can be eliminated from the scene), has banished his older brother.

CELIA: Why, cousin! why, Rosalind! Cupid have mercy! Not a word?
ROSALIND: Not one to throw at a dog.
CELIA: No, thy words are too precious to be cast away upon curs; throw some of them at me; come, lame me with reasons.
ROSALIND: Then there were two cousins laid up, when the one should be lamed with reasons and the other mad without any.
CELIA: But is all this for your father?
ROSALIND: No, some of it is for my child's father. O, how full of briers is this working-day world!
CELIA: They are but burrs, cousin, thrown upon thee in holiday foolery. If we walk not in the trodden paths, our very petticoats will catch them.
ROSALIND: I could shake them off my coat. These burrs are in my heart.
CELIA: Hem them away.
ROSALIND: I would try, if I could cry 'hem,' and have him.
CELIA: Come, come; wrestle with thy affections.
ROSALIND: O! they take the part of a better wrestler than myself!
CELIA: O, a good wish upon you! You will try in time, in despite of a fall. But, turning these jests out of service, let us talk in good earnest. Is it possible, on such a sudden, you should fall into so strong a liking with old Sir Rowland's youngest son?

ROSALIND: The duke my father loved his father dearly.

CELIA: Doth it therefore ensue that you should love his son
dearly? By this kind of chase, I should hate him, for my
father hated his father dearly; yet I hate not Orlando.

ROSALIND: No, faith, hate him not, for my sake.

CELIA: Why should I not? Doth he not deserve well?

ROSALIND: Let me love him for that; and do you love him,
because I do. Look, here comes the duke.

CELIA: With his eyes full of anger. *(Enter Duke Frederick, [with Lords].)*

DUKE FREDERICK: Mistress, dispatch you with your safest haste.
And get you from our court.

ROSALIND: Me, uncle?

DUKE FREDERICK: You, cousin.
Within these ten days if that thou be'st found
So near our public court as twenty miles,
Thou diest for it.

ROSALIND: I do beseech your Grace,
Let me the knowledge of my fault bear with me.
If with myself I hold intelligence.
Or have acquaintance with mine own desires,
If that I do not dream or be not frantic,—
As I do trust I am not,—then, dear uncle,
Never so much as in a thought unborn
Did I offend your Highness.

DUKE FREDERICK: Thus do all traitors.
If their purgation did consist in words,
They are as innocent as grace itself.
Let it suffice thee that I trust thee not.

ROSALIND: Yet your mistrust cannot make me a traitor.
Tell me whereon the likelihood depends.

DUKE FREDERICK: Thou art thy father's daughter; there's enough

ROSALIND: So was I when your Highness took his dukedom;
So was I when your Highness banish'd him.
Treason is not inherited, my lord;
Or, if we did derive it from our friends,
What's that to me? My father was no traitor.

Then, good my liege, mistake me not so much
To think my poverty is treacherous.
CELIA: Dear sovereign, hear me speak.
DUKE FREDERICK: Ay, Celia; we stay'd her for your sake;
Else had she with her father rang'd along.
CELIA: I did not then entreat to have her stay:
It was your pleasure and your own remorse.
I was too young that time to value her;
But now I know her. If she be a traitor,
Why so am I; we still have slept together,
Rose at an instant, learn'd, play'd, eat together;
And wheresoe'er we went, like Juno's swans,
Still we went coupled and inseparable.
DUKE FREDERICK: She is too subtle for thee; and her smoothness,
Her very silence and her patience,
Speak to the people, and they pity her.
Thou art a fool: she robs thee of thy name;
And thou wilt show more bright and seem more virtuous
When she is gone. Then open not thy lips.
Firm and irrevocable is my doom
Which I have pass'd upon her; she is banish'd.
CELIA: Pronounce that sentence then, on me, my liege:
I cannot live out of her company.
DUKE FREDERICK: You are a fool. You, niece, provide yourself.
If you outstay the time, upon mine honour,
And in the greatness of my word, you die.
(Exeunt Duke Frederick [and Lords].)
CELAI: O my poor Rosalind! whither wilt thou go?
Wilt thou change fathers? I will give thee mine.
I charge thee, be not thou more griev'd than I am.
ROSALIND: I have more cause.
CELIA: Thou hast not, cousin.
Prithee, be cheerful; know'st thou not, the duke
Hath banish'd me, his daughter?
ROSALIND: That he hath not.
CELIA: No, hath not? Rosalind lacks then the love

Which teacheth thee that thou and I am one.
Shall we be sunder'd? Shall we part, sweet girl?
No: let my father seek another heir.
Therefore devise with me how we may fly,
Whither to go, and what to bear with us:
And do not seek to take our change upon you,
To bear your griefs yourself and leave me out;
For, by this heaven, now at our sorrows pale,
Say what thou canst, I'll go along with thee.
ROSALIND: Why, whither shall we go?
CELIA: To seek my uncle in the forest of Arden.
ROSALIND: Alas, what danger will it be to us,
    Maids as we are, to travel forth so far!
    Beauty provoketh thieves sooner than gold.
CELIA: I'll put myself in poor and mean attire,
    And with a kind of umber smirch my face;
    The like do you. So shall we pass along
    And never stir assailants.
ROSALIND: Were it not better,
    Because that I am more than common tall,
    That I did suit me all points like a man?
    A gallant curtle-axe upon my thigh,
    A boar-spear in my hand; and,—in my heart
    Lie there what hidden woman's fear there will,—
    We'll have a swashing and a martial outside,
    As many other mannish cowards have
    That do outface it with their semblances.
CELIA: What shall I call thee when thou art a man?
ROSALIND: I'll have no worse a name than Jove's own page,
    And therefore look you call me Ganymede.
    But what will you be call'd?
CELIA: Something that hath a reference to my state:
    No longer Celia, but Aliena.
ROSALIND: But, cousin what if we assay'd to steal
    The clownish fool out of your father's court?
    Would he not be a comfort to our travel?

CELIA: He'll go along o'er the wide world with me;
      Leave me alone to woo him. Let's away,
      And get our jewels and our wealth together,
      Devise the fittest time and safest way
      To hide us from pursuit that will be made
      After my flight. Now go we in content
      To liberty and not to banishment.
      (Exeunt.)

The Beggar's Opera

John Gay

1728

Scene: The Peachum's House. Mrs. Peachum is angry because Polly has gotten married to Captain Macheath, a highwayman and womanizer. Polly is in love. Her parents scorn her attitude and behavior.

Peachum, ringleader of a gang of beggars and thieves.
Mrs. Peachum, his equally tough wife.
Polly Peachum, their daughter, romantic, lovely.

MRS. PEACHUM: *(In a very great passion.)* Our Polly is a sad slut! nor heeds what we have taught her.

I wonder any man alive will ever rear a daughter!

For she must have both hoods and gowns, and hoops to swell her pride.

With scarfs and stays, and gloves and lace; and she will have men beside;

And when she's dress'd with care and cost, all-tempting, fine and gay,

As men should serve a cowcumber, she flings herself away.

Our Polly is a sad slut, etc.

You baggage! you hussy! you inconsiderate jade! had you been hanged, it would not have vexed me, for that might have been your misfortune; but to do such a mad thing by choice! The wench is married, husband.

PEACH: Married! The captain is a bold man, and will risk anything for money; to be sure he believes her a fortune. Do you think your mother and I should have lived comfortably so long together, if ever we had been married? Baggage!

MRS. PEACH: I knew she was always a proud slut; and now the wench hath played the fool and married, because forsooth she would do like the gentry. Can you support the expense of a husband, hussy, in gaming, drinking, and whoring? Have you money enough to carry on the daily quarrels of man and wife about who shall squander most? There are not many husbands and wives who can bear the charges of plaguing one another in a handsome way. If you must be married, could you introduce nobody into our family but a highwayman? Why, thou foolish jade, thou wilt be as ill used, and as much neglected, as if thou hadst married a lord!

PEACH: Let not your anger, my dear, break through the rules of decency, for the captain looks upon himself in the military capacity, as a gentleman by his profession. Besides what he hath already, I know he is in a fair way of getting, or of dying; and both these ways, let me tell you, are most excellent chances for a wife.— Tell me, hussy, are you ruined or no?

MRS. PEACH: With Polly's fortune, she might very well have gone off to a person of distinction. Yes, that you might, you pouting slut!

PEACH: What, is the wench dumb? Speak, or I'll make you plead by squeezing out an answer from you. Are you really bound wife to him, or are you only upon liking?

(Pinches her.)

POLLY: *(Screaming.)* Oh!

MRS. PEACH: How the mother is to be pitied who hath handsome daughters! Locks, bolts, bars, and lectures of morality are nothing to them: They break through them all. They have as much pleasure in cheating a father and mother as in cheating at cards.

PEACH: Why, Polly, I shall soon know if you are married, by Macheath's keeping from our house.

AIR VIII: *(Grim king of the ghosts.)*

POLLY: Can love be controll'd by advice?
    Will Cupid our mothers obey?
Though my heart were as frozen as ice,
    At his flame 'twould have melted away.
When he kiss'd me so closely he press'd.

    'Twas so sweet that I must have comply'd:
So I thought it both safest and best
    To marry, for fear you should chide.

MRS. PEACH: Then all the hopes of our family are gone for ever and ever!

PEACH: And Macheath may hang his father and mother-in-law, in hope to get into their daughter's fortune.

POLLY: I did not marry him (as 'tis the fashion) coolly and deliberately for honour or money. But I love him.

MRS. PEACH: Love him! worse and worse! I thought the girl had been better bred. O husband, husband! her folly makes me mad! my head swims! I'm distracted! I can't support myself—oh! (Faints.)

PEACH: See, wench, to what a condition you have reduced your poor mother! a glass of cordial, this instant. How the poor woman takes it to heart! (Polly goes out and returns with it.) Ah, hussy, now this is the only comfort your mother has left!

POLLY: Give her another glass, Sir; my mama drinks double the quantity whenever she is out of order.—This, you see, fetches her.

MRS. PEACH: The girl shows such a readiness, and so much concern, that I could almost find in my heart to forgive her.

AIR IX: *O Jenny, O* Jenny, *where has thou been?*
O Polly, you might have toy'd and kiss'd.
By keeping men off, you keep them on.

POLLY: But he so teas'd me,
And he so pleas'd me,
What I did, you must have done.

MRS. PEACH: Not with a highwayman.—You sorry slut!

PEACH: A word with you, wife. 'Tis no new thing for a wench to take man without consent of parents. You know 'tis the frailty of woman, my dear.

MRS. PEACH: Yes, indeed, the sex is frail. But the first time a woman is frail, she should be somewhat nice, methinks, for then or never is the time to make her fortune. After that, she hath nothing to do but to guard herself from being found out, and she may do what she pleases.

PEACH: Make yourself a little easy; I have a thought shall soon set all matters again to rights. Why so melancholy, Polly? since what is

done cannot be undone, we must all endeavour to make the best
of it.

MRS. PEACH: Well, Polly; as far as one woman can forgive another, I
forgive thee.—Your father is too fond of you, hussy.

POLLY: Then all my sorrows are at an end.

MRS. PEACH: A mighty likely speech, in troth for a wench who is just
married!

AIR X: *Thomas, I cannot*

POLLY: I, like a ship in storms, was toss'd;
    Yet afraid to put in to land;
For seiz'd in the port the vessel's lost,
    Whose treasure is contraband.
        The waves are laid,
        My duty's paid.
Oh joy beyond expression!
     Thus, safe ashore,
     I ask no more,
My all is in my possession.

PEACH: I hear customers in t'other room. Go, talk with 'em, Polly; but
come to us again, as soon as they are gone.— But, hark ye, child,
if 'tis the gentleman who was here yesterday about the repeating
watch, say, you believe we can't get intelligence of it till tomorrow. For I lent it to Suky Straddle, to make a figure with it tonight
at a tavern in Drury Lane. If t'other gentlemen calls for the silver-
hilted sword, you know Beetle-browed Jemmy hath it on, and he
doth not come from Tunbridge till Tuesday night, so that it cannot be had till then.

The Rivals

Richard Brinsley Sheridan
1775

Scene: Mrs. Malaprop's Home. Lydia is in love with a poor ensign whom her aunt feels is an inappropriate choice for a suitor. Mrs. Malaprop and Sir Anthony enter the house.

Lydia Languish, a wealthy and headstrong young lady.
Mrs. Malaprop, her Aunt, who uses the language in unusual ways.
Sir Anthony Absolute

LYD: Never mind—open at *Sobriety.*—Fling me *Lord Chesterfield's Letters.*—Now for 'em.
(Enter Mrs. Malaprop and Sir Anthony Absolute.)
MRS. MAL: There, Sir Anthony, there sits the deliberate simpleton who wants to disgrace her family, and lavish herself on a fellow not worth a shilling!
LYD: Madam, I thought you once—
MRS. MAL: You thought, Miss! I don't know any business you have to think at all. Thought does not become a young woman. But the point we would request of you is, that you will promise to forget this fellow—to illiterate him, I say, quite from your memory.
LYD: Ah! Madam! our memories are independent of our wills. It is not so easy to forget.
MRS. MAL: But I say it is, Miss; there is nothing on earth so easy as to *forget*, if a person chooses to set about it. I'm sure I have as much forgot your poor dear uncle as if he had never existed—and I thought it my duty so to do; and let me tell you, Lydia, these violent memories don't become a young woman.
SIR ANTH: Why sure she won't pretend to remember what she's ordered not!—aye, this comes of her reading!
LYD: What crime, Madam, have I committed to be treated thus?
MRS. MAL: Now don't attempt to extirpate yourself from the matter; you know I have proof controvertible of it. But tell me, will you

promise to do as you're bid? Will you take a husband of your friend's choosing?

LYD: Madam, I must tell you plainly, that had I no preference for anyone else, the choice you have made would be my aversion.

MRS. MAL: What business have you, Miss, with *preference* and *aversion*? They don't become a young woman; and you ought to know, that as both always wear off, 'tis safest in matrimony to begin with a little *aversion*. I am sure I hated your poor dear uncle before marriage as if he'd been a blackamoor—and yet, Miss, you are sensible what a wife I made!—and when it pleased heaven to release me from him, 'tis unknown what tears I shed! But suppose we were going to give you another choice, will you promise us to give up this Beverley?

LYD: Could I belie my thoughts so far as to give that promise, my actions would certainly as far belie my words.

MRS. MAL: Take yourself to your room. You are fit company for noting but your own ill-humours.

LYD: Willingly, Ma'am—I cannot change for the worse.
(Exit Lydia.)

MRS. MAL: There's a little intricate hussy for you!

SIR ANTH: It is not to be wondered at, Ma'am—all this is the natural consequence of teaching girls to read. Had I a thousand daughters, by heaven! I'd as soon have them taught the black art as their alphabet!

MRS. MAL: Nay, nay, Sir Anthony, you are an absolute misanthropy.

SIR ANTH: In my way hither, Mrs. Malaprop, I observed your niece's maid coming forth from a circulating library! She had a book in each hand—they were half-bound volumes, with marble covers! From that moment I guessed how full of duty I should see her mistress!

MRS. MAL: Those are vile places, indeed!

SIR ANTH: Madam, a circulating library in a town is as an evergreen tree of diabolical knowledge! It blossoms through the year! And depend on it, Mrs. Malaprop, that they who are so fond of handling the leaves, will long for the fruit at last.

MRS. MAL: Fie, fie, Sir Anthony, you surely speak laconically!

SIR ANTH: Why, Mrs. Malaprop, in moderation, now, what would you have a woman know?

MRS. MAL: Observe me, Sir Anthony. I would by no means wish a daughter of mine to be a progeny of learning; I don't think so much learning becomes a young woman; for instance—I would never let her meddle with Greek, or Hebrew, or Algebra, or Simony, or Fluxions, or Paradoxes, or such inflammatory branches of learning—neither would it be necessary for her to handle any of your mathematical, astronomical, diabolical instruments;—but, Sir Anthony, I would send her, at nine years old, to a boarding school, in order to learn a little ingenuity and artifice. Then, Sir, she should have a supercilious knowledge in accounts—and as she grew up, I would have her instructed in geometry, that she might know something of the contagious countries—but above all, Sir Anthony, she should be mistress of orthodoxy, that she might not misspell, and mispronounce words so shamefully as girls usually do; and likewise that she might reprehend the true meaning of what she is saying. This, Sir Anthony, is what I would have a woman know—and I don't think there is superstitious article in it.

SIR ANTH: Well, well, Mrs. Malaprop, I will dispute the point no further with you; though I must confess that you are a truly moderate and polite arguer, for almost every third word you say is on my side of the question. But, Mrs. Malaprop, to the more important point in debate—you say you have no objection to my proposal.

MRS. MAL: None, I assure you. I am under no positive engagement with Mr. Acres, and as Lydia is so obstinate against him, perhaps your son may have better success.

SIR ANTH: Well, Madam, I will write for the boy directly. He knows not a syllable of this yet, though I have for some time had the proposal in my head. He is at present with his regiment.

MRS. MAL: We have never seen your son, Sir Anthony; but I hope no objection on his side.

SIR ANTH: Objection!—let him object if he dare! No, no, Mrs. Malaprop, Jack knows that the least demur puts me in a frenzy directly. My process was always very simple—in their younger days, 'twas "Jack do this,"—if he demurred—I knocked him down—and if he grumbled at that—I always sent him out of the room.

MRS. MAL: Aye, and the properest way, o' my conscience! —nothing is so conciliating to young people as severity. Well, Sir Anthony, I shall give Mr. Acres his discharge, and prepare Lydia to receive your son's invocations; and I hope you will represent *her* to the Captain as an object not altogether illegible.

SIR ANTH: Madam, I will handle the subject prudently. Well, I must leave you—and let me beg you, Mrs. Malaprop, to enforce this matter roundly to the girl; take my advice—keep a tight hand; if she rejects this proposal—clap her under lock and key—and if you were just to let the servants forget to bring her dinner for three or four days, you can't conceive how she'd come about! *(Exit Sir Anthony.)*

MRS. MAL: Well, at any rate I shall be glad to get her from under my intuition. She has somehow discovered my partiality for Sir Lucius O'Trigger—sure, Lucy can't have betrayed me! No, the girl is such a simpleton, I should have made her confess it.—*(Calls.)* Lucy!—Lucy—Had she been one of your artificial ones, I should never have trusted her.

A Doll's House

Henrik Ibsen

Scene: Norway. Winter. The living room of the Helmer home. Nora is entertaining Kristine Linde who has returned after many years. Nora is quite nervous as she shows Mr. Krogstad into her husband's study for she has secretly borrowed a large sum of money from him to take her husband on a much-needed holiday, but she has not paid him back. Torvald has just been named Bank Manager and Nora does not know the purpose of Krogstad's visit. Kristine recognizes him as he passes through the parlor.

Dr. Rank, 40s, family physician who has come to examine Torvald Helmer, a banker.

Nora Helmer, the pampered wife of Torvald, 30s.

Mrs. Linde, an old friend of Nora's, now a widow, 30s (Kristine).

NORA: Then would you please be good enough to step into his study? *(She nods indifferently and shuts the hallway door; then she goes and tends the stove.)*

MRS. LINDE: Nora—who was that man?

NORA: That was a lawyer named Krogstad.

MRS. LINDE: So it really was him.

NORA: Do you know that man?

MRS. LINDE: I used to know him—a long time ago. He was a law clerk for a while up in our area.

NORA: Yes, that's right, he was

MRS. LINDE: He certainly has changed.

NORA: He had a very unhappy marriage.

MRS.LINDE: And now he's a widower?

NORA: With several children. There we go, now it's burning. *(She closes the stove door and moves the rocking chair a little to the side.)*

MRS. LINDE: He's got himself involved in all kinds of businesses, they say.

NORA: Oh yes? Probably; I really wouldn't know. But let's not think about business—it's so boring!

(Doctor Rank comes out from Helmer's study.)

RANK: *(Still in the doorway.)* No, no, Torvald: I don't want to be in the way; I'd just as soon go talk to your wife for a while. *(Closing the door and noticing Mrs. Linde.)* I'm sorry—I'm in the way here too.

NORA: You certainly are not. *(Introducing him.)* Doctor Rank, Mrs. Linde.

RANK: Ah ha! That's an off-mentioned name in this house. I think I passed you on the stairs when I arrived.

MRS. LINDE: Yes, I don't handle stairs very well.

RANK: Ah ha—are you having some kind of trouble?

MRS. LINDE: Probably just overwork.

RANK: Nothing more? So you've probably come to town to catch your breath in the holiday parties.

MRS. LINDE: I'm looking for a job.

RANK: Is that the prescription for overwork?

MRS. LINDE: One has to live, Doctor.

RANK: Yes, there's general agreement on that point.

NORA: Oh, come on now, Doctor Rank, you want to live as much as anyone.

RANK: Yes, I really do. Wretched as I am. I really want to stretch my torment to the limit. All my patients feel the same way. And it's the same with the morally diseased—right now there's a terminal moral case in there with Helmer—

MRS. LINDE: *(Quietly.)* Ah—!

NORA: Who's that?

RANK: Oh, just a certain lawyer Krogstad, no one you'd know anything about. His character, my ladies, is rotten right down to the roots—but even he began making speeches—as if it were self-evident—that he had to *live.*

NORA: Oh? What did he want to talk to Torvald about?

RANK: I don't know for sure. All I heard was something about the bank.

NORA: I didn't know Krog—that this lawyer Krogstad had anything to do with the bank.

RANK: Yes, he's got some kind of position down there. *(To Mrs. Linde.)* I don't know if you have, in your part of the country, any of these moral detectives, these investigators who go around sniffing out moral corruption and then get their victims into a safe place where they can keep them under constant surveillance—it's a lucrative business these days. The healthy ones get left out in the cold—no room for them!

MRS. LINDE: And yet it's the sick ones who need to be brought inside.

RANK: *(Shrugs his shoulders.)* There you have it. That's the philosophy that's turning our whole world into a hospital.

(Nora, lost in thought, breaks into quiet laughter, clapping her hands.)

RANK: Why do you laugh? Do you really know what the world is?

NORA: What do I care about the boring old world? I was laughing at something else—something terribly funny. Tell me, Doctor Rank, all those people who work at the bank—are they all under Torvald now?

RANK: Is *that* what's so terribly funny to you?

NORA: *(Smiling and humming.)* Never mind! Never mind! *(Walking around the room.)* Yes, it is extremely amusing that we—that Torvald has so much influence over so many people. *(Takes a bag from her pocket.)* Doctor Rank, how about a little macaroon?

RANK: Ah ha! Macaroons! I thought they were illegal here.

NORA: Yes, but Kristine gave me these—

MRS. LINDE: What? I—?

NORA: Now, now, now, don't worry. How could you know that Torvald made a law against them? You see, he's afraid they'll rot my teeth. But, fuff—just this once—don't you agree, Doctor Rank? There you are! *(She pops a macaroon into his mouth.)* You too, Kristine. And I'll have one too, just a little one—or two at the most. *(Walking around again.)* Yes, now I am really tremendously happy. There's just one last thing in the world I have a tremendous desire to do.

RANK: Oh? What's that?

NORA: I have this tremendous desire to say something so that Torvald can hear it.

RANK: So why can't you say it?

NORA: No, I don't dare. It's too horrible.

MRS. LINDE: Horrible?

RANK: Well, then, maybe you'd better not. But with us—can't you? What do you want to say so Torvald can hear?

NORA: I have a tremendous desire to say: To hell with everything!

RANK: Are you crazy?

MRS. LINDE: For heaven's sake, Nora.

RANK: Say it—here he is.

NORA: *(Hiding the macaroons.)* Shh, shh, shh!

Miss Julie

August Strindberg
1888

Scene: In the kitchen of the Count's mansion. It is Midsummer's Night
in Sweden. A party is in progress outdoors. Kristin is at the stove.

Jean, the valet, aged 30, handsome, knows his job.
Kristin, the cook, aged 35, Jean's fiancée.
Miss Julie, aged 25, daughter of the Count, a wealthy landowner, a
horsewoman, headstrong and beautiful who has recently broken
her engagement to her fiancé.

JEAN: *(Angrily.)* Don't pull my hair! You know how sensitive I am.
KRISTIN: Now, now! It was only a little love-pull. *(Opens a bottle of
beer while Jean eats.)*
JEAN: Beer on Midsummer Eve! Thank you, no! I've got something
better! Right in here! *(Opens a table drawer and pulls out a bottle of red wine with yellow sealing wax on the cork.)* See that?
Yellow seal! Give me a glass—no, a wine glass—this is the real
stuff!
KRISTIN: *(Goes back to the stove and puts on a small pan.)* God save
the woman who gets you for a husband! What an old fussbud-
get!
JEAN: Listen to her! Get a man as good as me, and you'd be lucky!
And it hasn't hurt your reputation any them calling me your
boyfriend! *(Tastes the wine.)* Ah! Mm! Very good! Just not quite
room temperature. *(Warms the glass with his hands.)* This one we
bought in Dijon. Four francs the liter, unbottled, plus duty.
What're you cooking there? Smells like hell!
KRISTIN: Some damn concoction Miss Julie wants for Diana.
JEAN: Choose your words more carefully, Kristin. But why stand there
cooking for that bitch of a dog on Midsummer Eve? Is she sick?
KRISTIN: She's sick, all right! Stole out one night with the gamekeeper's mutt, and now there's trouble—and that's one thing the
young miss just doesn't want to handle.

JEAN: Our "young miss" is too stuck-up in some ways, if you ask me, and not proud enough in others. Just like the Countess when she was alive. She was most at home in the kitchen and the stables. All the same, one horse was never enough to draw her carriage for her. Dirty cuffs most of the time, yet every button was stamped with her coat of arms. Back to Miss Julie, though—she could take a lesson in self-respect—remember her position for a change. A little refinement is in order, to come right down to it. Just now, dancing in the barn? She grabbed the gamekeeper away from Anna and forced him to dance with her. We don't do things like that. But that's the way it is when aristocrats try to come down off their pedestals—they just go downright common! But she's magnificent, all right, no question! Figure—shoulders—etcetera, etcetera!

KRISTIN: I wouldn't overdo it if I was you. Just don't overdo it, you hear? I've heard Klara talk—and she dresses her. She should know.

JEAN: Klara, ah! You women are all jealous of each other! I've been out riding with her! And you should see her dance!

KRISTIN: Will you dance with me when I'm done here?

JEAN: Sure—why not?

KRISTIN: Promise?

JEAN: Promise! What I say, I do, and I will. Thanks for the food! It was the best! *(Puts the cork in the bottle.)*

MISS JULIE: *(Appears in the doorway, speaking to someone outside.)* I'll be right back—you wait there—*(Jean quickly replaces the bottle in the table drawer and rises respectfully. Miss Julie enters and goes to Kristin at the stove.)* Well, is it ready?

KRISTIN: *(Signals to her that Jean is present.)* Mm —

JEAN: *(Gallantly.)* I see the ladies will have their little secrets.

MISS JULIE: *(Flips her handkerchief in his face.)* Curious?

JEAN: Ah, lovely! The smell of violets—

MISS JULIE: *(Coquettishly.)* Impertinence! You know all about perfumes now, do you? You certainly do dance well! Now, now, no peeking! Shoo—

JEAN: *(Boldly but politely.)* A witches' brew to work magic on Midsummer Eve? A peek into the future for that future husband!

JULIE: *(Sharply.)* You'd need awfully good eyes to see *that! (To Kristin.)* Pour it into a bottle and cork it well. Come and dance a schottische with me now, Jean—

JEAN: *(Hesitantly.)* I don't mean to be impolite, but I promised this one to Kristin—

MISS JULIE: Oh, she can dance another one with you—can't you, Kristin? You'll lend me Jean, won't you?

KRISTIN: That's not for me to say, Miss. If Miss Julie condescends to dance, it's hardly for him to say no. You go on, Jean, and be grateful to Miss Julie for the honor.

JEAN: If I can speak frankly, Miss Julie, without meaning to hurt you, of course, I wonder if it's a good idea to dance twice in a row with the same partner, considering the way people talk—

MISS JULIE: *(Flaring up.)* Talk? What do you mean, talk!

JEAN: *(Submissively.)* Since you choose not to understand, Miss Julie, I'll have to speak more plainly. It doesn't look good to show a preference for one servant when they all hope to be similarly honored—

MISS JULIE: Preference! What an idea! I'm amazed! I, the mistress of the house, honor my servants' dance with my presence, and when I want to dance, I want to dance with someone who knows how to lead, and not with someone who'll make me look a fool!

JEAN: Whatever you say, Miss Julie. I'm at your command.

MISS JULIE: *(Softly.)* You needn't take it as a command. It's a holiday! We're celebrating! We're happy! Rank should be set aside. So give me your arm! Don't worry, Kristin! I won't steal your beau! *(Takes Jean's offered arm and is led out.)*

(The following scene is played in pantomime, as if the actress were really alone. When necessary, she should turn her back to the audience, not look in their direction, nor hurry as if afraid they are becoming impatient.—Kristin is alone. Faint violin music is heard in the distance: a schottische. She hums the tune as she clears the table after Jean, washes the plate at the sink, dries it and places it in the cupboard. She then removes her apron, pulls

a small mirror out of one of the table drawers, leans it against the jar containing the lilacs, lights a candle and heats a curling iron with which she curls the hair falling over her forehead. She then goes to the door and stands listening. Returning to the table, she notices the handkerchief forgotten by Miss Julie; picks it up and smells it; then, without thinking, spreads it out, smoothes it, folds it twice, etc.)

JEAN: *(Enters alone.)* She's wild! That's all there is to it! What a way to dance! People watching and grinning from behind doors—! What's got into her, Kristin!

KRISTIN: Oh, she's having her period, and that always makes her crazy. How about the dance?

JEAN: You mad at me for dancing the last one with her?

KRISTIN: Of course not. A little thing like that! Besides, I know my place—

JEAN: *(Puts his arm around her waist.)* You've got a good head on your shoulders, Kristin. You'd make a good wife.

MISS JULIE: *(Enters; unpleasantly surprised; with forced joviality.)* Some gentlemen you are—running out on your partner like that—

JEAN: Beg to differ, Miss Julie. As you can see, I hurried back to the partner I deserted.

MISS JULIE: *(Changing her tone.)* Nobody dances like you, Jean. I guess you know that, though. But why are you in uniform on a holiday? Take it off at once!

JEAN: In which case I'll ask you to step out for a moment, Miss Julie— my black coat's hanging over here in—*(Gestures as he goes right.)*

MISS JULIE: Do I embarrass you? You're only changing your coat! Well, then, go to your room and come back. Or stay, and I'll turn my back.

JEAN: With your permission, Miss Julie. *(Gets off right; his arm visible while changing coats.)*

MISS JULIE: *(To Kristin.)* Tell me, Kristin. Is Jean your fiancé? He's so familiar around you.

KRISTIN: Fiancé? Yes, if you like. We call it that, too, I guess.

MISS JULIE: Call?

KRISTIN: Yes, well, you've been engaged yourself, Miss Julie—

MISS JULIE: Yes, but *properly*—

KRISTIN: Still—it didn't come to anything, did it—?

(Jean enters wearing a black cutaway and a black bowler.)

MISS JULIE: *Très gentil, monsieur Jean! Très gentil!*

JEAN: *Vous voulez plaisanter, madame!*

MISS JULIE: *Et vous voulez parler français!* Where did you learn that?

JEAN: Switzerland. I was the wine steward in one of the biggest hotels in Lucerne.

MISS JULIE: You're quite the gentlemen in those tails! *Charmant! (Sits at the table.)*

JEAN: You're just flattering me!

MISS JULIE: *(Annoyed:)* Flattering you?

JEAN: My natural modesty forbids me to believe that you would actually compliment someone like me. I therefore took the liberty of assuming that you were exaggerating—or, as we call it, flattering.

MISS JULIE: Wherever did you learn to talk like that? You must have spent a lot of evenings at the theater.

JEAN: That, too. Yes, I've been around. Seen many places.

MISS JULIE: But you were born in the neighborhood, weren't you?

JEAN: My father was a tenant farmer on the estate next to yours. You never noticed me, of course, but I saw you often when I was a child.

MISS JULIE: No, really!

JEAN: Yes, and one time in particular—well, except I can't tell you about that.

MISS JULIE: Oh, of course you can! Come on! Make an exception!

JEAN: No, I'm afraid not. Some other time, perhaps.

MISS JULIE: Some other time means never. Why is now so dangerous?

JEAN: Not dangerous, no—I'm just not in the mood.—Look at her! *(Pointing at Kristin who has fallen asleep on the chair by the stove.)*

MISS JULIE: What a charming wife she'll make. Perhaps she even snores.

JEAN: Not really. But she does talk in her sleep.

MISS JULIE: *(Cynically.)* How do you know that?

JEAN: *(Coolly.)* I've heard her.

MISS JULIE: *(After a pause, during which they look at one another.)* Won't you sit?

JEAN: Oh, I couldn't ma'am, not in your presence.

MISS JULIE: If I order you?

JEAN: Then I obey.

MISS JULY: Well, then, sit down. No, wait. I'd like something to drink first.

JEAN: I'm not sure what's in the icebox. Only beer, I think.

MISS JULIE: "Only"? My tastes are very simple. I prefer it to wine.

JEAN: *(Takes a bottle of beer from the icebox, opens it and looks for a glass and plate in the cupboard; serves her.)* There you are!

MISS JULIE: Thank you! Won't you have some?

JEAN: I don't care much for beer, but if that's an order—

MISS JULIE: Order? Surely a gentlemen doesn't let a lady drink alone—

JEAN: I stand corrected—*(Opens a bottle and gets a glass.)*

MISS JULIE: Now drink to my health! *(Jean hesitates.)* Why, I do believe he's shy!

JEAN: *(Kneels in a parody of the romantic manner, and raises his glass.)* To my lady's health!

MISS JULIE: Bravo! Now kiss my shoe and it will be perfect! *(Jean hesitates, then boldly takes hold of her foot, kissing it lightly.)* Really splendid! You should have been an actor!

JEAN: *(Rising.)* This has got to stop, Miss Julie! Anyone could come in and see us!

MISS JULIE: And?

JEAN: People would talk is what. You should have heard their tongues wagging out there a minute ago—

MISS JULIE: What were the saying, I wonder? Tell me. Sit down—

JEAN: *(Sits.)* I wouldn't want to hurt your feelings, but they were saying things that—well—expressions, you know? Well, I know you know, you're not a child, and when they see a woman drinking alone with a man—and a servant to boot—at night—well—

MISS JULIE: Well, what? It's not as if we're alone. Kristin's here.

JEAN: Asleep!

MISS JULIE: Then I'll wake her! *(Gets up.)* Kristin! Are you asleep? *(Kristin mumbles something in her sleep.)* Kristin! Some sleeper!

KRISTIN: *(In her sleep.)* Count's boots polished—water for the coffee—right away, right away—mm—pish—ho—

MISS JULIE: *(Taking Kristin by the nose.)* Will you wake up?

JEAN: *(Severely.)* Let her sleep!

MISS JULIE: *(Sharply.)* What!

JEAN: Standing over a hot stove all day tires a person out by evening. Sleep should be respected—

MISS JULIE: *(Changing her tone.)* What a considerate thought—it does you credit—thank you! *(Holds out her hand to him.)* Come outside with me now—pick me some lilacs—

(Kristin wakens during the following dialogue and, stupefied with sleep, goes out right to lie down.)

JEAN: With you?

MISS JULIE: With me.

JEAN: No, I'm afraid not! We can't do that!

MISS JULIE: I don't understand. Surely you couldn't be imagining—

JEAN: Not me, no, the others—

MISS JULIE: What? That I'm in love with a servant?

JEAN: I'm not conceited, but such things have happened—and for these people nothing is sacred.

MISS JULIE: Goodness, you sound like you're stepping up in the world!

JEAN: Yes, I am.

MISS JULIE: And I'm stepping down—

JEAN: Take my advice, Miss Julie, don't come down. No one will believe you did so of our own free will. People will always say you fell—

MISS JULIE: It seems my opinion of people is higher than yours. Come on, let's see if I'm right! Come! *(Looks tenderly at him.)*

JEAN: You're a very strange person, Miss Julie—

Playboy of the Western World

John Millington Synge
1907

Scene: Christy has arrived in the village bragging of killing his father. He has taken refuge in Pegeen Mike's Tavern. The Widow Quin comes over to perhaps find herself a new husband.

Of Note: In this and other scenes where an accent is appropriate, it would be beneficial to try it, even if it comes out a bit strange. The attempt will add energy and authenticity to the scene, regardless.

Pegeen Mike, 20s.
Christy Mahon, 20s–30s.
Widow Quin, older.

PEGEEN: *(Putting her hand on his shoulder.)* Well, you'll have peace in this place, Christy Mahon, and none to trouble you, and it's near time a fine lad like you should have your good share of the earth.

CHRISTY: It's time surely, and I a seemly fellow with great strength in me and bravery of . . . *(Someone knocks. Clinging to Pegeen)* Oh, glory! it's late for knocking, and this last while I'm in terror of the peelers, and the walking dead.

(Knocking again.)

PEGEEN: Who's there?

VOICE: Me.

PEGEEN: Who's me?

VOICE: The Widow Quin.

PEGEEN: *(Jumping up and giving him the bread and milk.)* Go on now with your supper, and let on to be sleepy, for if she found you were such a warrant to talk, she'd be stringing gabble till the dawn of day. *(He takes bread and sits shyly with his back to the door.)* *(Opening door, with temper.)* What ails you, or what is it you're wanting at this hour of the night?

WIDOW QUIN: *(Coming in a step and peering at Christy.)* I'm after meeting Shawn Keogh and Father Reilly below, who told me of your curiosity man, and they fearing by this time he was maybe roaring, romping on your hands with drink.

PEGEEN: *(Pointing to Christy.)* Look now is he roaring, and he stretched out drowsy with his supper and his mug of milk. Walk down and tell that to Father Reilly and to Shaneen Keogh.

WIDOW QUIN: *(Coming Forward.)* I'll not see them again, for I've their word to lead that lad forward for to lodge with me.

PEGEEN: *(In blank amazement.)* This night is it?

WIDOW QUIN: *(going over)* This night. "It isn't fitting," says the priesteen, "to have his likeness lodging with an orphaned girl." *(To Christy.)* God save you, mister!

CHRISTY: *(Shyly.)* God save you kindly.

WIDOW QUIN: *(Looking at him with half-amused curiosity.)* Well, aren't you a little smiling fellow? It should have been great and bitter torments did rouse your spirits to a deed of blood.

CHRISTY: *(Doubtfully.)* It should, maybe.

WIDOW QUIN: It's more than "maybe" I'm saying, and it'd soften my heart to see you sitting so simple with your cup and cake, and you fitter to be saying your catechism than slaying your da.

PEGEEN: *(At counter, washing glasses.)* There's talking when any'd see he's fit to be holding his head high with the wonders of the world. Walk on from this, for I'll not have him tormented, and he destroyed travelling since Tuesday was a week.

WIDOW QUIN: *(Peaceably.)* We'll be walking surely when his supper's done, and you'll find we're great company, young fellow, when it's of the like of you and me you'd hear the penny poets singing in an August Fair.

CHRISTY: *(Innocently.)* Did you kill your father?

PEGEEN: *(Contemptuously.)* She did not. She hit himself with a worn pick, and the rust poison did corrode his blood the way he never overed it, and died after. That was a sneaky kind of murder did win small glory with the boys itself. *(She crosses to Christy's left.)*

WIDOW QUIN: *(With good humour.)* If it didn't, maybe all knows a widow woman has buried her children and destroyed her man is a wiser comrade for a young lad than a girl, the like of you, who'd go helter-skeltering after any man would let you a wink upon the road.

PEGEEN: *(Breaking out into wild rage.)* And you'll say that, Widow Quin, and you gasping with the rage you had racing the hill beyond to look on his face.

WIDOW QUIN: *(Laughing derisively.)* Me, it is? Well, Father Reilly has cuteness to divide you now. *(She pulls Christy up.)* There's great temptation in a man did slay his da, and we'd best be going, young fellow; so rise up and come with me.

PEGEEN: *(Seizing his arm.)* He'll not stir. He's pot-boy in this place, and I'll not have him stolen off and kidnapped while himself's abroad.

WIDOW QUIN: It'd be a crazy pot-boy'd lodge him in the shebeen where he works by day, so you'd have a right to come on, young fellow, till you see my little houseen, a perch off on the rising hill.

PEGEEN: Wait till morning, Christy Mahon. Wait till you lay eyes on her leaky thatch is growing more pasture for her buck goat than her square of fields, and she without a tramp itself to keep in order her place at all.

WIDOW QUIN: When you see me contriving in my little gardens, Christy Mahon, you'll swear the Lord God formed me to be living lone, and that there isn't my match in Mayo for thatching, or mowing, or shearing a sheep.

PEGEEN: *(With noisy scorn.)* It's true the Lord God formed you to contrive indeed. Doesn't the world know you reared a black ram at your own breast, so that the Lord Bishop of Connaught felt the elements of a Christian, and he eating it after in a kidney stew? Doesn't the world know you've been seen shaving the foxy skipper from France for a threepenny-bit and a sop of grass tobacco would wring the liver from a mountain goat you'd meet leaping the hills?

WIDOW QUIN: *(with amusement)* Do you hear her now, young fellow? Do you hear the way she'll be rating at your own self when a week is by?

PEGEEN: *(To Christy.)* Don't heed her. Tell her to go on into her pigsty and not plague us here.

WIDOW QUIN: I'm going; but he'll come with me.

PEGEEN: *(Shaking him.)* Are you dumb, young fellow?

CHRISTY: *(Timidly to* Widow Quin.*)* God increase you; but I'm potboy in this place, and it's here I liefer stay.

PEGEEN: *(Triumphantly.)* Now you have heard him, and go on from this.

WIDOW QUIN: *(Looking round the room.)* It's lonesome this hour crossing the hill, and if he won't come along with me, I'd have a right maybe to stop this night with yourselves. Let me stretch out on the settle, Pegeen Mike; and himself can lie by the hearth.

PEGEEN: *(Short and firecely.)* Faith, I won't. Quit off or I will send you now.

WIDOW QUIN: *(Gathering her shawl up.)* Well, it's a terror to be aged a score. *(To Christy.)* God bless you now, young fellow, and let you be wary, or there's right torment will await you here if you go romancing with her like, and she waiting only, as they bade me say, on a sheepskin parchment to be wed with Shawn Keogh of Killakeen.

CHRISTY: *(Going to Pegeen as she bolts door.)* What's that she's after saying?

PEGEEN: Lies and blather, you've no call to mind. Well, isn't Shawn Keogh an impudent fellow to send up spying on me? Wait till I lay hands on him. Let him wait, I'm saying.

CHRISTY: And you're not wedding him at all?

PEGEEN: I wouldn't wed him if a bishop came walking for to join us here.

CHRISTY: That God in glory may be thanked for that.

PEGEEN: There's your bed now. I've put a quilt upon you I'm after quilting a while since with my own two hands, and you'd best stretch out now for your sleep, and may God give you a good rest till I call you in the morning when the cocks will crow.

CHRISTY: *(As she goes to inner room.)* May God and Mary and St. Patrick bless you and reward you for your kindly talk. *(She shuts the door behind her. He settles his bed slowly, feeling the quilt with immense satisfaction.)* Well, it's a clean bed and soft with it, and it's great luck and company I've won me in the end of time—two fine women fighting for the likes of me—till I'm thinking this night wasn't I a foolish fellow not to kill my father in the years gone by.

The Hairy Ape

Eugene O'Neill
1922

Scene: Aboard ship. Mildred has declared that she is going below deck to see the workings of the ship.

Mildred, a wealthy and cultured young lady.
Aunt, arrogant.
Second Engineer, A steamship stoker, brutish, uneducated, a worker.

MILDRED: *(Protesting with a trace of genuine earnestness.)* Please do not mock at my attempts to discover how the other half lives. Give me credit for some sort of groping sincerity in that at least. I would like to help them. I would like to be some use in the world. Is it my fault I don't know how? I would like to be sincere, to touch life somewhere. *(With weary bitterness.)* But I'm afraid I have neither the vitality nor integrity. All that was burnt out in our stock before I was born. Grandfather's blast furnaces, flaming to the sky, melting steel, making millions—then father keeping those home fires burning, making more millions—and little me at the tail end of it all. I'm a waste product in the Bessemer process—like the millions. Or rather, I inherit the acquired trait of the by-product, wealth, but none of the energy, none of the strength of the steel made it. I am sired by gold and damned by it, as they say at the race track—damned in more ways than one. *(She laughs mirthlessly.)*

AUNT: *(Unimpressed—superciliously.)* You seem to be going in for sincerity today. It isn't becoming to you, really—except as an obvious pose. Be as artificial as you are, I advise. There's a sort of sincerity in that, you know. And, after all, you must confess you like that better.

MILDRED: *(Again affected and bored.)* Yes, I suppose I do. Pardon me for my outburst. When a leopard complains of its spots, it must sound rather grotesque. *(In mocking tone.)* Purr, little leopard.

Purr, scratch, tear, kill, gorge yourself and be happy—only stay in the jungle where your spots are camouflage. In a cage they make you conspicuous.

AUNT: I don't know what you are talking about.

MILDRED: It would be rude to talk about anything to you. Let's just talk. *(She looks at her wristwatch.)* Well, thank goodness, it's about time for them to come for me. That ought to give me a new thrill, Aunt.

AUNT: *(Affectedly troubled.)* You don't mean to say you're really going? The dirt—the heat must be frightful—

MILDRED: Grandfather started as a puddler. I should have inherited an immunity to heat that would make a salamander shiver. It will be fun to put it to the test.

AUNT: But don't you have to have the captain's—or someone's—permission to visit the stokehold?

MILDRED: *(With a triumphant smile.)* I have it—both his and the chief engineer's. Oh, they didn't want to at first, in spite of my social service credentials. They didn't seem a bit anxious that I should investigate how the other half lives and works on a ship. So I had to tell them that my father, the president of Nazareth Steel, chairman of the board of directors of this line, had told me it would be all right.

AUNT: He didn't.

MILDRED: How naïve age makes one! But I said he did, Aunt. I even said he had given me a letter to them—which I had lost. And they were afraid to take the chance that I might be lying. *(Excitedly.)* So it's ho! for the stokehole. The second engineer is to escort me *(Looking at her watch again.)* It's time. and here he comes, I think. *(The Second Engineer enters. He is a husky, fine-looking man of thirty-five or so. He stops before the two and tips his cap, visibly embarrassed and ill-at-ease.)*

SECOND ENGINEER: Miss Douglas?

MILDRED: Yes *(Throwing off her rugs and getting to her feet.)* Are we ready to start?

SECOND ENGINEER: In just a second, ma'am. I'm waiting for the Fourth. He's coming along.

MILDRED: *(With a scornful smile.)* You don't care to shoulder his responsibility alone, is that it?

SECOND ENGINEER: *(Forcing a smile.)* Two are better than one *(Disturbed by her eyes, glances out to sea—blurts out.)* A fine day we're having.

MILDRED: Is it?

SECOND ENGINEER: A nice warm breeze—

MILDRED: It feels cold to me.

SECOND ENGINEER: But it's not hot enough in the sun—

MILDRED: Not hot enough for me. I don't like Nature. I was never athletic.

SECOND ENGINEER: *(Forcing a smile.)* Well, you'll find it hot enough where you're going.

MILDRED: Do you mean hell?

SECOND ENGINEER: *(Flabbergasted, decides to laugh.)* Ho-ho! No, I mean the stokehold.

MILDRED: My grandfather was a puddler. He played with boiling steel.

SECOND ENGINEER: *(All at sea—uneasily.)* Is that so? Hum, you'll excuse me, ma'am, but are you intending to wear that dress?

MILDRED: Why not?

SECOND ENGINEER: You'll likely rub against oil and dirt. It can't be helped.

MILDRED: It doesn't matter. I have lots of white dresses.

SECOND ENGINEER: I have an old coat you might throw over—

MILDRED: I have fifty dresses like this. I will throw this one into the sea when I come back. That ought to wash it clean, don't you think?

SECOND ENGINER: *(Doggedly.)* There's ladders to climb down that are none too clean—and dark alleyways—

MILDRED: I will wear this very dress and none other.

SECOND ENGINEER: No offense meant. It's none of my business. I was only warning you—

MILDRED: Warning? That sounds thrilling.

SECOND ENGINEER: *(Looking down the deck—with a sigh of relief.)* There's the Fourth now. He's waiting for us. If you'll come—

MILDRED: Go on. I'll follow you. *(He goes.* Mildred *turns a mocking smile on her aunt.)* An oaf—but a handsome, virile oaf.

AUNT: *(Scornfully.)* Poser!

MILDRED: Take care. He said there were dark alleyways—

AUNT: *(In the same tone.)* Poser!

MILDRED: *(Biting her lips angrily.)* You are right. But would that my millions were not so anemically chaste!

AUNT: Yes, for a fresh pose I have no doubt you would drag the name of Douglas in the gutter!

MILDRED: From which it sprang. Good-bye, Aunt. Don't pray too hard that I may fall into the fiery furnace.

AUNT: Poser!

MILDRED: *(Viciously.)* Old hag! *(She slaps her aunt insultingly across the face and walks off, laughing gaily.)*

AUNT: *(Screams after her.)* I said poser!

A View from the Bridge

Arthur Miller
1955

Scene: In the Carbone apartment in Brooklyn. Catherine has just announced that she is getting a job. Eddie, very protective of her, objects. There has been unspoken tension between Eddie and Beatrice for a while as well.

Eddie Carbone, late 30s–40s, Italian-American, a stevedore, hard working.
Beatrice, his wife, 30s, a housewife.
Catherine, his niece whom he has raised and loves dearly, 17 years old.

EDDIE: *(He is strangely nervous.)* Where's the job? What company?
CATHERINE: It's a big plumbing company over Nostrand Avenue.
EDDIE: Nostrand Avenue and where?
CATHERINE: It's some place by the Navy Yard.
BEATRICE: Fifty dollars a week, Eddie.
EDDIE: *(To Catherine, surprised.)* Fifty?
CATHERINE: I swear.
EDDIE: *(Pause.)* What about all the stuff you wouldn't learn this year, though?
CATHERINE: There's nothin' more to learn, Eddie, I just gotta practice from now on. I know all the symbols and I know the keyboard. I'll just get faster, that's all. And when I'm workin' I'll keep gettin' better and better, you see?
BEATRICE: Work is the best practice anyway.
EDDIE: *(Pause.)* That ain't what I wanted, though.
CATHERINE: Why! It's a great big company . . .
EDDIE: I don't like that neighborhood over there.
CATHERINE: It's a block and a half from the subway, he says.
EDDIE: Near the Navy Yard plenty can happen in a block and a half. And a plumbin' company!—That's one step over the waterfront. They're practically longshoremen.

BEATRICE: Yeah, but she'll be in the office, Eddie.

EDDIE: I know she'll be in the office, but that ain't what I had in mind.

BEATIRCE: Listen, she's gotta go to work sometime.

EDDIE: Listen, Bea, she'll be with a lotta plumbers. And sailors up and down the street? So what did she go to school for?

CATHERINE: But it's fifty a week, Eddie.

EDDIE: Look, did I ask you for money? I supported you this long, I support you a little more. Please, do me a favor, will ya? I want you to be with different kind of people. I want you to be in a nice office. Maybe a lawyer's office someplace in New York in one of them nice buildings. I mean if you're gonna get outa here then get out; don't go into practically the same kind of neighborhood. *(Pause. Catherine lowers her eyes.)*

BEATRICE: *(To Catherine as she sits at L. of table.)* Go, Baby, bring in the supper. *(Catherine goes out to kitchen.)* Think about it a little bit, Eddie. Please. She's crazy to start work. It's not a little shop, it's a big company. Some day she could be a secretary. They picked her out of the whole class. *(He is silent, staring down at the tablecloth, fingering the pattern.)* What are you worried about?—She could take care of herself. She'll get out of the subway and be in the office in two minutes.

EDDIE: *(He is somehow sickened.)* I know that neighborhood, Bea, I don't like it.

BEATRICE: Listen, if nothin' happened to her in this neighborhood it ain't gonna happen no place else. *(She turns his face to her.)* Look, you gotta get used to it, she's no baby no more. Tell her to take it. *(He turns his head away.)* You hear me. *(She is angering.)* I don't understand you; she's seventeen years old, you gonna keep her in the house all her life?

EDDIE: *(He is insulted.)* What kinda remark is that?

BEATRICE: *(With sympathy but insistent force.)* Well, I don't understand when it ends. First it was gonna be when she graduated high school, so she graduated high school. Then it was gonna be when she learned stenographer, so she learned stenographer. So what're we gonna wait for now? I mean it, Eddie, sometimes I don't understand you; they picked her out of the whole class, it's an honor for her. *(Catherine enters from kitchen with food, which she silently sets on the table. After a moment of watching her face, Eddie breaks into a smile, but it almost seems that tears will form in his eyes.)*

EDDIE: With your hair that way you look like a Madonna, you know that? You're the Madonna type. *(She doesn't look at him, but continues ladling out food onto the plates.)* You wanna go to work, heh, Madonna?

CATHERINE: *(Softly.)* Yeah.

EDDIE: *(With a sense of her childhood, her babyhood, and the years.)* All right, go to work. *(She looks at him, then rushes and hugs him.)* Hey, hey! Take it easy! *(He holds her face away from him to look at her.)* What're you cryin' about? *(He is affected by her, but smiles his emotion away.)*

CATHERINE: *(She sits at her place R. of table.)* I just . . . *(Bursting out.)* I'm gonna buy all new dishes with my first pay! *(They laugh warmly.)* I mean it. I'll fix up the whole house! I'll buy a rug!

EDDIE: And then you'll move away.

CATHERINE: No, Eddie!

EDDIE: *(He's grinning.)* Why not?—That's life. And you'll come visit on Sundays, then once a month, then Christmas and New Year's.

CATHERINE: *(She gasps his arm to reassure him and to erase the accusation.)* No, please!

EDDIE: *(He smiles but he is hurt.)* I only ask you one thing—don't trust nobody. You got a good aunt but she's got too big a heart, you learned bad from her. Believe me.

BEATRICE: Be the way you are, Katie, don't listen to him.

EDDIE: *(To Beatrice—strangely and quickly resentful.)* You lived in a house all your life, what do you know about it? You never worked in your life.

BEATRICE: She likes people—what's wrong with that?

EDDIE: Because most people ain't people. She's goin' to work; plumbers; they'll chew her to pieces if she don't watch out. *(To Catherine.)* Believe me, Katie, the less you trust, the less you be sorry. *(He crosses himself and the women do the same, and they eat.)*

CATHERINE: First thing I'll buy is a rug, heh, Bea?

BEATRICE: I don't mind. *(To Eddie.)* I smelled coffee all day today. You unloadin' coffee today?

EDDIE: Yeah, a Brazil ship.

CATHERINE: I smelled it too. It smelled all over the neighborhood.

EDDIE: That's one time, boy, to be a longshoreman is a pleasure. I could work coffee ships twenty hours a day. You go down in the hold, y'know?—it's like flowers, that smell. We'll bust a bag tomorrow, I'll bring you some.

BEATRICE: Just be sure there's no spiders in it, will ya? I mean it. *(She directs this to Catherine, rolling her eyes upwards.)* I still remember that spider coming out of that bag he brung home—I nearly died.

EDDIE: You call that a spider? You oughta see what comes outa the bananas sometimes.

BEATRICE: Don't talk about it!

EDDIE: I seen spiders could stop a Buick.

BEATRICE: *(Clapping her hands over her ears.)* All right, shut up!

EDDIE: *(Laughs.)* Well, who started with spiders?

BEATRICE: All right, I'm sorry, I didn't mean it. Just don't bring none home again. What time is it?

EDDIE: Quarter nine. *(Puts watch back in his pocket. They continue eating in silence.)*

CATHERINE: He's bringin' them ten o'clock, Tony?

EDDIE: Around, yeah. *(He eats.)*

CATHERINE: Eddie, suppose somebody asks if they're livin' here. *(He looks at her as though already she had divulged something publicly. Defensively.)* I mean if they ask.

EDDIE: Now look, Baby, I can see we're getting' mixed up again here . . .

CATHERINE: No, I just mean . . . people'll see them goin' in and out . . .

EDDIE: I don't care who sees them goin' in and out as long as you don't see them goin' in and out. And this goes for you too, Bea. . . . You don't see nothin' and you don't know nothin'.

BEATRICE: What do you mean?—I understand.

EDDIE: You don't understand; you still think you can talk about this to somebody just a little bit. Now lemme say it once and for all, because you're makin' me nervous again, both of you. I don't care if somebody comes in the house and sees them sleepin' on the floor, it never comes out of your mouth who they are or what they're doin' here.

BEATRICE: Yeah, but my mother'll know . . .

EDDIE: Sure she'll know, but just don't you be the one who told her, that's all. This is the United States government you're playin' with now, this is the Immigration Bureau—if you said it you knew it, if you didn't say it you didn't know it.

CATHERINE: Yeah, but Eddie, suppose somebody—

EDDIE: I don't care what question it is—you—don't—know—nothin'. They got stool pigeons all over this neighborhood they're payin' them every week for information, and you don't know who they are. It could be your best friend. You hear? *(To Beatrice.)* Like Vinny Bolzano, remember Vinny?

BEATRICE: Oh, yeah. God forbid.

EDDIE: Tell her about Vinny. *(To Catherine.)* You think I'm blowin' steam here?—*(To Beatrice.)* Go ahead, tell her. *(To Catherine.)* You was a baby then. There was a family lived next door to her mother, he was about sixteen . . .

BEATRICE: No, he was no more than fourteen, 'cause I was to his confirmation in Saint Agnes. But the family had an uncle that they were hidin' in the house, and he snitched to the Immigration . . .

CATHERINE: The kid snitched?!

EDDIE: On his own uncle!

CATHERINE: What, was he crazy?

EDDIE: He was crazy after, I tell you that, boy.

BEATRICE: Oh, it was terrible. He had five brothers and the old father. And they grabbed him in the kitchen and pulled him down the stairs—three flights his head was bouncin' like a coconut. And they spit on him in the street, his own father and brothers. The whole neighborhood was cryin'

CATHERINE: Ts! So what happened to him?

BEATRICE: I think he went away . . . *(To Eddie.)* I never seen him again, did you?

EDDIE: *(He starts to rise during this, taking out his watch.)* Him? You'll never see him no more, a guy do a think like that?—how's he gonna show his face? *(To Catherine, as he gets up uneasily.)* Just remember, kid, you can quicker get back a million dollars that was stole than a word that you gave away. *(He is standing now, stretching his back.)*

CATHERINE: Okay, I won't say a word to anybody, I swear.

EDDIE: Gonna' rain tomorrow. We'll be slidin' all over the decks. Maybe you oughta put something on for them, they be here soon.

BEATRICE: I only got fish, I hate to spoil it if they ate already. I'll wait, it only take a few minutes; I could broil it.

CATHERINE: What happens, Eddie, when that ship pulls out and they ain't on it, though? Don't the captain say nothin'?

EDDIE: *(Slicing an apple with his pocketknife.)* Captain's pieced-off, what do you mean?

CATHERINE: Even the captain?!

EDDIE: What's the matter, the captain don't have to live? Captain gets a piece, maybe one of the mates, piece for the guy in Italy who fixed the papers for them, Tony here'll get a little bite . . .

BEATRICE: I just hope they get work here, that's all I hope.

EDDIE: Oh, the syndicate'll fix jobs for them; till they pay 'em off they'll get them work every day. It's after the pay off, then they'll have to scramble like the rest of us.

BEATRICE: Well, it be better than they got there.

EDDIE: Oh, sure, well, listen. So you gonna start Monday, heh, Madonna?

CATHERINE: *(She is embarrassed.)* I'm supposed to, yeah. *(He is standing facing the two seated women. First Beatrice smiles, then Catherine—for a powerful emotion is on him, a childish one and a knowing fear, and the tears show in his eyes—and they are shy before the approval.)*

EDDIE: *(He is sadly smiling, yet somehow proud of her.)* Well . . . I hope you have good luck. I wish you the best. You know that, kid.

CATHERINE: *(Rising, trying to laugh.)* You sound like I'm going' a million miles!

EDDIE: I know. I guess I just never figured on one thing.

CATHERINE: What? *(She is smiling.)*

EDDIE: That you would ever grow up. *(He utters a soundless laugh at himself, feeling his breast pocket of his shirt.)* I left a cigar in my other coat, I think. *(He starts for the bedroom.)*

CATHERINE: Stay there! I'll get it for you. *(She hurries out to bedroom. There is a slight pause, and Eddie turns to Beatrice who has been avoiding his gaze.)*

EDDIE: What are you mad at me lately?

BEATRICE: Who's mad? *(She gets up, clearing the dishes.)* I'm not mad. *(She picks up the dishes and turns to him.)* You're the one is mad. *(She turns and goes into the kitchen as Catherine enters from the bedroom with a cigar and a pack of matches.)*

Marty

Paddy Chayefsky

Scene: Marty and Clara are in the apartment that Marty shares with his Mother. Old-fashioned, overcrowded with lots of furniture and little religious statues.

Marty, late 30s, a butcher, Italian-American still living at home with his mother.
Mother, round, dark, late 50s, a strong woman.
Girl, Clara Davis, Marty's sweetheart, the first girl he's ever really cared for, 30s, plain, a teacher.

MARTY: Well, that's the history of my life. I'm a little, short, fat, ugly guy. Comes New Year's Eve, everybody starts arranging parties, I'm the guy they gotta dig up a date for. I'm old enough to know better. Let me get a packa cigarettes, and I'll take you home. He starts to rise, but doesn't . . . sinks back onto the couch, looking straight ahead. The girl looks at him, her face peculiarly soft and compassionate.

GIRL: I'd like to see you again, very much. The reason I didn't let you kiss me was because I just didn't know how to handle the situation. You're the kindest man I ever met. The reason I tell you this is because I want to see you again very much. Maybe, I'm just so desperate to fall in love that I'm trying too hard. But I know that when you take me home, I'm gong to just lie on my bed and think about you. I want very much to see you again. *(Marty stares down at his hands in his lap.)*

MARTY: *(Without looking at her.)* Waddaya doing tomorrow night?

GIRL: Nothing.

MARTY: I'll call you up tomorrow morning. Maybe we'll go see a movie.

GIRL: I'd like that very much.

MARTY: The reason I can't be definite about it now is my Aunt Catherine is probably coming over tomorrow, and I may have to help out.

GIRL: I'll wait for your call.

MARTY: We better get started to your house because the buses only run about one an hour now.

GIRL: All right. *(She stands.)*

MARTY: I'll just get a packa cigarettes. *(He goes into his bedroom. We can see him through the doorway, opening his bureau drawer and extracting a pack of cigarettes. He comes out again and looks at the girl for the first time. They start to walk to the dining room. In the archway, Marty pauses, turns to the girl.)*

MARTY: Waddaya doing New Year's Eve?

GIRL: Nothing. *(They quietly slip into each other's arms and kiss. Slowly their faces part, and Marty's head sinks down upon her shoulder. He is crying. His shoulders shake slightly. The girl presses her cheek against the back of his head. They stand . . . there is the sound of the rear porch door being unlatched. They both start from their embrace. A moment later the mother's voice is heard off the kitchen.)*

MOTHER: Hallo! Hallo, Marty? *(She comes into the dining room, stops at the sight of the girl.)* Hallo, Marty, when you come home?

MARTY: We just got here about fifteen minutes ago, Ma. Ma I want you to meet Miss Clara Davis. She's a graduate of New York University. She teaches history in Benjamin Franklin High School. *(This seems to impress the mother.)*

MOTHER: Siddown, siddown. You want some chicken? We got some chicken in the icebox.

GIRL: No, Mrs. Pillietti, we were just going home. Thank you very much anyway.

MOTHER: Well, siddown a minute. I just come inna house. I'll take off my coat. Siddown a minute. *(She pulls her coat off.)*

MARTY: How'd you come home, Ma? Thomas give you a ride? *(The mother nods.)*

MOTHER: Oh, it's a sad business, a sad business. *(She sits down on a dining room chair, holding her coat in her lap. She turns to the girl, who likewise sits.)*

MOTHER: My sister Catherine, she don't get along with her daughter-in-law, so she's gonna come live with us.

MARTY: Oh, she's coming, eh, Ma?

MOTHER: Oh, sure. *(To the girl.)* It's a very said thing. A woman, fifty-six years old, all her life, she had her own home. Now, she's just an old lady, sleeping on her daughter-in-law's couch. It's a curse to be a mother, I tell you. Your children grow up and then what is left for you to do? What is a mother's life but her children? It is a very cruel thing when your son has no place for you in his home.

GIRL: Couldn't she find some sort of hobby to fill out her time?

MOTHER: Hobby! What can she do? She cooks and she cleans. You gotta have a house to clean. You gotta have children to cook for. These are the terrible years for a woman, the terrible years.

GIRL: You mustn't feel too harshly against her daughter-in-law. She also wants to have a house to clean and a family to cook for.
(The mother darts a quick, sharp look at the girl—then looks back to her hands, which are beginning to twist nervously.)

MOTHER: You don't think my sister Catherine should live in her daughter-in-law's house?

GIRL: Well, I don't know the people of course, but, as a rule, I don't think a mother-in-law should live with a young couple.

MOTHER: Where do you think a mother-in-law should go?

GIRL: I don't think a mother should depend so much upon her children for her reward in life.

MOTHER: That's what it says in the book in New York University. You wait till you are a mother. It don't work out that way.

GIRL: Well, it's silly for me to argue about it. I don't know the people involved.

MARTY: Ma, I'm gonna take her home now. It's getting late, and the buses only run about one an hour.

MOTHER: *(Standing.)* Sure. *(The girl stands.)*

GIRL: It was very nice meeting you, Mrs. Pilletti. I hope I'll see you again.

MOTHER: Sure. *(Marty and the girl move to the kitchen.)*

MARTY: All right, Ma. I'll be back in about an hour.

MOTHER: Sure.

GIRL: Good night, Mrs. Pilletti.

MOTHER: Good night.

(Marty and the girl exit into the kitchen. The mother stands, expressionless, by her chair watching them go. She remains standing rigidly even after the porch door can be heard being opened and shut. The camera moves up to a close-up of the mother. Her eyes are wide. She is staring straight ahead. There is fear in her eyes.)

The Odd Couple
Neil Simon
1965

Scene: An apartment belonging to Oscar Madison. The Pigeon sisters
   have been invited for dinner and Felix is entertaining them as
   Oscar makes the drinks in the kitchen.

Felix Ungar, 30s–40s, separated from his wife, fastidious and polite.
Gwendolyn Pigeon, 30s, British, somewhat attractive.
Cecily Pigeon, her sister, 30s, somewhat attractive.

FELIX: Yes, I see. *(Ha laughs. They all laugh. Suddenly he shouts
   toward the kitchen.)* Oscar, where's the drinks?
OSCAR: *(Off stage)* Coming! Coming!
CECILY: What field of endeavor are you engaged in?
FELIX: I write the news for CBS.
CECILY: Oh! Fascinating!
GWENDOLYN: Where do you get your ideas from?
FELIX: *(He looks at her as though she's a Martian.)* From the news.
GWENDOLYN: Oh, yes, of course. Silly me . . .
CECILY: Maybe you can mention Gwen and I in one of your news
   reports.
FELIX: Well, if you do something spectacular, maybe I will.
CECILY: Oh, we've done spectacular things but I don't think we'd
   want it spread all over the telly, do you, Gwen? *(They both laugh.)*
FELIX: *(He laughs too, then cries out almost for help.)* Oscar!
OSCAR: *(Offstage.)* Yeah, yeah!
FELIX: *(To the girls.)* It's such a large apartment, sometimes you have
   to shout.
GWENDOLYN: Just you two baches live here?
FELIX: Baches? Oh, bachelors! We're not bachelors. We're divorced.
   That is, Oscar's divorced. I'm *getting* divorced.
CECILY: Oh. Small world. We've cut the dinghy loose too, as they say.
GWENDOLYN: Well, you couldn't have a *better* matched foursome,
   could you?

FELIX: *(Smiles weakly.)* No, I suppose not.

GWENDOLYN: Although technically I'm a widow. I was divorcing my husband, but he died before the final papers came through.

FELIX: Oh, I'm awfully sorry. *(Sighs.)* It's a terrible thing, isn't it? Divorce.

GWENDOLYN: It can be—if you haven't got the right solicitor.

CECILY: That's true. Sometimes they can drag it out for months. I was lucky. Snip, cut, and I was free.

FELIX: I mean it's terrible what it can do to people. After all, what is divorce? It's taking two happy people and tearing their lives completely apart. It's inhuman, don't you think so?

CECILY: Yes, it can be an awful bother.

GWENDOLYN: But of course, that's all water under the bridge now, eh? Er, I'm terribly sorry, but I think I've forgotten your name.

FELIX: Felix.

GWENDOLYN: Oh, yes. Felix.

CECILY: Like the cat. *(Felix takes his wallet from his jacket pocket)*

GWENDOLYN: Well, the Pigeons will have to beware of the cat, won't they? *(She laughs.)*

CECILY: *(Nibbles on a nut from the dish.)* Mmm, cashews. Lovely.

FELIX: *(Takes a snapshot out of his wallet)* This is the worst part of breaking up. *(He hands the picture to Cecily.)*

CECILY: *(Looks at it)* Childhood sweethearts, were you?

FELIX: No, no. That's my little boy and girl. *(Cecily gives the picture to Gwendolyn, takes a pair of glasses from her purse and puts them on.)* He's seven, she's five.

CECILY: *(Looks again.)* Oh! Sweet.

FELIX: They live with their mother.

GWENDOLYN: I imagine you must miss them terribly.

FELIX: *(Takes back the picture and looks at it longingly.)* I can't stand being away from them. *(Shrugs.)* But—that's what happens with divorce.

CECILY: When do you get to see them?

FELIX: Every night. I stop there on my way home! Then I take them on the weekends, and I get them on holidays and July and August.

CECILY: Oh! Well, when is it that you miss them?

FELIX: Whenever I'm not there. If they didn't have to go to school so early, I'd go over and make them breakfast. They love my French toast.

GWENDOLYN: You're certainly a devoted father.

FELIX: It's Frances who's the wonderful one.

CECILY: She's the little girl?

FELIX: No. She's the mother. My wife.

GWENDOLYN: The one you're divorcing?

FELIX: *(Nods.)* Mm! She's done a terrific job bringing them up. They always look so nice. They're so polite. Speak beautifully. Never, "Yeah." Always. "Yes." They're such good kids. And she did it all. She's the kind of woman who—Ah, what am I saying? You don't want to hear any of this. *(He puts the picture back in his wallet.)*

CECILY: Nonsense. You have a right to be proud. You have two beautiful children and a wonderful ex-wife.

FELIX: *(Containing his emotions.)* I know. I know. *(He hands* Cecily *another snapshot.)* That's her. Frances.

GWENDOLYN: *(Looking at the picture.)* Oh, she's pretty. Isn't she pretty, Cecy?

CECILY: Oh, yes. Pretty. A pretty girl. Very pretty.

FELIX: *(Takes the picture back.)* Thank you. *(Shows them another snapshot.)* Isn't this nice?

GWENDOLYN: *(Looks.)* There's no one in the picture.

FELIX: I know. It's a picture of our living room. We had a beautiful apartment.

GWENDOLYN: Oh, yes. Pretty. Very pretty.

CECILY: Those are lovely lamps.

FELIX: Thank you! *(Takes the picture.)* We bought them in Mexico on our honeymoon. *(He looks at the picture again.)* I used to love to come home at night. *(He's beginning to break.)* That was my whole life. My wife, my kids—and my apartment.

CECILY: Does she have the lamps now too?

FELIX: *(Nods.)* I gave her everything. It'll never be like that again. Never! I—I— *(He turns his head away.)* I'm sorry. *(He takes out a handkerchief and dabs his eyes. Gwendolyn and Cecily look at each other with compassion.)* Please forgive me. I didn't mean to get emotional. *(Trying to pull himself together, he picks up a bowl from the side table and offers it to the girls.)* Would you like some potato chips? *(Cecily takes the bowl.)*

GWENDOLYN: You mustn't be ashamed. I think it's a rare quality in a man to be able to cry.

FELIX: *(Puts a hand over his eyes.)* Please. Let's not talk about it.

CECILY: I think it's sweet. Terribly, terribly sweet. *(She takes a potato chip.)*

FELIX: You're just making it worse.

GWENDOLYN: *(Teary-eyed.)* It's so refreshing to hear a man speak so highly of the woman he's divorcing! Oh, dear. *(She takes out her handkerchief.)* Now you've got me thinking about poor Sydney.

CECILY: Oh, Gwen. Please don't *(She puts the bowl down.)*

GWENDOLYN: It was a good marriage at first. Everyone said so. Didn't they, Cecily? Not like you and George.

CECILY: *(The past returns as she comforts Gwendolyn.)* That's right. George and I were never happy. Not for one single, solitary day. *(She remembers her unhappiness, grabs her handkerchief and dabs her eyes. All three are now sitting with handkerchiefs at their eyes.)*

FELIX: Isn't this ridiculous?

GWENDOLYN: I don't know what brought this on. I was feeling so good a few minutes ago.

CECILY: I haven't cried since I was fourteen.

FELIX: Just let it pour out. It'll make you feel much better. I always do.

GWENDOLYN: Oh, dear; oh, dear; oh dear. *(All three sit sobbing into their handkerchiefs.)*

Waiting for the Bus

Ramon Delgado
1968

Scene: Edith and Andrew are at the Park. Cynthia enters.

Edith, an old, old woman.
Andrew, her husband, an old, old man.
Cynthia, an old woman, of ill-repute.
Toto, an imaginary dog.

EDITH: Oh, hello. How do you do.
CYNTHIA: Fine, sister. How about yourself.
EDITH: Rather well, thank you.
CYNTHIA: *(Sitting.)* Mind if I sit down?
EDITH: Not a bit. Be careful of Toto.
CYNTHIA: Who?
EDITH: Our dog.
CYNTHIA: Where?
EDITH: Right here, on the end of the leash.
CYNTHIA: *(Uneasily.)* Oh—sure. Pretty, ain't he?
EDITH: I don't know that you'd exactly call him pretty. Unique would
    be more correct.
CYNTHIA: Yeah, that's what I mean—a pretty unique dog. *(Pause.)*
    My name's Cynthia, what's yours?
EDITH: My name is Edith, and my husband's name is Andrew.
CYNTHIA: *(Nostagically.)* I knew an Andrew once—in Germany.
EDITH: *(Warily.)* In Germany—you don't say. When was that?
CYNTHIA: Near the close of the war.
EDITH: Which one? There have been so many through Germany.
CYNTHIA: I don't guess it was the same Andrew.
EDITH: He's been a soldier a good long time.
CYNTHIA: Well, I've been going around from country to country for a
    good long time too.
EDITH: And from man to man?
CYNTHIA: What makes you say that?

EDITH: I know your type. I can tell by the thick makeup. I've never understood that. Why does a woman in your "profession" cover herself with such heavy paint?

CYNTHIA: We have to work past our prime.

EDITH: Was it my Andrew you knew in Germany?

CYNTHIA: How do I know whether it was your Andrew or not. Men come and men go; and they don't leave their calling cards. There are Andrews all over the world.

EDITH: Did he tell you that he loved you?

CYNTHIA: They all say that.

EDITH: All of them?

CYNTHIA: *(Wistfully.)* They used to.

EDITH: My Andrew wouldn't. He wouldn't even look at you.

CYNTHIA: Lady, I'm not going to argue with you. I don't know your Andrew from Adam's house cat, and if I weren't so dog tired, I'd walk on to find another bench.

EDITH: You had been running, hadn't you?

CNYTHIA: I'm always running—from something or to something.

EDITH: You don't have to, you know. You could get married.

CYNTHIA: I'd rather run.

EDITH: On the average, marriage is good for people.

CYNTHIA: When you've seen as many unfaithful men as I have, you don't have much faith in marriage.

EDITH: But the family is the foundation of our society, and without marriage—

CYNTHIA: Look, lady, you ain't gonna reform me. I heard all the gospel I could stand in the last Graham crusade.

EDITH: Just the same— *(Andrew enter D.L., giggling to himself.)* *(Edith rises.)* Andrew, I want you to tell this woman— *(Crosses to Andrew's R.)* Andrew, what is the matter with you? Stop that silly giggling.

ANDREW: I've seen it—the writing on the wall.

EDITH: On the wall?

ANDREW: The verses and quotations, the scriptures and passages, the jokes and songs on the wall of the comfort station.

EDITH: Andrew, be serious. I want you to—

ANDREW: And I have made an important decision.

EDITH: Andrew, this woman—

ANDREW: And I am sure that history will prove that all important decisions were made by some great man sitting on the john.

EDITH: Andrew, that isn't very nice.

ANDREW: Hello—who is this?

EDITH: Her name is Cynthia. Will you please tell her to go away?

ANDREW: *(Crossing to* Cynthia's *L.)* No, indeed. Didn't you tell me we were all related? She may be my kissing cousin.

EDITH: Past desire, past hope?

ANDREW: Past desire, but not past hope.

EDITH: You mustn't even look at such a woman.

ANDREW: *(Crossing to R. end of bench.)* It doesn't do any harm to look.

EDITH: *(Crossing to Cynthia's L. and tugging her up by her arm.)* Run along, miss. Our bus will be here in just a little while.

CYNTHIA: I've got just as much right to be here as you have.

EDITH: We don't want you.

ANDREW: *(Crossing to* Cynthia's *R.)* Well, I want her. I want her to go on the bus trip with us. She would be delightful company.

CYNTHIA: See, lady, they're all alike.

EDITH: Miss, my dog needs walking. Would you be so kind.

CYNTHIA: I don't see why I shou—

EDITH: *(Giving Cynthia the leash.)* Here, take his leash and come back later. *(Showing Cynthia out D.L.)* Take him on a long walk.

CYNTHIA: Well, you don't have to shove.

EDITH: Go along with you.

CYNTHIA: All right, but I'll be back, and take my place on the bench. I've got just as much right as the rest of you. *(Cynthia exits with Toto's leash D.L.)*

EDITH: *(crossing to L. end of bench.)* Andrew, you should be ashamed. A man your age staring at lewd women.

ANDREW: *(Sitting R. end of bench.)* I don't see anything wrong—

EDITH: *(Crossing behind bench to Andrew's R.)* Did you know her in Germany?

ANDREW: In Germany? I don't think so.

EDITH: She said she knew an Andrew in Germany during the war.

ANDREW: There are hundreds—

EDITH: I know. Did you know her?

ANDREW: *(Rising.)* Now, love, you've been with me every time I went to Germany. *(Edith starts crying.)* Now what's the matter?

EDITH: I've never been to Germany. I've given you the best years of my life, and you have been unfaithful to me. And not only were you unfaithful, but you want her to go on the bus with us on our last trip together.

ANDREW: Now, now, Edith.

EDITH: And we had planned on it for so long.

ANDREW: There's not any good reason to get upset.

EDITH: And after this you were going to write your memoirs.

ANDREW: Now, Edith—

The Gingerbread Lady

Neil Simon

1971

Scene: A Brownstone Apartment in New York City, mid November. Jimmy has been fixing up Evy's apartment in order to welcome her back from her monthlong stay in rehab for alcoholism. Her friend, Toby, has gone to pick her up and bring her home. The phone rings.

Evy, 40s, just out of rehab.

Toby, early 40s.

Jimmy, early 40s portly, gay probably but not obviously.

JIMMY: *(Comes out with a can of coffee in his hand and crosses to the phone.)* Hello?. . . No, she's not, I'm expecting her home any minute. Who's calling, please? . . . Well, in regards to what? . . . Oh! Well, I'm sure Mrs. Meara hasn't not paid her phone bill intentionally, she's been away sick for the past ten weeks . . . But you're not going to cut it off, are you? She'll pay it as soon as she gets home . . . Fourth notice already, my goodness. . . . But you must realize she's good for it, I mean this is Evelyn Meara, the singer . . . It must be in by Tuesday, yes, I'll tell her that. Thank you very much, I appreciate that. *(Hangs up. To the phone)* Wait three years to get one but you rip 'em out fast enough, don't you? *(Continues opening the can. The front doorbell rings. Jimmy turns and looks at the door. He is extremely anxious. Puts the can of coffee down on chair, wipes his hands on his pants and crosses to door. Calls out without opening.)* Who is it?

WOMAN'S VOICE: It's us. We're home.

(Jimmy tries to open door but it doesn't work since he's forgotten that he bolted it. Tries to unbolt it but has a little difficulty at first.)

JIMMY: *(Calls out.)* Wait a second, I'm so damned nervous. *(Finally opens it and Toby Landau enters, a very pretty woman in her early forties, but you'd never believe it. That's because she spends most of her waking hours trying to achieve that effect. She is well dressed in a smartly tailored suit. She carries a large, heavy, but not very elegant suitcase.)* Look at me, I'm shaking.

TOBY: *(Entering.)* Don't complain to me. I just spent four hours in a taxi on the Long Island Expressway. Look out the window, you'll see a very rich cabdriver. *(Looks around the apartment.)*

JIMMY: Where is she? *(Looks out door.)* Evy? Where's Evy?

TOBY: She's saying hello to a neighbor . . . I thought you were going to clean the apartment. Didn't you say you would clean the apartment for Evy?

JIMMY: I tried rearranging the furniture, but it always came out like a bus terminal in Passaic. Where is she? Is she alright?

TOBY: Yes, but you're going to be shocked when you see her. She lost 42 pounds.

JIMMY: Oh, my God.

TOBY: I will tell you right here and now that a rest home for drunks is the most depressing place in the world.

JIMMY: I never thought she'd last it out. I'm so nervous. What do I say to her? How do I act in front of her?

TOBY: You hug her and love her and, above all, you must trust her.

JIMMY: I'll kill her if she ever takes another drink . . . Where the hell is she?

(We hear Evy's voice just outside the door.)

EVY: *(Offstage.)* I'm out in the hall. Are you ready?

JIMMY: Ready.

(Evy enters, in mink coat and carrying books.)

EVY: Alright, say it, I'm gorgeous, right?

JIMMY: Oh, my God, I don't believe it. Who is she? Who is this beautiful woman?

EVY: It better be me or I'm out twenty-seven hundred bucks.

JIMMY: Am I allowed to hug you?

EVY: You're allowed.

JIMMY: *(Rushes into her arms and hugs her. He feels her.)* It's true. It's gone. Forty-two pounds are gone. Where did it go?

EVY: You want it? It's in the suitcase.

JIMMY: I can't get over it. It's like talking to a stranger. Somebody introduce me.

TOBY: Jimmy, this is Evelyn Meara. Remember? She used to sing in clubs?

JIMMY: That fat lady? Who used to drink a lot? Use foul language? No. This is a nice, skinny woman. You put a dress on her, you can take her anywhere.

EVY: I don't want to go anywhere. I want to be right here in my own apartment . . . Oh, it's so good to be home. *(Looks around.)* Jesus, it look different when you're sober. I thought I had twice as much furniture.

TOBY: Will you sit down? She won't sit down. She stood all the way in the taxi coming home.

JIMMY: You must be starved. When did you eat last?

EVY: I had chicken salad in July. I'm not hungry.

TOBY: The doctors told me she worked harder than any patient there. Even the nurses were so proud of her.

EVY: It's the truth. I was the best drunk on my floor. . . . *(Looking at sectional.)* Christ, now it's coming back to me. I threw the other half of this out the window.

JIMMY: I want to make you something. Let me make you a tongue and Swiss on toast and a pot of coffee. Sit down. I'll be five minutes.

EVY: I thought my mother lived in Ohio. Leave me alone. I tortured myself to lose 42 pounds.

TOBY: Jimmy, stop it, you'll get Evy nervous.

JIMMY: I'm worried about her. If someone doesn't make it for her she doesn't eat.

EVY: There's plenty of time to eat next year. I'm alright. I'm home. Let me enjoy myself.

JIMMY: Who's stopping you? *(To Toby . . . softly.)* She look alright to you? *(Toby nods.)* Is there anything she has to take? Pills or something?

TOBY: Just some tranquilizers. She has them in her bag.

JIMMY: But nothing heavy? No serious stuff?

TOBY: Just a mile sedative to help her sleep.

EVY: *(At kitchen door.)* If you doctors want to be alone, I can go back to Happy Valley. What are you whispering about?

JIMMY: We're not whispering. We're talking softly.

EVY: You were whispering.

JIMMY: We were not whispering. We were talking softly.

EVY: Why were you talking softly?

JIMMY: Because we don't want you to hear what we're saying . . .

TOBY: Jimmy's worried about you, that's all.

EVY: If he's worried, let him worry a little louder. I can't stand whispering. Every time a doctor whispers in the hospital, the next day there's a funeral.

JIMMY: I'm sorry. I'm sorry.

EVY: It took ten weeks to cure me and five minutes for you to drive me crazy.

TOBY: Jimmy didn't mean it, darling.

EVY: What are you blaming him? You were whispering too.

TOBY: I had to. He whispered a question to me.

JIMMY: Alright, can we drop it?

TOBY: I didn't even bring it up.

EVY: Jesus, I got along better with the nuts on Long Island.

JIMMY: I'm sorry, Evy. Alright? I'm nervous I'm gonna say the wrong thing. I don't know how to act in front of somebody who just got home from the cure five minutes ago.

EVY: You act natural. The way you always acted with me.

JIMMY: This is the way I always acted with you.

EVY: Yeah? Well, maybe that's why I started to drink.

TOBY: My God, what a homecoming!

EVY: *(Wilts a little.)* Hey, listen, I'm sorry. Maybe I am nervous . . . Don't pay attention to me. Jimmy, you know what I'd love more than anything else in the world? A tongue and Swiss on toast and a pot of coffee.

JIMMY: Do you mean it?

EVY: I dreamt of it every night. First I dreamt of sex, then a tongue and Swiss on toast.

JIMMY: I'll bring you the sandwich. The rest I can't help you with. *(Exits into kitchen.)*

TOBY: *(Looking at herself in mirror.)* And what can I do, Evy?

EVY: You can stop looking at yourself and give me a cigarette.

TOBY: You *are* nervous, aren't you?

EVY: I hated that place so much I used to save up matches planning to burn it down. It was a Goddamn prison. And then when it came time to leave I was afraid to go. . . I suddenly felt comfortable there . . . Can I have my cigarette, please?

TOBY: That's almost a whole pack since we left the hospital. Are you sure they said it's alright to smoke?

EVY: Once you pay your bill and check out, they don't care if you get knocked up by a dwarf. *(Takes cigarette and smokes.)* I thought I'd have a million things to do once I got home. I'm here six minutes, I'm bored to death.

TOBY: You've got to give yourself time, Evy. And then you're going to start your life all over again and you're going to grow up to be a beautiful wonderful person like me.

EVY: What's that? What's that crap you're putting on your face?

TOBY: It's a special crap that protects the skin. Have you noticed you've never seen pores on me. As long as you've known me, have you ever seen a single pore on my face?

EVY: I've never even seen your face . . . Who are you anyway?

TOBY: A woman can never be too pretty. It's her feminine obligation. I love my looks, don't you?

EVY: You're gorgeous. If you went bald and lost your teeth, you'd still be cute looking. Leave yourself alone.

TOBY: I can't. Isn't it terrible? I'm obsessed.

EVY: You remind me of the psycho in the room next to me. She used to shampoo her eyelashes every night. Thought all the doctors were in love with her. An eighty-seven-year-old virgin screwball.

TOBY: What a sweet story. You just going to sit there forever? Aren't you going to unpack or something?

EVY: Unpack what? A pair of pajamas and a bottle of mineral oil? Besides, I'm never going in that bedroom again. I ruined half my life in there, the next half I'm playing it safe.

TOBY: I understand perfectly. But how will you get to the bathroom?

EVY: Over the roof and down the pipes. Just worry about your face, alright?

TOBY: I can worry about both. I wish I could stay with you tonight.

EVY: Then why don't you stay with me tonight?

TOBY: I have to meet Martin at Pavilion for dinner. It's business, I distract the client.

EVY: Some friend you are.

TOBY: Don't say it like that. I'm a wonderful friend. I'm sensitive. You want me to be hurt?

EVY: Don't pout. You'll crack your makeup and start an avalanche on your face.

TOBY: Anyway Jimmy can stay with you tonight.

'Dentity Crisis

Christopher Durang
1979

Scene: Living room. Jane is in a disheveled bathrobe. She is depressed and reading *Time* magazine.

Edith, 40s.
Jane, her daughter, late teens–20s.
Robert, her son, then, her husband.

VOICE: *(Offstage.)* Cuckoo. Cuckoo.
   (Enter Edith, carrying a bag of groceries and a dress in a dry cleaner's bag. Dress is very badly stained with blood.)
EDITH: Hello, dear, I'm back. Did you miss me? Say yes. *(Pause.)* Of course you missed me. A daughter always misses her mother. You're less depressed today, aren't you? I can tell. *(Puts bag down.)* I got your dress back. I'm afraid the stains didn't come out. You should have heard the lady at the cleaners. What did she do, slash her thighs with a razor blade? she said. I had to admit you had. Really, dear, I've never heard of anyone doing that. It was so awful when your father and I want into the bathroom together to brush our teeth and saw you perched up on the toilet, your pretty white dress over your head, slashing way at your thighs. I don't think your father had ever seen your thighs before, and I hope he never will again, at least not under those unpleasant conditions. I mean, what could have possessed you? No one in our family has ever attempted suicide before now, and no one since either. It's a sign of defeat, and no one should do it. You now what I think? Jane? Jane?
JANE: What?
EDITH: I don't think you ever attempted suicide at all. That's what I think.
JANE: How do you explain the stains then?
EDITH: I don't. *(Laughs merrily.)* I always say stains will explain themselves, and if they don't then there's nothing can be done about

it. *(Edith empties the grocery bag on the table. It is filled with loose potato chips, which Edith playfully arranges as if it is some sort of food sculpture.)*

JANE: I did attempt suicide.

EDITH: No, dear, you didn't. A daughter doesn't contradict her mother.

VOICE: Cuckoo, cuckoo.

JANE: Did you hear the voice of my therapist just then?

EDITH: No dear. *(Listens.)* Ah, now I hear it. He's saying what a fine daughter I have. *(Enter Robert.)*

ROBERT: Mother! I'm home.

EDITH: Oh, Jane, it's your brother. *(Edith and Robert kiss passionately and long. Jane is very upset and rips up the plastic covering on her dress.)*

ROBERT: Darling, darling.

EDITH: Oh, Dwayne, this is mad. We've got to stop meeting like this. Your father will find out.

JANE: I'll tell him!

EDITH: Jane, you'd never do anything like that.

ROBERT: I'm made for you. I find you . . . exciting. *(They kiss.)*

EDITH: *(Looking off.)* Quick, there's the postman. Act busy. *(Robert and Edith smash the potato chips on the table with their fists, then they brush the crushed chips into a wastebasket with a little broom.)*

EDITH: There, he's gone.

ROBERT: *(Holding her.)* Oh, why must you taunt me? Let's get married.

EDITH: We have different blood types.

ROBERT: Oh, Mother, I love you. *(They embrace.)*

EDITH: Oh, my God. Here comes your father. *(Robert, with no change of costume—and without exiting or re-entering—becomes the father.)*

ROBERT: Edith, what are you doing?

EDITH: Oh, Arthur, I was just finishing off my morning shopping.

ROBERT: And how is our daughter?

JANE: You're not my father.

EDITH: Don't contradict your father. You love your father, Jane.

JANE: He's my brother.

EDITH: Dwayne is your brother, dear.

ROBERT: Has she been seeing that psychologist of hers?

EDITH: Well, not socially.

ROBERT: Good *(Shouting at Jane.)* I don't ever want to hear of your dating a psychologist again.

JANE: I never have!

EDITH: Of course not, dear. You obey your father. You're a good daughter.

ROBERT: Not like some I could mention.

EDITH: No.

ROBERT: I could mention some.

EDITH: You could.

ROBERT: I could. I will.

EDITH: Now?

ROBERT: Now. Frances, Lucia, Henrietta, Charmant, Dolores, Loretta, and Peggy.

EDITH: Listen to your father, Jane.

ROBERT: No more of this slashing your thighs, young lady. I don't think that psychologist would ever go out with you again if he knew you were slashing your thighs.

JANE: I don't go out with my psychologist.

EDITH: Of course you don't. He has a wife and sixteen children. You're a good girl. You listen to your father.

JANE: *(To Robert.)* You're not my father.

EDITH: Jane, you know he's your father.

JANE: If you're my father, you must be close to fifty.

ROBERT: I am close to fifty.

JANE: Let me see your driver's license.

ROBERT: Here. *(Hands it to her.)*

JANE: *(Reads it.)* This says you're fifty. How did you get them to put that down?

EDITH: The truth is the truth no matter how you look at it, Jane.

JANE: How come you don't look fifty?

EDITH: Your father never looked his age. Most girls would be pleased that their father looked young.

ROBERT: Most girls are pleased.

EDITH: Jane's pleased you look young, aren't you, Jane? Don't you think Arthur looks young for his age, Grandad?

ROBERT: Eh? What?

EDITH: *(Shouting.)* Don't you think Arthur looks young, Grandad!

ROBERT: *(Smiling senilely.)* Yes, yes. Breakfast.

EDITH: Poor Grandad can't hear a thing.

JANE: Where's Father?

EDITH: Isn't he here? That's funny. I didn't hear the door close.

JANE: Grandad, Mother is having an affair with Dwayne!

ROBERT: *(Not hearing.)* What?

This One Thing I Do

Claire Braz-Valentine
1981

Scene: Time: 1901 Set: Elizabeth's bedroom with a comfortable sitting area and a fireplace. Arthur Brenton has come to interview Susan on the eve of her final public speech to the nation on behalf of women's suffrage. Susan enters in a bad mood.

Elizabeth Cady Stanton, at age 86.
Susan B. Anthony, at age 81.
Mr. Brenton, an eager young reporter.

SUSAN: It's so infernally cold in here! Never could figure out how that woman can stand it so cold. *(Yells through open doorway.)* And don't put any sugar in my tea, Elizabeth! I've known you for over fifty years and you still insist on sugaring my tea! I hate sugar in my tea! *(Throws logs on fire—rubs hands together. She sits and looks over at the table and notices a stack of newspaper clippings. She picks up a few of the clippings and reads them silently and disdainfully. She mutters under her breath and wads them up as she reads them and throws them one-by-one into the fireplace.)*
(Elizabeth Cady Stanton enters, looking very happy with herself. She carries a tray of tea things. She pretends she doesn't notice that Susan has found and burned the clippings.)
ELIZABETH: Susan! My God! Don't you think that fire is a little large?
SUSAN: No, I don't. And stop swearing.
ELIZABETH: *(Reaches over and holds Susan's hands.)* Your hands still bother you, don't they? All that campaigning in blizzards in open wagons! It's awful, Susan, that you still have to suffer from that.
SUSAN: I've got more than that on my mind. If all I had to worry about was how I feel, I'd feel just fine.
ELIZABETH: *(Preparing tea.)* Now Susan, don't get yourself all in a snit.
SUSAN: *(Grabs a handful of news clippings and waves them in the*

air.) I already am in a snit, and why not? Look at this press . . . all this hoopla over one little speech. You'd think I was the Pope.

ELIZABETH: Speaking of the press, Susan, there's a reporter in the kitchen.

SUSAN: *(Flatly.)* There's a what in where? *(Plops down in chair.)*

ELIZABETH: A perfectly delightful young reporter names Arthur Brenton. I told him he could have just one small interview. He's very interested in this final address of yours. *(Pats Susan's knee.)* I knew you wouldn't mind.

SUSAN: Of course I would mind. And there is no such thing as a delightful reporter, Elizabeth. The words don't even belong in the same sentence. *(Long crash in the kitchen.)*

SUSAN: What in heaven's name is he doing in your kitchen?

ELIZABETH: Well, the cookies were still in the oven. I believe he's watching them.

SUSAN: *(In disbelief.)* A reporter in your kitchen baking cookies.
(At this point Brenton comes through the door bearing a plate of cookies. Susan does not see him.)

SUSAN: If that doesn't beat all. I can't go anywhere anymore without reporters showing up. What I'd like to know is where were all those reporters for the last 50 years when I was trekking back and forth across America in broken-down wagons? When I think back to all those barns I slept in . . . those snowstorms I traveled in . . . where were those reporters then?

ELIZABETH: *(Notices Brenton but prompts Susan anyway.)* You tell me. Where were they?

SUSAN: In their nice warm newspaper offices with the rest of their male cronies, that's where, making up stories about how we were planning the murder of firstborn male sons.

BRENTON: I can't believe it. Susan B. Anthony and Elizabeth Cady Stanton and I'm in the same room with both of them. *(Susan gives him a look of disgust while he hurriedly puts down the tray of cookies and extends his hand.)*

SUSAN: Well it comes as much of a shock to me as it does to you. *(Extends her hand for a quick shake.)* Other than catering this little intimate gathering just what are you doing here, Mr. Brenton?

ELIZABETH: Here, Susan, have a cookie. It will calm your nerves. *(Elizabeth eats a cookie.)*

SUSAN: Cookies calm your nerves, not mine. I think better when I'm hungry. You eat them. *(Elizabeth happily takes a few more cookies and eats them.)*

BRENTON: *(Taking out a pad and penci.)* Do you mind if I take notes?

SUSAN: Of exactly what do you expect to take notes, young man?

BRENTON: Well, Mrs. Stanton kindly invited me to visit both of you today to give some publicity to your upcoming final address, Miss Anthony.

ELIZABETH: *(Taking another cookie.)* I knew you wouldn't mind, Susan.

SUSAN: *(Susan thinks for a minute and develops a plan.)* All right Mr. Brenton. Take a seat and take notes. *(Elizabeth is delighted. Susan turns to her.)*

SUSAN: Well then, you have decided to help me with the speech!

ELIZABETH: Oh no! We've settled that issue.

SUSAN: Of course we haven't settled it.

ELIZABETH: I can't help you with the speech because I'm retired and tired. Ever wonder why those words sound so much alike? Tired and retired? *(To Brenton.)* And don't take notes of this. This is not what I want you to write.

BRENTON: Yes Ma'am. *(Holds note pad off to side to secretly record conversation.)*

SUSAN: Don't talk balderdash, Elizabeth, and don't be lazy. You'll retire when suffrage passes . . . not before. Besides your speeches were always superior to mine. I never seemed to stick to the point, always got too angry. It seems to me that every time I wrote a speech without your help I got egged off the platform. Eighty-one is too old to get egged, Elizabeth.

BRENTON: I hear they're expecting around 3,000 people.

ELIZABETH: That's a lot of eggs. *(Thinks a minute.)* About 250 dozen to be exact . . . I suggest you wear a raincoat. *(Giggles and eat another cookie.)*

BRENTON: Mrs. Stanton, forgive me. But am I understanding correctly that after fifty years of teamwork you are simply refusing to work with Miss Anthony?

SUSAN: Very well said. Take notes of that!

ELIZABETH: Susan! Shame on you. That's distorting the facts. I told you I wouldn't help with the speech weeks ago. I've said everything already. I've written it all . . . shouted it . . . cried for it over and over. I have an attic filled with my writings. I go to sleep sometimes thinking my ceiling will fall in and I will be crushed to death by my own words . . . die in my own rhetoric. I'm so tired of trying to find yet another way to pound reason through thick skulls.

SUSAN: *(to Brenton.)* You see how she is? And the press calls me stubborn.

BRENTON: As I recall, the press called you more than that. I was going through the archives this morning and came upon these cartoons, Miss Anthony. I thought you might like to look at them again. *(Hands Susan the clippings.)*

SUSAN: Oh yes. Yes. This is one of my favorites. Look here, Elizabeth. This is the one where we're portrayed playing pool and we both have beards.

ELIZABETH: *(Grabs the clipping.)* How disgusting. You know, Susan, you don't look so bad in a beard. I look like a perverted Santa Claus. *(Studies the clipping and takes another cookie.)*

BRENTON: Do you think either of you would care to comment on what it was like in the old days when women had no rights?

SUSAN: My dear child, are you under the impression women now have rights?

BRENTON: Well, what about your victories? When you first started campaigning, women weren't even allowed to speak in public!

ELIZABETH: You call that victory? Why a dog was allowed to bark on the street corner, but a woman wasn't allowed to speak. That's not a victory. That's common decency! Take a note of that!

BRENTON: I will, Mrs. Stanton. And I would be delighted to try one of your delicious-smelling cookies.

ELIZABETH: *(Leans over to get the plate.)* Well, someone seems to have eaten them all. What do you know about that? *(Smiles.)*

SUSAN: *(Smiles.)* Elizabeth! *(Pleadingly.)* You can't tell me you've come this far to sit in front of a fire eating cookies and say you're too tired to help with this speech.

ELIZABETH: *(A little angry.)* And don't I deserve it? Look what happened when I rewrote the Bible. You'd think women would have been grateful. Were they?

BRENTON: Actually I was hoping to talk to you about that . . . that . . .

SUSAN: I think fiasco is the word you're searching for, Mr. Brenton. And I think enough has been said about it.

ELIZABETH: *(Changing subject.)* You know. I figured by this time I would be a retired Congresswoman, or a Supreme Court Justice, or at least a retired mayor, for God's sake. Any jackass can be a mayor. But here we sit, the same way we've sat . . . it seems forever . . . before a stack of blank paper.

SUSAN: *(Turns to Brenton.)* You're partially responsible for this you know. When I think of all those smut mongers printing those lies about us . . .

ELIZABETH: Oh Susan, it's not his fault. He was still in nappies when all that happened. We've arrived, Susan! The press loves us! They even serve us cookies! It's taken fifty years to get the reporters on our side. Now is certainly not the time to get angry with them.

SUSAN: What do you mean "get"? I've been angry for half a century and I don't intend to start loving them now.

ELIZABETH: Now, if you want to be angry, be angry with Congress. No telling how many more years it will take to win that bunch over. And in this "last" speech of yours, remind them that the 20th century has arrived, but the vote for women still hasn't. Now that—get angry over that.

BRENTON: Why don't *you* tell them Mrs. Stanton? You can't choose to sit and remain silent. One state after another is passing suffrage. The movement is gaining power every day. Why you're both being quoted every day, in textbooks, in newspapers, in speeches. Your names have become household words.

ELIZABETH: Why don't you be quiet, you young upstart. *(Under her breath.)* Household words, are we? Like garbage bin or scrub brush?

SUSAN: You'll have to forgive Elizabeth, Mr. Brenton. She always did get grumpy when the cookies ran out.

ELIZABETH: To hell with the cookies, Susan. I want the damn vote. At least the vote before I die. Is that too much to ask? How dare they deny me that?

BRENTON: Mrs. Stanton, you probably don't remember my grandmother, Mary Brenton. She never forgot you. She used to tell me stories about how women weren't even allowed to leave the house alone. She always quoted you. Do you know what her favorite quote was? "Remember that no one in power ever gives freely. Power must be fought for." She was with you at Seneca Falls. Heard your speech. She said it was a turning point in her life.

ELIZABETH: *(Softening, thinking back.)* At Seneca was she? And how is your grandmother these days? What does she think of the fact that women still can't vote?

BRENTON: She's been dead seven years, ma'am. I sure wish I could tell her about today though.

ELIZABETH: Dead is she? *(Looks at Susan.)* How many of us are there left, Susan, that really remember? Women today seem to think the rights we fought so hard for are their birthrights. We thought so too. That's why we fought so hard.

SUSAN: There's enough of us, dear. We're still here, aren't we?

This One Thing I Do

Claire Braz-Valentine
1981

Scene: A flashback to earlier years. Susan is a guest in the Stanton's home.

Elizabeth Cady Standon, age 40s.
Henry Stanton, her husband, 40s.
Susan B. Anthony, 40s.

ELIZABETH: It took you ten minutes to use the privy. I timed you.

SUSAN: How very clever of you.

ELIZABETH: I timed Henry. It takes him two.

SUSAN: It's biological, Elizabeth. It's easier for them, like everything else. I don't think it's an issue worth pursuing. We've got other things more pressing.

ELIZABETH: You know why it took ten minutes. It's these abominable clothes. I bet if Henry put on my clothes it would take him ten minutes also.

SUSAN: Call him in, let's ask him. I have something to discuss with Henry anyway that I know will interest you.

ELIZABETH: OK, I will, although I think the chances of getting Henry to wear a dress are extremely slight, Susan. *(Goes to bedroom door and opens it.)* Henry dear, would you mind joining us for a minute?

(Henry enters, kisses Elizabeth)

HENRY: I was reading, Elizabeth.

ELIZABETH: I know you were reading, dear, but Susan and I were wondering about the time it takes men to use the privy and the time it takes women.

HENRY: You're being vulgar, Elizabeth.

ELIZABETH: Oh Henry, vulgar is relative.

HENRY: *(Good naturedly.)* So you've disturbed my reading . . . what is it you want to do . . . to have a race in the water closet?

SUSAN: Henry . . . let's just ignore Elizabeth's obsession with nature's calling for a minute . . . Now, I know, Elizabeth, you've got something there in the back of your mind and I don't want, in any way, to slight your little experiment, but I've just returned from a meeting on the Equal Rights Amendment and I've had some very enlightening discussions with a few Congressmen. Henry, we need to talk and I need your honest and straightforward answers.

HENRY: *(Sitting.)* Well, Susan . . . I think I know what's on your mind and I'll be glad to discuss it with you.

ELIZABETH: What's going on? What's on your mind? What are you going to discuss?

SUSAN: We're in trouble, Elizabeth. Big trouble. We've been working ourselves silly on the property rights act . . .

ELIZABETH: But that passed, . . . don't tell me there's something gone amiss with that . . . my father just decided to re-inherit me . . . or whatever the opposite of disinherit is . . . no offense Henry, but if you run away with the maid I would like to be able to keep my father's estate instead of giving it over to you and Myna.

SUSAN: Elizabeth, my sweet . . . shut up! I think you are about to have the shock of your life and I am most certain you are pregnant again and a woman in your condition . . .

ELIZABETH: Tell me. Please! I can't stand it.

SUSAN: Tell her, Henry.

HENRY: *(Sadly.)* Elizabeth, . . . Susan . . . we've worked together for many years. I admit most of my focus has been on abolition . . . but I have backed you on every issue for the total equality of women. But you realize my first involvement was for the Negro. You know that. It always has been.

ELIZABETH: What difference does that make? Together we fight for equality . . . Negroes and woman. What purpose is there in separating the issue? Once the suffrage amendment is passed, all citizens of the United States will be free citizens and allowed the vote. I don't understand any separation of the issues. We're all people.

SUSAN: Evidently we're not, Elizabeth. *(Elizabeth looks a long time at Susan and then turns to Henry and stares at him.)*

ELIZABETH: Which of us is to be left out?

HENRY: All things come in time, Elizabeth.

ELIZABETH: And?

HENRY: Abolition will probably pass. Freedom for all Negroes. The probably suffrage. . . suffrage for . . . Negroes . . . Male Negroes.

ELIZABETH: *(Anguished.)* And so the Negro male slave in the South will choose my representatives . . . will vote on the issues that decide whether I can be educated . . . whether I can own a home . . . whether I can divorce or marry or live or die as a citizen with a voice . . . *(It is important during the following dialogue that Elizabeth's anger is not directed towards Henry. Henry is on their side and she knows it. Yelling.)* What is it? What is it that so terrifies the men in this country to give us at least the freedom they have? We ask nothing more. Nothing more than they have. Are they afraid that if a woman earns a salary comparable to men that they won't be a man anymore? Are they so afraid of us that the very race they treated so contemptibly they are now willing to put over us?

HENRY: Elizabeth, you sound racist and I don't like it.

ELIZABETH: I don't like it either, Henry . . . and I am sure all the women Negro workers for the movement wouldn't like it either. Wouldn't like it. *(Pause.)* Is the word *male* going to be written into the Constitution? Has it come to that?

SUSAN: I am afraid it has Elizabeth. The word *male* will be written. The last of the suppressed will finally be defined clearly and without any chance for error. Women. Women of any color, . . . of any age . . . of any intelligence. We have gone nowhere. We have run campaigns in various states and won small victories. We've been fools. Our victory won't be won through individual states. Our victory will be in the Congress. It will be an amendment to the Constitution. We've taken too much for granted.

ELIZABETH: I've always said if the word *male* appeared in our Constitution, it would be a hundred years before women win equality. *(Pause.)* We have lost a century.

HENRY: But the vote, Elizabeth . . . you may win the vote in a few years. The liquor lobbyists are your worst enemy. Once they realize all women are not for prohibition things could change rapidly . . .

ELIZABETH: My worst enemy? The vote? Who ever said all we wanted was the vote? When did it boil down to this, Susan? And where the hell do we go from here?

SUSAN: Where the hell can we go, but up? That's one good thing about being on the bottom. When you want to change direction you don't have to waste your time deciding where you're going to move.

HENRY: I'm sorry, Elizabeth. This is the Negroes' hour. No one thought the women would be left out. That's just the way it happened. You know if I could have had it different I would have.

ELIZABETH: I know Henry . . . and so would I . . . have had it different. *(Gets up.)* And if you both will excuse me, I am going to the commode and I am going to vomit. Women have more experience at vomiting. We do it well and we do it quickly . . . regardless of color. *(Looks at Susan.)* This one will be a girl, Susan. She will have your name and she will be a fighter. God knows she'll have to be. *(Elizabeth exits to the commode and Susan sits staring at Henry. Henry shakes his head and puts his head down in his hands. Susan gets up with great determination and walks over to the door where Elizabeth exited.)*

SUSAN: Elizabeth? Elizabeth . . . I've been meaning to talk to you about my latest speech . . .
(Toilet flushes. Blackout)

The Wash
Phillip Gotanda
1984

Scene: Kiyoko's restaurant. They are playing five-card stud and Blackie is working on his sixth beer, but is not drunk. They are discussing Nobu, Kiyoko's gentleman-friend.

Kiyoko, 55ish, originally from Japan, previously married to an American soldier, a widow.

Chiyo, originally from Japan, late 40s, owns a beauty parlor next door to Kiyoko's restaurant.

Blackie, Hawaiian Nisei, 55ish, speaks with thick pidgen English, a cook at Kiyoko's restaurant.

(Kiyoko's restaurant, three weeks later, night. Kiyoko, Chiyo, Blackie are playing five-card stud. When the scene starts they each have one card down and two up. Chiyo is in the process of dealing the next card, Kiyoko on her left, Blackie to her right. Chiyo wears a poker visor. Five empty bottles sit in front of Blackie, who is working on a sixth. He is not drunk, though. Hawaiian music is playing on his large portable tape player.)

CHIYO: *(Examining her hand.)* He's got a wife. You said so yourself.

KIYOKO: They're separated.

CHIYO: He wants to get back together. I know his kind. She left him. They can't get over that. He only wants you for one thing—your "tempura." Yeah. He's over your restaurant everyday, *desho* [isn't that so]? You feeding him. He's eating up all your profits.
(Chiyo and Kiyoko notice Blackie chugging down the rest of his beer, making strange gurgling sounds. They stare.)

BLACKIE: You gotta drink beer when you're playing poker or you aren't playing poker. You're just playing cards. I don't like cards, hate cards. *(Holds up another beer)* I *love* poker.

KIYOKO: Nobu is a good man.

CHIYO: You like to mother him, you like that kind of thing. But you don't know about men.

KIYOKO: And you do, heh?

CHIYO: You don't get out of this restaurant of yours. I tell you, "Go out, go out." "No, I gotta work, work . . ." *(Noticing something)* Wait, wait, someone didn't ante. We only bet once, a nickel, a nickel, right? *(Counting.)* See. Someone didn't ante.

KIYOKO: I did.

CHIYO: So did I.

(They turn to Blackie, who's guzzling a beer.)

BLACKIE: Huh? Oh, yeah. *(Innocently tosses money in.)*

CHIYO: *(Begins to deal; to Kiyoko.)* Two sixes—a pair of saxophones. *(To Blackie.)* A three of diamonds gives you . . . nothing. *(To self.)* Eight of puppy toes to the dealer, working on a possible club flush. *(To Kiyoko)* Pair of saxes high. I just can't see myself going out with him.

KIYOKO: Nobu is an honest man. Not like that guy you've been seeing. Check.

CHIYO: Ray, his name is Ray. Blackie.

BLACKIE: *(Carefully examining his cards.)* Yeah, I know.

KIYOKO: That time Blackie gave Nobu too much change. Remember? He walked all the way back from his house to return it—twenty-five cents.

CHIYO: Good investment. He gets a $4.50 combo plate free now. *(To Blackie)* Your bet.

BLACKIE: Don't rush me, don't rush me.

CHIYO: *(To Blackie.)* You're queen high, working on a possible nothing. *(Motioning to her own cards.)* Possible club flush here and . . . *(Pointing to Kiyoko's hand.)* A pair of saxes there, possible three-of-a-kind. *(To Kiyoko.)* I just think you can do better, that's all I'm saying. Besides, he's so old.

KIYOKO: I don't want to talk about it.

(Blackie finally decides to bet but Chiyo ignores him and goes right ahead.)

CHIYO: Dealer bets a nickel.

KIYOKO: He's not old.

CHIYO: Is he good in bed?

KIYOKO: He's sixty-eight years old, Chiyo. I raise you a dime.

CHIYO: So he really is old. See you and I bump you a quarter.

BLACKIE: I love it when the wahines talk dirt. *(They stare at him.)* Jeez, just joking. Don't lose your coconut.

(As Blackie begins putting in the bets he missed Kiyoko and Chiyo continue on.)

KIYOKO: *(Tossing quarter in.)* I call.

CHIYO: *(Starting to deal; to Kiyoko.)* Nine of spades. No help there. *(To Blackie)* A trois. Oh, a pair of threes. *(To self.)* And for the dealer . . . another club. Read'em and weep. Four puppy toes looking mighty pretty. Flush, very possible. *(To* Kiyoko.*)* Pair of saxes still high.

KIYOKO: Chiyo, you don't know him like I do. Check. *(She notices Blackie sucking on his beer.)* He checks, too.

CHIYO: I'm just saying you could find someone else. Someone younger, more fun.

KIYOKO: *(Irritated.)* You watch too many soap operas, Chiyo. Life's not like that. Men don't fall into your lap.

CHIYO: *(Upset at being lectured to.)* Fifty cents.

BLACKIE: *(Impressed.)* Fifty cents . . .

KIYOKO: I *like* Nobu. One dollar.

BLACKIE: *(In disbelief.)* One dollar . . .

CHIYO: All right, all right, white hair doesn't bother me. It's no hair I can't stand. *(Tosses in dollar.)* Call you. You got the three-of-a-kind?

KIYOKO: Pair of sixes, that's all. You got the flush?

CHIYO: Pair of eights! Hah!

(Kiyoko's disgusted. Chiyo's about to grab the pot when Blackie puts down his cards. Kiyoko and Chiyo stare in disbelief.)

BLACKIE: *(Puffing up like a rooster.)* Excusez-moi's, but I got three trois's.

CHIYO: Blackie . . .

(Blackie shovels the pot in. Kiyoko pushes the cards to Chiyo, who examines them skeptically.)

KIYOKO: *(To Chiyo.)* Your wash. *(To Blackie.)* Blackie, cut.

(Blackie cuts the shuffled deck and Kiyoko begins to deal.)

BLACKIE: *(Holding up beer.)* Hate cards. *Love* poker. *(He starts to guzzle)*

KIYOKO: *(Dealing.)* Today is the fifteenth, *neh* [isn't it]? *(Stops, reflecting.)* Harry would have been fifty-nine this week.

(Chiyo and Blackie exchange glances.)

Crossing Delancy

Susan Sandler
1984

Scene: Bubbie's dining room. The table is set for Sam to meet
Isabelle. She is late, he arrives on time, and Hannah is eating
everything in sight.

Bubbie (Ida), an elderly, loving Jewish Grandma to Isabelle.
Hannah, a middle-aged matchmaker, loud, outspoken.
Sam, late 20s–early 30s, attractive, a deli-owner. Hannah is trying to
match him with Ida's granddaughter, but Isabelle is put off by his
lowly profession despite how nice he is.

BUBBIE: How much you weigh, Henka?
HANNAH: *(Not breaking the rhythm of her meal.)* I don't know.
BUBBIE: I got a scale.
HANNAH: How old is she—your Isabelle?
BUBBIE: I'll ask her—you got enough to eat there?
HANNAH: Yeah, this is good— Just a snack.
BUBBIE: I wouldn't want you should starve.
HANNAH: Please, don't trouble yourself for me. A bite is good. Until
    supper.
BUBBIE: Herbie, may he rest in peace, did he ever sit down to eat with
    you?
HANNAH: What else?—He was my husband.
BUBBIE: All the yentas made blah-blah when he jumped from the six-
    teenth floor—such a nice, new apartment—why should he want
    to fly away?
HANNAH: *(Still not breaking her rhythm.)* He never got a chance to
    tell me. *(Bubbie crosses to the window.)* Ida—
BUBBIE: Yeah?
HANNAH: Something's bothering me—I got to know—why are they
    set up to meet by you tonight? Isabelle's so ashamed to show him
    where she lives it's so lousy?

BUBBIE: You stinker—she gives me a little nachas, this is her job. It's such a crime?

HANNAH: Excuse me for asking. *(Pause.)* She's coming right from work?

BUBIE: Yeah. You don't need to broadcast she works on shabbos.

HANNAH: Don't worry, I keep secrets like an old cocker keeps a young wife.

BUBBIE: For my money, she can work on Yom Kippur—honest work is honest work—but I don't want to shake up the little pickleman, fshtast?

HANNAH: The little pickleman is already plenty shook.

BUBBIE: It was the same with me—all the boys, they lost their tongues when they saw me. The poor schmendricks.

HANNAH: So tell me, Ida, satisfy my curiosity, why did your Isabelle decide to turn around and give him another look. You promise her something nice? Ain't I right? A little gelt maybe?

BUBBIE; I don't butt in. I don't operate this way.

HANNAH: So what happened?

(Doorbell.)

BUBBIE: In her dreams she saw pickles.

HANNAH: It's a match

BUBBIE: Not so fast. *(She crosses to the door.)*

HANNAH: It's a match.—I got to admit—sometimes I know what I'm doing in this life.

(Bubbie looks through the peephole and opens the door, Sam enters. He is wearing an oversized jacket and baggie pants with a cummerbund in the manner of the hip, young Japanese design-ers. The ensemble looks like it stepped off the cover of GQ. Wearing it, Sam, however, does not. The total effect on him is ludicrous. Bubbie does not move.)

HANNAH: *(Rises from the table and crosses to him.)* Sammy, Sammy. Come. Let's take a look. Ohhh la la—I don't know what to say. You take my breath and throw it away. *(She grabs his hand.)* Walk around, show it off. Let me see. *(Sam walks around the kitchen area, avoiding eye contact with both women.)* Very nice. Very nice. You look like a million. Don't let anybody tell you different.

BUBBIE: Who is the thief sold you these schmataz?

SAM: Max.

BUBBIE: Max?

SAM: Mrs. Mandelbaum's brother-in-law.

BUBBIE: I gotta hand it to you, Henka—you get them coming and going.

HANNAH: You think I get something from this? Not a penny. Not a dime. It's part of my job to know fashion. You got to package what you sell. Right, Sam?

BUBBIE: Sammy, you look like you missed the boat back to Pinsk—you understand what I'm saying?—This is not the way educated people dress.

HANNAN: *(Pulling Sam away from her.)* Leave him alone. Stop criticizing. You look terrific, Sammy. Take it from me. I know what's what with young people. Isabelle will like it. This is all that matters. What's in the bags?

SAM: Mrs. Mandelbaum, what are you doing here?

HANNAH: I'm a sucker for romance— This is my fate.

SAM: Mrs. Kantor—for you. *(He hands her a gift-wrapped box.)* And this is for Isabelle. *(He places a large bouquet of flowers wrapped in paper on the table.)*

HANNAH: Gold. Pure gold. The boy is gold—what did I tell you?

SAM: Aren't you going to open it, Mrs. Kantor?

BUBBIE: Now?

SAM: Please.

BUBBIE: *(She opens the package in her usual careful manner, untying the knots, winding the string, folding the paper, finally removing a bottle of schnapps from the box. As she pulls the bottle out)* Now you're talking. Let's have a drink, Sammy. What do you say. *(She brings the glasses to the table.)*

SAM: Shouldn't we wait for Isabelle?

BUBBIE: She only drinks milk. Come. *(Bubbie pours two very full glasses and one half full which she gives to Hannah.)*

HANNAH: *(As Bubbie pours.)* Sam, it's driving me crazy—I'm looking at you and I'm thinking—who could it be you remind me of dressed up so beautiful like this—

SAM: I can't help you with that one, Mrs. Mandelbaum—I feel like I'm breaking new ground here.

HANNAH: *Vincent Price!*—Vincent Price in *The House of Wax!* . . . oh, what a heartbreaker, huh?

BUBBIE: *(Holding up the glass for a toast.)* Good health, long life, and a heart full of happiness. *(All three clink glasses.)*

ALL: A-main. *(They all drink up, both Bubbie and Hannah draining their glasses quickly.)*

HANNAH: Ah! This is what I needed. Thank you, darling. *(She kisses Sam on the cheek.)* Oy! A zees kite!!—So where are you taking the date?

SAM: I thought I'd let Isabelle decide.

HANNAH: Sammy, something wrong? You look a little green.

BUBBIE: Of course he's green. That's some first-class garbage you put him in.

SAM: Maybe I should go home and change. It wouldn't take a minute. I'm just around the corner. When Isabelle comes you can tell her I'm on my way, all right?

HANAH: Don't listen to her. You look fine. Max gave you a good price? You told him you came from me?

SAM: Yes, Mrs. Mandelbaum.

(Phone rings.)

BUBBIE: *(Crosses to answer it.)* Hello—who's there?—Isabelle—you all right?—I can't hear you— —What?—Where are you?—ohhh— *(Spits.)* Ptu! You scared me—So why aren't you here, people are waiting . . . I don't like this. This I don't like. You make a date to be with someone, you don't mix it up.—So what time you come? Ach—you're some criminal. Here, talk to Sam. He's the lost one. *(She motions to Sam to take the phone.)*

SAM: Isabelle? You're not coming? . . . Oh, yes?—Yes . . . of course. This sounds important. Certainly. Please, don't rush. We'll wait. We're all relaxed. Anytime with your Bubbie is a good time.— — I understand . . . Good-bye. *(He hangs up.)* I understand.

The Duck Pond

Ara Watson

Scene: The bank of a pond that flows through the campus of a mid-America University. There is a park bench facing the pond (the audience) with a trash container near by.

Rachel, 20, twenty pounds overweight.
Elizabeth, 21, very clean cut.
John, 22, also very clean cut.

RACHEL: OK, here goes. *(She throws a piece of bread.)* Oh, come on. You can do better than that. You have to at least try. If I'm going to try, you have to try. One more time—and watch out for old Marmaduke there. OK. One—two—Oh, on the count of three. OK? OK. One—two—three *(She throws. Excited.)* No, no, to your left! To your—! Wha—? I don't believe it. How could you miss that one? Well, don't look at me. I threw it practically right to you. *(She eats a few bread pieces.)* Nope. No more special favors. You'll have to take your chances with the rest. *(Throws a handful.)* Bet you'll miss me next week, won't you? *(Elizabeth and John enter. They are a year or two older than Rachel. very "clean-cut," dressed neatly—Elizabeth in dress, low heels. They are carrying books.)* Well, I'll only be gone for a week. You won't—

ELIZABETH: *(Interrupting.)* Rachel?

RACHEL: *(Startled, she turns quickly, dropping her sack.)* What?

JOHN: *(Smiling.)* We've been looking for you, Rachel.

ELIZABETH: *(Smiling.)* We surely didn't mean to frighten you.

RACHEL: No . . . no. I was . . .

JOHN: You dropped your sack. *(Putting his books on the bench, he picks up the sack and the crumbs which have fallen out.)* Here. We better pick this up for you.

RACHEL: I can. *(But she doesn't.)*

ELIZABETH: *(Coming to her.)* It's a beautiful day, isn't it? I would say spring is definitely here. *(Kisses her on the cheek.)* I can certainly understand why you sneaked out of your study cubicle.

RACHEL: I didn't.

JOHN: *(Gently reprimanding her with a smile.)* Hey . . . Rachel.

RACHEL: I mean . . . I just took a little break, is all . . .

JOHN: *(Rising.)* You know what the regs say, though.

ELIZABETH: *(Pointing.)* Oh, would you look at that? *(laughs)* Aren't they wonderfully funny when they take off from the water? There are so many different kinds. Do you know much about them, Rachel?

RACHEL: I know . . . a little. I've . . . been studying them.

ELIZABETH: *(Looking all around her.)* I can never quite get over what a beautiful campus we have. So much space. We're very, very lucky.

JOHN: I think the word is fortunate, Elizabeth.

ELIZABETH: *(Smiles.)* Of course. *(To Rachel.)* And I, for one, am most grateful to be here.

RACHEL: Yes.

ELIZABETH: "Yes?"

RACHEL: I'm grateful, too.

ELIZABETH: See, John, I told you.

JOHN: Yeah, Yeah, I'm real glad to hear that. Good. Good.

ELIZABETH: *(To Rachel.)* Are you planning to go home for spring break next week?

RACHEL: *(Smiling.)* Yes. I haven't seen my folks since the fall.

ELIZABETH: Now, won't that be nice? See, I'm grateful, John—and I'm sure Rachel is, too—that we can live and work and learn here with God-fearing and God-loving people, with our family in Jesus.

JOHN: Praise the Lord.

ELIZABETH: Praise the Lord.

RACHEL: Praise the Lord.

ELIZABETH: We're given so much here and so little is asked of us in return.

JOHN: *(To Rachel.)* I've forgotten whether you went to State or University last year.

RACHEL: *(Quietly.)* State.

ELIZABETH: Now, John, don't bring all that up. That's past history. Rachel doesn't need to be reminded of how unhappy she was before she came here—how she didn't have any friends. Do you, Rachel? *(Rachel shakes her head.)* No, of course not.

RACHEL: I'm very happy here, Elizabeth.

ELIZABETH: That's wonderful to hear you say. *(She embraces Rachel).* I love you, Rachel. You're like a sister to me. You are a sister to me in the Lord.

RACHEL: I'm sorry, Elizabeth I . . . I won't break regs anymore.

ELIZABETH: Pray about it.

RACHEL: I will. Thank you. I'll go back in now.

(Rachel picks up her things from the bench as John and Elizabeth watch her. As she starts off, Elizabeth nods slightly to John.)

JOHN: Rachel. *(Rachel stops.)* We haven't finished our business with you.

RACHEL: But I promise—

JOHN: The Council sent us to talk to you and I'm afraid it's more serious than your bad study habits.

ELIZABETH: Would you like to sit down?

RACHEL: No.

JOHN: Sit down, Rachel. *(She does so.)* I think you ought to know that Elizabeth and I went way out on a limb for you today.

RACHEL: Why? How? What—?

ELIZABETH: You must let him finish.

JOHN: We didn't want to see you just kicked out.

RACHEL: Kicked out?!

ELIZABETH: Shhh.

JOHN: I don't know how you can sit there and act surprised. Did you think they were just going to forget about it? I'm telling you, it was very hard for Elizabeth and me to stand up in front of the other members of the Council and ask for a chance to come talk to you before final decision. It took a lot of courage on our part, Rachel—a lot of courage.

ELIZABETH: Everyone else was saying, "We've already given her a second chance—it didn't do any good. What good would another chance do?" But we said we were just sure there must be an explanation, a reason . . . That you were too precious to be—

JOHN: *(Interrupting.)* Stand up, Rachel. Go on. *(She does.)* When you came to us at the first of the year, we—the school, the Council—accepted you on one condition. Do you remember that condition? Well? Do you? *(Rachel stands with lowered head.)* Stand up! You know what I see when I look at you now? I sure don't see a Christian girl. I see a fat girl. I see a fat girl who has broken her word to all those who have loved and trusted her.

RACHEL: I didn't!

JOHN: What do you mean you didn't? How can you say that—"You didn't?" I was there, both of us were, when you signed that oath that by the end of this year you would be regulation weight. And, when you weren't losing any by the end of last semester and we talked to you and you said you were trying, but it was slow, you were changing your eating habits, you'd be down by the middle of the next semester, et cetera, et cetera, we believed you. We trusted you. Were you lying from the beginning? Were you just sitting back laughing at all our help, all our concern for you?

RACHEL: I've tried! I have tried! It's my metabolism.

JOHN: Meta—! You see, Elizabeth. She's going to go right on deceiving. *(He picks up the second paper sack and dumps out two candy bars and a cupcake.)* The body is the temple of the Lord and if you don't care about your body, then you don't care about the Lord. Come on, Elizabeth. We're going to have to go face the Council with this.

ELIZABETH: I'm very hurt, Rachel.

RACHEL: I wasn't gong to eat it.

JOHN: Were you going to feed it to the ducks? *(Toward her.)* You know what the Council will decide after they get our report?

ELIZABETH: You will be asked to leave, Rachel.

JOHN: You'll be told to leave.

RACHEL: No, I don't want to go. I can't . . .

JOHN: You won't have any choice. God needs a strong arm. We don't have any room for liars and weaklings.

ELIZABETH: You'll never be able to come back. We will never speak your name again. We will erase you from our minds and our hearts.

RACHEL: Oh, don't. Please, please, I can. I know I can. I promise. I
  promise. I promise, I promise!
JOHN: You promised before.
RACHEL: And I tried! Nobody ever believes me! I tried!
JOHN: You see? You're still lying!
RACHEL: No, I'm—
ELIZABETH: John, maybe—
JOHN: Not while she's still lying! We won't accept another promise
  born in a lie!
ELIZABETH: *(Gently.)* Rachel, admit you lied and ask for forgiveness.
JOHN: She doesn't want to be forgiven.
RACHEL: I do!
ELIZABETH: Then ask before it's too late. Now. Ask now.
RACHEL: I do ask.
ELIZABETH: You must say the words.
RACHEL: *(Quietly.)* Forgive me.
JOHN: What? I can't hear your.
ELIZABETH: Louder, Rachel.
RACHEL: I did.
ELIZABETH: Louder, Rachel.
RACHEL: *(A little louder.)* Forgive me.
JOHN: For what, Rachel? "Forgive me" for what?
RACHEL: *(The crying begins.)* For . . . you know . . . for lying.
JOHN: And for what else?
RACHEL: *(Confused.)* For . . . for . . . I don't . . .
JOHN: Don't you want to be forgiven for being fat? For letting the Devil
  have control of your mind and your body? You're fat, aren't you?
  Aren't you?! *(Rachel nods.)* You've got a fat, ugly body! Say it!
RACHEL: *(Mumbling.)* I'm . . . fat.
ELIZABETH: Louder, Rachel. Cast Satan out with the truth.
RACHEL: I'm fat.
JOHN: Again.
RACHEL: *(Louder.)* I'm fat.
ELIZABETH: Again!
RACHEL: *(Louder.)* I'm fat! I'm fat! *(Louder.)* I'm fat! *(Almost yelling.)*
  I'm fat and I'm fat and I'm fat!

ELIZABETH: *(Under.)* Praise God!

RACHEL: And I'm fat and I'm ugly! I'm ugly! I'm—

(Rachel breaks down sobbing. John and Elizabeth stand and look at her a moment, then smile at each other. Elizabeth slowly moves in and enfolds her.)

ELIZABETH: Praise the Lord. There, there. You've faced it. You have stood up to it. It's all right now. Just feel the cleansing power of the Lord. *(She smiles at John.)* We love you, Rachel. God loves you. We'll talk to the Council and see what we can do. You can stay here at school during spring break. You won't have to go home. We'll help you. We'll be with you and pray with you *(Elizabeth nods to John who comes over and puts his arm around Rachel and begins leading her off.)* Go with John, now. Go with John to the Prayer Temple.

JOHN: *(Exiting, he quietly talks to Rachel, who is still crying and is now clinging to John.)* Jesus will help you. You know that. You've seen it over and over again. He loves you and he wants to keep you with his chosen, but you must learn that a good soldier is an obedient soldier, and the Lord needs good, healthy soldiers . . . *(Off.)* *(During John and Rachel's exit, Elizabeth has been gathering the things on the bench. She finds there are still crumbs in the sack, so she walks closer to the pond and throws them in. She watches as the ducks gobble them up and she smiles warmly at them.)*

ELIZABETH: You don't care, do you? You big old fat lazy things. *(And, with a smile, she turns and exits.)*

(Lights. The End.)

Last Day of Camp

Jeffrey Sweet
1989

Scene: Time: The Present, evening, end of summer. Place: Outside, at a summer camp.

Craig
Lillian
Fiona

CRAIG: They do twinkle

LILLIAN: Isn't that amazing? They really do.

CRAIG: You didn't know that?

LILLIAN: Not really.

CRAIG: Come on, you must know the song. Everybody knows the song.

LILLIAN: Which?

CRAIG: "Twinkle, Twinkle, Little Star." You don't know that?

LILLIAN: Sure.

CRAIG: Where do you think they got that from? I mean, art imitates life, right?

LILLIAN: I don't know. There's a lot of bullshit in songs. The only stars I ever saw twinkle were in Disney cartoons or Christmas pageants. Till this summer. I guess it's pretty hard to twinkle through all that guck in the city.

CRAIG: So you've had an educational summer, hunh?

LILLIAN: You're laughing at me.

CRAIG: Not really.

LILLIAN: That's OK.

CRAIG: I'm not laughing.

LILLIAN: You aren't?

CRAIG: No.

LILLIAN: I'm glad. But it would have been OK if you were. I mean, I like you.

CRAIG: Well, that goes both ways. And I wasn't laughing at you.

LILLIAN: *(Pretending to be embarrassed.)* Well, gosh and shucks, Craig. *(A beat.)* So quiet now. I've gotten so used to hearing kids' voices. Now they're gone, it all sounds sort of naked.

CRAIG: You packed?

LILLIAN: I'm putting it off.

CRAIG: I know, it's a drag, isn't it?

LILLIAN: No, it's not that. I think I just don't want to admit that it's over.

(Fiona enters.)

FIONA: Well, Lucy Bernell's mother finally showed up.

CRAIG. About time.

LILLIAN: What's this about?

FIONA: One of my little monsters in cabin three. Her mother was supposed to pick her up and she was late or something.

CRAIG: The mother or the kid?

FIONA: Who cares? They're both gone and out of our hair. They're all gone, thank God.

LILLIAN: You really like kids, don't you?

FIONA: Let's just say that when it comes to Hansel and Gretel, my sympathies are with the witch.

LILLIAN: Which is why of course you took a job in a summer camp

FIONA: I heard there was a lake here. Thought with luck I might see one drown.

CRAIG: What a pleasant thought.

FIONA: I'm a meanie, didn't you know that?

CRAIG: Sure.

FIONA: I am.

CRAIG: I believe you.

FIONA: OK, don't say I didn't warn you.

CRAIG: Guess what I got for a tip?

FIONA: Most I got was a twenty.

LILLIAN: That's not bad.

FIONA: It's OK, but nothing spectacular. Divide that down by the hours I spent making sure they didn't break an ankle or get eaten by a bear, comes to pretty cheap baby sitting.

LILLIAN: What were you saying, Craig?

CRAIG: This guy hands me an envelope and right away I can feel there's something other than money in it. I open it up and it's maybe an ounce of grass.

LILLIAN: Whose daddy was that?

CRAIG: You know Dave Greenberg?

FIONA: The little freak?

CRAIG: A clear case of like son, like father.

FIONA: OK, let's see.

CRAIG: See what?

FIONA: Isn't he cute when he plays innocent? Your tip.

CRAIG: I'll show you mine if you show me yours.

FIONA: You know what I'll bet, I'll bet it's some of that anemic home-grown stuff.

CRAIG: Only one way to find out.

FIONA: All right then, break it out and let's put it to the test.

CRAIG: Don't have it with me.

FIONA: Where is it?

CRAIG: Back in my cabin, in my secret hiding place.

FIONA: I'll bet.

LILLIAN: You'll want to be careful.

CRAIG: What about?

LILLIAN: Remember what happened to Leonard.

CRAIG: Leonard was a different case entirely.

LILLIAN: They caught him with dope.

CRAIG: They caught him turning on the kids in his cabin. That was Leonard's fatal mistake.

FIONA: Yeah, but till they kicked him out, he was the most popular counselor in the camp.

CRAIG: I think what tipped them off was the water pipe one of his kids made in arts and crafts.

LILLIAN: I'm just saying be careful.

CRAIG: I appreciate your concern. But we're leaving tomorrow, so it's not like there's any great danger.

FIONA: You going to turn him in, Lillian?

LILLIAN: Of course not. Why would you say a thing like that?

FIONA: Maybe you don't approve.

LILLIAN: It's not a matter of my approving or disapproving . . .

FIONA: She said disapprovingly.

LILLIAN: It's not. Just because I don't do it, I'm not laying anything on anyone else.

CRAIG: You've never smoked?

LILLIAN: Sure, I've smoked, but not anymore.

FIONA: Got to protect those chromosomes.

LILLIAN: No, it's just I didn't enjoy it.

CRAIG: You're kidding.

LILLIAN: Why am I kidding?

CRAIG: You didn't enjoy it at all?

LILLIAN: What, is this the new taboo—you don't admit you don't enjoy dope? You say it like it's something I should be ashamed of.

CRAIG: No.

LILLIAN: If you enjoy it, terrific.

CRAIG: Well, I do.

LILLIAN: Terrific. It's not often you find something you really enjoy. Only we all enjoy different things. If we didn't, what would be the point of being different people?

FIONA: Bet you I know why you don't like dope.

LILLIAN: I just don't.

FIONA: It scares you.

LILLIAN: No.

FIONA: You feel those inhibitions slipping away, you're afraid of what you might do. What wild, disgraceful things you might do. Maybe dance or tell dirty jokes or take your clothes off.

LILLIAN: I can do all those things without smoking.

FIONA: Yeah, but *do* you?

LILLIAN: Is that what you think of me—that I'm some virginal square hard-ass?

FIONA: What I think is you're a lady who hasn't investigated her full potential for having a good time.

LILLIAN: OK, yeah, right. There you have me nailed into one pithy sentence.

FIONA: Just telling you what I see.

LILLIAN: Thank you very much.

FIONA: OK, take it the wrong way if you want to.
LILLIAN: Don't you worry about what kind of time I'm having.
FIONA: OK.
LILLIAN: I'm having a fine time.
FIONA: If you say so.

Every effort has been made to locate the proper copyright holder for each excerpt published in this anthology. Any discrepancies or exclusions are unintentional.

Permission Acknowledgments

reading, permission for which must be obtained from the author's agent in writing. Reprinted by permission of Smith and Kraus. All inquiries should be sent to P.O. Box 127, Lyme, NH 03768.

CLIZIA by Nicolo Machiavelli, translated by Robert Cohen. Copyright 1994 by Mayfield Publishing Co. CAUTION: Professionals and amateurs are hereby warned that performance of CLIZIA is subject to royalty. It is fully protected under the copy right laws of the United States of America and of all countries covered by the International Copyright Union (including the Dominion of Canada and the rest of the British Commonwealth), and all by the Pan-American Copyright Convention and the Universal Copyright Convention, the Berne Convention and of all countries with which the United States copyright relations. All rights, including professional, amateur/motion picture stage rights, recitation, lecturing, public reading, radio broadcasting, television, video or sound recording, all other forms of mechanical or electronic reproduction, such as CD-ROM, CD-1, information storage and retrieval systems and photocopying, and the rights of translation into foreign languages are strictly reserved. Particular emphasis is laid upon the matter of reading, permission for which must be obtained from the author's agent in writing. Reprinted with permission by Robert Cohen. All inquiries should be sent to Robert Cohen at cohen@uci.edu.

COVER by Jeffrey Sweet. Copyright 1989 by Jeffrey Sweet with Stephen Johnson and Sandra Hustie. CAUTION: Professionals and amateurs are hereby warned that performance of COVER is subject to royalty. It is fully protected under the copy right laws of the United States of America and of all countries covered by the International Copyright Union (including the Dominion of Canada and the rest of the British Commonwealth), and all by the Pan-American Copyright Convention and the Universal Copyright Convention, the Berne Convention and of all countries with which the United States copyright relations. All rights, including professional, amateur/motion picture stage rights, recitation, lecturing, public reading, radio broadcasting, television, video or sound recording, all other forms of mechanical or electronic reproduction, such as CD-ROM, CD-1, information storage and retrieval systems and photocopying, and the rights of translation into foreign languages are strictly reserved. Particular emphasis is laid upon the matter of reading, permission for which must be obtained from the author's agent in writing. Reprinted with permission by Samuel French, Inc. All inquiries should be sent to Samuel French, Inc., 45 W. 25th St., New York, NY 10010.

CRIMES OF THE HEART by Beth Henley. Copyright 1982 by Beth Henley CAUTION: Professionals and amateurs are hereby warned that performance of CRIMES OF THE HEART is subject to royalty. It is fully protected under the copy right laws of the United States of America and of all countries covered by the International Copyright Union (including the Dominion of Canada and the rest of the British Commonwealth), and all by the Pan-American Copyright Convention and the Universal Copyright Convention, the Berne Convention and of all countries with which the United States copyright relations. All rights, including professional, amateur/motion picture stage rights, recitation, lecturing, public reading, radio broadcasting, television, video or sound recording, all other forms of mechanical or electronic reproduction, such as CD-ROM, CD-1, information storage and retrieval systems and photocopying, and the rights of translation into foreign languages are strictly reserved. Particular emphasis is laid upon the matter of reading, permission for which must be obtained from the author's agent in writing. Reprinted by permission of Gilbert Parker, William Morris Agency. All inquiries should be sent to 1325 Avenue of the Americas, New York, NY 10019.

CROSSING DELANCY by Susan Sandler. Copyright 1984, 1987 Susan Sandler. CAUTION: Professionals and amateurs are hereby warned that performance of CROSSING DELANCY is subject to royalty. It is fully protected under the copy right laws of the United States of America and of all countries covered by the International Copyright Union (including the Dominion of Canada and the rest of the British Commonwealth), and all by the Pan-American Copyright Convention and the Universal Copyright Convention, the Berne Convention and of all countries with which the United States copyright relations. All rights, including professional, amateur/motion picture stage rights, recitation, lecturing, public reading, radio broadcasting, television, video or sound recording, all other forms of mechanical or electronic reproduction, such as CD-ROM, CD-1, information storage and retrieval systems and photocopying, and the rights of translation into foreign languages are strictly reserved. Particular emphasis is laid upon the matter of reading, permission for which must

Particular emphasis is laid upon the matter of reading, permission for which must be obtained from the author's agent in writing. Reprinted with permission by Samuel French, Inc. All inquiries should be sent to Samuel French, Inc., 45 W. 25th St., New York, NY 10010.

FRIENDS by Kobe Abe, translated by Donald Keene. Copyright 1969 by Grove Press, Inc. CAUTION: Professionals and amateurs are hereby warned that performance of FRIENDS is subject to royalty. It is fully protected under the copy right laws of the United States of America and of all countries covered by the International Copyright Union (including the Dominion of Canada and the rest of the British Commonwealth), and all by the Pan-American Copyright Convention and the Universal Copyright Convention, the Berne Convention and of all countries with which the United States copyright relations. All rights, including professional, amateur/motion picture stage rights, recitation, lecturing, public reading, radio broadcasting, television, video or sound recording, all other forms of mechanical or electronic reproduction, such as CD-ROM, CD-1, information storage and retrieval systems and photocopying, and the rights of translation into foreign languages are strictly reserved. Particular emphasis is laid upon the matter of reading, permission for which must be obtained from the author's agent in writing. Reprinted with permission by Grove/Atlantic, Inc. All inquiries should be sent to Grove/Atlantic, Inc., 841 Broadway, New York, NY 10003.

GHOSTS by Henrik Ibsen. Copyright 1995 by Rick Davis and Brian Johnston. CAUTION: Professionals and amateurs are hereby warned that performance of GHOSTS is subject to royalty. It is fully protected under the copy right laws of the United States of America and of all countries covered by the International Copyright Union (including the Dominion of Canada and the rest of the British Commonwealth), and all by the Pan-American Copyright Convention and the Universal Copyright Convention, the Berne Convention and of all countries with which the United States copyright relations. All rights, including professional, amateur/motion picture stage rights, recitation, lecturing, public reading, radio broadcasting, television, video or sound recording, all other forms of mechanical or electronic reproduction, such as CD-ROM, CD-1, information storage and retrieval systems and photocopying, and the rights of translation into foreign languages are strictly reserved. Particular emphasis is laid upon the matter of reading, permission for which must be obtained from the author's agent in writing. Reprinted with permission by Smith and Kraus. All inquiries should be sent to P.O. Box 127, Lyme, NH 03768.

GOLDEN ACCORD by Wole Soyinka. Copyright 1980. CAUTION: Professionals and amateurs are hereby warned that performance of GOLDEN ACCORD is subject to royalty. It is fully protected under the copy right laws of the United States of America and of all countries covered by the International Copyright Union (including the Dominion of Canada and the rest of the British Commonwealth), and all by the Pan-American Copyright Convention and the Universal Copyright Convention, the Berne Convention and of all countries with which the United States copyright relations. All rights, including professional, amateur/motion picture stage rights, recitation, lecturing, public reading, radio broadcasting, television, video or sound recording, all other forms of mechanical or electronic reproduction, such as CD-ROM, CD-1, information storage and retrieval systems and photocopying, and the rights of translation into foreign languages are strictly reserved. Particular emphasis is laid upon the matter of reading, permission for which must be obtained from the author's agent in writing. Reprinted by permission by Samuel French, Inc. All inquiries should be sent to 45 W. 25th St., New York, NY 10010.

HEADS by Jon Jory. Copyright MCMLXXXIII by Jon Jory. Printed in the United States of America. *All Right Reserved.* (UNIVERSITY). CAUTION: Professionals and amateurs are hereby warned that performance of HEADS is subject to royalty. It is fully protected under the copy right laws of the United States of America and of all countries covered by the International Copyright Union (including the Dominion of Canada and the rest of the British Commonwealth), and all by the Pan-American Copyright Convention and the Universal Copyright Convention, the Berne Convention and of all countries with which the United States copyright relations. All rights, including professional, amateur/motion picture stage rights, recitation, lecturing, public reading, radio broadcasting, television, video or sound recording, all other forms of mechanical or electronic reproduction, such as CD-ROM, CD-1, information storage and retrieval systems and photocopying, and the rights of translation into foreign languages are strictly reserved. Particular emphasis is laid upon the matter of reading, permission for which must be obtained from the author's agent in writing. Reprinted with permission by Dramatic Publishing. All inquiries should be sent to Dramatic Publishing, 311 Washington St., Woodstock, IL, 60098.

I HATE HAMLET by Paul Rudnick. Copyright 1991 by Paul Rudnick. CAUTION: Professionals and amateurs are hereby warned that performance of I HATE HAMLET is subject to royalty. It is fully protected under the copy right laws of the United States of America and of all countries covered by the International Copyright Union (including the Dominion of Canada and the rest of the British Commonwealth), and all by the Pan-American Copyright Convention and the Universal Copyright Convention, the Berne Convention and of all countries with which the United States copyright relations. All rights, including professional, amateur/motion picture stage rights, recitation, lecturing, public reading, radio broadcasting, television, video or sound recording, all other forms of mechanical or electronic reproduction, such as CD-ROM, CD-1, information storage and retrieval systems and photocopying, and the rights of translation into foreign languages are strictly reserved. Particular emphasis is laid upon the matter of reading, permission for which must be obtained from the author's agent in writing. The stage performance rights in I HATE HAMLET (other than first class rights) are controlled exclusively by Dramatists Play Service, 440 Park Avenue South, New York, NY 10016. No professional or non-professional performance of the Play (excluding first class professional performance) may be given without obtaining in advance the written permission of Dramatists Play Service, and paying the requisite fee. Reprinted with permission by Helen Merrill, Ltd. on behalf of the Author. All other inquiries should be sent to Helen Merrill, Ltd., 435 West 23rd St., New York, NY 10011.

LAST DAY OF CAMP by Jeffrey Sweet. Copyright 1992 by Jeffrey Sweet. CAUTION: Professionals and amateurs are hereby warned that performance of LAST DAY OF CAMP is subject to royalty. It is fully protected under the copy right laws of the United States of America and of all countries covered by the International Copyright Union (including the Dominion of Canada and the rest of the British Commonwealth), and all by the Pan-American Copyright Convention and the Universal Copyright Convention, the Berne Convention and of all countries with which the United States copyright relations. All rights, including professional, amateur/motion picture stage rights, recitation, lecturing, public reading, radio broadcasting, television, video or sound recording, all other forms of mechanical or electronic reproduction, such as CD-ROM, CD-1, information storage and retrieval systems and photocopying, and the rights of translation into foreign languages are strictly reserved. Particular emphasis is laid upon the matter of reading, permission for which must be obtained from the author's agent in writing. Reprinted with permission by Samuel French, Inc. All inquiries should be sent to Samuel French, Inc., 45 W. 25th St., New York, NY 10010.

MADWOMAN OF CHAILLOT by Jean Giraudoux. Copyright 1945. CAUTION: Professionals and amateurs are hereby warned that performance of MADWOMAN OF CHAILLOT is subject to royalty. It is fully protected under the copy right laws of the United States of America and of all countries covered by the International Copyright Union (including the Dominion of Canada and the rest of the British Commonwealth), and all by the Pan-American Copyright Convention and the Universal Copyright Convention, the Berne Convention and of all countries with which the United States copyright relations. All rights, including professional, amateur/motion picture stage rights, recitation, lecturing, public reading, radio broadcasting, television, video or sound recording, all other forms of mechanical or electronic reproduction, such as CD-ROM, CD-1, information storage and retrieval systems and photocopying, and the rights of translation into foreign languages are strictly reserved. Particular emphasis is laid upon the matter of reading, permission for which must be obtained from the author's agent in writing. Reprinted by permission of Dramatists Play Service Inc. All inquiries should be sent to 440 Park Avenue South, New York, NY 10016.

OEDIPUS AT COLONUS by Sophocles translated by Carl Mueller. Copyright 2000 by Smith and Kraus. CAUTION: Professionals and amateurs are hereby warned that performance of OEDIPUS AT COLONUS is subject to royalty. It is fully protected under the copy right laws of the United States of America and of all countries covered by the International Copyright Union (including the Dominion of Canada and the rest of the British Commonwealth), and all by the Pan-American Copyright Convention and the Universal Copyright Convention, the Berne Convention and of all countries